BOMBER
COMMAND
HANDBOOK

1939–1945

JONATHAN FALCONER

SUTTON PUBLISHING

First published in 1998 by
Sutton Publishing Limited · Phoenix Mill
Thrupp · Stroud · Gloucestershire · GL5 2BU

This paperback edition first published in 2003

British Library Cataloguing in Publication Data
A catalogue record for this book is available from the British Library.

ISBN 0 7509 3171 X

Typeset in 10/13 pt Baskerville.
Typesetting and origination by
Sutton Publishing Limited.
Printed in Great Britain by
J.H. Haynes & Co. Ltd, Sparkford.

CONTENTS

CONTENTS

ACKNOWLEDGEMENTS

The help of the following individuals and organisations in the preparation of this book is gratefully acknowledged: my schoolfriend Lauren Ash and her mother Anne Beard for allowing me to photograph items of RAF escape kit in their possession; Don Darbyshire for allowing me to refer to his article on Roberts Dunstan, and Victor Doree for his kind permission to reproduce the photograph of Dunstan; Arthur Eyton-Jones DFC, navigator, 226 Squadron; Howard Farmiloe DSO, pilot, 61 Squadron; the *Glasgow Herald*; Isabel Wilson of Hitchin Museum, Hertfordshire; Vera Sherring, Denis Field, Gerry Blacklock, Colin Pateman, Peter R. March and Brian Strickland; fellow authors Philip Birtles, Martin Bowman, Roy Conyers Nesbit, Philip Jarrett and Alfred Price for kindly allowing me the use of photographs from their personal collections; Frances Russell and Alex Thomson of the British Society of Cinematographers, and in particular Jim Wilde, for biographical details of RAF Film Unit cameraman 'Skeets' Kelly; Piers Whitley, son of Air Marshal Sir John Whitley, for assistance with biographical information on his late father. The *Daily Telegraph* Library; Sebastian Cox and Graham Day of the MOD Air Historical Branch; Peter Elliott of the RAF Museum, Hendon; the Defence Estate Organisation, Waterbeach and Farnborough offices; the Public Record Office, Kew; Imperial War Museum; US National Archives; North Kesteven District Council Tourist Information Department, Lincolnshire; the Commonwealth War Graves Commission, Maidenhead, Berkshire; Larry Monuk of the Canadian National Defence Headquarters Library, Ottawa, and the staff of the Department of National Defence's Directorate of History and Heritage, also in Ottawa.

INTRODUCTION

As we approach the millennium, ebbing morale is in danger of robbing the RAF of highly trained air and groundcrews. A succession of deep and far-reaching cuts imposed by the Treasury and apparently accepted by the Ministry of Defence have done more damage to the fabric of the Service than Hitler's Luftwaffe managed to achieve in six years of total war.

One RAF Tornado pilot is on record in the national press as saying that in his view in 1998 'the average American supercarrier has more aircraft at readiness than the whole of Fighter Command'. Many others believe that the RAF of the late 1990s is little better than a Third World air force: a sad reflection, indeed, on the condition of 'the' air force on which, for a long time, most others were modelled.

During the folly years of appeasement in the 1930s the RAF faced similar damaging cuts to its establishment and efficiency. A two-pronged assault – Treasury-inspired cuts to its front line and a threat to its very existence from a jealous Army and Navy – put its future in the balance. When war broke out in 1939 the RAF's squadrons went into battle with second-rate aircraft and a shortage of aircrews.

Bomber Command had been conceived in 1936 as a daylight bomber force along the lines of contemporary strategic thought that 'the bomber would always get through'. The reality was very different. Unsustainable heavy losses quickly forced most of the Command's efforts into a night offensive, for which its crews were poorly prepared or trained, and which lasted for almost six years. Its small force of daylight bombers continued to fly suicide missions against targets in enemy-occupied Europe, suffering dreadful losses in the process. Yet by the end of the Second World War Bomber Command had adapted to the new operational requirements and was equipped with some of the best aircraft in the world, manned by well-trained aircrew with high morale.

This book does more than simply illustrate the six-year transition of Bomber Command from a small and ill-equipped handful of squadrons in 1939 into a numerically and technologically superior weapon of war by 1945. It sets the six-year offensive against the background of the cult of the bomber in the 1930s, and then goes on to describe the organisation and control of Bomber Command, from the policy developed at War Cabinet level, handed down through the tiers of command via the Air Ministry, Command, Group and finally to the Squadron – the sharp end. It looks at the airfield construction programme that made the bomber offensive possible, and shows how these airfields were organised to serve the squadrons they supported.

The training of different aircrew trades is examined and a review of their survival chances are set against tour lengths and the spectre of LMF. Offensive and defensive armament is described, along with the means by which crews found their way to a target and then bombed it. A typical night raid is described in detail to reveal just what was involved in a 'maximum effort' operation. The human side of operational life is also discussed, with details of uniforms and insignia, flying clothing and equipment, communications, and escape and evasion matters.

Bomber Command was not simply a fleet of aircraft commanded and crewed by automatons: it was an organisation made up from the cream of British youth, directed on the whole by an educated and highly experienced cadre of commanders. Published here for the first time are full biographical details of the high and group commanders, complemented by short biographies of a representative selection of the men who made up Bomber Command.

Four detailed appendices include a comprehensive war diary of Bomber Command actions from 1939 to 1945, a full listing of bomber squadrons and their commanders (available here for the first time), the airfields and orders of battle.

Fifty years after the end of the war there are dozens of museums and exhibitions scattered the length of England, dedicated to the men and women of Bomber Command and the six-year offensive they fought by day and by night. Full details of these sites are included to enable readers to plan visits.

It is reassuring to trust in the belief that 'cometh the hour cometh the man' – and this saying can be applied to both 'Bomber' Harris and his air and groundcrews of Bomber Command. But it is alarming to think that in 1939 it took a world war to bludgeon politicians and civil servants into accepting the old truism 'if you want peace, prepare for war'. Let us hope today that those in whom we have placed our trust for the defence of the nation have heeded the warnings of history.

Sadly, I believe that in Great Britain most of our political leaders and civil servants – apparently blind to the wisdom of hindsight, keen to cash in on the post-Cold War peace dividend (from which we are yet to reap any benefits) and not blessed with the imagination of foresight – fail to realise that unless they reverse the dangerous cuts in our armed forces we may be edging ever closer to repeating the lessons of recent history.

A cartoon in a national newspaper of May 1945 sums up the price of peace, bought with the lives of millions of men and women. A figure of Victory handing a wreath of olive leaves to a British soldier, set against the backdrop of a devastated landscape, says: 'Here it is, don't lose it again.'

Jonathan Falconer
Bradford-on-Avon
September 1998

REAPING THE WHIRLWIND

THE RISE OF THE BOMBER

The cult of the bomber was very much a phenomenon of the interwar period. Its new mass destructive role witnessed during the closing stages of the First World War strongly affected military thinking in the years that immediately followed. Three men in particular can be credited with the original theories of air warfare: General Giulio Douhet of Italy, Air Marshal Sir Hugh Trenchard of Great Britain, and Brigadier-General William ('Billy') Mitchell of the USA. The early air theorists argued that the object of war was to destroy the will of the enemy nation as well as his ability to resist, and then to impose one's own will upon him. In the conflict of the future these three men believed naval and ground forces would no longer have the decisive role. With the advent of the aeroplane, the obstacle of the enemy's surface forces could be jumped and attacks could be staged by air to hit at the enemy's population, or at the industry and economy that supported it. Gone were the days of air forces being merely auxiliary to the Army or Navy.

In Douhet's view, the best way to attain victory was to destroy air bases, supply points and centres of production on which the enemy depended. His strategic bomber force would have two separable functions: it must be able to win command of the skies, and be able to exploit that command. The immediate aim of air warfare, as Douhet clearly saw, was the need to defeat totally the opposing air force.

Trenchard's theory was that the heart of air power lay in strategic bombing of an independent character. He argued that operations in direct support of the Army and Navy were subsidiary and diversionary.

However, 'Billy' Mitchell made a big mistake: his advocacy of autonomy for the air arm aroused American democracy's strong distaste for the military establishment and its theories of total war. This effectively put paid to any ideas of an independent air force in America until after the Second World War.

Throughout the interwar period various international conventions were held with the intention of banning the bomber. In 1922 the Washington Conference on the Limitation of Armaments strongly condemned aerial bombardment. The Hague Rules of Aerial Warfare of 1923, although never ratified, attempted to provide definition of what constituted a military target, what could be suitably subjected to air bombardment, and what could not. Military targets included:

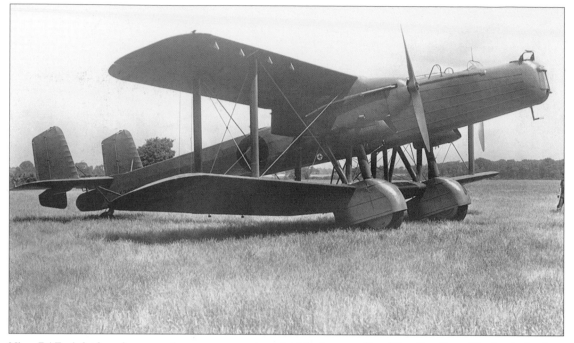

Nine RAF night bomber squadrons were equipped with the gangling Handley Page Heyford, the last biplane heavy bomber to join the RAF. It was on the Heyford that many of the RAF's regular officer pilots, who were to play a key role in Bomber Command's fledgling offensive in the first year of the Second World War, flew their first tours. K3490 was the second production Heyford and was allocated to the first squadron to equip with the type, 99 Squadron at Upper Heyford, in November 1933.

'. . . military forces, works, establishments or depots, factories constituting important and well-known centres engaged in the manufacture of guns, munitions or distinctively military supplies; lines of communication or transportation for military purposes'.

One of the important reasons for the failure to reach an agreement can be attributed to the fact that the Hague Rules saw aerial bombardment as legitimate, but only when directed against military objectives. The difficulty lay in defining and reaching agreement on what constituted a military objective. The rules therefore left it to the discretion of the attacker as to whether a military target was important enough to warrant a bombardment. In 1928 Trenchard produced a paper in which he acknowledged that although bombing of civilians could be contrary to the rules of warfare, 'it is an entirely different matter to terrorise munitions workers (men and women) into absenting themselves from work or stevedores into abandoning the loading of a ship with munitions through fear of air attack upon the factory or dock concerned'.

From the early 1930s much of Britain lived in fear of a catastrophic blow from the air by bombers. The politician Harold Macmillan wrote in his memoirs: 'We thought of air warfare in 1938 rather as

The Boulton Paul Overstrand medium bomber was the first RAF aircraft to have a power-operated enclosed gun turret when it entered service with 101 Squadron in 1934. Power-operated turrets were to become a common defensive feature on most RAF bombers of the Second World War. Overstrand K4561 served with 101 Squadron at Bicester from 1935 to 1938, when it was replaced by the Bristol Blenheim monoplane.

people think of nuclear warfare today.' Further attempts to restrict air warfare failed in 1932 when a disarmament conference organised by the League of Nations assembled in Geneva. By the time Germany withdrew from the conference in 1933 there had been no significant progress. It became increasingly obvious to Baldwin and his Cabinet that Germany, under Hitler, was rearming at a rapid rate and preparing for war.

In 1934 the British Army's allocation of money was halved in the new rearmament programme, since it was decided to rely primarily on the deterrent effect of a larger air force. By 1938 the RAF's share of the combined services budget had risen from 17 per cent to a massive 40 per cent, with the bomber-building programme taking the lion's share. The plans were for the UK-based air force to be increased to eighty-four squadrons by March 1939, as detailed in Expansion Scheme 'A' for the RAF which was approved by the Cabinet in July 1934. To concur with the policy of the Air Staff, forty-one bomber squadrons – but only twenty-eight fighter squadrons – were to be included. However, these figures were revised upwards and downwards at least eight times between 1933 and 1939 and were based on somewhat ambiguous information supplied to parliament by the Air Ministry.

In July 1936 Bomber Command came into existence when the Air Defence of

Great Britain was replaced by four new commands: Fighter, Bomber, Coastal and Training. In the same year, the trio of twin-engined monoplane medium and heavy bombers that would eventually bear the brunt of the RAF's early bomber offensive made their maiden flights. The Whitley, Wellington and Hampden were ground-breaking designs of their time and were conceived as the aircraft with which Bomber Command would undergo its expansion. While the factories were tooling up to mass produce these aircraft, important decisions were being taken by the Air Staff leading to the design and production of the next generation of heavy bombers that would see Bomber Command successfully through the Second World War – the four-engined Stirling, Halifax and Lancaster.

In the meantime, before the first trio of medium and heavy bombers entered squadron service, an odd assortment of monoplane bombers entered limited production and equally limited service with Bomber Command. These were the Vickers Wellesley, Fairey Hendon and Handley Page Harrow, all of which were obsolete even before they had been taken on strength by the RAF. Although the Vickers Wellesley medium bomber offered a vast improvement in performance over the Fairey Gordon and Hawker Audax biplanes which it replaced, it quickly became apparent to its crews that it was neither fast enough nor sufficiently well armed to survive in combat against the new German fighter aircraft. The first Wellesleys entered squadron service in April 1937 but most had been transferred to squadrons in the Middle East before war broke out. Only one bomber squadron was equipped with the five-man Fairey Hendon, the RAF's first low wing monoplane heavy bomber. Fourteen production Hendon IIs entered RAF service in November 1936 with 38 Squadron at

Mildenhall and later at Marham, and remained operational until January 1939 when they were superseded by Wellingtons. The Harrow was the last of the stop-gap bombers intended to equip RAF heavy bomber squadrons during the expansion period. They served with five bomber squadrons and the first aircraft was delivered to 214 Squadron at Feltwell in April 1937. Harrows were replaced in late 1939 by Wellingtons and then reassigned to RAF transport squadrons. It was not entirely surprising, therefore, that in 1935 no British bomber then in service could reach the nearest target in Germany, drop a bomb larger than 500lb, and return to its base in England. These lamentable shortfalls in quality, quantity and strike capability existed up until 1938, when the Wellington and Hampden began to arrive on the squadrons.

With the bomber cast to play the leading role in the Air Staff's plans for any future war, such a large increase in the RAF's bomber force would inevitably cause problems with airfield accommodation. At the end of the First World War there had been some 300 military aerodromes in the UK, yet by 1924 this number had dwindled to 27. The need clearly existed for a rapid programme of airfield construction to accommodate the growing air force.

Even before the echoes of a bitter conflict yet to come had reverberated around the Geneva Armament Conference, plans were afoot at home to construct new airfields for the RAF. In the early 1930s the Air Ministry Works Directorate (AMWD) was formed as the body responsible for the planning and organisation of these new airfields. A subsidiary of the AMWD was created in 1934, known as the Air Ministry Aerodromes Board (AMAB). Its task was to work in close liaison with the Air Ministry Lands Branch (AMLB) in the selection of suitable sites for new airfields. An important part of the

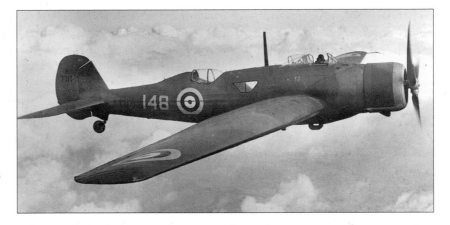

Stop-gap bomber 1:
Vickers Wellesley
K7717 served initially
with 148 Squadron
before conversion to a
very long range trials
aircraft.

Stop-gap bomber 2:
Fairey Hendon
K5085 was the first of
the fourteen
production aircraft.

Stop-gap bomber 3:
Handley Page Harrow
K6937 is pictured
prior to delivery to
214 Squadron in 1937,
minus its gun turrets.

AMAB's brief was to create a standard architectural style for both airfield and domestic facilities, and to prepare plans for the modification of existing airfields.

The environmental impact of all this new land development, much of it in the heart of the English countryside, attracted the attentions of a number of monitoring groups. All plans for permanent buildings on new airfields had to be approved by the Royal Fine Arts Commission while the siting of airfields in the countryside involved consultations with the Society for the Preservation of Rural England.

In 1935 the RAF's Expansion Scheme really took off. With a carefully planned airfield building programme totalling some 100 new military airfields, it continued unabated up to the outbreak of war four years later. Scheme 'C', approved in March that year, emphasised the need for the bomber force to be able to reach Berlin in a latitudinally straight line, so the eastern counties of England, in particular Lincolnshire and Yorkshire, became the obvious choice for the construction of these new airfields, sowing the seeds for the rapid growth of what later became known as the 'Bomber Counties' of the Second World War. Work on the first of the Expansion Scheme bomber stations – Cranfield, Feltwell, Harwell, Marham, Stradishall and Waddington – was begun in 1935. At the same time a number of existing bomber stations, like Upper Heyford, underwent a modernisation programme. More new permanent stations were started in 1936: Dishforth, Driffield, Finningley, Hemswell, Leconfield, Scampton, Upwood and Wyton – names that would soon assume well-earned places in the RAF's history book.

The last permanent bomber stations to be built before the outbreak of war included Binbrook, Bramcote, Coningsby, Leeming, Middleton St George, Newton, North Luffenham, Oakington, Oulton, Swanton Morley, Swinderby, Syerston, Topcliffe and Waterbeach. The stage was now set and it was not long before the first act was played out in September 1939, but the main act that followed was an offensive that would last six long years.

THE SIX-YEAR OFFENSIVE

When war was declared on Germany in September 1939, the RAF was faced with the problem of how to wage a viable strategic air offensive with so few and inadequate aircraft, of which about 280 were serviceable and with crews on a given day. Air Chief Marshal Sir Edgar Ludlow-Hewitt, who was then Commander-in-Chief of Bomber Command, tried in vain to open the eyes of the Air Staff to the serious shortcomings in aircraft, armament and equipment, and not least aircrew training to even the most basic level. After the first costly daylight bombing raids on enemy targets in September and December 1939, the pre-war theory that the bomber would always get through was quickly proved wrong and Bomber Command realised that if it wanted to avoid heavy casualties, the only way to pursue an effective bombing campaign was under the cover of darkness.

Over the winter of 1940–1, it was believed that raids on the small but vital enemy oil refineries would reduce Germany to impotence, but the attacks proved a dismal failure. The first signs of the 'area' offensive yet to come became visible on 16 December 1940 when the centre and suburbs of Mannheim were bombed. By March 1941, however, the U-boat menace in the Atlantic had reached crisis point and Bomber Command was diverted for three months from direct attacks on Germany to bomb enemy naval targets elsewhere, in the hope of relieving the enemy's stranglehold on Atlantic supply routes to Britain.

Bomber Command's first sortie of the Second World War was flown on the day war broke out. A Bristol Blenheim IV of 139 Squadron made a successful photo-reconnaissance sortie north of Wilhelmshaven where it spotted the German fleet. The Blenheim in this photograph has just returned from a reconnaissance sortie early in the war.

A Merlin-engined Whitley V is bombed up with 250lb GP bombs at Linton-on-Ouse during the summer of 1940. The Whitley in the foreground is probably N1426 'O-Orange', frequently flown by Flg Off S.B.I. Bintley and crew. The aircraft in the background, 'N-Nan', is either N1442 (FTR 20 June 1940) or its successor P4991. (IWM CH227)

Concentrations of invasion barges massing in the Channel ports during September 1940 were the subject of repeated and largely successful attacks by aircraft of Bomber Command. This photograph of Dunkirk was taken on 19 September by a Blenheim of 82 Squadron in a combined recce and bombing sortie and shows bomb damage to wharves and barges. (Roy Conyers Nesbit collection)

Heavy losses sustained on the early daylight operations owing to enemy action forced Bomber Command to review its tactics and conduct its main offensive under cover of darkness. As dusk falls and the shadows lengthen, a Wellington crew board their aircraft before setting off on a night raid. (Roy Conyers Nesbit collection)

Home from the first RAF bombing raid on Berlin on the night of 25/26 August 1940, Wellington crews of 149 Squadron pose for the camera at their base at Mildenhall. (IWM HU44271)

Even though operating by night, Bomber Command's losses in men and machines continued to mount since many crews were unused to night flying. This is the wreckage of a British bomber, probably a Hampden or Whitley, brought down over Berlin during the latter half of 1940.

Bomber Command's principal targets in Germany.

With its aircrew untrained and untried in night bombing, it was not until mid-1941 that Bomber Command was forced to face up to its grave shortcomings. The Butt Report of August 1941, commissioned by Churchill's scientific adviser, Lord Cherwell, revealed that few if any of its bombers had reached what they thought was the target, and fewer still had actually dropped their bombs anywhere near it. Hundreds of brave aircrew had died in the process, and to little effect, but with the formation in 1942 of a specialist target finding and marking force, 8 (Pathfinder) Group, the first of several measures were taken to remedy this situation. The Pathfinders' task was to guide squadrons of the main force to the target, which they had marked in advance with coloured flares and target indicators, thereby enabling accurate bombing to take place.

However, the problems encountered by the Command's heavy bomber squadrons of

While Bomber Command's heavy bomber groups operated by night, the Blenheim light bombers of 2 Group continued to fly daring low-level operations in daylight against heavily defended targets in Germany and occupied Europe. On 12 August 1941 fifty-four Blenheims attacked the important Quadrath and Knapsack power stations at Cologne in western Germany, for the loss of ten aircraft. (Roy Conyers Nesbit collection)

finding and hitting a target by night did not stop the medium bomber squadrons of 2 Group from continuing to mount daring but often costly daylight raids against enemy targets in occupied Europe and in Germany itself. Locating a target in daylight and hitting it from low level did not pose the same problems for navigation and bombing accuracy as a bombing operation by night over a longer distance and at higher altitude. From May 1943, control of 2 Group passed from Bomber Command to the 2nd Tactical Air Force in preparation for the Allied invasion of north-west Europe and from thereon in the Command became an exclusively 'heavy' force.

In the latter half of 1941, Bomber Command suffered increasingly heavy losses. The exceptionally harsh winter that followed was doubtless to blame for some of these casualties, but when on 7 November 1941 37 aircraft failed to return from a force

Blenheim crews of 114 Squadron pictured on 13 February 1942, the morning after the Channel Dash operation against the German battle cruisers *Scharnhorst* and *Gneisenau*, and the light cruiser *Prinz Eugen*. In the largest daylight operation of the war so far, 242 sorties were flown by every type of aircraft in the Bomber Command inventory (except the Whitley) in an effort to prevent the German warships passing through the English Channel en route to Germany from Brest. Most bombers were unable to find the ships in the poor weather conditions, and those that did scored no hits. All three ships reached the safety of German ports.

Left to right: ? Kendrick, John Newberry, Wg Cdr J.F.G. Jenkins (CO 114 Squadron), ? King, Flg Off H.P. Brancker, and Flt Sgt C.H. Gray. (Mrs Vera Sherring)

of 400 dispatched, Churchill ordered that bombing operations be suspended until the following spring. In some respects this gave the Command a welcome respite, with time to regroup and reassess the direction of the bomber offensive, but it also served to show it up to its critics in the Admiralty and the War Office as being a bottomless pit into which considerable resources had been thrown, and to little effect.

However, it was not all gloom for Bomber Command in 1941, for the first of the new generation of four-engined bomber aircraft that would transform its striking power began to come on stream with front-line squadrons, beginning in February with the Short Stirling, followed swiftly in March by the Handley Page Halifax, and by the Avro Lancaster in March 1942. They gradually replaced the obsolescent twin-engined Wellington, Whitley and Hampden that had so valiantly borne the brunt of the early offensive.

On 22 February 1942 Bomber Command and the bomber offensive gathered fresh momentum with the appointment of a new and dynamic commander-in-chief, Air Marshal Sir Arthur 'Bomber' Harris. He immediately set about stifling criticism from his detractors by launching the first 1,000-bomber raid in May the same year, which simultaneously proved to the Germans and enemies nearer home that Bomber Command meant business and was far from being a spent force.

During 1942, three scientific research projects began to reach fruition, enabling Bomber Command to improve radically its navigation and bombing accuracy. These were 'Gee' which first saw use in February 1942, followed later that year in December by 'Oboe', and in January 1943 by 'H2S'.

The year 1943 marked the watershed for the fortunes of Bomber Command. At this midpoint in the war it possessed a heavy bomber force made up almost exclusively of four-engined aircraft, flown by better-trained crews using the latest in radar technology for navigation and target finding, and guided over land and sea by the Pathfinders, enabling them to drop their bombs fairly and squarely on target, thanks to accurate target marking, improved bombsights and better bombs.

During the war not all of Bomber Command's efforts were channelled into mass attacks on urban targets. A number of high-profile precision raids on key targets were flown both in daylight and at night by small forces of heavy bomber aircraft. Perhaps the most widely known was the attack on the Ruhr dams in May 1943 by

Bomber Command's principal targets in France.

Lancasters of 617 Squadron led by Wing Commander Guy Gibson. The Dambusters, as they became known, continued to bomb high prestige targets from mid-1943 until the end of the war in Europe, accompanied later by the Lancasters of 9 Squadron.

Bomber Harris believed that bombing held the key to the defeat of Germany. Strategic bombing on a large enough scale, relentlessly pressed home, would lead to the collapse of German industry and the morale of its population. The Casablanca Directive, drawn up by the Combined Chiefs of Staff in January 1943, gave him the authority he required to prove his contention with a sustained assault on German cities. In the first of a series of carefully planned area attacks, the industrial cities of the Ruhr were pounded in thirty-one major raids between March and July, causing huge material damage and heavy loss of civilian life, but at the cost to Bomber Command of

The salvation of Bomber Command and the RAF's strategic bomber offensive, the Avro Lancaster entered squadron service in 1942 and by the war's end equipped sixty out of eighty heavy bomber squadrons.

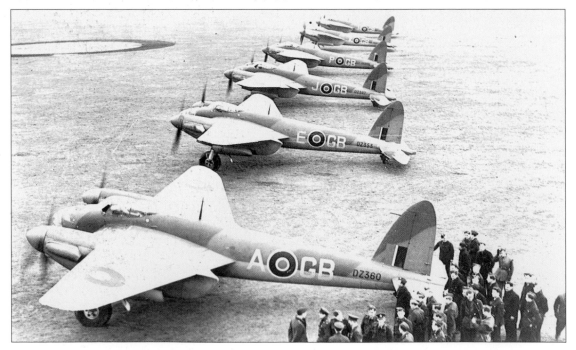

Another new bomber also entered service with the RAF in 1942. Called the Mosquito, it was unarmed and built mainly of wood – but was capable of carrying a 4,000lb bomb to Berlin.

To silence critics at home and prove to Hitler that Bomber Command meant business, the Commander-in-Chief of Bomber Command, Air Marshal Sir Arthur Harris, launched the first ever 1,000-bomber raid on 30/31 May 1942, the target Cologne. Such was the raid's success that it commanded the front pages of Britain's daily papers the following morning.

Throughout the Second World War Britain's factories turned out thousands of aircraft for Bomber Command. In this photograph, taken in March 1943, semi-completed Stirling III fuselages can be seen on the production line at Rover's Longbridge shadow factory, one of many across the country turned over to aircraft manufacture. (Rover)

1,045 aircraft and more than 5,500 aircrew killed or missing.

The climax of the area bombing campaign came in July and August the same year when the RAF launched four major night attacks on Hamburg, raising a terrific firestorm that devastated the city and killed more than 41,000 people. Speaking after the war, Hitler's Armaments Minister, Albert Speer, remarked that further attacks of this nature straight away on six more cities might have forced Germany into defeat, but Harris failed to grasp the significance of the

repetitive attacks which had made the immense destruction possible.

In the meantime, the state of the U-boat war had improved greatly and a change in bombing priorities was authorised by the Combined Chiefs of Staff. The Pointblank Directive issued on 10 June 1943 amended the earlier Casablanca Directive, making the German aircraft industry first priority during the autumn of 1943, but Harris ignored the implication to attack specific key, or 'panacea' targets as he called them. Instead, in August he launched the battle of

Although largely committed to the area bombing of Germany, several squadrons in Bomber Command were tasked with mounting precision attacks against key enemy targets. Probably the best known is 617 Squadron – the 'Dambusters' – for its highly publicised attacks against the Ruhr dams on 16/17 May 1943. This dramatic photograph shows the Möhne dam soon after the attack by Lancasters of 617 Squadron, the large breach in its structure pouring much of the reservoir's 134 million cubic metres of water into the Ruhr valley below. (US National Archives)

Wg Cdr Guy Gibson, who led the dams raid, discusses its success with HM King George VI on the occasion of the king's visit to RAF Scampton where he met the squadron. (US National Archives)

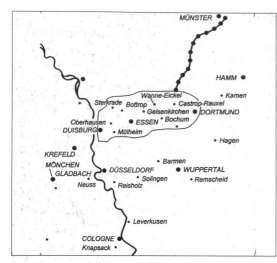

Targets in the Ruhr and environs.

Berlin (although sustained bombing of the capital did not actually get under way until mid-November). What he had done to Hamburg could be repeated on the capital of the Reich, and he believed it would cost Germany the war.

The greater part of the battle was fought in atrocious winter weather conditions against a target at the extreme range of the bombers' endurance. The sheer size of the city and the strength of its formidable defences created serious problems for the aircrews, but in spite of concentrating the offensive on a decisive target the predicted collapse in German morale did not materialise. Although huge areas of the capital had been devastated, Bomber Command's loss rate was disastrous: in 19 major raids between August 1943 and March 1944, more than 600 aircraft were lost and 2,690 aircrew killed. But worse was still to come. When 795 aircraft of Bomber Command raided Nuremberg on 30/31 March, 95 of their number failed to return, making it the Command's heaviest single loss of the war. Mistakes in route planning at Bomber Command headquarters and freak meteorological conditions encountered on the journey to Nuremberg combined to serve up the bomber force on a plate to waiting German nightfighters.

The strategic offensive was curtailed from March to September 1944 while the squadrons of Bomber Command were switched to bombing communications targets in France and Belgium in the run-up to Operation 'Overlord', the Allied invasion of north-west Europe. In the weeks and months following the Normandy landings on 6 June, they were used in the tactical bombing role to support Allied troops in their breakout from the beach head, and against the V-1 flying bomb sites in the Pas de Calais area. The diversion from bombing Germany was almost total, with only 8 per cent of the tonnage dropped in June being upon Germany itself.

By the time strategic operations resumed in strength in the late summer, the RAF and USAAF had succeeded in gaining a measure of air superiority over mainland Europe. Long-range fighters like the American P-51 Mustang provided powerful escort defence for daylight raids as far afield as Berlin. This development enabled Bomber Command's heavies to attack German targets by day with a greatly diminished risk of assault by enemy fighters, although the Command continued to operate extensively by night.

By far the greatest damage inflicted upon Germany was achieved in the last six months of war, at which point Bomber Command was able to strike massive and highly destructive blows against both area and precision targets. On 14 and 15 October 1944, it flew more than 2,000 sorties to Duisburg in less than 24 hours. Towards the end of November 1944 precision attacks on communications and oil targets were beginning to paralyse German industry, while area attacks continued to lay waste the industrial cities of the Ruhr. By the end of January 1945, Germany's national grids of gas, electricity and water were wrecked, the

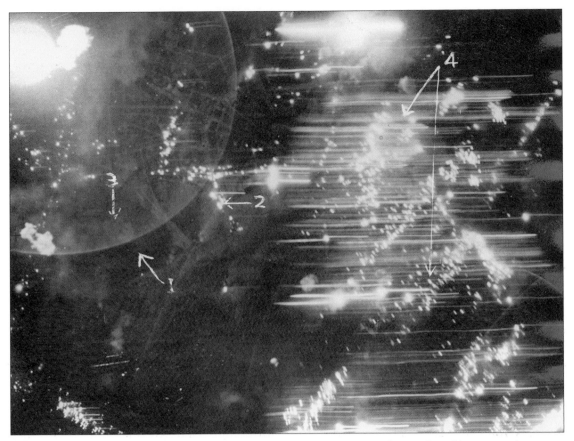

Under 'Bomber' Harris, Bomber Command became locked into a costly area bombing campaign against German cities. A series of four fire raids against Hamburg in late July/early August 1943 demonstrated the awesome levels of destruction that could be achieved by blast bombs and incendiaries. This photograph shows the city ablaze. It was taken from an RAF bomber on the first raid of the series, on the night of 24/25 July. Illuminated by photo-flash bombs and fires, it shows: 1. Aussen Alster; 2. the bridge leading to the main railway station; 3. flak position on a lake; 4. burning incendiaries and fires. (Roy Conyers Nesbit collection)

This Halifax was shot down on a raid to Hamburg, probably in 1943. The RAF's heavy bomber crews paid a high price in the unrelenting bomber offensive against Germany.

Silhouetted against an evening sky Stirling bombers prepare to take off for a heavy raid on Berlin, 23/24 August 1943. 'Bomber' Harris predicted that he could wreck Berlin from end to end and bring Germany to her knees by a series of sustained heavy attacks. In the Battle of Berlin that raged between August 1943 and March 1944, nineteen major raids were dispatched against the city and over 30,000 tons of bombs were dropped for the loss of more than 600 aircraft and their crews. But despite the huge material and human destruction visited on the German capital, the war continued for at least another year. (Roy Conyers Nesbit collection)

Back from raiding Germany, Stirling crews of 149 Squadron unwind with cigarettes and mugs of tea before their debriefing at Lakenheath early in 1944. (IWM CH12689)

Bomber Command's squadrons played an important part in the defeat of the German V-weapons programme in 1944. Flying bomb and rocket sites in the Pas-de-Calais, Somme and Normandy areas were heavily bombed, but the Germans still managed to bring new sites into service at the same rate as the destruction. This photograph shows the cratered landscape of the V-1 flying bomb storage site at Siracourt in the Pas-de-Calais, the result of heavy and sustained bombing attacks by the RAF and USAAF. (Roy Conyers Nesbit collection)

rail network was in chaos, and every type of fuel was in very short supply. High octane aviation fuel became increasingly scarce and it was not long before most of the *Luftwaffe*'s fighter force had been grounded due to lack of fuel.

In the spring of 1945, Bomber Command reached its peak wartime strength with an average daily availability of 1,609 aircraft with crews, but this period was also the most controversial of the war in terms of the morality of the RAF's bomber offensive. For many, the destruction of the medieval city of Dresden on 13/14 February 1945 represented the moral balance rejected. A city of minor industrial significance crammed with refugees, it was razed by a terrific aerial bombardment and the ensuing firestorm incinerated between 35,000 and 135,000

In the closing weeks of the war, Allied air superiority over Europe was such that large daylight raids could be flown to targets in Germany. Here, Lancasters attack the coastal gun batteries on the German island of Wangerooge on the approaches to Bremen and Wilhelmshaven. (US National Archives)

A ruined land: by the war's end much of Germany had been reduced to heaps of smouldering rubble. This is a post-war view of bomb damage in Düsseldorf. (IWM CL2439)

people; the exact number remains undetermined. Dresden was one of the few remaining large, built-up but unbombed German cities and was thus singled out for destruction because there were few selective targets left.

Although Bomber Command could smash Germany's cities to rubble and dust it failed to break the will of its people, just as the *Luftwaffe* had failed to break the inhabitants of London in the Blitz of 1940–1. On 16 April 1945 the Chiefs of Staff announced the ending of area bombing. Ironically, Bomber Command's final sorties of the war were humanitarian in nature, dropping much needed food supplies to the starving population of Holland and the repatriation of Allied former prisoners of war from camps in Europe.

The hard-fought six-year bomber offensive against Germany had cost the lives of 55,000 Bomber Command aircrew and more than 8,000 aircraft had been destroyed. It had brutally remodelled the face of urban Germany and caused much material damage to the towns and cities of France and the Low Countries. Whether it hastened the end of the war in Europe remains a hotly debated issue, but the bravery of the men who flew by day and night with Bomber Command is an undisputed fact.

CHAPTER 1

ORGANISATION

THE CHAIN OF COMMAND

From the outbreak of war, bombing policy directives were handed down from the Chief of the Air Staff at the Air Ministry to the Commander-in-Chief Bomber Command. These directives invariably stemmed from the higher authority of the War Cabinet (later, the Defence Committee) which received advice from the Chiefs of Staff of the three services. In January 1943 policy directives for Bomber Command became subject to the authority of the Combined Chiefs of Staff in the wake of the Casablanca Directive, that set in motion plans for a combined RAF and USAAF bomber offensive. These plans received final endorsement by the Combined Chiefs of Staff at the Trident conference in Washington in May 1943.

In the first instance the general policy directives handed down from the Air Ministry were received by the commander-in-chief at Bomber Command's subterranean headquarters at High Wycombe in Buckinghamshire. From them the C-in-C interpreted his response and chose the way, means and timing of operations. His staff then communicated the general plan to individual group headquarters, each of which was commanded by an air vice-

marshal. The group commanders were responsible for drawing up detailed orders to be handed down to their squadrons. These orders contained details of the target for attack, the number of aircraft to be dispatched, the weight and composition of the bomb load, the route into and out of the target, etc. Group commanders were given a considerable degree of autonomy within the limits set in planning an attack.

The next tier of command was at station level, each of which was commanded by a group captain or, when the 'base' system came into existence, an air commodore. Late in 1942, with the rapid growth in the number of bomber airfields, it became apparent that it would be impracticable to control efficiently up to fifteen airfields from a single group headquarters, and that some form of intermediate link was required. Thus in the spring of 1943 the base system came about to ease this strain and to offer greater local control to stations and their satellite airfields. Centred around a parent or base station, usually one of the pre-war permanent types hosting the base administrative apparatus for the control of six heavy bomber squadrons (or three HCUs), two substations of temporary wartime construction were located close by, each commanded by a group captain. The base system enabled the centralisation of many specialist and administrative functions previously undertaken on an individual station basis, although 8 (PFF) and 100 (BS) Groups were the exceptions to this rule. These stations were organised on an independent basis due to the widely varying tasks of their resident squadrons, although a form of centralised major servicing was introduced for their aircraft. From 1943 the PFF operated a scheme of planned maintenance for its Lancasters and Mosquitoes which kept the number of aircraft available for operations at a higher level than any other group in the Command.

Each base headquarters was identified by a two-digit code, the first digit identifying the parent group and the second the base itself. For example, Pocklington in Yorkshire was designated as 42 Base Headquarters and its four satellite stations, Elvington, Full Sutton, Snaith and Burn, each became known as a 42 Base Substation. From 16 September 1943 until the end of the war, all bases were known by number and not their geographical location.

At any one time RAF bomber stations could house either one or two squadrons, an operational training or heavy conversion unit, and/or a number of smaller miscellaneous units. However, front-line and training units would never have occupied the same station simultaneously, except for a short spell in 1941–2 when squadron conversion flights existed alongside their operational parent to convert new crews onto four-engined bombers. Each individual station provided its resident squadrons or units with technical and domestic housing, mess facilities, flying control, emergency and medical services and airfield security.

A squadron, usually commanded by a wing commander and with a total complement (on average) of some twenty-four aircraft with three in reserve, was responsible for its own aircraft maintenance and administration. But from July 1944, administrative functions were centralised at

Sir Archibald Sinclair succeeded Sir Samuel Hoare as Secretary of State for Air in May 1940.

station level whereby the station was organised into three wings: flying, administrative and servicing. All personnel not directly involved with flying were taken off the squadron and reallocated to either the administrative or servicing wings and therefore came under control of the station for all purposes. The squadron was now composed of operational commanders, aircrew, and a handful of specialist and administrative personnel, thus reducing it in effect to a flying echelon incapable of undertaking operations independently of the station organisation.

At the sharp end of the squadron, individual aircraft, aircrews and groundcrews were allocated to a particular flight – A, B or C – each made up of some eight aircraft and occupying its own assigned corner of the airfield. Individual aircraft had their own

The subterranean nerve centre of Bomber Command headquarters at High Wycombe where operations were planned, pictured here in 1941. The C-in-C, Sir Richard Peirse, sits at the desk in the foreground, watched on his left by his SASO Sir Robert Saundby. (Roy Conyers Nesbit collection)

dispersal pan situated on the airfield perimeter, with an aircrew of seven (generally) and a dedicated groundcrew staff with a flight sergeant ('chiefy') in charge.

All routine servicing, fuelling, arming and bombing-up was carried out in the open air on the dispersal pan, whatever the weather and time of day, night or year. An aircraft would only return to the hangars on the airfield's technical site for major maintenance. However, Bomber Command ground servicing staff were hampered by inadequate technical accommodation and

equipment up until the end of the war, but to a large extent this situation was alleviated from 1943.

Once the squadron had been briefed for operations and the aircraft readied for the task ahead, the crews would embark and the aircraft would be marshalled from the dispersal pans by their groundcrews onto the perimeter track, around which they would taxi to the threshold of the runway in use. Once there they would await their turn for the green light from the airfield controller's caravan, clearing them for take-off and sending them hurtling down the runway and off into the night. For a two-squadron Lancaster station, like Mildenhall in September 1944 operating 15 and 622 Squadrons, it would have taken a little over half an hour on a maximum effort raid to get all aircraft of both squadrons airborne.

THE CHAIN OF COMMAND 1939–45
(Dates of appointment in parenthesis)

WAR CABINET
Prime Minister
Secretary of State for Air

AIR COUNCIL
Secretary of State for Air
Sir Kingsley Wood (May 1938)
Sir Samuel Hoare (Apr. 1940)
Sir Archibald Sinclair (May 1940)

Parliamentary Under-Secretary of State for Air
Capt Harold Balfour (May 1938)
Lord Sherwood (July 1941)
Cdr R.A. Brabner (Nov. 1944)
Maj Quintin Hogg (Apr. 1945)

AIR STAFF
Chief of the Air Staff
ACM Sir Cyril Newall (Sept. 1937)
ACM Sir Charles Portal (Oct. 1940)

Vice-Chief of the Air Staff
AM Sir Richard Peirse (Apr. 1940)
ACM Sir Wilfred Freeman (Nov. 1940)
AVM C. Medhurst (Acting) (Oct. 1942)
AM Sir Douglas Evill (Mar. 1943)

AIR MINISTRY
Air Member of Personnel
AM Charles Portal (Feb. 1939)
AM Sir Ernest Gossage (Apr. 1940)
AM Philip Babington (Dec. 1940)
AM Sir Bertine Sutton (Aug. 1942)
AM Sir John Slessor (Apr. 1945)

Air Member for Supply and Organisation
AM W. Welsh (Sept. 1937)
AM Sir Christopher Courtney (Jan. 1940)

Air Member of Training
AM Alfred Garrod (July 1940)
AM Sir Peter Drummond (Apr. 1943)

Permanent Under-Secretary of State of Air
Sir Arthur Street (June 1939)

BOMBER COMMAND
Commander-in-Chief – Air Marshal

GROUP
Air Officer Commanding – Air Vice-Marshal

BASE
Commanding Officer – Air Commodore

STATION
Commanding Officer – Group Captain

SQUADRON
Commanding Officer – Wing Commander

THE GROUPS

In September 1939 Bomber Command's front-line force was made up of twenty-nine home-based squadrons divided between four groups and spread across seventeen airfields from Yorkshire to Oxfordshire. Each group was equipped with a particular type of twin-engined bomber aircraft dedicated specifically to the light, medium or heavy bombing roles.

No. 2 Group was based in the Norfolk area and equipped with the shapely Bristol Blenheim light bomber; 3 Group's squadrons were centred on the Cambridge and Huntingdon areas and were equipped with Dr Barnes Wallis's 'geodetic' medium bomber, the Vickers

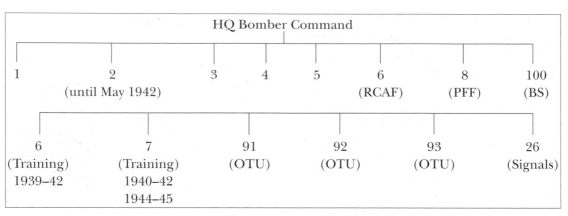

			HQ Bomber Command				
1	2	3	4	5	6	8	100
	(until May 1942)				(RCAF)	(PFF)	(BS)
6	7	91	92		93		26
(Training)	(Training)	(OTU)	(OTU)		(OTU)		(Signals)
1939–42	1940–42						
	1944–45						

Front and second line groups under the operational control of Bomber Command, 1939–45.

The location of RAF bomber groups in England and Scotland, 1939–45.

Wellington; the North and West Riding of Yorkshire-based 4 Group's mainstay was the slab-sided Armstrong Whitworth Whitley heavy bomber; 5 Group was based in south Lincolnshire and Nottingham-shire and was equipped with the 'flying panhandle' – the Handley Page Hampden medium bomber. No. 1 Group, with ten squadrons of single-engined Fairey Battle light bombers, had moved to France on 1 September to form part of the Advanced Air Striking Force (AASF) and did not come under Bomber Command's operational control again until June 1940, whereafter its squadrons were based in south Yorkshire and north Lincolnshire.

From comparatively small beginnings at the onset of war, by 1945 Bomber Command had grown into an awesome leviathan capable of laying waste to Nazi Germany's cities and industrial might. In September 1939, the Command could muster a daily average of 280 aircraft with crews flying from 27 grass airfields; in the closing months of the war it could field a daily average of 1,069 aircraft with crews, drawn from 96 squadrons flying from more than 60 airfields (all but 2 of which had paved runways) and under the control of 7 operational groups. By this late stage of the war it was a predominantly heavy bomber force.

Looking at the disposition of its groups in 1945, the geographical locations of the groups was little changed from 1939; but what had changed was the Command's sheer size and destructive power. No. 1 Group operated an all-Avro Lancaster force; 2 Group's light bombers had been hived off in May 1943 to join the 2nd Tactical Air Force, in preparation for the D-Day landings in June 1944; 3 Group, like 1 Group, was an all-Lancaster affair; 4 Group's squadrons flew Handley Page Halifaxes while 5 Group was predominantly an all-Lancaster force although it did operate a number of de Havilland Mosquitoes in the target marking role, for which it was unique in the Command. This target marking force was made up of three squadrons 'on loan' from 8 (PFF) Group. The decision to amputate a vital part of the PFF's body and transplant it elsewhere in the Command was the source of some considerable displeasure at 8 (PFF) Group's headquarters. But this was just a continuation of the infighting between the main force groups and the PFF which had begun in 1942 when four of the best squadrons, one drawn from each of the four front-line groups, had been allocated to the newly formed 8 (PFF) Group.

Moving up country to the North Riding of Yorkshire and Co. Durham, the Canadian squadrons of 6 (RCAF) Group flew a mixed force of Halifaxes and Lancasters. Bomber Command's specialist target marking force was 8 (PFF) Group – the Pathfinders – which flew a mixed force of Lancasters and Mosquitoes from airfields around Ely in Cambridgeshire's fenlands. Finally, another specialised force existed for bomber support duties in the shape of 100 (BS) Group, which flew electronic and radio countermeasures and intruder sorties with a mixed force of Mosquitoes, Halifaxes, Lancasters, Stirlings, Liberators and Flying Fortresses from airfields in north Norfolk.

FRONT-LINE GROUPS

No. 1 Group

Formed at Abingdon, Berkshire, on 1 May 1936, 1 Group began life with three stations and ten squadrons; by the war's end this had risen to fourteen of each. On the outbreak of war the group moved to France with its Fairey Battle squadrons where it became HQ Advanced Air Striking Force. After suffering severe losses in the battle of France, the AASF returned to England in June 1940 and 1 Group was then re-formed at Hucknall, Nottinghamshire, as a main force bomber group with bases in the East Midlands and Lincolnshire. By the end of the year its squadrons were in the middle of casting off their obsolete Fairey Battles for Vickers Wellingtons. In January 1942 the group comprised ten Wellington squadrons, of which four were Polish and two Australian. Group headquarters was moved again in July 1941, this time to Bawtry Hall in Yorkshire, and the group eventually established its wartime bases in Lincolnshire and Yorkshire. By the end of November 1942 its squadrons had begun to convert to Lancasters which they retained for the duration of the war. No. 1 Group flew a total of some 57,900 sorties during the war and dropped 238,356 tons of bombs, for the loss of 8,577 aircrew.

Air Officers Commanding
(with dates of appointment)
AVM A.C. Wright – Sept. 1939
Air Cdre J.J. Breen – June 1940
AVM R.D. Oxland – Nov. 1940
AVM E.A.B. Rice – Feb. 1943
AVM R.S. Blucke – Feb. 1945

No. 2 Group

Formed on 20 March 1936, also at Abingdon, 2 Group then comprised just two squadrons, one each of Hawker Harts and Hinds.

On 3 September 1939 it made history by dispatching the first operational sortie of the war, and the next day mounted the first bombing raid on Germany. In October the group consisted of ten squadrons of Bristol Blenheims and finally settled its headquarters at Castlewood House, Huntingdon, where it was to remain for the next four years. No. 2 Group was established as a medium bomber group and equipped variously with the Bristol Blenheim, de Havilland Mosquito, Lockheed Ventura, Douglas Boston and North American Mitchell. (The exception to this was 90 Squadron which was equipped with the Boeing Fortress I heavy bomber between May 1941 and October 1942.) The achievements and exploits of the group are many and varied, but the more daring include the first daylight raid on Berlin, several precision attacks on Gestapo and SS buildings in occupied Europe and Scandinavia, and the low-level daylight raid on Bremen in which Wing Commander Hughie Edwards won the VC. At the end of May 1943, 2 Group was transferred from Bomber Command to the newly formed 2nd Tactical Air Force in preparation for the invasion of Europe. The group flew over 57,000 sorties during the war for the loss of 2,671 aircrew.

Air Officers Commanding
(with dates of appointment)
AVM C.T. Maclean – May 1938
AVM J.M. Robb – Apr. 1940
AVM D.F. Stevenson – Feb. 1941
AVM A. Lees – Dec. 1941
AVM J.H. D'Albiac – Dec. 1942
AVM B.E. Embry – June 1943 (2 TAF)

No. 3 Group

Formed at Andover, Hampshire, on 1 May 1936, 3 Group headquarters moved to Mildenhall before finally settling in Exning, Suffolk, in March 1940. The group achieved a number of firsts early in the war. It was the first group to be completely equipped with the Wellington; 115 Squadron made the RAF's first attack on a mainland target, Stavanger/Sola airfield, on 11/12 April 1940; and 7 Squadron became the first in Bomber Command to equip with one of the new generation of four-engined heavy bombers, the Short Stirling, in August 1940. No. 3 Group was equipped variously with the Vickers Wellington, Short Stirling and Avro Lancaster and its squadrons flew as part of the main force for the whole of the war, taking part in all of Bomber Command's campaigns. During 1943–4 its Stirling aircraft played an important role in resistance operations, dropping agents and equipment into occupied Europe and Scandinavia. The group also played a leading part in the introduction of the radar bombing aid G-H in November 1943 and was later earmarked to become Bomber Command's sole G-H-equipped heavy bomber group. No. 3 Group flew some 66,613 sorties during the war for the loss of 1,668 aircraft.

Air Officers Commanding
(with dates of appointment)
AVM J.E.A. Baldwin – Aug. 1939
AVM The Hon R.A. Cochrane – Sept. 1942
AVM R. Harrison – Feb. 1943

No. 4 Group

Formed on 1 April 1937 at Mildenhall, Suffolk, the group headquarters moved twice more before settling at Heslington Hall near York in April 1940. At the outbreak of war the group's eight heavy bomber squadrons were equipped with the Armstrong-Whitworth Whitley and based in Yorkshire. They flew the first night sorties of the war when they dropped leaflets on German cities on 3/4 September 1939. Further leaflet and anti-shipping sorties followed before 4 Group made its first attack on a land target, Hornum on the island of Sylt, in March 1940. In June, five squadrons of Whitleys made the first long-range bombing raid of the war on an Italian target, Turin. As part of the main force, the group's squadrons flew on all of Bomber Command's campaigns of the war including tactical bombing in support of the invasion of Europe. Equipped initially with the Whitley, 4 Group began to re-equip with the four-engined Halifax in early 1941, the aircraft type with which it remained for the duration of the war. Two Wellington squadrons also formed part of the group in 1941–2. In summer 1944 two all-French squadrons, 346 and 347, joined the group and flew Halifaxes from Elvington until the end of the war. In May 1945 the group transferred from Bomber to Transport Command with which it remained until disbanded in 1948. In total, 4 Group's squadrons flew 57,407 sorties during the war and dropped more than 200,000 tons of bombs for the loss of 1,509 aircraft.

Air Officers Commanding
(with dates of appointment)
AVM A. Coningham – July 1939
AVM C.R. Carr – July 1941
AVM J.R. Whitley – Feb. 1945

No. 5 Group

Formed on 1 September 1937 at Mildenhall, Suffolk, as an offshoot of 3 Group, 5 Group's wartime activities became more widely publicised than any of its rivals. The group contributed not only to the main heavy bomber offensive but was also responsible for many of the more specialised and most dramatic attacks of the war. These included the Ruhr dams raid by 617 Squadron, successive breachings of the Dortmund–Ems canal, the daylight raid on Augsburg and the sinking of the *Tirpitz*. At the outbreak of war, with its headquarters at St Vincents in Grantham, 5 Group controlled five stations and ten squadrons equipped with the Handley Page Hampden. By the war's end it had seventeen squadrons of Lancasters and one of Mosquitoes under its command. The group pioneered target marking (it had its own independent target marking force) and minelaying techniques and was the only group in Bomber Command to use the 12,000lb Tallboy and 22,000lb Grand Slam earthquake bombs operationally, and in daylight. After VE-Day, 5 Group prepared for service in the Far East with the 'Tiger Force', but the dropping of the atom bomb put paid to this and the group was finally disbanded in December 1945. During the war it had been equipped variously with the Hampden, Manchester, Lancaster and Mosquito, and had flown 70,357 sorties for the loss of 1,888 aircraft.

Air Officers Commanding
(with dates of appointment)
Air Cdre W.B. Calloway – Aug. 1937
AVM A.T. Harris – Sept. 1939
AVM N.R. Bottomley – Nov. 1940
AVM J.C. Slessor – May 1941

AVM W.A. Coryton – Apr. 1942

AVM The Hon Sir R.A. Cochrane – Feb. 1943

AVM H.A. Constantine – Feb. 1945

No. 6 (RCAF) Group

Formed on 25 October 1942 at Allerton Park, near Knaresborough in Yorkshire, 6 (RCAF) Group was unique in Bomber Command, being manned almost entirely by Canadians and paid for by the Canadian government.

In January 1943 the group became operational with nine heavy bomber squadrons equipped with the Wellington, some of which were detached to the Middle East from June to November. Flying from airfields in North Yorkshire and Co. Durham, 6 (RCAF) Group's squadrons played a full part in the bomber offensive up until the very end of the war in Europe; the group was disbanded in August 1945. Equipped variously with the Wellington, Halifax and Lancaster, the group flew 39,584 sorties and dropped 126,122 tons of bombs and mines for the loss of 784 aircraft and almost 10,000 aircrew.

Air Officers Commanding
(with dates of appointment)
AVM G.E. Brookes – Oct. 1942
AVM C.M. McEwen – Feb. 1944
Air Cdre J.L. Hurley – June 1945

No. 8 (Pathfinder Force) Group

Formed on 15 August 1942 with head-quarters at Wyton in Huntingdonshire and known as the Path-finder Force, the group was officially redesignated 8 (PFF) Group on 13 January 1943. Its headquarters later moved in June 1943 to Castle Hill House, also in Huntingdonshire. Created at the instigation of the Air Ministry with the intention of leading the main force and marking the target – although initially opposed by Bomber Harris who feared the creation of a *corps d'élite* would lead to the fostering of jealousy within the other groups of his command – it was made up of five squadrons, one from each of the operational bomber groups. By April 1945 the force comprised nineteen operational squadrons. At first the constituent squadrons of the group flew their original aircraft (Wellington, Stirling, Halifax, Lancaster and Mosquito) but eventually it standardised on the Lancaster and Mosquito only. Pathfinder crews were all volunteers who were experts in their respective aircrew trades and who had agreed to fly another tour of operations – volunteers within a volunteer force. The navigational skills of the Pathfinder Force were legendary and, combined with navigational and blind bombing aids such as Oboe and H2S, they perfected target marking techniques. With the use of coloured pyrotechnics they made possible the visual pinpointing and accurate bombing of targets by the main force crews who followed. Pathfinder Mosquitoes were also part of the Light Night Striking Force which flew high-speed nuisance raids against German industrial centres armed with 4,000lb HC 'cookies'. By the war's end, the Pathfinders had flown 51,053 sorties against 3,440 targets, for the loss of more than 3,700 aircrew and 675 aircraft. It was disbanded in December 1945.

Air Officers Commanding
(with dates of appointment)
AVM D.C.T. Bennett – Jan. 1943

(Bennett, as an Air Cdre, had been appointed to command the PFF in Aug. 1942.)

AVM J.R. Whitley – May 1945

No. 100 (Bomber Support) Group

Formed on 23 November 1943 at Radlett, Hertfordshire, the headquarters of 100 (BS) Group finally settled at Bylaugh Hall near Swanton Morley in Norfolk. This specialist – and very secret – group was an eclectic mix of heavy bomber and nightfighter aircraft and crews whose task was to wield a host of newly invented electronic and radio counter-measures equipment to confound the German nightfighter and air defence systems, thereby reducing the losses being inflicted upon Bomber Command's main force and Pathfinder squadrons. Using air and ground radars, homing and jamming equipment, and special radio and navigational aids, the group's bomber aircraft jammed and deceived the German defences, while its nightfighter intruder aircraft roamed the night skies over Europe to seek out and destroy *Luftwaffe* nightfighters. By the war's end 100 (BS) Group had largely succeeded in paralysing the German nightfighter network. With thirteen squadrons equipped with Halifax, Fortress, Stirling, Liberator, Wellington, Mosquito, Beaufighter and Lightning aircraft, the group operated from a clutch of airfields in north Norfolk. By the end of the war it had flown 7,932 radio countermeasures sorties for a loss of 47 aircraft, and 8,814 'Serrate' and intruder sorties for the loss of 75 aircraft, and suffered more than 500 aircrew casualties. The group was disbanded in December 1945 but its contribution to the 'new' war of electronic countermeasures had far-reaching implications for conflicts yet to come.

Air Officer Commanding
(with date of appointment)
AVM E.B. Addison – Nov. 1943

TRAINING GROUPS

No. 6 (Training) Group

Formed on 2 September 1939 at Abingdon, Berkshire, 6 (Training) Group controlled fourteen so-called 'group pool' squadrons responsible for the operational training of newly trained aircrew. Aircraft of the same type as those in current use with front-line squadrons were allocated to the group. From early in 1940 these group pool squadrons became known as operational training units. On 11 May 1942, 6 (Training) Group became 91 (OTU) Group.

Air Officers Commanding
(with dates of appointment)
Air Cdre W.F.McN. Foster – Sept. 1939
Gp Capt H.S.P. Walmsley – Mar. 1942

No. 7 (Training) Group

On 15 July 1940 a second operational training group, No. 7, was formed with headquarters at Bicester, Oxfordshire, to cope with the increase in demand for operational training. Its headquarters moved to Winslow Hall, Buckinghamshire, on 1 September 1941 where it was renumbered 92 (OTU) Group on 11 May 1942. No. 7 (Training) Group was re-formed on 20 September 1944 with headquarters at St Vincents, Grantham, Lincolnshire, to control the growing number of Bomber Command heavy conversion units that were previously under the control of individual bomber groups. The group was finally disbanded on 21 December 1945 and control of its units passed to 91 (OTU) Group.

Air Officers Commanding
(with dates of appointment)
Acting Air Cdre L.H. Cockey – July 1940
AVM E.A.B. Rice – Feb. 1945

No. 91 (OTU) Group

Formed on 11 May 1942 at Abingdon, Berks, by renumbering 6 (Training) Group, 91 Group continued to administer bomber operational training units until its disbandment in March 1947.

Air Officers Commanding
(with dates of appointment)
Gp Capt H.S.P Walmsley – Mar. 1942
AVM J.A. Gray – Feb. 1944

No. 92 (OTU) Group

Formed on 14 May 1942 at Winslow Hall, Bucks, by renumbering 7 (Training) Group, 92 Group continued to administer bomber operational training units until its disbandment on 15 July 1945.

Air Officers Commanding
(with dates of appointment)
Gp Capt H.A. Haines – May 1942
AVM H.K. Thorold – Mar. 1943
AVM G.S. Hodson – Feb. 1945

No. 93 (OTU) Group

Formed on 15 June 1942 at Egginton Hall, Derby, 93 Group became the third operational training group to be established in order to cope with the huge demands for bomber aircrew operational training. With the eventual downturn in requirements as the war drew to a close, the group was absorbed into the remaining two OTU groups in January 1945.

Air Officers Commanding
(with dates of appointment)
Gp Capt C.E. Maitland – June 1942
Air Cdre A.P. Ritchie – Feb. 1943
AVM O.T. Boyd – Feb. 1944
AVM G.S. Hodson – Aug. 1944

THE SQUADRONS

At various times 130 bomber squadrons flew with Bomber Command in north-west Europe during the Second World War. Some could trace their lineage with pride back to the early years of the First World War, before the formation of the RAF in 1918.

The RAF's squadron numbering system began with the formation of the service on 1 April 1918 and the initial numbering sequence for RAF squadrons was from 1–299, but with the rapid expansion of the RAF during the Second World War and the incorporation of individual Commonwealth and Allied personnel and units, new block sequences of squadron numbers were made available, as follows: 300–52 Allied (e.g., Polish, Dutch, French); 353–99 RAF; 400–49 Canadian; 450–84 Australian; 485–99 New Zealand; 500–9 Special Reserve; 510–99 RAF; 600–16 Auxiliary Air Force; 617–50 RAF; 651–73 Army; 674–99 RAF.

Under Article XV of the British Commonwealth Air Training Plan it was agreed that trained Canadian, Australian and New Zealand air and groundcrews would be provided to serve with the RAF, but in return the RAF had to pay and equip them. These squadrons were actually RCAF, RAAF and RNZAF, but served under British operational control for the duration of the war and were therefore regarded as being part of the RAF's organisation. Twenty-five such squadrons served at various times with Bomber Command and constituted a quarter of the Command's effective strength. Australian squadrons were the most numerous, with eight, and then there were two New Zealand squadrons, but the contribution from the antipodes was topped by the RCAF which supplied a whole bomber group (No. 6) of – ultimately – fifteen squadrons, from January 1943.

Bomber Command was a truly cosmopolitan organisation during the Second World War, with squadrons manned by personnel from the Dominions and Nazi-occupied countries serving alongside British aircrew. The most numerous were the Canadians with their own bomber group, No. 6, flying from airfields in the North Riding of Yorkshire. Wg Cdr Joe Lecomte was the popular commander of 425 (Alouette) Squadron, RCAF. The Alouettes were a French-Canadian unit and flew from Dishforth and Tholthorpe. (DND/UK)

The only Czech bomber unit in the RAF, 311 (Czech) Squadron, flew Wellingtons from Honington and East Wretham between July 1940 and April 1942. This young Czech pilot sports RAF pilot's wings above his left breast pocket, and those of the Czech Air Force on the right pocket. (Roy Conyers Nesbit collection)

Although fewer in number, the nine squadrons from Allied countries overrun in the opening stages of the war contributed in no small way to Bomber Command's campaign. To some extent, their men had a stronger and more personal reason to hit back at Nazi Germany. Of these squadrons, four were Polish, four French (although two went to 2nd TAF in May 1943, soon after their formation in the UK) and one Czech. For a number of reasons – political, security and simple prejudice – the use by the RAF of personnel from Allied countries, particularly Czechoslovakia, was the source of much high-level discontent in the British government and at the Air Ministry.

Some squadrons had a name incorporated into their titles. Allied squadrons like 311 (Czech) Squadron incorporated their nationality, while others adopted a regional title from their mother country, e.g., the Free French 342 (Lorraine) Squadron. RAF squadrons manned largely by personnel from a Commonwealth country incorporated this recognition in their title, e.g. 44 (Rhodesia)

Squadron or 139 (Jamaica) Squadron. Canadian squadrons incorporated the names of wild animals, birds – usually ones indigenous to Canada – or native Indian tribes, e.g. 429 (Bison) Squadron, or the name of an adoptive city, e.g. 405 (Vancouver) Squadron. The practice established during the First World War of naming RAF squadrons after countries who had presented aircraft or made gifts of money to fund a particular squadron, continued during the Second World War, e.g. 97 (Straits Settlement) Squadron and 214 (Federated Malay States) Squadron.

THE AIRFIELD BUILDING PROGRAMME

By the end of the war in Europe in May 1945, over 170 airfields in England and Scotland had seen use by Bomber Command at various times in the six-year-long offensive against Nazi Germany, but the RAF's massive airfield building programme had begun in earnest in 1939. It was in that fateful year that the Emergency Powers (Defence) Act was passed to enable the Air Ministry to requisition suitable land for airfield construction. Civilian building contractors were invited to tender for contracts and the ambitious programme quickly got under way.

Big construction companies like Laing, Taylor-Woodrow, Costain and Wimpey, which are well known today as house and road builders, were involved in the airfield building programme. A greater number of smaller contractors were also involved and where individual firms possessed insufficient plant of their own, machinery was loaned to them by the AMWD so that all companies – big and small – could play their part in the massive undertaking.

Once tenders had been accepted and issued, work began on clearing and levelling sites. Armies of workmen with heavy plant moved in to remodel the English rural landscape into launch pads for hundreds of Allied bomber aircraft, and homes for thousands of RAF personnel.

If the inevitable labour shortages occasioned by such a large construction programme in wartime were not enough, two knotty problems continued to thwart the AMWD in its desire to maintain a smooth-running programme. Air Ministry policy changes concerning the dimensions and levels of accommodation on bomber airfields meant that alterations in airfield layout and dispersal schemes had to be made in mid-contract, with all the disruption to work and the re-tendering of contracts this entailed; the intense pressure on contractors to work faster meant that concrete and tarmac laying was often carried out under unsuitable weather conditions, like frost or heavy rain. The result was the disintegration of substandard runways and perimeter tracks through the constant pounding by heavy bomber aircraft taking off and landing day and night.

At the outbreak of war, Bomber Command was operating from twenty-seven permanent airfields in England and Scotland, all of which were grass surfaced. A significant number of large, permanent airfields were also nearing completion, legacies of the RAF's pre-war Expansion Scheme. As a result of the changes in Air Ministry requirements already described, major extensions were undertaken at these half-finished airfields to provide additional barrack blocks, bomb stores and ancillary buildings. Comprehensive camouflage schemes were put into operation using paint, netting and other materials, to make runways, hangars and other buildings as inconspicuous as possible from the air.

The RAF's Expansion Scheme stations

Construction workers and plant at work on runway construction 'somewhere in England' during the Second World War. Such was the rate of construction that in the peak year of 1942 one new airfield was coming into use with the RAF every three days. (John Laing Plc)

were characterised by their distinctive and comfortable neo-Georgian headquarters buildings, messes and quarters, and solid C-Type aircraft hangars. Technical buildings were generally located alongside and to the rear of the hangars. Accommodation was centralised and laid out to a roughly circular arrangement and not dispersed over a large area like the dozens of hostilities-only 'prefab' bomber stations built during the course of the Second World War.

Because of the large aircraft they operated, bomber stations needed bigger hangars and more technical accommodation than fighter stations, although what they did have remained inadequate for much of the war. In fact, the rapid expansion of the bomber force and the growing complexity of

its new and heavier aircraft outstripped a hoped-for parallel growth in ground support services and equipment. As a result, powerplant, workshop and other technical accommodation fell far short of the Command's minimum requirements, at least until the end of 1943.

Bomber airfields built before the war had no paved runways, and grass landing strips were the norm. With the introduction to service of heavier bomber aircraft the need for paved runways to allow an unhindered all-weather operational capability became clear. Grass airfields were generally quite adequate in the summer, but with the onset of winter poor drainage of surface water led to waterlogging and serious problems for an airfield's operational effectiveness. The

All routine servicing of bomber aircraft was carried out in the open air on the dispersal pans. Here, fitters work on the port inner Merlin engine of 431 Squadron's Halifax V, LK640 'Q-Queenie', at Tholthorpe, Yorkshire, in 1943. 'Queenie' failed to return from Mannheim on 19 November 1943, crashing in the sea with the loss of all her crew, skippered by Flg Off G.O. Carefoot RCAF. (DND/PL26140)

advantages of tarmac and concrete runways became apparent and in 1939 work began to gradually re-equip most of the command's airfields with a new three-runway layout, perimeter tracks and concrete dispersal pans.

The new dispersal pan system allowed squadron aircraft to be scattered around an airfield perimeter to save them from damage or destruction in the event of enemy air attack. Aircraft were usually only returned to the central maintenance area or the hangars for major engineering or repair work, although a shortage of hangars was the principal reason behind this practice.

From December 1940 all new bomber airfields were constructed with one paved main runway of 1,400 yd and two subsidiaries each of 1,100 yd in length. By February 1941 this scale was amended with

Wellington Ic T2470 'K-King' is towed into the hangars at Mildenhall for major servicing in the summer of 1940. (IWM CH1415)

an increase in length of the main runway to 1,600 yd. In October the same year the requirements had changed still further, extending the main runway length to 2,000 yd with subsidiaries each of 1,400 yd, thereby setting the standard for runway dimensions until the end of the war. In practice the subsidiary runways were rarely used and towards the end of the war doubts were expressed about the need for a three-runway layout on heavy bomber stations.

As the war progressed, so too did the pace of the airfield construction programme. The need for the rapid construction of airfields led to the development of a range of prefabricated building designs such as the Nissen and Romney hut, and the T-Type hangar, all of which combined ease and speed of erection with cost-effectiveness and durability. The need also became clear for a standard night-landing lighting system on all airfields in the Command. The result was the Mk II system which was controlled from the watch office and was highly effective in reducing the time taken to land heavy bombers at night. It also increased the number of aircraft which it was possible to operate from one airfield.

The pace of runway construction also gathered momentum, with an average completion time from foundations down to receiving the first bomber aircraft of five to seven months. It would take about eighteen months for a 1,000-strong labour force to complete an entire 'A' class (Heavy Bomber) airfield with all facilities. Such was the rapid rate of construction that in the peak year of 1942 an average of one new airfield every three days was coming into use with the RAF, at an average cost of about £1 million each.

During 1943, the RAF identified a number of its airfields as suitable for improvement to Very Heavy Bomber (VHB) standard in order to take the expected Boeing B-29 Washington (or Superfortress in USAAF parlance) and the projected Vickers Windsor (never to enter service). Lakenheath, Marham and Sculthorpe were earmarked to become the first VHB airfields and were closed for major reconstruction work during 1944–5.

Within months of peace being declared in the summer of 1945, the RAF began to wind down its huge force of men and machines, airfields and weapons. Squadrons were disbanded, air and groundcrews demobbed; hundreds of aircraft were scrapped and thousands of redundant bombs dumped into the seas around Britain; and dozens of airfields which had once been home to the most powerful conventional bomber force the world had yet seen were returned to the ploughshare and mother nature, from whence they had come.

CHAPTER 2

THE MEN

THE BOMBER CREW

Bomber Command and the aircrews who served in it were probably unique in the history of warfare. The Command itself was a truly cosmopolitan affair, attracting men from the far corners of the empire and from the Nazi-occupied countries of Europe and Scandinavia. A typical RAF bomber crew was a microcosm of Bomber Command itself, reflecting this broad international and social mix of humanity. In fact by January 1945 nearly half of Bomber Command's pilots were from Canada, Australia or New Zealand.

All RAF bomber aircrew were volunteers, and in the case of the Pathfinder Force many were volunteers within a volunteer force. Canada contributed a complete bomber group, No. 6, while other countries contributed entire squadrons. By the war's end most of Bomber Command's aircrew was made up of men who were volunteers (that is, not regulars) and who at the beginning of the war had still been at school. Those who had been regulars in the pre-war RAF and who had survived the culling of six years of war, were by now in a distinct minority.

BOMBER AIRCREW TRADES

At the outbreak of war the aircrew of a typical twin-engined light bomber such as the Blenheim Mk IV was made up of a pilot,

an observer/bomb-aimer and a wireless operator/air gunner. By the war's end the crew of a four-engined heavy bomber like the Lancaster could number up to eight men: pilot, navigator, flight engineer, bomb-aimer, wireless operator, mid-upper gunner, tail gunner, and perhaps an extra gunner, navigator or 'special operator'.

As the war gathered momentum the growing size and complexity of bomber aircraft made it necessary to restructure the bomber crew, bringing in new and specialised crew trades while revising the duties of existing ones. In 1939 a medium or heavy bomber like the Wellington or Whitley had two pilots, one the captain and the other a novice gaining experience under his instruction. This practice was later considered wasteful and discontinued in 1942 because the Air Ministry insisted that it was impossible to train sufficient pilots to carry two per aircraft in Bomber Command. A single pilot policy was therefore adopted throughout the Command, but Don Bennett, AOC of the Pathfinder Force, took a very different view of this change in policy which was beginning to have its greatest effect just when the PFF was created: 'Had junior pilots been brought in to act as flight engineers for, say, fifteen trips before they went for their final conversion training to fly in command of heavies, a tremendous improvement in efficiency and a reduction in losses would have resulted.' Nevertheless, this was but one of the ways in which the role of the bomber pilot gradually evolved from the pre-war duties of flying and navigating the aircraft to one of purely piloting, the other jobs being taken over by specialist aircrew trades.

The pilot was identified by the flying brevet with two wings either side of a laurel wreath surrounding the letters RAF, surmounted by a king's crown. The same design applied to pilots from Canada, Australia and New Zealand, with the letters replaced by RCAF, RAAF or RNZAF respectively.

Defence of the bomber against enemy fighters lay in the hands of the air gunner. Before the war he was an armament tradesman who could be called upon to fly as an air gunner, for which he was paid only for the time he spent in the air. He wore a brass winged bullet on each sleeve, but for him flying was a secondary duty. Not until May 1940 did the Air Ministry officially decree that all aircrew tradesmen (that is, air gunners and wireless operator/air gunners) should be promoted from the ranks to the minimum rank of sergeant. This promotion applied to all other ranks who had completed training in their aircrew trade category and who were flying operationally. There were two aircrew trades that came under the air gunner category: wireless operator/air gunner and straight air gunner. Both were identified by the twelve-feather half-wing brevet with a laurel wreath surrounding the letters 'AG'. Wireless operators were identified by the addition of 'sparks' badges on each sleeve above their stripes, although a few 'WAG' brevets were issued.

With the move to night operations in 1940, bomber aircraft began flying ever increasing distances and it became clear that a navigation specialist was required. Although the aircrew category of observer

The romantic notion of the dashing pilot attracted many young men to volunteer for aircrew duties: 'a job that calls for fitness, dash, initiative, intelligence, responsibility'. Many were found unsuitable for their first choice as pilot, but were trained in other aircrew trades.

(designated by the flying 'O' half-wing brevet, but without the laurel wreath) had been around since the First World War and performed the duty of second aircrew member responsible for navigation, bomb-aiming and any other task called upon to do

A typical RAF heavy bomber crew: seven men comprising pilot, navigator, bomb-aimer, wireless operator, flight engineer and two gunners. These men with their skipper, Flt Lt John Arthur Ingham, have just returned from bombing Berlin on the night of 23/24 August 1943. (Roy Conyers Nesbit collection)

A typical RAF light bomber crew: four men comprising pilot, navigator, wireless operator and air gunner. They are standing beside their Ventura of 464 (RAAF) Squadron.

by the pilot, it was clearly insufficient because the pilot was still the primary navigator. Not until the introduction of the specialist navigator category in 1942, identified by the 'N' half-wing brevet, did the situation change. Now that the roles of pilot and navigator had been more clearly defined, a requirement for further specialist categories became apparent – that of the air bomber ('B') and flight engineer ('E').

A greater range of bombs were now in use by the RAF and with them came more complex bombsights and bomb-release mechanisms. Analysis of early raids had identified the need for two specialists in a bomber crew: the navigator to take the bomber to the target area and an air bomber to take over and make the final run-in to the actual target where he would release the bombs. Along with the flight engineer category, that of the air bomber was introduced at about the same time as the navigator.

The advent of the four-engined bomber, the first of which was the Short Stirling, led to the creation of the flight engineer trade to handle the mechanical, hydraulic, electrical and fuel systems during flight. He also acted as a link between the aircrew and the groundcrew. The first officially trained flight engineers began arriving on the squadrons in April 1941, although it was not until September 1942 that official recognition was forthcoming with the introduction of the specialist 'E' flying brevet.

Up until the autumn of 1944 flight engineers for Canadian heavy bomber squadrons in England were in short supply because the RCAF did not train aircrew in this trade. As a palliative for this situation the RAF supplied trained flight engineers on attachment to 6 Group's bomber squadrons. Towards the end of 1943 the Canadians began training their own flight engineers in response to an Air Ministry request for this aircrew category to serve with RCAF heavy bomber crews, but it was late in 1944 before the first appeared on the squadrons.

From mid-1943 the importance of radio countermeasures to the bomber offensive became increasingly plain. To the newly designated special duty squadrons of 100 (BS) Group a new aircrew category was added. Known as a 'special operator', or 'spec op' for short, his duty was to operate the onboard electronic jamming equipment with which to jam German communications. Spec ops were selected from all aircrew categories and every man was a German language speaker; some were German-born, others were German Jews, who took an extra personal risk whenever they flew over enemy territory.

On the main force squadrons it was also not uncommon for an extra (eighth) crew member to be carried to operate the H2S set. He was usually a navigator and was known as the 'Y' operator, 'Y' equipment being another code name for the H2S radar.

BOMBER AIRCREW COMMISSIONING POLICY

Since the earliest days of the RAF when it became clear that more than one person was needed to crew a large aircraft, the most important figure in any aircrew has always been the pilot. In most cases he was a commissioned officer and was designated the captain of the aircraft. Along with two other key crew members – the navigator and the bomb-aimer – the leadership qualities of these three men were vital to the cohesion of a Second World War RAF bomber crew.

The Air Ministry's aircrew commissioning policy, which held good for much of the Second World War, reflected this need for leadership, and was based largely on its pre-war perception of the RAF as a small elite band of regular officers, the question of who was in charge of a bomber aircraft, and its views on social class which reflected those of British society in the 1940s. The benchmark for an aircrew commission in the RAF during the pre-war years had been leadership – or displaying 'officer-like qualities' – which reflected strongly the public school ethos of the period. But during the Second World War when NCOs made up the greater part of the RAF's bomber crews, change was forced onto a reluctant Air Ministry.

More pilots, navigators and bomb-aimers were commissioned on completion of their flying training than were the other aircrew categories – the so-called 'tradesmen' like air gunners, wireless operators and flight engineers. Of those who were commissioned out of the former group, many were likely to have been educated at public school. More than a few who served in RAF bomber aircrew during the war suspected that the 'old school tie' network lay behind commissioning policy, but it is equally true to say that many officers in the RAF and Bomber Command in particular were not public school educated. In an aircraft piloted by an NCO where there were commissioned officers in the crew, in some instances the navigator or bomb-aimer (who was commissioned) would be designated as the captain of the aircraft. However, it was not uncommon to find all-NCO aircrews. But in any case, if a man survived a tour of thirty bomber operations he would almost certainly be put forward for a commission, the reasoning probably being that he must have had officer-like qualities to get him through a tour unscathed – a back-handed compliment if ever there was one.

The RCAF, who from 1942 was a large supplier of trained bomber aircrew to the RAF, suggested there should be more fairness in granting commissions to all who shared the same dangers as aircrew, arguing that NCO rank was not compatible with the heavy responsibilities of a pilot. Needless to say the Air Ministry was unconvinced by the argument. But the need for aircrew continued to grow as the bomber offensive gained momentum and the original supply of public school candidates soon diminished, forcing the RAF to open its aircrew ranks to a wider social catchment. Soon, it was the turn of men who were products of the grammar and secondary modern schools to swell the ranks of the RAF's bomber crews. Young men like Michael Beetham and Ivor Broom joined up almost straight from school and served the RAF well. They each became distinguished bomber pilots in their own right during the war and rose to high office in the postwar RAF – Sir Michael Beetham became Marshal of the RAF, Sir Ivor Broom an air marshal and group commander in Strike Command.

TRAINING NEW CREWS

At the outbreak of war one of the main tasks of Bomber Command's small regular force of officers and men was to train the huge influx of aircrew volunteers. Some of the older volunteers for flying duties had experience of flying from before the war with University Air Squadrons or the Volunteer Reserve, but the vast majority had never flown before.

To train these volunteers, from August 1939 thirteen squadrons were reserved for operational training duties and became known as Group Pool Squadrons under the control of 6 (Training) Group, although from April 1940 they were renamed Operational Training Units (OTU). They provided six-week courses in which individuals were welded into crews and converted onto type; 55 hours of flying for those earmarked for heavy bombers, 60 for light/medium bombers. In July 1940 a second OTU group, No. 7, was formed to cope with the increase in demand for operational training. These two groups were later renumbered 91 and 92 Groups when a third OTU group, No. 93, was formed in May 1942. (With the downturn in operational training requirements as the war drew to a close, 93 (OTU) Group's flying units were eventually absorbed into the remaining two training groups in January 1945.) Bombers of the same types as those being used in the front-line squadrons were allocated to the OTUs and tour-expired aircrew were 'rested' at them as instructors to pass on their first-hand knowledge of operational flying to the novice crews. Training crews for heavy bombers made the biggest demand on the OTU system, with only two from an average total of twenty-two OTUs supplying trained crews to the light bomber squadrons of 2 Group.

However, before volunteers could be posted to Bomber Command they needed to undergo basic theoretical and flying training in Training Command. Aircrew basic training was undertaken at one of the many Initial Training Wings (ITW) scattered across England, where drill and PT were combined with classroom work to prepare minds and bodies for the next stage in the training programme. After completion of the passing-out examinations, and various psychological and aptitude tests, successful graduates were shipped overseas for flying training. As a result of the Empire Air Training Agreement much of this was carried out at Service Flying Training Schools (SFTS) thousands of miles away from the shores of Great Britain in the safer and less congested skies of the dominions and the USA. (The exception was for flight engineers who trained at 4 School of Technical Training at St Athan in South Wales.) Those bomber crews who trained overseas will never forget the colourful names of their training airfields in the dominion countries like Canada, for

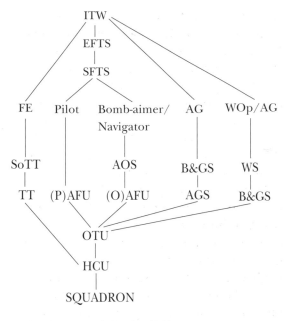

RAF aircrew training in 1944.

example – airfields named Moose Jaw, Medicine Hat and Portage la Prairie, set in the dramatic flatlands of Canada's prairies.

At the peak of the scheme in September 1943, there were 333 Flying Training Schools of which 153 were in the UK, 92 in Canada, 26 in Australia, 25 in South Africa, 10 in South Rhodesia, 9 in India, 6 each in New Zealand and the Middle East, and one in the Bahamas. Five were in the USA. Of course, these schools trained aircrew for the RAF as a whole, but Bomber Command was a major recipient.

Flying Training Command produced pilots, navigators, bomb-aimers, wireless operators and air gunners, and handed them over to Bomber Command whose job it then was at the OTUs to fuse them into fighting crews and then convert them onto the operational types they would soon be flying into battle.

The 'crewing up' process at OTU was a haphazard affair but was in most cases highly successful. Hundreds of young men fresh out

Much aircrew training was undertaken overseas in the dominions. These RAF pilots under training are pictured in the crew room of 31 EFTS at Calgary on the western prairies of Canada in July 1941. They were the first RAF course to pass through 31 EFTS following its formation only the month before.

of flying training were herded into hangars and told to sort themselves out into crews. What attracted individuals to one another ranged from physical appearance to smoking or drinking habits and the crews that resulted from this strange 'marriage' of individuals were often of mixed nationality and social background, comprising men from the four corners of the empire and from all walks of life. Once on a squadron the very nature of their shared experiences and mutual danger quickly bonded them into tightly-knit crews who grew together. Even after fifty years these bonds are still as strong in many of those who survived; in early 1943 only about 17 per cent of RAF bomber crews could expect to finish a thirty-operation tour.

By early 1942, the length of the OTU training stood at 80 hours during a ten-week course, a figure which it remained at more or less for the rest of the war. Intakes were fortnightly with between eleven and sixteen crews arriving at a time. The principal – and

most numerous – aircraft type on which crews trained at OTU was the Wellington and a single OTU would have on strength some fifty aircraft. In the main these were hand-me-downs from the front-line squadrons, worn out and in need of considerable engineering support to keep them flying safely. Needless to say, the exigencies of war meant that many OTU aircraft were kept flying long after they should have been grounded and became virtual death traps. This, combined with the youthful inexperience of their crews, meant that fatal accidents during operational training were high: some classes lost as many as 25 per cent of their strength in three or four months. The churchyards of many a small town in the Vales of Evesham and York pay mute testimony to the thousands of trainee aircrew who never made it onto an operational squadron, victims of clapped-out aircraft and their own inexperience.

With the downturn in operational training requirements as the war drew to a close, 93 (OTU) Group's flying units were eventually absorbed into the remaining two training groups in January 1945.

Two problems arose when the new four-engined bombers started arriving on the squadrons at an ever quickening pace to replace the twin-engined Whitleys, Wellingtons and Hampdens. The first problem was to convert the operational crews from the old type to the new by withdrawing the squadron from the line, but after that the new incoming crews also had to be converted. The second problem concerned the Wellingtons which now predominated at the OTUs, because they had neither mid-upper turrets nor flight engineers, both of which were features and requirements of the new four-engined bombers. Thus the conversion of new crews onto four-engined bombers was soon beyond the practical capability of front-line squadrons.

Before the entry into service of the four-engined heavy bombers which necessitated a further special (heavy conversion) course, the final stage of training was completed at an OTU where individual aircrew trades all came together for the first time and formed themselves into crews. Pictured here are graduates of 2 Crew, 3 Course, 20 OTU, at Lossiemouth in September 1940.

With ever more squadrons converting to four-engined bombers an interim solution was arrived at where one heavy conversion unit (HCU) per bomber group was established, plus one conversion flight (CF) of four aircraft per squadron, generally equipped with Halifaxes or Stirlings. This second stage in the operational training chain converted crews onto the heavy bomber types they would soon fly operationally. In a course lasting five weeks which covered a variety of skills and procedures combined with 20 hours of flying instruction, it enabled pilots to achieve a minimum of 350 hours before joining a heavy bomber squadron. This was also the point at which the flight engineer joined the crew from his trade training at St Athan in South Wales. (By mid-1944, the flying element of the course had risen to nearer 40 hours, while the grand total had risen to an average of 440 hours for pilots; navigators received some 200 hours of flying – over twice that provided in 1941.)

A further review of Bomber Command's advanced training took place in 1942 which led to the disbandment of individual squadron conversion flights and the amalgamation of their resources to form heavy conversion units. These HCUs had a mixture of aircraft types which comprised Halifax, Manchester, Stirling and Lancaster, but within a few months they had been resolved into units containing, for the most

The final link in the aircrew training chain came at heavy conversion units where novice crews were 'converted' onto four engined aircraft. This crew is pictured at 1664 HCU, Lindholme, Yorkshire, in late 1943.

part, one type only. Like those on the OTUs, most of these aircraft were worn out hand-me-downs with poor serviceability records and this, combined once again with the novice crews' inexperience, could have tragic results.

When the first Lancasters came into service in 1942 the problems of conversion training became even more complicated. There was a natural reluctance on the part of Bomber Command to relegate any of these fine – and at first fairly scarce – aircraft to conversion training, and so a number of HCUs were established with fifty-fifty Halifax and Lancaster strengths, but this was soon found to be unsatisfactory and the

arrangement was abandoned in 1943. The Lancasters were withdrawn and crews being posted to Lancaster squadrons were sent for a short period to Lancaster Finishing Schools for a further 12 hours of flying. This practice ceased at the end of 1944 when the supply of Lancasters became better and the appropriate HCUs were equipped with them.

The number of HCUs increased steadily during 1943 and many moved to satellite stations where they could continue the crew conversion process unimpeded by the demands of an operational station. Each bomber group allocated a base station and a number of satellites for use by the HCUs associated with it. For example, 4 Group in Yorkshire allocated Marston Moor as 42 Base Station (1652 HCU), with its satellites at Rufforth (1663 HCU) and Riccall (1658 HCU). With a daily serviceability rate of about forty aircraft, the strength of a typical HCU was considerably higher than that on an operational bomber squadron, but HCUs also suffered much the same troubles as OTUs with the dangerous mix of clapped-out aircraft and inexperienced crews, as the following personal diary excerpt reveals. It was kept by nineteen-year-old flight engineer Sergeant Les Fry while he was undergoing conversion training onto Halifaxes at 1666 HCU, Wombleton, in the early summer of 1944:

Saturday 27 May: We had only been here 5 minutes when I saw the first plane I have seen go up in flames. It was burning for almost an hour. There were three F/Es in it: one of them had his leg broken and the other his jaw. The rest of the crew got out OK.
Monday 5 June: Another kite crashed. Everyone was OK.
Wednesday 7 June: Another kite crashed. All were killed.
Sunday 11 June: The kite we were on last night was lousy. We had to change kites because we had an oil leak.
Wednesday 14 June: Tonight I did my first solo if one can call it that. It was about 5 hours, but we had to change kites. I have not been in a kite yet that is first class.
Thursday 22 June: We got about nine hours in today and are going hard at it. I had an engine cut out on landing yesterday, but it picked up a bit when we started to level off.
Friday 23 June: On fighter affil for four hours this afternoon. I had the hydraulic system go U/S.
Monday 26 June: They lost another kite on

Saturday night. Only the first F/E and the tail gunner got out. The rest were killed.

By mid-1944, the length of an HCU course had been increased to five weeks, with one week of ground instruction and four weeks of flying training. The flying element of the HCU course had risen to nearer 40 hours (nearly double when compared to the syllabus used in 1942), while the cumulative total across the whole flying training process had risen to an average of 440 hours for pilots, and some 200 hours of flying for navigators – over twice that provided in 1941. During the summer months, ten to eleven new crews were posted in every week although this figure usually dropped to about seven during the winter.

The Mosquito squadrons in Bomber Command presented a particular problem when it came to conversion training. Like the Lancaster, the 'Wooden Wonder' was an aircraft in short supply and therefore could not be spared from the front-line squadrons. Another problem arose due to its high performance because there was nothing comparable to a Mosquito for conversion training purposes – except of course another Mosquito. The interim solution was to form a small Mosquito Training Unit (No. 1655, from the Mosquito Conversion Unit) in the Pathfinder Force in October 1942 where only pilots and navigators with previous operational experience, and who were likely to learn quickly, were sent in. Once the supply situation had improved sufficiently, an existing OTU (No. 16) was re-equipped with Mosquitoes in late 1944.

Other special training units were formed from time to time to give particular instruction on new equipment and techniques, for example G-H and H2S training, and the Pathfinder Navigation Training Unit (formed in June 1943) which gave special instruction in target marking techniques.

TOUR LENGTH, SURVIVABILITY AND LMF

Based on the British Army's combat experience in the First World War, the RAF of the Second World War soon realised that to sustain a bomber offensive over a long period of time some form of front-line crew rotation would be necessary. At first 200 hours of operational flying was established by the Air Ministry as the cut-off point whereafter a bomber crew could be rested at an operational training unit, or other flying training establishment. In 1941 the notion of an absolute number of operations constituting a tour of duty came into being: thirty sorties, not exceeding 200 flying hours, was regarded as sufficient for completion of a tour, with a six-month break from operations at a flying training establishment followed by a second tour. Pathfinder Force crews committed themselves to a forty-five sortie tour. On the medium bomber squadrons of 2 Group, however, a tour of daylight operations was set at twenty during the autumn of 1942, with few crews actually getting beyond fifteen. Whether this twenty-op limit had been set 'unofficially' at group or squadron level is not known, but it would

Main force first tours were set at thirty operations, Pathfinders at forty-five. In 1943 fewer than one-fifth of all heavy bomber crews would survive their first tour; one in forty would survive a second. This was often the last glimpse anyone saw of a crew as they began their take-off run down the runway. In this atmospheric twilight scene, 102 Squadron's Halifax V DT743 'O-Orange' prepares to take off from Pocklington to attack the Schneider armament works at Le Creusot in eastern France on the night of 19 June 1943. (Roy Conyers Nesbit collection)

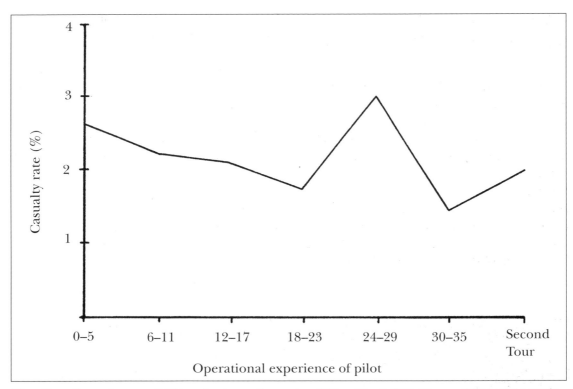

The effect of experience on RAF bomber losses, September 1944 to March 1945. (Source: PRO AIR14/1847)

certainly reflect the high level of casualties experienced at the time by crews flying daylight sorties.

The grim realities of operational flying put the survival prospects for bomber crews into sharp perspective. In 1942 less than half of all heavy bomber crews would survive their first tour; one in five would live to survive a second. By 1943 the odds against survival had lengthened further still with one in six expected to survive their first tour, while a slim one in forty would survive two tours.

Aircrew survival depended upon many different factors which included the operational experience of a crew, their degree of alertness and vigilance when flying, the type of aircraft and whether day or night operations were being flown, the time of the war at which they were operating – and luck.

Once a heavy bomber crew had completed twelve operations, their chances of going on to complete a full tour of thirty ops without becoming casualties was good.

To improve their chances of survival, they might have taken some of the following precautions: observing strict RT procedure; flying a gentle weaving course, rather than remaining straight and level for long periods; gently banking the aircraft from side to side to enable the gunners to check the blind spots beneath the wings for an enemy fighter moving into position for attack; gunners keeping a constant look-out for enemy nightfighters, continually scanning the night sky while traversing their turrets from side to side; maintaining a high level of concentration on the way home, when the temptation was to relax.

A Blenheim crew operating in daylight during 1940–1 would have had a very slim

FLYING-OFFICER PETER BALL

COALVILLE RUGGER FAMILY: ANOTHER SON MISSING

Fate has dealt a cruel blow to Mr. and Mrs. A. G. Ball, of Green-hill-road, Coalville, who, after receiving news that one son was missing and another killed, have now learned that a third is missing. All the boys were bomber-pilots in the Royal Air Force.

The latest news that Flying-Officer Peter Ball, D.F.M., is officially reported missing, came as a great shock to the family and friends.

Mr. and Mrs. Ball had all their children, five sons, serving in the Forces, and it was a happy day when three of them gained the coveted silver wings as sergeant-pilots of the Royal Air Force.

Two County Players

The Ball brothers made a name for themselves on the Rugby field, and two of them secured their county caps, including Leslie, who was posted missing after a raid last year.

There was another happy gathering when Peter received the Distinguished Flying Medal from the King at Buckingham Palace, but some months later came the news that Ken, or "Tin," as he was affectionately known, had been killed on active service. He was a sergeant-pilot and did part of his training in Canada, where he received his wings. Ron., another brother, is a commissioned officer, serving abroad, whilst Jack, a County Rugby player, is in the Home Forces.

The father, Mr. A. G. Ball, the Coalville rating and valuation officer, is secretary of the Coalville Rugby F.C., and on more than one occasion he and his five sons have turned out for the club.

Flying Officer Peter Ball, who is 22 years of age, was formerly employed at the Sun Ray shirt factory at Coalville. He was the second Coalville airman to receive the D.F.M., the other being Sergt. Eric Neal, who is also missing.

Above.

In common with an earlier generation in the First World War, there were few families in the Second who remained untouched by the ravages of war. The Ball family of Coalville in Leicestershire suffered grievously, losing three of their five sons. Brothers Leslie and Peter Ball are pictured here shortly after gaining their pilot's wings. Leslie (left) was a 23-year-old sergeant pilot with 49 Squadron; his Hampden, X3024 'H-Harry', failed to return from bombing Lutzkendorf on 19/20 November 1940. Peter was a 22-year-old flying officer when he and his 44 Squadron Lancaster crew were lost without trace on operations to Essen on 4/5 August 1942. Another brother, Ken, also a bomber pilot, had been killed on active service four months earlier.

Right.

For reasons of security, relatives of missing aircrew and the editors of newspapers that carried casualty reports were requested not to disclose specific details of date, place and circumstances, or the unit of the casualty.

CONFIDENTIAL NOTICE

The names of all who lose their lives or are wounded or reported missing while serving with the Royal Air Force will appear in the official casualty lists published from time to time in the Press.

Any publication of the date, place or circumstances of a casualty, and particularly any reference to the unit concerned, might give valuable information to the enemy, and for this reason, only the name, rank and Service number are included in the official lists.

Relatives are particularly requested, in the national interest, to ensure that any notices published privately do not disclose the date, place or circumstances of the casualty, or the unit.

The Press have been asked to co-operate in ensuring that no information of value to the enemy is published.

Any premature reference in the Press to those reported missing may jeopardise their chances of evading capture, if they have survived without falling into enemy hands.

Above.

The local newspaper said that Peter had been reported missing on operations, a depressingly common feature in the wartime press the length and breadth of the country.

Some aircraft made it home despite suffering serious damage at the hands of flak and fighters. This Lancaster II of 115 Squadron survived a determined attack by two Focke Wulf Fw 190 nightfighters when returning from Cologne on 29 June 1943. The rear turret and its gunner were completely shot away in the ensuing combat, but the Lancaster's gunners claimed one Fw 190 as a probable. (IWM CE79)

chance of survival, whereas a Mosquito crew flying operationally in the spring of 1945 would have stood a very high chance of coming through unscathed.

Although the Lancaster was the best of the RAF's trio of heavy bombers, it was more difficult to bale out of quickly and successfully than either the Halifax or the Stirling.

Why did a crew that followed all of the precautions listed above suddenly 'fail to return' one night? Why did highly experienced and successful bomber pilots like Alec Cranswick, Charles Pickard and Guy Gibson – who between them had well over 300 operations to their credit – eventually die on operations? Why did a

Lancaster gunner survive a fall from 20,000ft without a parachute after his aircraft had been blown apart, his fall broken by the snow-laden branches of a fir tree? Is it all down to luck, fate, a confluence of circumstances? There is no answer.

LACK OF MORAL FIBRE

Although all RAF bomber aircrew were volunteers, the process did not work in reverse which meant that one could not 'volunteer out' if flying was not to one's liking, if the pressures were too great, or if an individual later found himself psychologically unsuited to flying duties.

The sheer elation of surviving another bombing sortie shows on the faces of these Halifax crews from 51 Squadron at Snaith, Yorkshire, as they hand in their parachutes after returning from a raid on the Ruhr in 1943. (IWM CH10293)

In the company of the AOC of 6 (RCAF) Group, AVM 'Black Mike' McEwen, Wg Cdr Bill Swetman, CO of 426 Squadron (fourth from left), and his crew celebrate beating the odds on completion of their tour. (DND/UK 9426)

The tremendous strains of operational flying imposed on aircrew affected all men to greater or lesser degrees, but some took it worse than others. Operational twitch, loss of nerve, emotional exhaustion, shell-shock – it took many forms and descriptions – was not entertained by those in positions of authority within the RAF. The official term was 'Lack of Moral Fibre' (simply abbreviated to LMF) and those branded as such were humiliated and vilified by the RAF before being drummed out of the service. LMF was thought to be contagious and had to be dealt with swiftly to avoid 'contamination', so an 'infected' man was posted off a bomber station immediately. By the standards of the 1990s, the punishment dispensed to those who could no longer take the strain of operations was harsh and inhumane, the intention being to prevent others of questionable morale from avoiding combat duties. Nevertheless, the RAF was very loathe to court-martial a man accused of LMF for fear of the adverse publicity such a trial might generate. In fact some high-ranking officers and politicians, including the Secretary of State for Air, considered parts of the LMF policy were indefensible from a popular point of view.

At operational level the treatment of LMF cases varied from station to station. Some commanding officers preferred to deal with the matter discreetly by posting away the offender on other grounds, while others took a more Draconian view and followed the Air Ministry's ruling on LMF cases to the letter. The latter approach meant offenders were posted to the Aircrew Disposal Unit (initially at Uxbridge, later at Chessington and finally at Keresley Grange near Coventry) to await adjudication of their cases. If found guilty of cowardice, aircrew officers were cashiered, NCO aircrew reduced to the ranks or discharged from the service; some were transferred to either the Army, the Navy or sent down the mines. Flying badges were forfeited since they were regarded by the air force as signs of continuing qualification rather than symbols of training graduation. However, the humiliation of the letters LMF did not stop there, because they were stamped on personal records and would follow a man wherever he went in service life thereafter.

Where there was hope of rehabilitating an offender, he was sent to an Aircrew Refresher Centre which was essentially an open arrest detention barracks, at Eastchurch or Sheffield. If the authorities later deemed him 'cured', he might be remustered to ground duties on his release, or in some instances returned to flying duties.

The policy's harshness accounts for the comparatively small number of LMF cases in Bomber Command during the Second World War, which ran at approximately 200 per year, although surviving records are not sufficiently comprehensive to confirm this figure. However, the true figure is probably higher because many men who experienced psychological problems associated with combat flying, but who were fearful of being branded LMF, kept their fears bottled up and either completed their tours – or simply failed to return. Many should not have continued to fly, their state of mind making them a danger for safety reasons to the rest of their crews. Compared with the USAAF's more enlightened attitude that most LMF cases were psychological in origin and should therefore be treated medically, the RAF's policy, based as it was on its questionable views on character deficiency and cowardice, was harsher and designed to act as a deterrent. Yet at no time in the war was the problem of LMF significant enough to compromise Bomber Command's operational effectiveness, even during the battles of the Ruhr and Berlin in 1943–4 when casualties among aircrew ran high.

CHAPTER 3

THE AIRCRAFT

Although the Avro Lancaster flew the highest number of sorties of any of its contemporaries and equipped the majority of Bomber Command's heavy squadrons by the war's end, it was but one of fourteen different types of bomber aircraft used at various times by the wartime Command between 1939 and 1945. The Lancaster and the Halifax bore the brunt of the strategic night offensive, ably supported by the Mosquito, but the early marks of Halifax and Stirling were not such good performers.

In the role of day bomber, the Blenheim light bomber single-handedly bore the brunt of the early daylight offensive until the arrival in 1941 of the first of a trio of replacement American bombers, the Boston, Ventura and Mitchell. Although faster and better armed, the American trio continued to receive the same savage losses suffered by the Blenheims at the hands of flak and fighters. This was not so much through poor aircraft design and armament, as through a blind adherence to a daylight offensive by Bomber Command strategists in the face of increasingly effective enemy defences.

As the war progressed, new types of bomber aircraft entered service, gradually replacing those that had served the RAF from the outbreak of war. With their arrival the definition and classification of what constituted a light, medium or heavy bomber aircraft changed. In 1940, the twin-engined Wellington and Hampden were classed as medium bombers, while the Armstrong-Whitworth Whitley was classed as a heavy. The Whitley could fly 1,630 miles with a 3,750lb bomb load at a cruising speed of 165mph. When it was eventually phased out of front-line service in 1942 successors to the appellation of heavy bomber were the four-engined Stirling, Halifax and Lancaster. Undisputably the best of the new breed of heavies, the Lancaster began to enter squadron service in January 1942 and could carry a 14,000lb bomb load up to 1,660 miles at a cruising speed of 216mph at 20,000ft.

Of the same period, the powerful twin-engined de Havilland Mosquito BXVI was classed as a light bomber, yet it was capable of carrying a 4,000lb bomb load 1,370 miles at 400mph at 28,000ft. By comparison, its predecessor in 1940 was the underpowered single-engined Fairey Battle which could carry a 1,000lb bomb load, 1,000 miles at 200mph at 15,000ft.

These comparisons are not entirely fair because they illustrate successive generations of aircraft design, and the Air Ministry planners and aircraft designers of the early 1930s could not have foreseen the demands of air offensive to come. However, they do serve to show how the exigencies of war acted as a powerful accelerant to bomber design.

The effort and effectiveness of Bomber Command aircraft compared*

Type	Total sorties flown	Total failed to return	Bomb load delivered (tons)	Losses: % of sorties
Manchester	1,185	69		5.80
Stirling	18,440	606	27,821	3.81
Blenheim	12,214	443	3,028	3.62
Ventura	997	38	726	3.60
Whitley	9,169	288		3.10
Wellington	47,409	1,332	41,823	2.80
Mitchell	221	6		2.70
Hampden	15,771	417	9,115	2.60
Boston	1,609	40	952	2.48
Halifax	82,773	1,830	224,207	2.28
Lancaster	156,192	3,340	608,612	2.13
Lightning	101	2		2.0
Fortress	1,517	7		0.46
Liberator	615	3		0.5
Mosquito	39,795	254	26,867	0.63

*Sources: Sharp and Bowyer, *Mosquito* (London, Faber, 1967), p. 324 and Middlebrook and Everitt, *The Bomber Command War Diaries* (London, Viking, 1985), pp. 782–4

ARMSTRONG-WHITWORTH WHITLEY

Characterised by its distinctive nose-down flying attitude in level flight, Armstrong-Whitworth designer John Lloyd's ungainly looking twin-engined AW 38 (later named Whitley) was the first of the modern generation of monoplane heavy bombers to enter squadron service with the RAF in 1937. It also became the first to fly offensive night operations over Germany in the Second World War and could carry a greater bomb load than its contemporary the Vickers Wellington. The Whitley Mk V became the main production version of which a total of 1,445 were eventually built to equip fifteen squadrons.

Alongside the Wellington and the Hampden, the Whitley bore the brunt of Bomber Command's early night offensive against Germany. Whitleys flew on the RAF's first bombing raid against Berlin on 25/26 August 1940 and later against some of the longer-range targets in Czechoslovakia and Italy. Its last bombing operation was on 29/30 April 1942 against Ostend, but the type continued to see service with bomber OTUs.

Despite a slow cruising speed and an inability to carry anything larger than the standard 1,000lb bomb in its small main bomb bay, the Whitley soldiered on as a heavy bomber with Bomber Command's 4 Group until the last squadron relinquished its Mk Vs for the four-engined Halifax in the spring of 1942.

Specification

Type: twin-engined five-man mid-wing heavy night bomber

Powerplant: Mk I, two 795hp Armstrong Siddeley Tiger IX 14-cylinder air-cooled radial engines; Mk II and III, 845hp Tiger VIII; Mk IV, two Rolls-Royce Merlin IV 12-cylinder

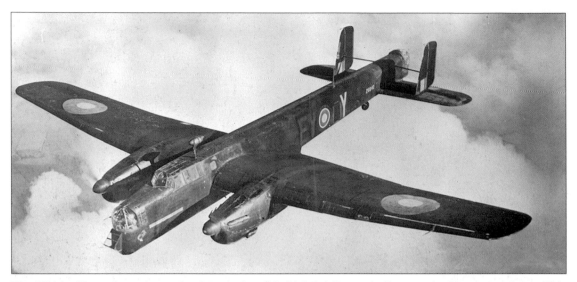

The Whitley V was the main production version, of which 1,445 were built to equip fifteen squadrons. This example, V6640, served with 78 Squadron and completed twenty-eight operations before its relegation to second-line duties in early 1942. It is seen here when serving with 1484 Target Towing Flight at Driffield.

liquid-cooled two-stage supercharged in-line engines; Mk V, 1,145hp Merlin X

Dimensions: span 84ft 0in, length 69ft 3in (Mk V 70ft 6in), height 15ft 0in, wing area 1,137 sq ft

Weights: Mk II and III, empty 15,475lb, loaded 22,900lb; Mk V, empty 19,350lb, loaded 33,500lb

Performance: Mk II and III, max speed 209mph at 16,400ft, service ceiling 23,000ft, range 1,315 miles. Mk V, max speed 230mph at 16,400ft, service ceiling 26,000ft, range 1,500 miles

Armament, defensive: 1 x .303in Browning mg in Nash and Thompson nose turret, 4 x .303in Browning mgs in Nash and Thompson tail turret. *Offensive*: max bomb load 7,000lb

Production: 1,811 (excl. prototypes)

AVRO LANCASTER

The four-engined Lancaster probably did more than any other British aircraft of the Second World War to take the fight back to the German heartland. Lancasters spearheaded Bomber Command's night offensive against Germany and flew thousands of sorties against targets the length and breadth of enemy-occupied Europe. By the end of 1942, seventeen heavy bomber squadrons had converted to the Lancaster; by the war's end the type equipped sixty out of Bomber Command's eighty heavy bomber squadrons, with both Pathfinder and main forces.

Contrary to popular belief, the Lancaster did not come about as the result of the failure of the twin-engined Manchester. The Ministry of Aircraft Production decided to go ahead with the four-Merlin Manchester III (later known as the Lancaster) months before the Vulture engine showed signs of trouble. The outcome was arguably the most successful Allied heavy bomber of the Second World War.

The first production Lancasters entered front-line service with 44 (Rhodesia) Squadron at Waddington on Christmas Eve 1941 and their first operation was a raid against Essen on 10/11 March 1942. The following month Lancasters of 44 and 97

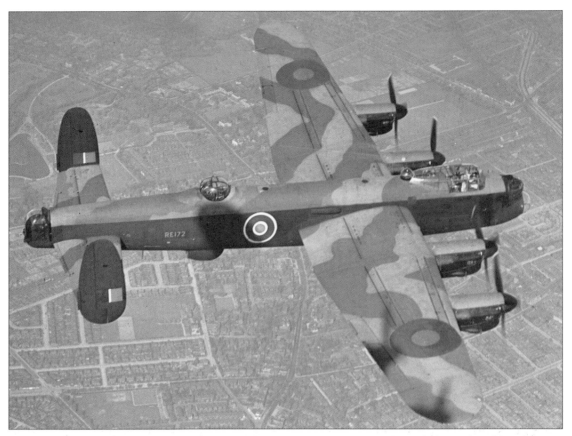

Probably the best-known British bomber of all time, the Lancaster was the only heavy bomber of the Second World War capable of carrying the 22,000lb Grand Slam. This example, RE172, is a Mk III and was one of a batch of eighty-seven built by A.V. Roe at Yeadon and delivered in the closing weeks of the war. It served with 37 Squadron until it was SOC on 3 June 1947.

Squadrons staged a spectacular daylight low-level deep-penetration raid against Augsburg near Munich. Specially converted Lancasters of 617 Squadron attacked the Ruhr dams in May 1943 and went on the achieve lasting fame with further precision bombing operations. As a weight-lifter the Lancaster's capabilities were unmatched. Over short ranges it could carry a bomb load of 14,000lb and it was the only heavy bomber of the Second World War capable of carrying the 12,000lb Tallboy and 22,000lb Grand Slam bombs.

Few changes were made to the basic Lancaster design throughout the Second World War and of nearly 7,000 Lancasters delivered during this period, almost half were lost on operations. Eleven VCs were awarded to Lancaster crew members.

Specification
Type: four-engined seven/eight-man mid-wing monoplane heavy night bomber
Powerplant: Mk I and III, four 1,460hp Rolls-Royce Merlin XX, 22, 38 or 224, 12-cylinder liquid-cooled, supercharged in-line engines;

Mk II, four 1,650hp Bristol Hercules VI 14-cylinder air-cooled two-row radial engines
Dimensions: span 102ft 0in, length 69ft 6in, height 20ft 4in, wing area 1,297 sq ft
Weights: empty 36,457lb, loaded 68,000lb. With 22,000lb bomb, 72,000lb
Performance: 287mph at 11,500ft, cruising speed 210mph at 12,000ft, service ceiling 24,500ft (without bomb load), range with 14,000lb bomb load 1,660 miles
Armament, defensive: 2 x .303in Browning mgs each in Frazer-Nash nose and dorsal turrets, four in Frazer-Nash tail turret; some aircraft had 2 x Browning mgs in downward firing ventral turret. *Offensive*: max bomb load 14,000lb. Special aircraft, either 1 x 22,000lb or 12,000lb deep penetration bombs, 1 x 9,500lb Upkeep bouncing mine.
Production: 7,373

AVRO MANCHESTER
Designed to Air Ministry specification P13/36 for a medium bomber, the Manchester was built around two 1,760hp Rolls-Royce Vulture engines and offered a good range and load-carrying performance. At the end of 1937 an initial order for 200 Manchesters was placed with Avro, although the first prototype did not fly until July 1939. 207 Squadron became the first to receive the new bomber in November 1940 and deliveries continued to 5 Group squadrons throughout 1941 and into early 1942. The underdeveloped Vulture engine led to frequent engine failures and,

Underpowered and unreliable, the Manchester failed to live up to expectations when it entered service with Bomber Command in November 1940. L7427 'Q-Queenie' served initially with 97 Squadron in 1941 before she was taken on strength by 83 Squadron in whose markings she is seen here. 'Queenie' went missing on operations to Hamburg on 8/9 April 1942. (Roy Conyers Nesbit collection)

combined with a troublesome hydraulic system and poor handling at fully loaded weight, the Manchester became an operational liability. Thus, from early in 1942, efforts were made to phase the type out of service for eventual replacement by the Lancaster and Halifax. The last operational use of the Manchester was on the 1,000-bomber raid against Bremen on 25/26 June 1942, after which the type was withdrawn. Many continued to see use as training aircraft with some of Bomber Command's heavy conversion units up until late in 1943.

Specification

Type: twin-engined seven-man mid-wing monoplane heavy night bomber
Powerplant: two 1,760hp Rolls-Royce Vulture I 24-cylinder liquid-cooled 'X' engines

Dimensions: span 90ft 1in, length 68ft 10in, height 19ft 6in, wing area 1,131 sq ft
Weights: empty 29,432lb, loaded 50,000lb
Performance: max speed 264mph at 17,000ft, cruising speed load 205mph, service ceiling 19,300ft, range with 8,100lb bomb load 1,630 miles
Armament, defensive: 2 x .303in Browning mgs each in Frazer-Nash nose and dorsal turrets, four in Frazer-Nash tail turret.
Offensive: max bomb load 10,350lb
Production: 200

BOEING B-17 FLYING FORTRESS

More popularly known for its key role in the USAAF's daylight bomber offensive against Germany, twenty of the B-17C version were delivered to the RAF in May 1941 as the Fortress I. They were used operationally by 90 Squadron on high altitude daylight

Twenty B-17C Flying Fortresses were delivered to the RAF in May 1941 and were trialled operationally by 90 Squadron.

bombing operations, but serious technical problems and several losses caused the RAF to conclude that the type was unsuitable for Bomber Command's purpose. Further supplies to the RAF of the Fortress E, F and G models under 'Lend-Lease' were diverted to Coastal Command for long-range maritime reconnaissance. The last production Fortress was the B-17G, of which 85 were delivered to Bomber Command's 100 (BS) Group as the Fortress III in January 1944, and were used by 214 and 223 Squadrons in the radio countermeasures role.

Specification (B-17G/Fortress BIII)

Type: four-engined ten-man mid-wing monoplane heavy bomber
Powerplant: four 1,200hp Wright Cyclone R-1820-97 air-cooled radial engines
Dimensions: span 103ft 9in, length 74ft 9in, height 19ft 1in, wing area 1,420 sq ft
Weights: empty 36,135lb, loaded 72,000lb
Performance: max speed 302mph at 25,000ft, cruising speed 160mph, service ceiling 35,600ft, max range 3,400 miles
Armament, defensive: 12 x .50in Browning mgs, two each in chin, dorsal, ventral and tail turrets, one each in the cheek and beam positions. *Offensive*: max bomb load 7,600lb

BRISTOL BLENHEIM

As the first RAF aircraft to fly over German territory within hours of the Second World War being declared, and the first to make a bombing attack on a German target, the Bristol Blenheim quickly carved for itself a place in history. In common with other RAF bombers of the expansion period the Blenheim was ordered straight off the drawing board, with the first two production aircraft serving as prototypes.

A development of the Bristol Type 142, 'Britain First', the first Blenheim I was delivered to 114 Squadron in March 1937 and was hailed as one of the fastest bombers

in the world. By the end of 1938 another fifteen bomber squadrons in 2 Group had re-equipped with the type although by September 1939 they were in the process of converting to the much improved long-nosed Mk IV version. Blenheim squadrons were based in France in early 1940 as part of the Air Component of the BEF and suffered heavy losses due to their light defensive armament and suicidal low-level attacks against the advancing German Army.

During 1941 and 1942 the Blenheim squadrons of 2 Group continued to carry out low-level daylight bombing raids against targets in occupied Europe, and suffered grievous losses in the process. In the daring raid on Bremen by Blenheims of 105 and 107 Squadrons on 4 July 1941, the leader Wing Commander Hughie Edwards was awarded the VC. By early in 1942 the Blenheim was slowly being replaced in 2 Group by the Douglas Boston, Lockheed Vega Ventura and North American Mitchell, the last aircraft being withdrawn from 18 Squadron in October 1942. Of the 1,012 Blenheims used by 2 Group between 1939 and 1942, 403 were lost on operations, 86 were damaged beyond repair and 96 were destroyed in flying accidents.

Specification (Blenheim Mk IV)

Type: twin-engined three-man mid-wing monoplane light bomber
Powerplant: two Bristol Mercury XV 9-cylinder air cooled radial engines
Dimensions: span 56ft 4in, length 42ft 9in, height 12ft 9in, wing area 469 sq ft
Weights: Empty 9,700lb, loaded 13,500lb
Performance: max speed 266mph at 11,000ft, cruising speed 225mph, service ceiling 22,500ft, range 1,450 miles with full bomb load
Armament, defensive: 1 x fixed .303in Browning mg in port wing, 2 x .303in Browning mgs in Frazer-Nash undernose

The Blenheim IV bore the brunt of the RAF's daylight bomber offensive until it was gradually phased out of front-line service in 1942, replaced by the American Boston, Mitchell and Ventura. Pictured here are Blenheim IVs of 13 OTU, which trained pilots, observers and air gunners for 2 Group and overseas squadrons. R3607 in the foreground had a surprisingly long operational career with 59, 57, 40 and 18 Squadrons, before joining 13 OTU in June 1941, but finally crashed on 13 March 1942.

mounting, 2 x Browning mgs in Bristol dorsal turret. *Offensive*: max bomb load 1,000lb, but additionally up to 350lb of light bombs on external racks

CONSOLIDATED B-24 LIBERATOR

Also better known for its role alongside the B-17 in the USAAF's daylight bomber offensive, the B-24 Liberator was chosen by the RAF as an electronic warfare platform for its 100 (BS) Group because of its capacious fuselage capable of carrying RCM equipment. Two units, 223 Squadron and 1699 Flight, operated some thirty-three Liberators, mainly

the B-24H and J versions, in the radio countermeasures and RCM training roles from early 1944 until the war's end.

Specification (B-24J/Liberator BVI)
Type: four-engined ten-man shoulder-wing monoplane heavy bomber
Powerplant: four 1,200hp Pratt & Whitney R-1830-65 air-cooled radial engines
Dimensions: span 110ft, length 67ft 2in, height 18ft, wing area 1,048 sq ft
Weights: empty 36,500lb, loaded 56,000lb
Performance: max speed 300mph at 28,000ft, range 2,100 miles, service ceiling 30,000ft

Liberators were used in small numbers by 100 (BS) Group in the radio countermeasures role. This example, belonging to 223 Squadron, had its bomb racks removed to enable radar and radio jamming equipment to be installed.

Armament, defensive: 10 x .50in mgs, two each in nose, dorsal, ventral and tail turrets, one each in beam position. *Offensive*: max bomb load 8,800lb

DE HAVILLAND MOSQUITO

Nicknamed the 'Wooden Wonder' by virtue of its largely wooden construction, the Mosquito was one of the most versatile and successful combat aircraft of the Second World War. It saw service in most theatres of operations and in a variety of different roles, most notably in north-west Europe with Bomber, Fighter and Coastal Commands. Although the 'Mossie' made an important contribution in the pathfinding role with Bomber Command, it was with the squadrons of the Light Night Striking Force that it achieved the most dramatic results.

The maiden flight of the first prototype was made in November 1940 and 105 Squadron became the first RAF bomber squadron to receive the aircraft in November 1941. Initial deliveries were of the PR Mk I but the first B Mk IV arrived on the squadron in May 1942. A second 2 Group squadron, No. 139, became operational on the Mosquito in November and for several months these two units flew specialised low-level precision attacks in daylight against high prestige targets. When 2 Group became part of 2nd Tactical Air Force on 1 June 1943, these operations ceased and the two Mosquito squadrons were transferred to 8 (PFF) Group, serving alongside 109 Squadron in the Pathfinder role. They continued to mount nuisance raids and 'spoofs' to divert attention from the main force targets and re-equipped progressively with the B Mk IX and XVI.

De Havilland's 'Wooden Wonder' was probably the most successful and versatile Allied bomber of the Second World War. It was with Bomber Command's Light Night Striking Force that the Mosquito achieved the most dramatic results, often flying to Berlin and back twice in one night to drop 4,000lb 'Blockbuster' bombs. Pictured here are a pair of Mosquito IVs, DZ353:E and DZ367:J, of 105 Squadron from Marham, the first unit in Bomber Command to equip with the Mossie.

In early 1944, the Light Night Striking Force (LNSF) was formed in 8 (PFF) Group, initially with 139, 627 and 692 Squadrons, although 627 soon left to join 5 Group's marker force. Later, 128, 571 and 608 Squadrons joined the LNSF and participated in the force's frequent nocturnal roving over Germany, guided to their targets by Oboe-equipped PFF Mosquitoes, and bombed with a precision seldom achieved by the main force heavies. Between January and May 1945, the LNSF Mosquitoes dropped 1,459 Blockbusters on Berlin alone, and 1,500 on other targets.

The famous Dambuster squadron, No. 617, used a variety of different marks of Mosquito (Mk IV, IX, XVI, XX and 25) for low-level target marking, while Mossies were also used by the bomber and fighter squadrons of 100 (BS) Group for radio countermeasures and intruder work.

A specially modified Mosquito, the B Mk IV (Special), was fitted with a bulged bomb bay to enable it to carry a 4,000lb Blockbuster bomb all the way to Berlin. Later marks of Mossie were factory fitted with the new bulged bomb bays and 100-gallon drop tanks, the definitive version being the B Mk XVI which also boasted a pressure cabin giving it an operational ceiling of 37,000ft and a maximum speed of 408mph loaded.

Bomber Command statistics for the Mosquito at the end of the war showed a total of 39,795 sorties flown for the loss of 254 – the lowest loss rate of any type operated by the Command.

Specification

Type: twin-engined two-man mid-wing monoplane bomber

Powerplant: Mk I and IV, two 1,460hp Rolls-Royce Merlin 21, 22 or 25 12-cylinder liquid-cooled supercharged in-line engines; Mk IX and XVI, two 1,680hp Merlin 72 and 73 or 1,710hp Merlin 76 and 77 engines

Dimensions: span 54ft 2in, length 40ft 6in, height 12ft 6in, wing area 454 sq ft

Weights: Mk IV, empty 13,400lb, loaded 21,462lb; Mk IX, empty 14,570lb, loaded 22,780lb

Performance: Mk IV, max speed 380mph at 17,000ft, service ceiling 29,100ft, range 2,100 miles. Mk XVI, max speed 415mph at 28,000ft, service ceiling 37,000ft, range with max bomb load 1,485 miles

Armament, defensive: none. *Offensive*: Mk IV, max bomb load 2,000lb; Mk IX and XVI, max bomb load 4,000lb, plus 2 x 500lb bombs under wings

Production: 7,781, of which 1,690 were completed as unarmed bombers

DOUGLAS A-20 BOSTON

Rugged, versatile and dependable, this American twin-engined design was used principally by the USAAF, US Navy, RAF and Soviet Air Force in the attack bomber, night intruder and nightfighter roles. The DB-7B model, identical to the USAAF's A20-A, was ordered by the RAF as a replacement for the Blenheim and in the guise of the Boston III it eventually equipped three squadrons in 2 Group, Nos 88, 107 and 226. Although faster than the Blenheim, better armed, with a nosewheel undercarriage and clean aerodynamic form, its range was not as good.

The first Boston entered service with 88 Squadron in July 1941, followed in early 1942 by Nos 107 and 226. Some 132 Bostons were used by the RAF on daylight bombing

Regarded by its pilots as a delight to fly, the Boston equipped three squadrons in 2 Group between July 1941 and August 1943 and it was faster and better armed than the Blenheim it replaced. Boston III AL754 'D-Donald' (pictured) flew on the famous Eindhoven raid on 6 December 1942 but suffered flak damage and was nursed home to a crash-landing at Great Massingham by its pilot Flt Sgt 'Nick' Nicholls.

operations until the last aircraft was withdrawn in August 1943, to be replaced by the Mitchell.

In all, 30 Bostons were lost on operations; 8 were written off as the result of battle damage, and 10 were lost through flying accidents.

Specification

Type: twin-engined four-man mid-wing monoplane day bomber

Powerplant: two 1,600hp Wright Cyclone GR-2600-23 air-cooled radial engines

Dimensions: span 61ft 4in, length 48ft 0in, height 15ft 10in, wing area 465 sq ft

Weights: empty 16,650lb, loaded 21,700lb

Performance: max speed 304mph at 13,000ft, cruising speed 200mph at 15,000ft, service ceiling 24,250ft, max range 1,240 miles with 2,000lb bomb load

Armament, defensive: 4 x .303in Browning fixed mgs in nose, 2 x .303in Browning hand-operated mgs in dorsal turret, 1 x .303in Browning ventral mg. *Offensive*: max bomb load 2,000lb

Production: 132 Boston Mk III and Mk IIIa used by 2 Group

FAIREY BATTLE

By the time the Second World War had started in September 1939, the single-engined two-man Fairey Battle was already obsolete as a bomber. It had been designed in the mid-1930s as a monoplane replacement for the Hawker biplane bombers and featured state-of-the-art construction for its day with light alloy and stressed kin. The prototype first flew in

Already obsolete as a light bomber when the Second World War started, the Fairey Battle equipped seventeen bomber squadrons in September 1939 but suffered grievous losses in the Battle of France that quickly followed. K7602 served with 52 Squadron at Upwood and is pictured here in its pre-war markings that display the squadron number on the fuselage. No. 52 Squadron received its full complement of Battles at the end of 1937.

March 1936, ten months after an initial order for 155 aircraft had been placed for an unenthusiastic RAF. But the pressing need to expand the RAF and a political wish to keep defence contractors busy meant that this unsatisfactory aircraft with its performance shortcomings was foisted on the RAF. No. 63 Squadron was the first to receive its Battles in May 1937 and within two years there were seventeen squadrons so equipped.

On the outbreak of war ten Battle squadrons of 1 Group moved to France as the bomber element of the Advanced Air Striking Force but suffered grievous losses due largely to their poor performance and ineffective armament. On 20 September 1939 a Battle gunner of 226 Squadron claimed the first German aircraft shot down in the Second World War, and on 11 May 1940 the RAF's first two VCs of the war were won by a Battle crew of 12 Squadron. The RAF's Battle squadrons were finally withdrawn to England in June 1940 although eight squadrons continued to use the aircraft for bombing the Channel ports from airfields in England before the type was eventually withdrawn from Bomber Command's front-line inventory in the autumn. Those Battles that had survived were transferred to training and target-towing duties.

Specification

Type: single-engined two-man low-wing monoplane light bomber
Powerplant: one 1,030hp Rolls-Royce Merlin I 12-cylinder liquid-cooled in-line super-charged engine (also Merlin II, III and V)
Dimensions: span 54ft 0in, length 42ft 4in, height 15ft 6in, wing area 433 sq ft
Weights: empty 6,647lb, loaded 10,792lb
Performance: max speed 257mph at 15,000ft, 210mph at sea level, service ceiling 23,500ft, range at 200mph, 1,000 miles
Armament, defensive: 1 x fixed Browning .303in mg in starboard wing, 1 x Vickers K GO mg in rear cockpit. *Offensive*: max bomb load 1,000lb
Production: 2,200

HANDLEY PAGE HALIFAX

Designed to Air Ministry specification P13/36, the Halifax became the second of the four-engined heavies to enter service with Bomber Command. The first Merlin-engined Mk I was delivered to 35 Squadron in November 1940 but it was not until 10 March 1941 that the first operation was flown by six Halifaxes when Le Havre was bombed. The British public had to wait until July to learn of the new bomber's existence, following a successful daylight attack on the battleship *Scharnhorst* at La Pallice. However, increasingly effective enemy defences soon led to the Halifax being confined to night bomber operations.

By early in 1942, four of 4 Group's heavy bomber squadrons had converted to the Halifax and re-equipment continued apace until by 1944 it became the exclusive equipment of 4 Group and 6 (RCAF) Group, and was also used in smaller numbers by 100 (BS) Group in the RCM role. The Halifax flew on virtually all the main raids of the night offensive between 1942 and 1945, and the last occasion when Bomber Command Halifaxes operated in strength against the enemy was in the raid on coastal gun batteries at Wangerooge on 25 April 1945.

The earlier Merlin-engined marks of Halifax, the Mk I, II and V, suffered heavier losses than the Lancaster on account of their inferior speed and operational ceiling. They also suffered from an incurable rudder lock-over problem which could lead to an unrecoverable and therefore fatal deep stall developing. When the first examples of the much improved Hercules-engined Mk III entered service in

The Halifax became the exclusive equipment of 4 and 6 (RCAF) Groups for the latter part of the war. The example pictured here is a B Mk II Series Ia of 78 Squadron, pictured on an air test from its base at Breighton, Yorkshire, in the autumn of 1943. It features Modification 814, the enlarged rectangular vertical tail surfaces that cured the potentially lethal rudder lock-over problem. (Roy Conyers Nesbit collection)

November 1943, the small triangular tail fins were replaced by new and larger rectangular ones which cured once and for all the lock-over problem. The performance of the Halifax was now good enough for it to hold its own against the Lancaster, and although it could carry up to 13,000lb of bombs the heaviest single weapon it could carry was the 8,000-pounder.

A longer-range Halifax with an extended wingspan, designated the Mk VI, was fitted with the Hercules 100 engine and a redesigned fuel system and issued to several squadrons in 4 Group to supplement the Mk IIIs in the last months of the war. Airframes built as Mk VIs, but fitted with the Hercules XVI, were designated Mk VII and entered service with three squadrons in 6 (RCAF) Group from June 1944.

A total of 6,179 Halifaxes had been built by the time production ceased, with Bomber Command's squadrons flying 82,773 operational Halifax sorties during the Second World War for the loss of 1,833 aircraft.

Specification

Type: four-engined seven/eight-man mid-wing monoplane heavy night bomber
Powerplant: Mk I, four 1,145hp Rolls-Royce Merlin X 12-cylinder liquid-cooled super-charged in-line engines. Mk II and V, 1,280hp Merlin XX. Mk III and VII, 1,650hp Bristol Hercules XVI 14-cylinder air-cooled sleeve-valve supercharged radial engines. Mk VI, 1,800hp Hercules 100
Dimensions: early production aircraft, span 98ft 10in, length 70ft 1in, height 20ft 9in, wing area 1,250 sq ft. Late production aircraft, span 104ft 2in, length 71ft 7in, height 20ft 9in, wing area 1,275 sq ft
Weights: Mk I, empty 36,000lb, loaded 60,000lb; Mk III, empty 38,240lb, loaded 65,000lb; Mk VI, empty 38,900lb, loaded 68,000lb

Performance: Mk I, max speed 280mph at 16,500ft, service ceiling 19,100ft, range with 8000lb bomb-load 1,060 miles. Mk III, max speed 282mph at 13,500ft, service ceiling 18,600ft, range with max bomb load 1,030 miles
Armament, defensive: Mk III, 1 x Vickers K GO mg in nose, 4 x .303in Browning mgs each in Boulton Paul dorsal and tail turrets.
Offensive: max bomb load 13,000lb
Production: 6,135

HANDLEY PAGE HAMPDEN

Faster than the Whitley or Wellington, the Hampden was a joy to fly and possessed a good range and a respectable bomb load. In company with the Wellington it was classed as a medium bomber, and with the Whitley

Faster than the Whitley or Wellington, the Hampden possessed near-fighter handling and was a joy to fly. However, its narrow fuselage made for cramped conditions inside. These Hampdens belong to 16 OTU from Upper Heyford, Oxfordshire. P5304 in the foreground later transferred to 455 Squadron in Coastal Command but crashed in Sweden in September 1942 during a transit flight to Vaenga, near Murmansk, Russia, to protect Arctic convoys.

it formed the backbone of Bomber Command.

Built to Air Ministry specification B9/32 for a twin-engined day bomber, the Hampden was developed in parallel with the Wellington and made its maiden flight six days later than its cousin on 21 June 1936. The twin-Bristol Pegasus radial-engined monoplane boasted a number of novel design features, the most prominent of which was its narrow but deep flat-sided forward fuselage – no more than 3ft wide at its broadest point – and a slender twin-boom tail.

An order for 180 Hampdens was placed two months after the prototype had flown and deliveries to the squadrons of 5 Group commenced in August 1938 with 49 Squadron at Scampton being the first to convert onto the new bomber. In September 1939, ten squadrons of Hampdens were equipped and ready. Aircraft from 44, 49 and 83 Squadrons were dispatched in daylight on 4 September to seek and attack German shipping in the Schillig Roads, but before long and in common with the RAF's other medium and heavy bombers, the Hampden was confined to night operations.

No. 5 Group's Hampden squadrons became increasingly committed to bombing German land targets and were involved in attacks on German invasion barges in the Channel ports during the summer and autumn of 1940. They continued to fly operations against a variety of enemy targets through 1941 and early 1942, but it was inevitable that with the Manchester and Lancaster beginning to come on stream in 1942, the Hampden should be withdrawn from front-line bomber operations. The last Hampden sortie in Bomber Command was flown on 14/15 September 1942 by 408 Squadron against Wilhelmshaven.

Hampdens flew a total of 16,541 bombing sorties and dropped 9,115lb of bombs for the loss of 413 aircraft, and a further 194 to other causes.

Specification
Type: twin-engined four-man mid-wing monoplane medium bomber
Powerplant: two 1,000hp Bristol Pegasus XVIII 9-cylinder air-cooled radial engines
Dimensions: span 69ft 2in, length 53ft 7in, height 14ft 11in, wing area 688 sq ft
Weights: empty 11,780lb, loaded 18,576lb
Performance: max speed 254mph at 13,800ft, service ceiling 19,000ft, range 1,885 miles with 2,000lb bomb load, 1,200 miles with 4,000lb bomb load
Armament, defensive: 1 x fixed .303in Browning in nose, 1 x Vickers K GO gun in nose, dorsal and ventral positions. Later modified to take twin Vickers K Rose-mounting in dorsal position. *Offensive*: max bomb load 4,000lb
Production: 1,451

LOCKHEED VEGA VENTURA

A military development of the Lockheed Lodestar civil transport, the twin-engined Ventura was intended for the RAF as a successor to the Hudson, to which it bore a striking similarity. As well as the bulbous twin .303in Boulton Paul dorsal turret, it featured a stepped underside to the rear fuselage to accommodate a gun position armed with two .303in guns. At 2,500lb its bomb carrying capability was disappointing and it was not long before 2 Group crews realised that the Ventura light bomber did little more than the Hudson, except consume more fuel. Only three squadrons were equipped with the Ventura I and II from May 1942 (Nos 21, 464 and 487), but due to its low speed and insufficient armament to withstand a determined fighter attack the type suffered heavy casualties on daylight bomber operations

Known to RAF bomber crews as the 'Pig' because of its ungainly appearance, the Lockheed Ventura equipped three RAF bomber squadrons. Although it was quite heavily armed the Ventura still suffered heavy casualties. (Philip Jarrett collection)

over north-west Europe and was withdrawn by late 1943. Of the 136 Venturas that saw service with 2 Group, 31 were lost on operations, 9 written off through battle damage, and 8 destroyed in flying accidents.

Specification
Type: twin-engined four-man mid-wing monoplane light bomber
Powerplant: two 2,000hp Pratt & Whitney Double Wasp R-2800-31 air-cooled radial engines

Dimensions: span 65ft 6in, length 52ft 7in, height 14ft 3in, wing area 551 sq ft
Weights: empty 17,468lb, loaded 26,700lb
Performance: max speed 289mph at 16,000ft, cruising speed 212mph at 11,000ft, service ceiling 24,800ft, range 925 miles with full bomb load
Armament, defensive: 2 x .50in fixed mgs on top of nose, 2 x .303in mgs in nose on flexible mounts, 2 x .303in mgs in Boulton Paul dorsal turret, tunnel gun position with 2 x .303in manually trained mgs. *Offensive*: max bomb load 2,500lb

Armed with six .50in machine guns in four positions, the Mitchell could also carry a 4,000lb bomb load. Four squadrons in 2 Group operated the Mitchell. This example is Mk II FL218 of 180 Squadron. (Roy Conyers Nesbit collection)

NORTH AMERICAN B-25 MITCHELL

The third of the trio of American twin-engined designs intended as replacements for the Blenheim, the Mitchell II (equivalent to the USAAF's B-25C and D) was used by four squadrons of 2 Group (Nos 98, 180, 226 and 320) between September 1942 and the end of the war. A five-man light bomber with a nosewheel under carriage and a range of more than 900 miles, the Mitchell could carry a 4,000lb bomb load. In May 1944, the heavier Mk III arrived on the squadrons but it proved to be much less popular with its crews. In total, 85 Mitchell IIs were lost on operations, 26 written off due to battle damage, and 22 lost in flying accidents.

Specification (Mitchell II)

Type: twin-engined five-man mid-wing monoplane light bomber
Powerplant: two 1,700hp Wright Cyclone GR-2600-13 air-cooled radial engines
Dimensions: span 67ft 6½in, length 54ft 1in, height 15ft 9½in, wing area 610 sq ft

Weights: empty 16,000lb, loaded 26,000lb, max 30,000lb

Performance: max speed 294mph at 15,000ft, cruising speed 237mph at 10,000ft, service ceiling 26,700ft. Range with 4,000lb bomb load 925 miles at 15,000ft

Armament, defensive: 2 x .50in mgs each in dorsal and ventral Bendix turrets, 1 x .303in mg in one of four ball-and-socket mountings in nose. *Offensive*: max bomb load 4,000lb

SHORT STIRLING

Of the eight heavy bomber types in service with the principal combatant nations during the Second World War, the RAF's Short Stirling was unique in several respects: it was the tallest at 22ft 9in, the longest at 87ft 3in and the slowest at a maximum speed of 260mph; at 99ft 1in it had the shortest wingspan, at 44,000lb the greatest empty weight, and the shortest range with a maximum payload, at 740 miles.

Of the three British 'heavies' the Stirling was the only one to be designed from the outset to take four engines, and the only one to have full dual control. It was introduced into RAF service in August 1940 with 7 Squadron and by the time the type was eventually withdrawn in July 1946, a total of 2,371 had been built, all of which were flown by the RAF. At the zenith of its operational career with Bomber Command in 1943, twelve squadrons of 3 Group were equipped with the Stirling, but with the introduction of the Halifax and Lancaster to most main force and Pathfinder squadrons by the end of that year, the Stirling quickly became the poorer relation in the RAF's trio of four-engined heavies, principally for its poor altitude performance and high attrition rate. It was therefore relegated to

The Stirling was the first four-engined heavy bomber to enter squadron service with the RAF in August 1940. This Stirling I, W7455 'B-Beer', of 149 Squadron, the third squadron to equip with the Stirling, is pictured bombing-up at Lakenheath in January 1942. (Roy Conyers Nesbit collection)

second-line duties and lightly defended short-range targets in France during the run-up to D-Day, with 149 Squadron flying the final Bomber Command Stirling sortie against Le Havre on 8 September 1944.

Specification

Type: four-engined seven/eight-man mid-wing monoplane heavy night bomber
Powerplant: Mk I, four 1,590hp Bristol Hercules XI 14-cylinder air-cooled sleeve-valve radial engines, Mk III, 1,650hp Hercules XVI
Dimensions: span 99ft 1in, length 87ft 3in, height 22ft 9in, wing area 1,460 sq ft
Weights: Mk III, empty 43,200lb, loaded 70,000lb
Performance: Mk III, max speed 260mph at 14,500ft, cruising speed 200mph at 10,000ft, range 2,010 miles with 3,500lb bomb load, 740 miles with 14,000lb bomb load
Armament, defensive: Mk III, 2 x .303in Browning mgs each in Frazer-Nash nose and dorsal turrets, 4 x Browning .303in mgs in Frazer-Nash tail turret. *Offensive*: max bomb load 14,000lb
Production: 2,369

VICKERS-ARMSTRONG WELLINGTON

The twin-engined Wellington became one of the outstanding bomber aircraft of the Second World War and was renowned for the amount of battle damage it could soak up. This was due largely to its unique geodetic construction that had been

Thanks largely to its unique geodetic construction, the Wellington was able to withstand an enormous amount of battle damage and still make it home. Only 410 examples of the Merlin-engined Mk II (illustrated) were built and equipped eight medium bomber squadrons, although the Mk II was less popular with crews than the radial-engined versions. In the foreground is W5461 'R-Robert' of 104 Squadron, captained by Sqn Ldr H. Budden DFC, which failed to return from Berlin on 12/13 August 1941. All the crew survived to become prisoners of war.

specially designed by Dr Barnes Wallis of 'bouncing bomb' fame. The first prototype flew in June 1936 and in October 1938 the first production aircraft entered service with Bomber Command's 99 Squadron. At the outbreak of war, eight operational bomber squadrons in 3 Group were equipped with the Wellington. 'Wimpys' flew the first bombing raid of the war against the German fleet at Wilhelmshaven on 4 September 1939, although from December the same year they were switched to night operations and became the RAF's principal night bomber until sufficient numbers of the Stirling, Halifax and Lancaster had reached the squadrons in 1942. The Wellington was the first RAF bomber to drop the 4,000lb Blockbuster.

The main production versions that saw service principally with Bomber Command's 1 and 3 Groups were the Mk I, Ia and Ic (Bristol Pegasus X and XVIII), the Mk II (Rolls-Royce Merlin X, 400 built), Mk III (Bristol Hercules XI, 1,519 built), the Mk IV (Pratt & Whitney Twin Wasp, 221 built), and the Mk X (Bristol Hercules VI, 3,804 built). Total Wellington production reached 11,460 aircraft, with many examples seeing service with Coastal Command, as trainers at bomber OTUs, and as engine and armament test-beds.

Specification

Type: twin-engined five-man mid-wing monoplane medium night bomber

Powerplant: Mk I, two 1,000hp Bristol Pegasus X and XVIII air-cooled radial engines. Mk II, 1,145hp Rolls-Royce Merlin X in-line liquid-cooled in-line engines. Mk III, 1,500hp Bristol Hercules XI sleeve-valve radials. Mk X, 1,675hp Bristol Hercules VI/XVI radials

Dimensions: span 86ft 2in, length 64ft 7in, height 17ft 5in, wing area 840 sq ft

Weights: Mk Ic, empty 18,556lb, loaded 28,500lb. Mk X, empty 22,474lb, loaded 36,500lb

Performance: Mk Ic, max speed 235mph at 15,500ft, service ceiling 18,000ft. Mk III, max speed 255mph at 12,500ft, service ceiling 18,000ft. Range with 4,500lb bomb load 1,540 miles

Armament, defensive: Mk Ic, 2 x .303in Browning mgs in Frazer-Nash nose and tail turrets, 2 x manually operated Browning .303in mgs in beam positions. *Offensive*: max bomb load 4,500lb. Mk III, *defensive*: 2 x Browning .303in mgs in Frazer-Nash nose turret, four in Frazer-Nash rear turret, 2 x manually operated Browning .303in mgs in beam positions. *Offensive*: max bomb load 4,500lb

Production: 11,460

CHAPTER 4

ARMAMENT

BOMBS AND AERIAL MINES

In the years that followed the First World War, very little money was made available by the British government for armament research and development purposes. It was not until 1935, when the possibility of another war looked increasingly likely, that the government began to turn its attention towards developing new bomb designs for the RAF. But when Bomber Command eventually went to war in 1939 it found itself equipped with a very limited and inadequate arsenal of high explosive general purpose (GP) bombs. It quickly became apparent that the GP range of bombs were poor performers with their low charge-to-weight ratio of 34 per cent and many simply failed to detonate on impact. The GP range was gradually replaced over a period of three years by the newly developed medium capacity (MC) range of weapons which proved very effective. As the war gathered pace, so new and heavier bombs were designed to meet the needs of the growing offensive, finding their apotheosis in the specialist Tallboy and Grand Slam 'earthquake' bombs designed by Dr Barnes Wallis, who was also co-designer of the Vickers Wellington.

By early 1942, Bomber Command was in the process of changing over from small twin-engined bombers like the Hampden and Blenheim which carried comparatively light bomb loads, to heavy four-engined bombers like the Halifax and Lancaster capable of carrying far greater loads over longer distances. In 1939 the heaviest bombs that could be carried as part of a load were 500-pounders; by the war's end it was common for a bomber to carry individual high explosive MC and HC bombs weighing between 2,000 and 4,000lb each.

The three principal types of bomb that Bomber Command employed in its offensive against Germany (apart from the specialist weapons) were the incendiary (or fire bomb) filled with either thermite pellets or a mixture of phosphorus and rubberised benzol; the high capacity (blast) bomb; and the medium capacity (for general bombardment) bomb, the latter two being filled with one of several high explosive (HE) charges then available which included RDX, Minol, Amatol, Amatex and Torpex. Used together, HE and incendiary produced devastating results when the blast bombs blew apart buildings and the incendiaries then set fire to the scattered contents. At the beginning of the war HE bombs were considered the best weapons to use, with incendiaries employed in small quantities as a harrassment measure; but in the final years of the war Bomber Command dropped mixed loads comprising a much higher ratio of incendiary to HE.

Armourers transport a train of 250lb General Purpose (GP) bombs from the bomb dump to waiting aircraft during the summer of 1940. The GP range of high explosive bombs with which the RAF found itself lumbered in 1939 were poor performers with a low charge-to-weight ratio.

In 1940, bomb loads included no more than 6 per cent by weight of incendiaries, but as the bomber offensive gathered momentum and the intensity of attacks grew ever greater, the value of incendiaries for fire-raising became appreciated. In fact, one of the great success stories of the war for the RAF was the small hexagonal stick-shaped 4lb incendiary bomb, of which Bomber Command dropped nearly eighty million during the course of the Second World War. By mid-1942 incendiaries comprised up to 40 per cent of a bomb load and later during the Battles of the Ruhr and Berlin in 1943–4 they could account for up to 66 per cent. It was from this point in the war that the combination of high explosive blast

bombs like the 4,000lb HC, used in conjunction with incendiaries, flattened many of Germany's urban centres and caused the terrible and uncontrollable firestorms that devastated the cities of Hamburg, Dresden, Kassel and Darmstadt.

The second of the three principal types of bomb was the high capacity range of weapons that were essentially modernised versions of those used with some effect by the newly formed RAF against German targets towards the end of the First World War. The HC came in three sizes, all of which were cylindrical in shape, their thin steel casings packed with high explosive. With their high charge-to-weight ratio of more than 70 per cent, the HC blast bombs

Groundcrew at RAF Wattisham refuel and re-arm a 110 Squadron Blenheim IV during the summer of 1940. The armourers manhandle a 250lb GP bomb ready for winching into the bomb-bay. On the trolley in the foreground can be seen a pair of bomb containers, each holding four 40lb GP bombs, which will eventually be loaded complete into the fuselage bomb-bay. This particular aircraft, R3600, flew forty-eight sorties before failing to return from a shipping strike on 6 May 1941. (IWM CH364)

had a devastating effect against most targets. The first of the Blockbuster 4,000lb HC bombs appeared in the spring of 1941 and from then on, supplemented with incendiaries, they became the standard area load for Bomber Command's heavy bombers. The 8,000lb and 12,000lb versions of this bomb were in effect 4,000lb sections bolted together. With the development of a new and powerful high explosive filling called Minol, the blast effect of these awesome weapons was further increased and their incendiary side effects enhanced, making them a most successful range of bombs.

The third type of bomb was the medium capacity (MC), developed between 1940 and 1943 to supersede the unreliable and ineffective GP series with which the RAF was equipped at the outbreak of war. Based on the German SC range of bombs, the British MCs came in three sizes – 500, 1,000 and 4,000lb. All had a charge-to-weight ratio of 50 per cent, were designed with streamlined steel casings with pointed noses, and clip-on or bolt-on tail units. The MC range was sufficiently robust to withstand the impact stresses and subsequent penetration of most structures, except for reinforced concrete. The 500-pounder was mainly for tactical bombing and was used to great effect in low-level attacks against the Philips radio and valve factory in Eindhoven in December 1942, the breaching of the walls of the Amiens prison in February 1944 and one month later against the Gestapo headquarters in Copenhagen. The 1,000 and 4,000-pounders were for general bombardment purposes, the 4,000-pounder being used mainly for high-level attacks although Mosquitoes of 8 (PFF) Group used them

By 1945 the RAF had specially designed 'Tallboy' and 'Grand Slam' ballistic 'earthquake' bombs of hitherto unimaginable destructive power. 'Tallboys' and 'Grand Slams' burst on and around the Arbergen railway bridge over the River Weser near Bremen on 25 March 1945. A Lancaster BI (Special) of 617 Squadron is pictured having just released its bomb. Note the absence of nose and dorsal turrets, both of which have been removed and faired over to save weight. (US National Archives)

effectively at low-level in 1944-5. The 500 and 1,000-pounder MC bombs outperformed all the other general bombardment bombs used by the RAF and, following their introduction in 1943, the 1,000-pounder became Bomber Command's first choice, with 17,500 being dropped in 1943, 203,000 in 1944 and 36,000 in 1945.

FUSING

Two types of bomb fusing were employed: bomb pistols and bomb fuses. The former was relatively simple and provided detonation by the direct action of a mechanical pistol, while the latter contained its own integral striker and detonator mechanism. Fuses could also be more complex and often incorporated barometric, clockwork, pyrotechnic or hydrostatic processes which provided a variety of options including airburst and underwater use. Where penetration of the target was desired the bomb was fused with a slight time delay, for example, of 0.04 or 0.025 seconds.

Bombs could be fitted with either nose or tail fuses, or both. Those intended for instantaneous detonation were usually fused at the nose end, but with a standby fuse in

A typical 'area' bomb load of 1,000lb Medium Capacity (MC) high explosive and 30lb incendiary clusters, seen here in the main fuselage and wing bomb-cells of a Merlin-engined Halifax, probably in early 1943. (IWM CH17361)

A scene of total devastation in the German city of Frankfurt after two heavy raids with high explosive and incendiary, each attack involving more than 800 heavy bombers of RAF Bomber Command, on 18/19 and 23/24 March 1944. (Roy Conyers Nesbit collection)

the tail end just in case the nose fuse failed. Delayed action bombs were only ever fused at the tail end.

BOMB-HANDLING EQUIPMENT

Due to continual increases in the variety of weapons available and the bomb loads carried, for much of the war bomb-handling equipment on RAF bomber stations lagged a stage behind the operational requirements. Bombs dumps were located on airfield perimeters and could store up to 200 tons of weapons at any one time. Bombs were 'picked' to order and loaded on to bomb trolleys which were then towed by David Brown or Fordson tractor to aircraft awaiting bombing-up on the dispersals. All HE bombs were handled in the bomb dumps simply by rolling, but the large MC bombs like the Tallboy and Blockbuster had to be handled by crane. Incendiary bombs were delivered from ordnance factories to bomb dumps in packs, where they were laboriously transferred by hand into small bomb containers and stored on end in Nissen huts until required. Pistols and fuses were fitted to bombs on the dispersals prior to hoisting the weapons into the bomb bays.

All bomb trolleys (except the Type H) had a low rectangular chassis with small pneumatic tyres at each corner, and adjustable chocks on which to locate the bombs. In 1942 there were two standard bomb trolleys in use, the Type B which was able to carry 4 x 500lb bombs, and the Type D for 1 x 4,000lb HC bomb. The Type B was slowly replaced with the Type C capable of carrying up to 6,000lb, and the Type F with a maximum load of 8,000lb. Towards the end of 1943 the Type E trolley was introduced for HC bombs up to 12,000lb, and in 1944 the Type H entered service for the large MC bombs, equipped with a cradle capable of being winched up to enable the bomb to be hoisted into the aircraft.

HIGH EXPLOSIVE BOMBS

40lb, 250lb, 500lb, 1,000lb, 1,900lb and 4,000lb GP

During the first two years of war GP bombs, which were really the products of pre-war thinking, formed the greater part of the RAF's armoury. All GP bombs suffered from the same shortcomings of too much metal and too little explosive and their effectiveness was questionable across the entire range, the 1,900 and 4,000-pounders being particularly suspect. They began to be superseded by the superior MC range from the end of 1941 onwards, although in the summer of 1944 many 250 and 500lb GP bombs were resurrected to make up for the serious shortage of MC bombs. The 4,000-pounder saw limited use between May 1942 and November 1943 after which date it was deleted from Bomber Command's inventory owing to fusing problems.

500lb, 1,000lb and 4,000lb MC

Introduced at the end of 1941, the 500lb MC contained about twice the HE content of the GP bombs then in use. Stocks were always inadequate of the 1,000-pounder which was a very effective weapon following its introduction in the spring of 1943. During 1944 the shortage reached crisis point and stocks had to be rationed with the greatest of care. Intended originally for use in low-level bombing operations, the 4,000lb MC introduced in January 1943 never became widely used by Bomber Command, partly because only one could be carried by Lancaster aircraft and none by Halifaxes. During the autumn of 1944, the weapon was used by Mosquito aircraft for high altitude night bombing.

American bombs

During 1944 large quantities of American bombs were used. These were the ANM 44, 58 and 64 (500lb) and ANM 59 and 64 (1,000lb). The 58 and 59 were SAPs while the others were equivalent to the British MC range.

A selection of High Capacity (HC) and MC bombs available to Bomber Command in early 1944. The 12,000lb HC became available in February 1944 and could only be carried by the Lancaster. An 8,000lb bomb with a third section bolted to the rear of the body, it possessed huge destructive power, but its sheer size created problems during ground handling and bombing-up; the 4,000lb HC was the first of the so-called blast bombs to be designed. Known as the 'Cookie' it was probably the most effective bomb used by the RAF in the Second World War and made its first appearance in the spring of 1941, closely followed by the 2,000lb HC. The HC range used in conjunction with incendiary bombs was responsible for laying waste to much of urban Germany from 1943 onwards. The 500lb and 1,000lb MC bombs became the best-performing general bombardment bombs to be used by the RAF during the Second World War, particularly the 1,000-pounder which was introduced in February 1943. (Roy Conyers Nesbit collection)

A Lancaster's bomb-load – a 4,000lb 'Cookie', four 250lb GP and twelve 500lb MC bombs – hurtles earthwards during a daylight raid on a German 'area' target in the spring of 1945.
(US National Archives)

A shortage of MC bombs in the summer of 1944 resulted in Bomber Command using American 500 and 1,000-pounders. Their box tails caused accommodation problems inside the bomb-bays of British bombers, drastically reducing the number that could be carried. A Lancaster of 106 Squadron is pictured here at its base at Metheringham in the summer of 1944 with American 1,000-pounders in the left foreground.

These bombs were quicker and easier to fuse and tail than their British-made equivalents, and gave good service, but the American box-type tails drastically reduced the number which could be carried in British aircraft.

Armourers winch a 4,000lb 'Cookie' up into the bulged bomb-bay of Mosquito IV DZ637 of 692 Squadron in the spring of 1944. (IWM CH12622)

2,000lb AP

This weapon saw very limited use against the German battlecruisers *Scharnhorst* and *Gneisenau* at Brest in 1942, and against underground oil storage plants in France in 1944. The results were disappointing and faulty fusing led to a large number of duds.

SAP bombs

Few semi-armour-piercing (SAP) bombs were used between 1942 and 1945 because suitable targets were seldom available, but with the grave shortage of HE bombs experienced in the summer of 1944 some SAP bombs were used against V-1 flying bomb sites in France.

2,000lb, 4,000lb, 8,000lb and 12,000lb HC

Initial use with a parachute attachment in early 1942 rendered the 2,000lb HC virtually unaimable. A request from Bomber Command for a fitted ballistic tail resulted in new supplies arriving in August the same year. The 4,000-pounder was formally introduced into service in January 1942, although more than 400 had been dropped on German targets in the previous nine months. It was followed later by the two larger weapons of which the 12,000-pounder was used mainly for special precision targets. In the event of a take-off crash, all of these bombs were liable to detonate owing to the delicate nose pistols.

SPECIALIST HIGH EXPLOSIVE BOMBS

'Upkeep'

This was the famous bouncing bomb designed by Dr Barnes Wallis and used with success by 617 Squadron against the Ruhr dams in May 1943. It was essentially an air-dropped rotating cylindrical 9,150lb mine filled with a high explosive called Torpex and fitted with a hydrostatic fuse. It was used by one squadron only and on one occasion operationally.

'Johnnie Walker'

Supplies of this air-dropped oscillating 500lb mine became available during 1943 but were not used operationally until 15 September 1944 when the *Tirpitz* was attacked as she lay in Kaa Fjord, Norway. This was the only occasion on which the weapon was deployed operationally.

12,000lb and 22,000lb MC

These so-called 'earthquake' bombs designed by Dr Barnes Wallis marked a major advance in bomb design and ballistics. They penetrated deep into the ground before detonation and the resulting shockwaves destroyed the target at its foundations, rather than relying on surface destruction which required a direct hit. Becoming available in the summer of 1944,

'Upkeep' was the famous 'bouncing bomb' (strictly speaking, a rotating mine) designed by Dr Barnes Wallis and used by Lancasters of 617 Squadron against the Ruhr dams in May 1943. In this photograph can be seen the two side-swing callipers used to clasp the mine beneath the belly of the aircraft, and the drive belt attached to the hydraulic motor in the forward end of the bomb-bay, by which means the mine was back-spun before release. (US National Archives)

The Lancaster was the only Allied bomber capable of carrying the 12,000lb and 22,000lb MC deep penetration bombs, their streamlined casings made from high quality steel with specially hardened nose sections. These revolutionary new ballistic bombs depended upon shock waves set up by their detonation – either underground or underwater – to demolish a target from its foundations. Also known as the 'Tallboy', the 12,000-pounder was stabilised in flight by four tail fins inclined at an angle of 5 degrees that caused it to spin about its axis as it fell. If dropped from the optimum height of 18,000ft the 'Tallboy', filled with 5,200lb of Torpex high explosive, took 37 seconds to reach the ground where it impacted at 750mph and penetrated some 25 feet into the surface before exploding. The first 'Tallboys' were dropped on 8/9 June 1944 on a railway tunnel near Saumur in France by Lancasters of 617 Squadron. By the war's end some 854 of these weapons had been dropped on targets that ranged from shipping, submarine and E-boat pens, to viaducts, canals and V-weapon sites. This 12,000lb 'Tallboy' was photographed moments after its release and just before its nose points earthwards. (US National Archives)

Virtually identical in appearance to the 'Tallboy', the 22,000lb 'Grand Slam' contained 9,135lb of Torpex and needed a specially strengthened Lancaster, fitted with more powerful Merlin 24 engines and with many weight-saving modifications. 'Grand Slam' was first dropped operationally on 14 March 1945 by a Lancaster of 617 Squadron on the Bielefeld viaduct in Germany from 16,000ft with spectacular success. Between them, the 'Tallboy' and 'Grand Slam' were probably the most effective air-dropped weapons used during the Second World War (apart from the atomic bomb). This Lancaster BI (Special) of 617 Squadron is about to release a 22,000lb 'Grand Slam'. (US National Archives)

An empty Dortmund–Ems canal, victim of a 'Tallboy' attack on the night of 23/24 September 1944.
Pictured here on 2 October, the tremendous damage caused by the bombs is plain to see, with two
direct hits causing breaches at 'A' and evidence of where the water flooded over the broken
embankments at 'B'. (Roy Conyers Nesbit collection)

these weapons were used to devastating effect against key targets which included the *Tirpitz*, U-boat pens and viaducts.

INCENDIARY BOMBS (IB)

4lb, 30lb, 30lb J-Type, 250lb IB

Dropped from small bomb containers (SBC) the 4lb magnesium incendiary bomb (IB) was the mainstay of Bomber Command throughout the war. However, it suffered badly from a lack of aimability which meant that incendiary attacks could become widely dispersed downwind from the target, and friendly aircraft in the stream were susceptible to damage from showers of loose bombs over the target area.

Various marks of the 30lb aimable phosphorus-filled IB were used from 1941 to late 1944 when use of this range was abandoned in preference of the 4-pounder, although by this time over 3 million had been dropped.

Operational trials of the 30lb J-Type conducted between April and August 1944 showed that it was only half as effective per ton as the 4lb IB, so it was not adopted. The J-Type produced a spectacular 2ft-wide jet of flame out to a distance of 15ft for one minute and more than 400,000 were used in bombing attacks.

Using a light casing originally designed for being filled with chemical warfare agents, the 250lb IB was first used in 1940 and saw several years of service in the IB role before later being converted for use as a target marker filled with coloured pyrotechnic substances. The 500lb IB was a scaled-up version of the 250-pounder, filled

Dozens of Small Bomb Carriers (SBC) filled with 4lb magnesium incendiary bombs, ready to be towed out to the dispersals and the waiting aircraft. (IWM CH6276)

with liquid phosphorus and designed mainly for special low-level missions by Mosquitoes.

Probably the least well-known weapon in the IB range, the 2,700-pounder was a 4,000lb HC bomb case filled with incendiary substance which first saw use in 1944 for low-level attacks on special targets by Mosquitoes.

CLUSTER PROJECTILES

In May 1943, at the instigation of Bomber Harris, a requirement was raised with the Air Ministry for a delivery device for IBs which could not be aimed individually with the Mk XIV bombsight. This device would also prevent trail-back of incendiary attacks and protect friendly aircraft from showers of IBs scattered

from SBCs. However, protracted development, supply problems and operational difficulties meant that by the war's end only a limited number of clustered incendiary projectiles had seen operational use.

AIR-DROPPED SEA MINES

A Mk I–IV 1,500lb and 1,850lb, A Mk V 1,000lb, A Mk VI 2,000lb and A Mk VII 1,000lb mines

Introduced in April 1940, the A Mk I–IV mine was robustly designed to withstand delivery from an aircraft flying at 200mph and from heights of between 100 and 15,000ft. It contained approximately 750lb

A Stirling of 75 Squadron is loaded with an A Mk I–IV 1,500lb mine early in 1944.

of explosive and incorporated a number of triggering options. Together with the A Mk V and VII, it became the predominant air-dropped mine to be used throughout the war. The A Mk I-IV was superseded by the A Mk VI 2,000-pounder in 1944.

The A Mk V 1,000lb mine was a smaller version of the A Mk I-IV and contained between 625 and 675lb of explosive. It was introduced during 1940–1 and was deployed predominantly in the magnetic mode. The A Mk VII 1,000lb mine was an upgraded version of the A Mk V mine and was introduced in 1944.

GUNS AND POWER-OPERATED TURRETS

Of all the air arms of the combatant nations in the Second World War, it was the RAF and the USAAF which made the greatest use of power-assisted multi-gun turrets to defend their bomber aircraft. Although British manufacturers pioneered their development and first use operationally, it was the Americans who ultimately produced the better armed and armoured designs.

Experimental designs for power-assisted enclosed gun turrets had been worked on during the 1930s, mainly by Boulton & Paul Aircraft Ltd, the Bristol Aeroplane Company and independent design engineers Archibald Frazer-Nash and Gratton Thompson. Although the Boulton Paul and Bristol-designed turrets saw use in Bomber Command aircraft in the Second World War, the designs for hydraulic gun control systems by Frazer-Nash and Thompson were adopted on a far larger scale in the .303in Browning-armed power-assisted turrets.

Much time and money was spent on the design and development of these gun turrets with great hopes pinned on their effectiveness against enemy fighters. Yet despite them, Bomber Command suffered such heavy losses in the early daylight raids that its heavy bombers were soon restricted to night operations. This situation persisted until after D-Day when the Command began a partial return to daylight operations with its heavy bombers, and by which time long-range escort fighters could be provided in sufficient numbers to protect the bomber streams.

As already stated, Nash and Thompson and Frazer-Nash designs became the most widely used of the war. The turrets themselves were manufactured at the Parnall Aircraft Company factory at Yate in Gloucestershire (acquired by Frazer-Nash and Thompson), while design and development was undertaken at Tolworth in Surrey. Their turrets were fitted to the Avro Manchester and Lancaster, Short Stirling, Vickers-Armstrong Wellington and Armstrong-Whitworth Whitley, and their use in service exceeded 50,000 turrets. Boulton Paul turrets were also widely used for the Handley Page Halifax. Bristol turrets were fitted to the Blenheim IV, while small numbers of Preston Green mid-under turrets were used in the Halifax III, and the Rose Brothers' twin .50in tail gun turret in the Lancaster.

It was the tail and mid-upper turrets that were most used in combat and where the gunners needed to remain for the entire trip. The nose turret was mainly used for observation purposes, although sometimes it could be used to engage overshooting enemy fighters and was therefore not manned continuously. In roomy aircraft like the Stirling there was ample space in the front end of the fuselage to accommodate the turret and its gunner, but in the Wellington and Lancaster where space was at a premium the nose gunner's feet often dangled down over the bomb-aimer in the compartment below.

Gunners in the remote tail turrets had the coldest and most dangerous position of all, seated for hours on end on a hard seat with no turret heating. To compound their discomfort the turret Perspex often misted over and then froze up completely, causing the gunner to smash out the sighting section to give a better view of approaching enemy fighters. Tail turrets were also the most vulnerable to attack since the nightfighter's favoured attacking position was from astern and slightly below. However, the lot of the air gunner – and that of the 'tail-end charlie' in particular – was gradually improved as the war progressed, with better heated clothing to wear and extra armour protection fitted to the turret.

The turret itself was a minor marvel of hydraulic and mechanical engineering. Each turret was mounted on a pair of concentric circular metal rings, the inner one rotated by a hydraulic rotation motor which derived its power from an engine-driven pump, thereby traversing the turret. Nash and Thompson, Frazer-Nash and Bristol turrets were fully hydraulic and reliant on huge lengths of copper piping transmitting high-pressure fluid from the aircraft power source to the turret. Those of Boulton Paul were electro-hydraulic which meant that their hydraulic power unit was self-contained inside the turret and electrically driven.

The elevation or depression of the guns, and the traversal of the whole turret, was achieved hydraulically by operation of a pair of control handles mounted close together on a common control column, or on each side of the turret outboard of the guns. The guns themselves were fired by hydraulic units and electrical solenoids in hydraulic and electrically operated turrets respectively, operated by triggers or push-buttons on the turret control handle. Sighting was almost exclusively with the Mk III Reflector Sight although the Mk IIC Gyro Sight was also used in conjunction with AGLT-equipped turrets from the autumn of 1944.

Ammunition was belt-fed to each turret along metal tracks from ammunition tanks contained in the aircraft fuselage, which meant that the gunner could fight his turret without having to reload magazines or drums of ammunition. The belt-feed system was not without its drawbacks, however, mainly in the form of belt breakages which led to gun stoppages which were not easy to rectify in the air.

GUNS

Three marks of gun were used operationally during the Second World War by aircraft of Bomber Command for defensive purposes. These were the Vickers .303in gas-operated Mk I no. 1, the Browning .303in, and the Browning .50in.

Vickers gas-operated .303in
Designed to replace the Lewis gun in the rear cockpits of day bombers, the Vickers gas operated .303in gun was looked upon as a stop-gap until hand-held guns were finally phased out of service. Known in RAF parlance as the VGO, the design was based on a French light infantry machine gun in use at the end of the First World War and first entered RAF service in 1937. It used a drum magazine and was as reliable as the Browning .303in gun, but much easier to maintain.

At the outbreak of war in 1939, the VGO was used singly in the front turret of the Whitley, in the nose of the Hampden, the rear cockpit of the Battle, and in the side gun hatches of the Wellington. But with the gradual withdrawal of these types from front-line use and their replacement by aircraft fitted with Browning gun turrets, by 1943 the VGO was almost obsolete in RAF

Twin-Vickers K Rose mounting fitted in the dorsal gunner's position of a Hampden of 83 Squadron. The air gunner is Sgt John Hannah, who was awarded Bomber Command's second VC of the war for his exceptional bravery during a raid on Antwerp docks on the night of 15/16 September 1940. (Roy Conyers Nesbit collection)

service, but this was not the end of the story. Its self-contained design, which needed no belt boxes, ensured its continued use up to the war's end in the nose position of all the later marks of Halifax.

Browning .303in

The Browning .303in gun was one of the two most important guns used by the RAF in the Second World War, and became the standard bomber armament for defence in multi-gun power-assisted turrets when they were introduced. The other weapon was the Hispano 20mm gun which was the subject of extensive pre-war development trials by Boulton & Paul but which was finally considered too large to fit any existing gun turret. However it did see extensive and highly effective service with Fighter Command.

Paradoxically the .303in gun remained the principal defensive armament for the bomber from its adoption in 1934 until the

Fixed twin .303in and .50in machine guns in the nose of a Ventura.

end of the war, despite its comparatively short range and hitting power. The reasons for this lie in the early days of the war when more heavily armed turrets had actually been designed, but were shelved when it became clear that maximum aircraft production was essential if the RAF was to pose a credible threat to Germany. Any interruption of the production lines caused through the introduction of new or modernised equipment was therefore not desirable. When Bomber Command was forced to switch to night operations the comparatively short range of the .303in machine gun was not considered a pressing issue, and many believed that a battery of four Brownings blazing away from a turret would be sufficient deterrent to any nightfighter looking for an easy kill.

When German fighters became armoured against rifle-calibre bullets, the RAF's .303in gun turrets became largely ineffective and little use was made of the bombers' defensive armament. G.T. Wallace, a technical officer with the Directorate of Armament Development, had this to say on their effectiveness: '. . . 90 per cent of Lancaster sorties were made without contact with enemy fighters, but of the 10 per cent that were intercepted approximately half were shot down despite their armament.'

Browning .50in
Towards the end of the war when the *Luftwaffe* began to increase further still the armour protection fitted to its fighters, several designs for turrets using twin 13.5mm or .50in guns were produced for potential use in Bomber

Flexible mounted .50in machine gun in the waist position of a Fortress I of 90 Squadron.

Command aircraft, but only one entered service operationally. This was the Rose Brothers' .50in Browning turret of which several hundred saw operational use and then only in the closing months of the war, although air gunners appreciated the extra firepower it brought to bear. Most were fitted to Lancasters in 1 and 5 Groups. The Model M2 version of the 'fifty-cal.' was the standard defensive armament fit on most American warplanes of the Second World War.

The Nash and Thompson FN82 and Boulton Paul D turret designs also incorporated twin .50in Brownings which would have seen widespread use by Bomber Command had the war continued longer.

The American experience on daylight bombing raids showed that turrets fitted with heavier .50in machine guns made little difference to the survivability of a heavy bomber aircraft in combat when pitted against a fast, manoeuvrable and heavily armed fighter aircraft. That said, the US 8th Air Force's gunners gave good accounts of themselves.

Hispano 20mm cannon

Fitted as a fixed gun to Mosquito aircraft in 100 (BS) Group, this weapon gave satisfactory service. It was also intended for use in the Bristol Type B.17 mid-upper turret under development, but which was too late to see war service.

POWER-ASSISTED GUN TURRETS

BOULTON PAUL

Type A Mk VIII nose turret

Mid-upper used with low profile fairing and fitted to the Halifax from the B Mk II Series Ia onwards.

The twin .303in Browning Boulton Paul Type C nose turret in a Halifax I. This fitting was used on the Mk I and Mk II, but discontinued from the Mk II Series I Special onwards.

Power system: BP electro-hydraulic
Armament: 4 x Browning .303in Mk II guns
Ammunition: 600 rpg from boxes in turret
Sighting: Mk IIIa reflector sight

Type C Mk I nose turret
Nose turret used in Halifax B Mk I and II only. Caused problems with control of the aircraft when turret was traversed in flight.
Power system: BP electro-hydraulic
Amament: 2 x Browning .303in Mk II guns
Ammunition: 1,000 rpg
Sighting: Mk IIIa reflector sight

Type C Mk II dorsal turret
Mid-upper fitted to the Halifax B Mk II only. Reduced the speed of the aircraft in flight

and was dispensed with altogether on the suivant Mk II Series I (Special).
(Specification as Type C Mk I)

Type E Mk I-III tail turret
This tail gun turret fitted to all Halifax B Mks I, II, III and V proved to be one of the most successful turrets ever produced and was popular with gunners. In common with the Type A design, the Type E had the facility for high-speed rotation and elevation for rapid tracking of targets.
Power system: BP electro-hydraulic
Armament: 4 x Browning .303in Mk II guns
Ammunition: 2,500 rpg
Sighting: MK III reflector sight

One of the most successful turrets ever produced, the bulbous Boulton Paul Type E tail turret provided rear defence for the RAF's Halifax and Liberator II aircraft. It is seen here installed in a Halifax Mk II Series I.

Type K ventral turret
Only twenty-seven examples of this under turret were manufactured. Adverse reports from the squadrons led to their removal from the early Halifax B Mk I.

BRISTOL

BI Mk IE, II, IIIA, IV dorsal turret
This mid-upper turret was specifically designed for and fitted to the Blenheim Mk IV. When not in use the cupola could be partially retracted to reduce drag, but the turret design quickly became outdated.
Power system: Bristol hydraulic
Armament: 1 x Vickers .303in GO (Mk IE, II); 2 x Vickers .303in GO (Mk IIIA); 2 x Browning .303in Mk II (Mk IV)
Ammunition: 400 rpg
Sighting: Mk III, Mk IIIA reflector sights

Single rearward-firing Browning .303in gun mounting beneath the nose of a Blenheim IV in 1940. (IWM CH366)

With a rate of fire of eighty rounds per second, the four-Browning Nash and Thompson FN4A tail turret was the most heavily armed turret in the world in 1940. The guns are early Browning Mk Is without the chromed bore and cooling vanes which prevented muzzle fouling. The FN4 was fitted to the Whitley IV and V, Manchester I and Ia, Stirling I and Wellington III, and is seen here in a Whitley V during 1940. (IWM C913)

FRAZER-NASH

Nash and Thompson FN4A tail turret

Designed originally for the Whitley IV and V, the FN4 was a milestone in bomber defensive armament offering a rate of fire of eighty rounds per second from its four Brownings. The FN4 was also fitted to the Manchester I and Ia, the early Stirling I, and the Wellington III.

Power system: Frazer-Nash (FN) hydraulic
Armament: 4 x Browning .303in Mk II
Ammunition: 1,000 rpg stored in turret
Sighting: Mk IIIa reflector sight
Armour: none

Nash and Thompson FN5 nose and tail turret

Designed originally for the Wellington I, the FN5 was also selected as the front turret for the Stirling (FN5), Manchester and Lancaster (FN5A). The FN5 was the most widely used of the Parnall turrets.

Power system: Nash and Thompson (N&T) hydraulic

The Nash and Thompson FN5 front turret is seen here on Stirling EF390 'T-Tommy' of 7 Squadron in 1943. FN5s were also fitted to the Lancaster (front) and Wellington (front and rear). (Colin Pateman)

Armament: 2 x Browning .303in Mk II
Ammunition: 1,000 rpg (nose), 2,000 rpg (tail in Wellington only)
Sighting: Mk III reflector sight
Armour: none

Nash and Thompson FN7 dorsal turret

Designed originally for the Blackburn Botha, the egg-shaped FN7 was not popular with gunners due partly to its cramped layout and difficult escape route. Its asymmetric shape put a heavy strain on the rotation motor and made it difficult to follow a target accurately. It was fitted as a mid-upper turret to more than 700 Stirling Is and over 200 Manchesters.
Power system: FN hydraulic from electrically driven pump
Armament: 2 x Browning .303in Mk II
Ammunition: 500 rpg from boxes in turret

Sighting: Mk IIIa reflector sight
Armour: none

Nash and Thompson FN16 nose turret

Adapted from the FN11 design used in the Sunderland flying boat, the FN16 was redesigned especially for the Whitley as a single-gun nose turret. It offered gunners an excellent field of view and was probably unique among gun turrets in being virtually draught-free and waterproof.
Power system: N & T hydraulic
Armament: 1 x Vickers .303in GO Type K
Ammunition: 5 x 50-round drums
Sighting: Norman Vane (early models), Mk IIIa reflector sight
Armour: none

Nash and Thompson FN17 ventral turret

This power-operated under turret was designed to provide the Whitley with 360-

degree protection to its underbelly against attack from fighters. The reality was somewhat different. Poor visibility for the gunner, a marked drag effect on the aircraft's performance when extended, and the tendency to extend unintentionally during flight, led to its withdrawal. The FN17 was not fitted to any Whitleys after the Mk IV.

Power system: hydraulic
Armament: 2 x Browning .303in
Ammunition: 500 rpg
Sighting: Mk IIIa reflector sight
Armour: none

Nash and Thompson FN20 tail turret

This rear defence turret was fitted to the Stirling, Whitley, Wellington, Manchester and Lancaster and was popular with gunners. It was also the most important in the Parnall range, being the standard tail defence turret of the Lancaster. The FN20 was essentially a redesigned FN4, the main improvements being in the provision of an armoured shield, a clear vision panel and greatly improved ammunition supply.

Power system: hydraulic
Armament: 4 x Browning .303in Mk II
Ammunition: 2,500 rpg. 1,900 in fuselage boxes, 600 in feed tracks
Sighting: Mk III reflector sight or GGS Mk IIc
Armour: 9mm plates when fitted

Nash and Thompson FN21 ventral turret

The FN21 was fitted to the Manchester and like the FN17 it was largely a failure. When extended it slowed the aircraft by 15mph, weighed a quarter of a ton and was not liked by gunners. Its one saving grace was that it gave the gunner a good field of view but was soon withdrawn from operational use and replaced by the mid-upper FN7.

Power system: N & T hydraulic
Armament: 2 x Browning .303in
Ammunition: from boxes on top of the turret
Sighting: Mk IIIa reflector sight

Nash and Thompson FN25 ventral turret

The specification for the cylindrical FN25 under defence turret designed for and fitted to the Wellington Mk I was almost identical to the FN17 fitted to the early marks of Whitley. The same unwelcome characteristics that plagued the FN17 (poor visibility and drag penalty) alas applied to the FN25 and it was soon consigned to the scrap heap. Unused turrets were later converted to take the anti-submarine Leigh Light.

Power system: N & T hydraulic
Armament: 2 x Browning .303in
Ammunition: 500 rpg
Sighting: Mk IIIa reflector sight

Parnall FN50 dorsal turret

Based on the mechanism for the FN5 nose turret, the FN50 was a replacement for the unliked FN7 turret fitted to the Manchester and early marks of Stirling. Roomy, comfortable and with an excellent all-round field of vision, the twin-Browning FN50 was fitted to the Stirling Mk I Series III and Mk III, but was used exclusively as the mid-upper turret for the Lancaster Mk I, II and III. A metal fairing was installed around the base of the turret to prevent damage to the fuselage.

Power system: N & T hydraulic
Armament: 2 x Browning .303in
Ammunition: 1,000 rpg, from boxes on each side of the gunner
Sighting: Mk IIIa reflector sight
Armour: 7mm plate to front aspect, from the turret ring down

Nash and Thompson FN54 undernose rear-firing mounting

Developed in response to a need to protect the Blenheim Mk IV against fighter attack from behind and below, the FN54 was a rear-firing twin-Browning turret fitted beneath the nose of the aircraft and

Parnall FN50 mid-upper turret as fitted to the Stirling III and the Lancaster I, II and III. It is seen here fitted to a Stirling III of 90 Squadron in 1944. (D. Field)

manually operated by the bomb-aimer with a pair of control handles and a periscopic sight. In event of an emergency the whole turret assembly could be jettisoned to allow the gunner to escape from the aircraft.

Power system: manual

Armament: 2 x Browning .303in

Ammunition: 1,000 rpg, stored in a box behind the turret

Sighting: periscopic reflector sight

Nash and Thompson FN64 ventral turret

Early production Lancasters were fitted with this rear-firing under turret, but its use was discontinued until reintroduced in mid-1944 by a handful of 1 Group squadrons in place of the H2S housing. The gunner sat facing to the rear and sighted the twin-Browning guns by means of a periscopic

sight. Apart from being hydraulically driven, the whole system was identical in practice to the FN54 used in the Blenheim IV and the gunner suffered problems with sighting due to the turret's poor field of vision.

Power system: N & T hydraulic

Armament: 2 x Browning .303in

Ammunition: 500 rpg, from boxes on either side of the gunner

Sighting: periscopic reflector sight

Nash and Thompson FN82 tail turret

Developed during 1943 and 1944 to replace the existing Nash and Thompson and Boulton Paul tail turrets, the FN82 was built to the same specification as the Boulton Paul Type D and was designed to take two .50in Mk 2 Browning guns which were sighted using the highly effective Type IID gyro

AGL(T) 'Village Inn' installation fitted to a Nash and Thompson FN121 tail turret on a Lancaster. The radar scanner housed inside the black dome moved in elevation with the four Brownings and detected approaching aircraft. It then fed direction and range data to the navigator and tail gunner who coordinated the gunner's response. Note the rearward-looking aerial array above the turret which gave the crew notice that they were being tracked by *Würzburg* or *FuG 202/212* transmissions.

sight. The FN82 was adapted to take the AGL(T) blind firing system and promised to be a potent tail defence turret. Fitted to the Lancaster in small numbers, had the war continued longer it would undoubtedly have seen wider use than it actually did.

Power system: N & T hydraulic
Armament: 2 x Browning .50in
Ammunition: 500 rpg, from boxes in mid-fuselage
Sighting: Mk IIc gyro gunsight
Armour: 9mm plates to gunner's front

Nash and Thompson FN120 tail turret
A modified version of the FN20 for the Lancaster, produced in late 1944 and featuring an improved heating system, electric ammunition feed and gyro gunsight

Nash and Thompson FN121 tail turret
A modified version of the FN120 fitted with Automatic Gun Laying (Turrets) (AGL(T)) and redesignated FN121. Initially fitted to Lancasters of 49 and 460 Squadrons the device first saw operational use in July 1944,

although before the end of the war AGL(T) was taken away from 460 Squadron. By May 1945 it was fitted to Lancasters of 35, 49, 582 and 635 Squadrons in 5 and 8 (PFF) Groups.

Nash and Thompson FN150 dorsal turret

A modified version of the FN50 for the Lancaster, sharing the same design improvements as the FN120.

BENDIX

Model A dorsal turret

Used only in the North American B-25 Mitchell, the Bendix Model A was electrically powered and provided effective all-round defence. However, it was not very comfortable for the gunner whose movements and field of vision were fairly restricted.

Power system: Amplidyne electrical
Armament: 2 x M2 .50in Browning guns
Ammunition: 400 rpg, from cans inside turret
Sighting: Type N8 retiflector or Type N6A reflector
Armour: armoured apron to gunner's front

PRESTON GREEN

Preston Green ventral turret

Mounted in the fuselage floor aft of the bomb bay and where the H2S cupola would have been, the rear-facing Preston Green under defence turret provided valuable protection to the Halifax III from attack from below by

Fitted only to the Halifax III, the Preston Green ventral mounting for a single 0.50in Browning Mk II gun can be seen here beneath the belly of Halifax III LL596 'U-Uniform' of 425 (Alouette) Squadron, pictured at Tholthorpe in 1944. Much to the disappointment of bomber crews, the turrets were taken out and replaced with H2S radar scanners when production of the latter had increased sufficiently. (DND/PL40185)

Schräge Musik nightfighters. However, once H2S production had increased the turrets were removed and replaced by the radar scanners, target identification presumably being deemed more important than the survival of a bomber and its crew.

Power system: manual

Armament: 1 x .50in Browning Mk II

Ammunition: 250 rounds, stored in box beside gunner

Sighting: Mk III reflector sight

Armour: none

ROSE BROTHERS

Rose Rice tail turret

The Rose Rice twin .50in Browning tail turret was the result of an unusual collaboration between Group Captain A.E. Rice of 1 Group and Alfred Rose of Rose Brothers Engineering in Gainsborough, Lincolnshire. It added greater firepower to the defence of the Lancaster with its hard-hitting .50in machine guns. The turrets were fitted only to the Lancaster, mostly in 1 Group, and were first used operationally in June 1944 by 101 Squadron.

Power system: Nicholls hydraulic

Armament: 2 x Browning .50in guns

Ammunition: 335 rpg, from boxes in turret base

Sighting: Mk IIIa reflector sight

Armour: none

CHAPTER 5

FINDING THE TARGET

NAVIGATIONAL AND BOMBING AIDS

At the outbreak of the Second World War Bomber Command was dependent upon non-radar aids to safety and air navigation, such as position-fixing medium and high frequency direction-finding (MF and HF D/F) stations, which required the use of wireless equipment and a wireless operator. The 'Darky' system was another position-fixing procedure, but which used R/T (radio) so that the pilot of an aircraft could speak to a ground station when over England and ask for his position. He would be given either his approximate position or courses to steer and distances from ground station to ground station until eventually he found his own airfield. Darky was intended for use by aircraft that were lost or in distress over Great Britain and was eventually superseded to a large extent by Gee.

From 1942, the new generation of radio and radar aids to navigation and bombing played an increasingly crucial part in Bomber Command's ability to find and then hit a target. It could deceive or jam the German Y (Listening) Service radar interception systems, but the only way it could completely deceive them when it came to the radar components of the system was to switch off all the transmitting equipment in its aircraft. However, Bomber Command's reliance on electronic navigational

aids such as Gee and H2S to find its targets made this option virtually impossible. From late 1944, however, a partial solution came with the imposition of a total radio and radar silence on all bombers until the stream had crossed over the enemy coast.

Gee was the first of the three principal radio navigational aids to be developed and introduced into Bomber Command. It first saw use on 8/9 March 1942 in an attack on Essen when leading aircraft of the 211-strong force were fitted with the aid. Initially, Gee was a highly effective device that enabled bomber crews to reach the general area of a target within its range (about 350 miles) and for longer distance targets it set them well on track after which navigators could recompute courses with confidence. However, the Germans quickly discovered how to jam Gee and it soon became impossible to obtain fixes east of the Dutch coast. Nevertheless, navigators still used it to maintain an accurate track outbound over the North Sea; on the final leg of the journey home it was effective for homing to base. One of the great advantages of Gee was that it was passive, requiring only a receiver and no transmitter, so any aircraft that used it did not risk giving away its position to the enemy.

From three widely spaced ground transmitter stations situated on a baseline of about 200 miles in length, radiated sequential radio pulses laid down an invisible grid over the target. One of the Gee transmitters was known as the 'A' or Master station, while the other two were 'B' and 'C' or Slave stations. Each Slave transmission was locked on to a Master transmission. By measuring the differences in the time taken by the A and B and A and C signals to reach the aircraft, the aircraft could be located on two position lines – or Gee coordinates – and its ground position coincided with the point at which these coordinates (printed as a grid on special Gee charts) intersected. The data was displayed on a cathode ray tube on the navigator's table in the aircraft and a good navigator could obtain a fix in less than a minute, with an accuracy of between ½ mile and 5 miles, depending on his skill.

Because Gee depended upon transmissions from ground stations in England its effective range was limited by the curvature of the earth to about 350 miles (the Ruhr was just included within this range limitation). The general rule of thumb for Gee was the greater the range, the lesser the accuracy.

Oboe was similar to Gee in that it depended upon transmissions from a pair of ground stations in England. Its accuracy was such that an Oboe-equipped aircraft flying at 28,000ft over the Ruhr could release its bombs within 120yd of the selected target. The drawback was that only one aircraft at a time could be controlled by a pair of Oboe transmitters every ten minutes, but later in the war this was partly solved by the use of multiple pulse frequencies.

Each Oboe ground station transmitted pulses and received them back from a suitably equipped aircraft, thus enabling the ground stations to measure the distance of the aircraft from them. One station (known as the Cat) controlled the track of the aircraft over the target, while the other

station (the Mouse) calculated the point on that track when the bombs should be released. Oboe pulses travelled at a tangent to the earth's surface and for this reason its range was limited only by the height that could be reached by the controlled aircraft.

Because of the higher service ceiling of the Mosquito when compared to its contemporaries in Bomber Command, it was invariably used with the Oboe system and for this reason – combined with the time and numbers limitations already described – it was used almost exclusively by the Pathfinder Force. Towards the end of the war the device was also used by Lancasters and Mosquitoes acting as Oboe leaders in formation bombing, where other aircraft in the formation bombed on a visual cue from their leader.

H2S was the only one of the three wartime navigational aids which was self-contained in the bomber and not limited in any way by range or altitude. Radar transmissions from a downward-looking rotating radar transmitter, fitted in the belly of the aircraft, scanned the terrain below and the echoes that 'bounced' back to receiving equipment in the aircraft were displayed on a television-type screen in the navigator's compartment, painting a radar impression of the ground over which the aircraft was flying. The contrast between land and water was particularly clear, less so built-up areas. Over large urban areas like Berlin and its suburbs it was virtually impossible to identify anything on the screen.

In conditions of total darkness and complete cloud cover, a blind bombing run could be made with a good degree of accuracy using H2S, and the bombs dropped blindly, but this method was not as accurate as Oboe bombing.

However, H2S was a blessing in disguise because it also worked against the interests of the bomber stream in two dangerous ways. From January 1944, H2S transmissions could be detected and the bombers homed

H2S was not affected by distance because both the transmitting and receiving equipment were carried in the aircraft. The H2S dome can be clearly seen beneath the rear fuselage of this Halifax II of 35 Squadron. (Roy Conyers Nesbit collection)

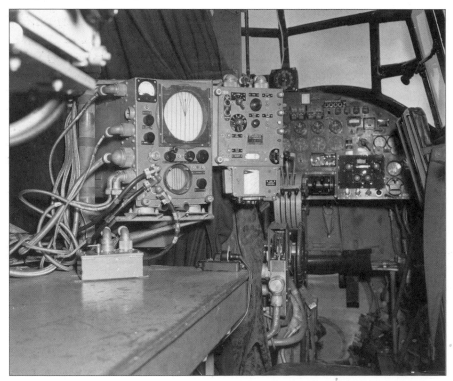

A Type 184 indicator (left) and Type 207 switch unit used in an H2S Mk IIB installation positioned at the navigator's station inside a Lancaster.

onto by German nightfighters fitted with a specialised search apparatus called '*Naxos*'. The Germans also developed a highly sensitive ground-based detection device called '*Korfu*' which enabled them to keep a constant plot of the bomber stream, from take-off to landing. It was so sensitive that it could even detect H2S test transmissions from a bomber aircraft parked on its dispersal pan at its airfield in England.

G-H was a combination of Gee and Oboe (or H, which was similar to Oboe but which functioned in reverse), performing much the same job as Oboe and at much the same range. Its big advantage was that it could be operated by some 100 aircraft at a time, but its drawback was that unlike Gee or H2S it could not be used simultaneously by the whole force.

An aircraft fitted with G-H transmitting and receiving equipment depended upon transmissions to and from a pair of ground stations. The ground position of an aircraft could be measured by plotting the point at which the two lines from the two ground stations intersected. Although the range of G-H was limited, unlike Gee its accuracy did not diminish with increasing distance. It was not until June 1944 that Bomber Command began to make extensive use of G-H for formation daylight bombing and an urgent requirement was made for all Lancaster aircraft of 3 Group to be equipped with the system. However, progress was slow and by October insufficient aircraft had been re-equipped. In order to make full use of the equipment, G-H crews were trained to undertake marking duties for night raids and act as formation leaders for daylight attacks.

Similar in operation to Gee, Loran was an American hyperbolic navigational aid designed originally for use over water and with a range of 1,400 miles. Code-named 'Skywave Synchronised' or 'SS Loran', the device was first used operationally on 11/12 November 1944 against Hamburg,

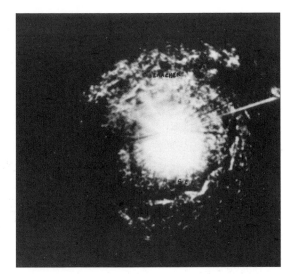

The trace left on an H2S screen revealing sketchy detail of the ground below. Although impossible to identify without a map and other intelligence information, this is actually Koblenz and environs. Coastal areas showed up with much more clarity on H2S than urban landscapes did. (US National Archives)

but its use was restricted and SS Loran was only fitted to aircraft of 5 and 8 (PFF) Groups, and the heavy aircraft of 100 (BS) Group. SS Loran suffered from a number of technical shortcomings and was very susceptible to enemy jamming, but its value to Bomber Command was never fully exploited. Had the war lasted longer its potential as a long-range navigational aid might well have come into its own.

MAPS AND CHARTS FOR AIR NAVIGATION

Although the new radio and radar aids made the job of the navigator that much easier, a high level of navigational skill was still needed and Bomber Command's navigators still had to rely on conventional maps for plotting courses and map reading.

They also used maps specially produced with intelligence requirements in mind.

The maps they used came in three scales: large for intelligence and target identification (1:63,360 or 1 in to the mile); medium for air map reading over strategically important regions on the Continent (1:500,000 or 1 in to 7.89 miles and 1:250,000 or 1 in to 3.95 miles) – the latter being especially useful for the industrial centres of the Continent where important detail was abundant; and small (1:1,000,000 or 1 in to 15.78 miles) where the

scale provided a useful general picture of any large area and could be used for plotting. A specially prepared plotting chart was also produced for navigators over which was printed a grid of Gee lattice lines for accurate course plotting and position checking at any time during a flight.

The large- and medium-scale maps were printed to a very high standard in full colour on a good quality paper with particular attention paid to lettering and the amount of detail shown. Small-scale plotting maps were

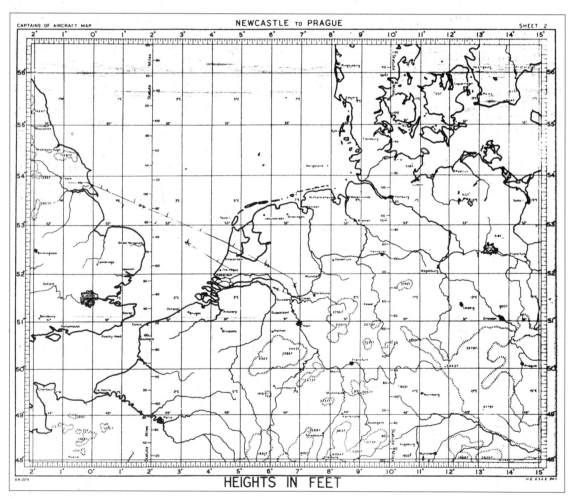

Small-scale Captains' of Aircraft Map on which has been marked the outward and homeward routes to be followed from a 4 Group airfield in the Vale of York. The German armaments manufacturing centre at Essen was the target on 27/28 May 1943, at the height of the Battle of the Ruhr.

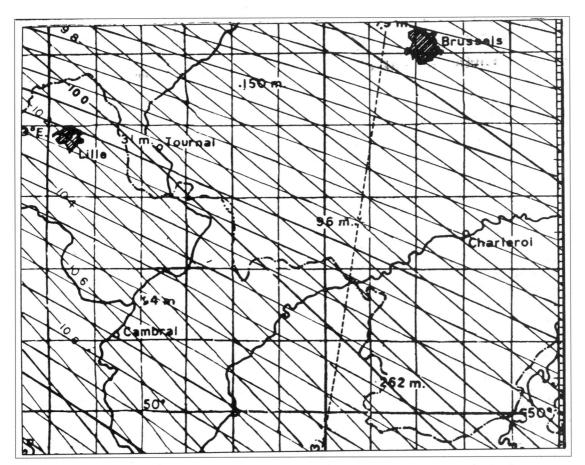

Detail from a navigator's Gee lattice chart of an area over Belgium. The lattice lines are further apart than they would be if the aircraft were nearer to the two transmitter stations in England. With Gee, accuracy decreased with distance.

generally printed in black or red on white and only few of the features of the ground were shown. Because they were intended for use at the rate of one map per sortie, they needed to be cheap to produce and were printed on an inexpensive grade of paper.

BOMBSIGHTS

For an aircraft loaded with bombs and navigated across land and sea to a target hundreds of miles distant, its crew need some

kind of sighting device to enable them to drop their bombs fairly and squarely on a target. Known as a bombsight, this device tells the crew at which point – usually some distance from the target – their bombs should be released. As the Second World War progressed, the bombs in use became more complex, and so too did the problems associated with their sighting. New, more advanced bombsights were therefore designed and for the most part provided effective solutions.

Between 1939 and 1945 the RAF used two basic types of bombsight in its bomber aircraft: the vector sight and the tachometric sight. The first had been in existence since 1918, with modifications, and required the bomb-aimer to compute and then feed in data before the attack for the aircraft's speed, altitude, the ballistic performance of the bomb, and estimated wind speed and direction. On a small reflecting screen in front of him the bomb-aimer referred to a sighting cross made either from crossed wires or lines of light. As the aircraft made its bombing run, the right moment to release the bombs was when the centre of the sighting cross corresponded with the target beneath. The vector sight was simple and effective, but it was only as accurate as the data fed into it and only if the aircraft made a straight and level approach to the target. The reality was that data was not always accurate and a straight and level approach in the presence of flak and fighters was courting disaster for the bomber crew.

The tachometric sight was a very different device to the vector type in that it computed wind velocity and direction automatically. A motorised sighting telescope was focused on a stabilised glass screen mounted beneath it. Linked to a gyro-stabilised platform the telescope enabled the bomb-aimer to view the target during the bombing run. Having programmed the analogue sighting computer with the aircraft's altitude and the bomb's ballistic performance, the bomb-aimer adjusted a pair of electric knobs connected to an electric motor to maintain the telescope's sighting graticule over the target, as viewed through the stabilised glass screen. Because the movement of the telescope relative to the platform was relayed to the sighting computer by the gyro stabilisation system, the computer in turn generated a stream of signals which were relayed to the pilot (or directed into the autopilot if it was engaged). These were displayed on a directional indicator on his instrument panel for corrections to be made in the aircraft's heading, thereby maintaining the sighting graticule accurately over the target. As the aircraft neared the target the angle of the telescope on the bombsight progressively reached a vertical position. Once it had reached the release angle calculated by the sighting computer, a pair of electrical contacts closed to form a circuit and the bombs were released automatically.

The following are the principal bomb-sights used by Bomber Command during the Second World War, with the exception of the Dann sight which was a one-off design for use only by 617 Squadron on the Ruhr dams raid.

MK IX COURSE SETTING BOMBSIGHT

From the outbreak of war, the Mk IX CSBS was in general use throughout Bomber Command. It was a pre-set vector sight used for night bombing of static targets when darkness prevented the target from being seen until the last minute. The sight was unsuitable for bombing while the aircraft was taking evasive action and its efficacy very much depended on the accuracy of wind computations.

In January 1942 a modified version, the Mk IXA incorporating the Fourth Vector (moving target attachment), was designated for use in all Halifaxes and Stirlings; Bostons and Mosquitoes were fitted with the CSBS Mk IXE* (without the Fourth Vector attachment), and all other aircraft were equipped with CSBS Mk IXA* (also without the Fourth Vector attachment). Low-level attachments for the CSBS were issued to the light bomber squadrons of 2 Group in May 1942 to replace their hand-held low-level Mk I bombsight.

MK XIV STABILISED VECTOR SIGHT

Introduced in the summer of 1942, initially to the Halifax-equipped 35 (Pathfinder)

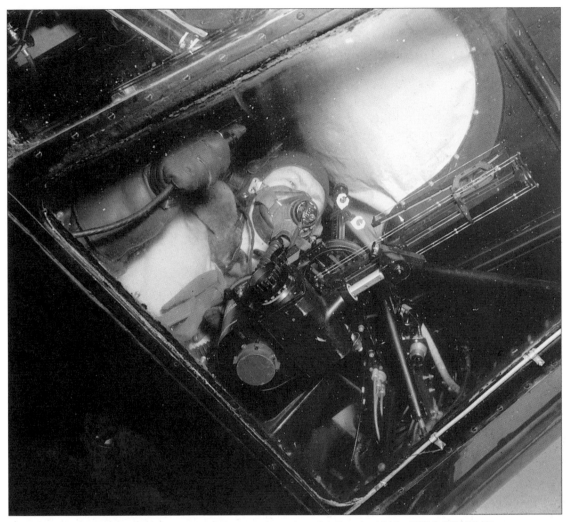

Mk IX Course Setting (Vector) bombsight seen here in a Stirling in 1943. (IWM CH11542)

Squadron, the Mk XIV stabilised vector sight – sometimes referred to as the 'area sight' – worked on similar principles to the CSBS but was more fully automatic, simpler to operate and better suited to use under war conditions. Later versions of the sight would serve RAF bomber squadrons well into the jet age. Evasive action could be taken up to the moment of bomb release and bombs could be released even with the aircraft making a banking turn to avoid flak or fighters, and even when climbing or gliding. In February 1943 use of the sighting head only was extended to Bostons, Mitchells and Mosquitoes of 2 Group, in place of their CSBS Mk IXE. By the middle of 1944 most operational heavy bomber aircraft in the Command had been fitted with the Mk XIV sight.

A modified version of the sight known as the Mk XIVA offered an increased height limitation and was trialled in July 1943 by

Mk XIV (Stabilised Vector) bombsight in a Lancaster in 1944. It was more fully automatic and simpler to operate than the Mk IX CSBS. (IWM CH12283)

8 (PFF) Group. The Mk XIVA increased the operational height at which the sight could be used, to 25,000ft, and was first employed operationally in August 1944 by Mosquitoes of 8 (PFF) Group.

T1 BOMBSIGHT

This American-built copy of the British Mk XIV sight differed little from the original except in minor details of construction, and by the end of 1943 it was in use by all operational Wellington squadrons in the Command. By the spring of 1944 it was beginning to replace the Mk XIV sighting head installations on OTU aircraft.

The T1A bombsight was the American-built copy of the Mk XIVA, and first saw use in the Command in July 1944 when Canadian-built Lancaster X aircraft arrived

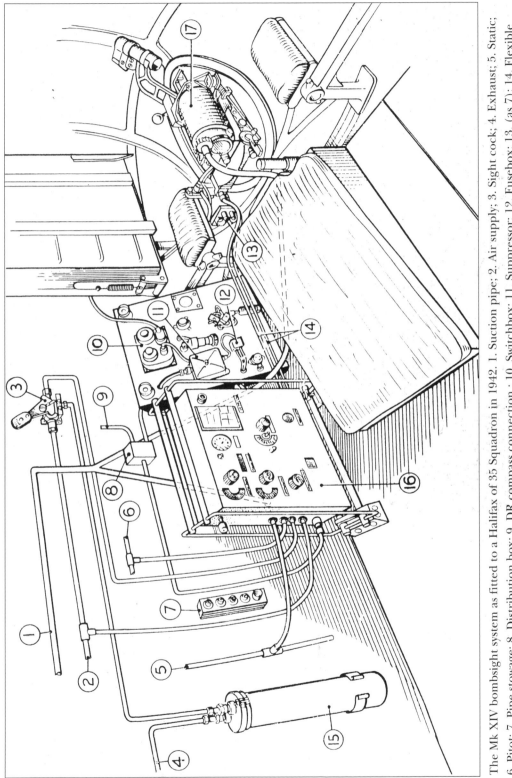

The Mk XIV bombsight system as fitted to a Halifax of 35 Squadron in 1942. 1. Suction pipe; 2. Air supply; 3. Sight cock; 4. Exhaust; 5. Static; 6. Pitot; 7. Pipe stowage; 8. Distribution box; 9. DR compass connection ; 10. Switchbox; 11. Suppressor; 12. Fusebox; 13. (as 7); 14. Flexible drives; 15. Air drier; 16. Computer; 17. Sighting head.

from North America ready fitted with the sight. T1A sights were also fitted in the Mosquito in January 1945 in place of the Mk XIVA which were then in short supply.

MK II STABILISED AUTOMATIC BOMBSIGHT (SABS)

This precision tachometric bombsight was similar to the American Norden sight used in USAAF bomber aircraft. The Mk II SABS had been fitted to aircraft of 97 and 207 Squadrons by February 1943, and 61, 83 and 106 Squadrons each had three aircraft equipped with the sight. Although it was more accurate than the Mk XIV stabilised vector sight, the Mk II SABS was withdrawn from use because the area bombing technique used by the RAF on night raids did not require a precision sight. In any case the need for a straight and level approach to the target was deemed a disadvantage at the height of the area offensive. Thus the Mk II sight was withdrawn from 5 Group's squadrons and replaced by the Mk XIV sight which was quite adequate for the job of area bombing. From August 1943, only 617 Squadron was equipped with a modified version, the Mk IIA SABS, for special precision bombing operations. By the war's end their operational experience using this sight was such that they could bomb a target from 20,000ft with an average error of only 80yd.

MK III LOW-LEVEL (ANGULAR VELOCITY) BOMBSIGHT

Designed for use at up to 1,000ft and developed primarily for the bombing of submarines at low level, the Mk III low-level bombsight was also very effective against land targets. It was introduced into service with Bostons of 2 Group in May 1943 and also saw

use – but only once – by Lancasters of 617 Squadron in 1944. Because Coastal Command had absolute priority on the issue of this sight, Bomber Command's operational use of it during the war was minimal. A few examples were acquired by 627 Squadron and the Mosquitoes of 8 (PFF) Group.

DANN SIGHT

This simple hand-held wooden bombsight was designed by Wing Commander C.L. Dann at A&AEE Boscombe Down for use by bomb-aimers of 617 Squadron on the Ruhr dams raid in May 1943. In order to achieve an accurate release point for the Upkeep weapon, Dann used calculations based on the width between the sluice towers of the Möhne dam to make a simple triangular wooden sight. With a sighting peephole at the apex and two nails at the extremities of the base, the bomb-aimer held the sight by a wooden handle attached to the underside of the apex and looked through the peephole. On the bombing run, when the twin towers of the dam coincided with the two nails the bomb-aimer pressed the bomb release mechanism.

However, the Dann sight had its drawbacks. Buffeting of the aircraft at low level by thermals meant that it was near impossible for a bomb-aimer to hold the sight steady with both hands and still maintain his balance in the bomb-aiming compartment. Some bomb-aimers dispensed with the Dann sight altogether and experimented with their own sighting devices, which included chinagraph pencil marks on the clear-vision panel and lengths of string attached to screws each side of the panel to create a large triangle. Laying prone on the floor of the aircraft supported by their forearms, some bomb-aimers saw this as a more stable position to adopt during the bombing run.

CHAPTER 6

BOMBER TACTICS

The tactics used during the Second World War by the squadrons of Bomber Command can be divided roughly into three: those that helped find and mark the target (the Pathfinders), those that involved the use of electronic and radar devices to confound and destroy enemy defences (100 Group), and those employed by individual bomber aircraft as a means of finding their way to and from the target and evading enemy defences.

LEADING THE WAY: THE PATHFINDERS

From its formation in the summer of 1942 the wartime exploits of Bomber Command's 8 (PFF) Group, better known as the Pathfinders, soon became synonymous with skill and bravery of the highest order to both friend and foe alike.

Poor navigation and bombing accuracy in the opening years of the war had led Bomber Command's senior commanders to the conclusion that specialist squadrons were needed to lead bombing raids. The Butt Report of August 1941, commissioned by Prime Minister Winston Churchill's scientific adviser Lord Cherwell, reached the alarming conclusion after analysing 4,065 night bombing photographs, that only one in four crews who claimed to have bombed a target in Germany were found to have been within 5 miles of the target.

Worse still, one-third of all crews dispatched could not claim to have even reached the target area. Added to these depressing revelations were the facts that Gee had not yet produced any great improvements in target finding and bombing accuracy, and aircrew losses continued to mount.

The idea of a specialist target marking force was the brainchild of Group Captain Syd Bufton, Director of Bomber Operations at the Air Ministry. Earlier in the war, Bufton had commanded 10 Squadron where he had pioneered attempts using his best crews to locate their targets with flares and then attract other crews to them by firing off Verey lights. He convinced his fellow staff officers at the Air Ministry of the very real need for a target finding force for the whole of Bomber Command and the idea was put to Bomber Harris as soon as he assumed control in April 1942. Harris rejected it, vehemently opposing the concept of an elite group within Bomber Command. Arguments for and against the proposal rumbled on through the summer of 1942 but eventually Portal overruled Harris and ordered him to prepare the new force.

Four bomber squadrons, one taken from each of Bomber Command's heavy groups and used to form the new pathfinding force, moved to their new bases in Huntingdonshire and Cambridgeshire on 17 August 1942. These were 156 Squadron with Wellingtons from 1 Group, 7 Squadron with

Mosquito IX LR503 'F-Freddie' of 105 Squadron flew with the Pathfinder Force and completed a staggering total of 213 operational sorties before the end of the war. The aircraft is pictured here with its crew, Flt Lt Maurice Briggs (right) and Flg Off John Baker.

Stirlings from 3 Group, 35 Squadron with Halifaxes from 4 Group, and 83 Squadron from 5 Group. Lancasters and Mosquitoes gradually replaced these older types of aircraft on the squadrons.

The new force did not immediately have group status but instead worked under the direct control of Bomber Command headquarters plans staff, with orders passing through the headquarters of 3 Group. Group Captain Basil Embry was initially suggested as the commander of the force but for unknown reasons he was not released from Fighter Command and the

job went instead to Air Commodore Donald Bennett. The crews themselves were all volunteers and were generally recruited direct from the main force squadrons after completing their first tour, although a few were on their second or third tours of operations. Occasionally crews who had passed out of the training system with the highest marks on their courses were posted straight to a Pathfinder squadron. A pathfinder tour was set at forty-five operations and qualified aircrew were entitled to wear the coveted gilt eagle of the Pathfinders on their left breast pocket.

On 8 January 1943 the Pathfinder Force was redesignated 8 (PFF) Group and in the steady expansion that followed, completed by January 1945, it grew to a total of nineteen squadrons, of which three were permanently detached to 5 Group for its own target marking force.

OPERATIONAL DUTIES

There were eight designated Pathfinder duties and all crews were expected to be able to fulfil the various tasks if and when required. The duties themselves were applied to the aircraft and not to the crews, although certain crews that excelled at a given duty were invariably selected for that particular task. Essentially, the Pathfinders were a team and the success of a raid depended very much upon the teamwork of the different duties.

1. When a new crew joined a PFF squadron it was sent to the target area as a 'Supporter' with the first group of the marker force to increase the number of aircraft over the target at the beginning of the raid.
2. 'Windowers' went in ahead of the marker force to drop window and hopefully confuse enemy radar, thereby giving marker crews a better chance.
3. 'Backers-up' (later called 'Visual Centerers') were required to estimate the mean point of impact (MPI) of all the primary markers and then aim their target indicators (TIs) at this point with the aid of their Mk XIV bombsight.
4. 'Route Markers' dropped TIs at important turning points leading to the target to help the main force maintain a stream.
5. 'Blind Illuminators' used H2S to navigate to the target and then dropped flares blindly to help the 'Visual Markers' in 'Newhaven' attacks.

6. 'Primary Visual Markers' aimed their TIs visually using the Mk XIV bombsight. This was the most difficult of all the PFF duties and only selected crews were allocated to this task.
7. 'Blind Markers ' used either H2S or Oboe to drop their TIs and sky markers.
8. 'Recenterers' arrived over the target halfway through a raid and marked it blindly using H2S, the idea being to overshoot with their markers to compensate for the gradual creep-back in bombing from the main force as the raid progressed.

Two further duties introduced later in the war by the Pathfinder Force were 'Master Bomber' and 'Deputy Master Bomber', devised to reduce the multiplication of errors as an attack progressed. Their aircraft orbited high above the bomber stream over the target area and used VHF radio to correct marking errors and advise Backers-up where they should drop their TIs, or instruct the main force to ignore this fire or bomb that.

Bennett's Pathfinder Force operated at high altitude and could mark any target, for any size of bomber force, and in any weather conditions, but 5 Group operated its own independent target marking force. For this task it used Mosquitoes and borrowed American Mustangs to mark for small bomber forces in clear weather conditions and at low level. This tactic was developed by Leonard Cheshire and advocated by Cochrane, but one to which Don Bennett could not subscribe because he feared for the safety of his crews at such low levels. It was not surprising, then, that a friendly rivalry should have persisted between 8 and 5 Groups throughout the war.

ROUTE AND TARGET MARKING

The Pathfinders used three methods of marking a target. These were code-named 'Parramatta', 'Newhaven' and 'Wanganui'.

Although the choice of code names sounds obscure, the last two were named after the home towns of Bennett's confidential WAAF clerk and one of his air staff officers respectively, while Bennett himself chose the town of Parramatta in Australia for the former 'just to keep the balance with New Zealand'.

The first method was 'Parramatta', or blind ground marking, which fell into two categories: 'Parramatta' and 'Musical Parramatta'. In the former, crews using H2S performed the initial marking and dropped their TIs blind on the target, and then the Backers-up aimed TIs of a contrasting colour at the mean point of impact of all the original markers. The main force crews following were instructed to aim at the centre of the secondary markers and ignore the initial markers (if there were no secondaries burning). In the latter, 'Musical Parramatta', Oboe crews were responsible for the primary marking. Backers-up aimed visually at the primary markers which were dropped at intervals during the attack. The main force was instructed to bomb the primary markers and ignore the secondaries unless no Oboe TIs were visible. However, blind ground marking using H2S was never as accurate as visual marking using the Mk XIV bombsight, or 'Musical' marking using Oboe.

The second method was 'Newhaven', for which selected Pathfinder crews were needed, initially to identify the aiming point and then to mark it visually using the Mk XIV bombsight. Blind Illuminators (using H2S) were invariably sent in ahead of the Visual Markers to release bundles of flares at intervals in the target area to help the Visual Marker crews to see the ground.

The third, and invariably the least accurate of the three marking methods, was 'Wanganui', or sky marking. Flares were dropped blindly by marker crews and fused to burst above the expected height of the cloud found in the target area. The main force crews were instructed to release their bombs when bomb-aimers had a flare in their bombsights, and on a required course given at briefing, but it was difficult for them to aim accurately at a moving target which was prone to drift with the wind.

DECEIVING THE ENEMY: 100 (BS) GROUP

The continuing growth and successes of the German nightfighter force in 1943 led to the formation of a dedicated new bomber group in November that year. No. 100 (Bomber Support) Group was the last operational group to be formed in Bomber Command during the Second World War and was commanded by Air Commodore Edward Addison, a specialist in electronics and signals. It combined all the radio countermeasures squadrons that already existed elsewhere in the Command as well as several Mosquito fighter squadrons that had been transferred from Fighter Command.

The group's role was clearly defined as giving direct intruder support to night bombing operations by attacking enemy nightfighter aircraft in the air or on the ground, and the use of airborne and ground-based radio countermeasures (RCM) equipment to deceive or jam enemy radio navigation aids, radar systems and wireless signals. In so doing it was hoped to reduce Bomber Command's escalating losses that were reaching a new high during the battle of Berlin that was being fought at this time.

To help them in their aim of confounding the enemy's defences, the aircraft of 100 (BS) Group were fitted with a variety of ingenious electronic and radar devices. Most were exclusive to the group, but some were in general use by main force and Pathfinder squadrons, like Window and Monica.

JAMMING DEVICES

There were two main types of jamming device which numbered some thirty-two different pieces of equipment in total. The first type of device generated electronic 'noise' and was aimed at the enemy's early warning (EW), ground-controlled interception (GCI), gun-laying (GL) and airborne interception (AI) radars. The second produced audio interference which disrupted the enemy's radio telephone (R/T) communication channels.

Window – the single most important RCM device of the war introduced by the RAF was used by all its heavy bomber groups including 100 (BS) Group. Window was strips of metallised paper cut to a particular length and dropped from bomber aircraft in clumps to produce spurious responses on enemy EW, GCI, GL and AI radar screens. It was first used over Hamburg on 24/25 July 1943.
Airborne Cigar (**ABC**)– designed to disrupt enemy R/T control channels on spot frequencies.
Carpet – designed to jam enemy GCI and GL *Würzburg* radars in the 300–600 MHz waveband.
Jostle – designed for continuous wave jamming of German R/T transmissions, but fitted only to 100 (BS) Group's B-17 and B-24 aircraft.
Mandrel – designed in both ground and airborne forms to jam enemy early warning radar, it first entered service in December 1942.
Piperack – an American-developed device designed to jam enemy AI radars. Also known as Dina.
Shiver – designed to jam enemy GCI and

GL *Würzburg* radars by transmitting a continuous squittering signal.
Tinsel – a microphone assembly fitted in the engine nacelle and connected to a transmitter which could be tuned to the enemy's R/T frequency by a German-speaking crew member and switched on, flooding it with engine noise.
Tuba – designed to jam enemy EW radars.

HOMING AND WARNING DEVICES

As the war progressed so too did the number of airborne radar and other transmitting devices in use by both sides. It was inevitable, therefore, that both sides would soon develop homing receivers to give a bearing on a transmission source. Warning devices were also invented to alert crews to the presence of other aircraft in their corner of the sky. All twelve of these devices used by 100 (BS) Group (except for the tail warning radar Monica for use against enemy interceptors) were passive, that is they did not produce any signal themselves.

Boozer – a rearward-looking aerial fitted in the tail of a bomber introduced in 1943, it gave crews notice of when their aircraft was being monitored by ground-based *Würzburg* radar, and by *FuG 202/212* transmissions from a nightfighter AI radar.
Monica – an active tail warning device first used in 1943, it was fitted to aircraft of most heavy bomber squadrons to give warning of nightfighters stalking them from behind. It was largely withdrawn by 1944 when it was found that its transmisions could be homed onto by the German *FuG 227 Flensburg* airborne homing device.
Perfectos – designed to trigger enemy IFF sets and then produce a bearing on the transmission.

Bundles of 'Window' go down from a British bomber en route to the Ruhr during a daylight raid late in the war. (US National Archives)

Mosquito nightfighter squadrons of 100 (BS) Group flew bomber support missions over occupied Europe and Germany in the last year of the war. DZ228 'D-Dog' was an F.Mk II and flew from Little Snoring with 23 Squadron. (Philip Birtles)

Serrate – designed to give a bearing on transmissions from enemy AI radars, used by Mosquitoes of 100 (BS) Group and also by Fighter Command/ADGB.

AIRBORNE INTERCEPTION RADAR

AI radar had a range of between 4 and 6 miles on average and was used in bomber support fighter aircraft like the Beaufighter and Mosquito to intercept German nightfighter aircraft preying on the bomber stream. There were four types of AI radar used by these aircraft: AI Mk IV, AI Mk VIII, AI Mk X and AI Mk XV.

SAFETY IN NUMBERS: THE BOMBER STREAM AND OTHER SURVIVAL TACTICS

When in the early years of the war bomber crews were briefed on the operation they were about to fly, they were given details of where the target was and individual captains were left to plan their own routes to and from it. At this stage in the war when the RAF's offensive was in its infancy and the enemy defences had yet to develop, it was very much a case of every man for himself. But with the

The end of a Messerschmitt Bf110 nightfighter, destroyed over Germany by a patrolling Mosquito nightfighter of 100 (BS) Group in November 1944. (US National Archives)

advent of the German Kammhuber Line of defence in 1942, the approaches to Germany and its occupied territories were protected by a defensive early warning network divided into radar-controlled fighter boxes. Its principal shortcoming was that its fighter boxes could only control one interception at a time, so Bomber Command's planners devised the bomber stream where as many aircraft as possible were funnelled over a given point in the shortest time possible in order to swamp the enemy defences. A force of some 600 aircraft could be spread over an area of sky 150 miles long, 6 miles wide and 2 miles deep. This concentration of bombers, all flying in the same direction in darkness, was not achieved by the pilots using visual contact to maintain formation. The reality was that each navigator was given route and timing points to follow at the briefing and instructed to follow them as best they could. With such a concentration of aircraft flying virtually blind in darkness, there was an ever-present risk of mid-air collisions. By the end of the war, bomber streams had become four times as dense as this. The Germans countered these tactics by deepening the Kammhuber Line and increasing the capacity of each box so that two or more nightfighters could be handled at once.

Corkscrewing and ample good luck enabled this 51 Squadron Halifax to make it home after a determined attack by a German nightfighter. (IWM CE114)

Other tactics introduced by the Germans to counter the bombers were the *Wilde Sau* (Wild Boar) method whereby single-seat fighters concentrated over the bombers' target and used searchlight illumination for target acquisition; and the *Zahme Sau* (Tame Boar) where freelance nightfighters infiltrated the bomber stream and used their own radars to find targets for themselves.

If a prowling German nightfighter was spotted in time by a bomber crew, the standard fighter evasion manoeuvre developed by Bomber Command for the protection of its heavy bombers was put into action. It was known as the 'corkscrew' and the order to 'Corkscrew port [or starboard] go!' could be given to the pilot by any bomber crew member who saw that a fighter attack was imminent. The constant changes

in direction, speed and altitude of this manoeuvre proved highly effective in hampering accurate deflection shooting by the pursuing nightfighter. However, the physical exertion required of a pilot to 'corkscrew' a heavy bomber about the sky was immense and a successful manoeuvre often left him drenched in sweat and aching from the sheer physical effort.

For bomber crews, the bomber stream continued to provide them with relative safety in numbers, but thanks to developments in interception techniques by the Germans it became necessary to stream bombers over the target in as little as 15 to 20 minutes by mid-1943. Because early identification of a target was important for enemy fighter controllers to direct *Wilde Sau* fighters, the RAF sought to keep them guessing for as long as possible by mounting 'spoof' raids to targets in the opposite direction to the intended one, and by the main force flying elaborate dog-leg courses to their target, only turning towards the true objective at the last minute. Control of *Wilde Sau* fighters depended upon ground-to-air R/T communication which could be electronically jammed, or subjected to spoof counter-orders by German-speaking RAF controllers of 100 (BS) Group.

Despite the best efforts at protecting the RAF's bomber force, these defensive tactics did not prevent the carnage of the Berlin raid of 24/25 March 1944, and the Nuremberg raid on 30/31 March, when 72 and 96 bombers respectively were lost, most to marauding nightfighters.

By the spring of 1944, the German nightfighter force was in the ascendancy after its temporary setbacks in 1942–3. A new command and control system, better ground and airborne radar equipment, and improved aircraft armament, meant that it remained a formidable defensive organisation up until the end of 1944. By this point in the war, the RAF's use of RCM and spoof tactics, combined with intruder and bomber support operations, had tipped the balance in favour of the bombers once again and there it remained until the end of the war.

An important aid to the survival of wartime RAF bomber crews, weary at the end of a gruelling flight, was a device codenamed FIDO. In the early years of the war, bomber crews often returned home only to discover their airfields completely fog-bound. Usually short of fuel and occasionally disabled by battle damage, the many crash-landings that resulted took a savage toll in valuable aircraft and crews.

After the personal intervention of Winston Churchill this deadly hazard was largely overcome by the government's Petroleum Warfare Department. The result was the development of FIDO – Fog Investigation and Dispersal Operation. Lines of burners fuelled by thousands of gallons of petrol were installed beside runways to literally burn the fog off the airfields, thereby allowing aircraft to take off and land in relative safety.

A countrywide FIDO system at fifteen British airfields covering most RAF and USAAF frontline commands was in place by the end of 1944. Ten Bomber Command airfields were equipped with the system: Carnaby, Downham Market, Fiskerton, Foulsham, Graveley, Ludford Magna, Melbourne, Metheringham, Sturgate and Tuddenham. By the time of the Ardennes offensive in the winter of 1944/45, FIDO had enabled more than one thousand Allied aircraft and their crews to make safe landings despite dense fog over Britain and the Continent.

CHAPTER 7

'TARGET FOR TONIGHT'

The description that follows is of a typical day and night for an RAF heavy bomber station during 1944, as station headquarters staff, ground and aircrews, plan and launch a 'Goodwood' or maximum effort raid to a target 'somewhere in Germany'.

After breakfast, aircrew report to their flight officers, and are told whether operations are planned for the coming night or if there will be a stand-down.

From the moment that details of the target for the coming night come through on the telephone from group headquarters, to the point some eighteen hours later when the last few aircraft land back at their home base, activity on a heavy bomber station to get their squadrons airborne was intense. Meanwhile, in station headquarters the group broadcast has come through on the telephone requiring a 'Goodwood' (maximum effort) and details of the target for tonight. The bomb load and H-Hour along with route details will follow shortly, but first of all the station intelligence officer notifies everyone who needs to know, from the station, squadron and flight commanders, through to flying control and the bomb dump.

Now that it is official that ops are planned, the crews go out to their dispersals to check on the serviceability of their aircraft, and if necessary fly air tests. The groundcrews busy themselves preparing the aircraft; tradesmen from the various sections check instruments, radar and electrical equipment; and the aircraft is fuelled, armed and bombed-up. The aircrews have lunch in their respective messes before the Tannoy announces the times for operational meals of bacon and eggs and the briefing.

Later in the afternoon, crews congregate outside the briefing room before finally entering. Once inside they sit on long wooden forms facing the end wall where a large map of Europe, shrouded from view by a blackout curtain, hangs on the wall above the raised platform from which the briefings are conducted. Once it has been ascertained by a roll-call of pilots' names that all crews are present, the whole assembly rises to its feet and stands smartly to attention when the platform party enters the room, comprising the station and squadron commanders, and the senior flight commanders. The briefing room doors are closed by an RAF policeman who then stands guard outside. Already present on the stage are the station intelligence officer, the met officer, the base engineering officer, and the flying control officer.

The station intelligence officer opens the briefing by unveiling the map to reveal the target for the night, with the route to be followed marked with red tape. Known flak

```
.+ GPF
V GFA  GFA 11/14 OF OP                    B/3rd              Return to
T W R IN ADD                                                 Base Int.
FROM HQ 1 GROUP.   141305A
      TO 12. 13. 14 AND 15 BASES AND ALL OPS STATIONS.
      INFO 71 BASE. HWBC. AND HQ 6 GROUP.
      SECRET WWX BT
A. FORM B SERIAL NO 1617 TASK NO 1729
B. 14TH JANUARY 1945.
C. SEE CURRENT INT SIGNAL A TOTAL OF 509 PLUS P.F.F. A/C WILL
   BE ATACKING THIS TARGET.
D. TO COMPLETE DESTRUCTION OF SYNTHETIC OIL PLANT.
E. NIGHT OF 14/15TH JANUARY 1945.
F. 12 BASE = 63 A/C
   13 BASE = 68 A/C
   14 BASE = 61 A/C (INCLUDING 8 ABC)
   15 BASE - 66 A/C
                  _____
                  258 AIRCRAFT.
N
.  ''GH 1515''
        AIMING POINT - 031H 094V ON ILLUSTRATION 15/14.
I AND H2 NIL.
. RESULTS OF THE RAID BY MEANS OF PHOTOGRAPHS AND PILOTS REPORTS.
  ALL A/C ARE TO CARRY PHOTOFLASHES
. AND L. (A) BASES - (B) READING - (C) BEACHY HEAD - (D) 5000N
          0120E - (E) 5000N 0400E - (F) 5010N 0740E - (G) 5105N
          0915E - (H) 5105N 1100E - TARGET - (I) 5115N 1210E -
          (J) 5045N 1145E - (K) 5020N 1000 E - (L) 5050N 0840E -
          (E) 5000N 0400E - (M) 5100N 0250E - (N) ORFORDNESS
          (A) BASES -
1. 'H' HOUR WILL BE 0001 HOURS.
2. 1ST WAVE .                      'H' TO 'H' PLUS 3.
   ----------                      --------------------
        12 BASE = 21 A/C. 13 BASE = 23 A/C - 14 BASE = 18 A/C.
        15 BASE = 22 A/C.
   2ND WAVE.                        'H' PLUS 3+ TO 'H'  PLUS 7
   ---------                        -------------------------
        12 BASE = 21 A/C. 13 BASE = 22 A/C. 14 BASE = 17 A/C.
        15 BASE = 22 A/C.
        PLUS 33 LANCS OF 6 GROUP.
   3RD WAVE.                        'H' PLUS 7 TO 'H' PLUS 10.
   ---------                        --------------------------
        12 BASE = 21 A/C. 13 BASE = 23 A/C. 14 BASE = 18 A/C.
        15 BASE = 22 A/C.
   . 8 A/C OF 101 SQUADRON ARE TO BE SPREAD EVENLY OVER THE PERIOD OF
     THE ATTACK.
1-. PETROL.      =   2154 GALLONS FOR ALL AIRCRAFT.
    ------
N2. BOMB LOAD.  1 X 4000 H.C.
                12 X 500 MC/GP.
                FUSING = TD 0.025 SECS.
                10% OF 500 LBS BOMBS ARE TO BE FUSED L.D. 6 TO 144 HOURS.
N3. DISTRIBUTOR SETTINGS.
    --------------------
        FOR A/C CARRYING HE LOAD = 0.25 SECS
        FOR A/C CARRYING ''CLUSTER LOAD'' = 0.1 SECS
        FOR A/C CARRYING S.B.C. LOAD = 0.2 SECS
```

Secret teleprinter orders from 1 Group Headquarters forwarded to 12, 13, 14 and 15 Bases on 14 January 1945, with full details of the coming night's operation to the synthetic oil refineries at Leuna near Leipzig.

N4. SECURITY.

SIGNALS AND RADAR SILENCE. INCLUDING ABC A/C IS TO BE MAINTAINED
AS FAR AS 0500E ON THE OUTWARD JOURNEY. AFTER THIS POINT
H2S IS TO BE SWITCHED ON FOR THE REMAINDER OF THE TRIP.

N5. OTHER GROUPS.
----

4 GROUP = 100 HALIFAX ON ''GQ2022'' H HOUR = 2320.
5 GROUP= 200 LANCS ON ''GQ1515'' H HOUR = 2100
6. GROUP = 53 LANCS ON ''GQ1515'' H HOUR = 0001
137 HALIFAX ON GSGS 4416 H HOUR = ~~1935XXXXX~~ 1935.

N6. METHOD.

(A) METHOD FOR TONIGHT WILL BE CONTROLLED ''NEWHAVEN'' WITH
EMERGENCY ''WANGANUI''

(B) PFF A/C WILL OPEN ~~THE TXXXX~~ THE ATTACK WITH STICKS OF
ILLUMINATING FLARES AT H MINUS 6. OTHER PFF A/C WILL MARK THE
AIMING POINT VISUALLY WITH LARGE SALVOES OF MIXED RED AND
GREEN T.I'S. AND SOME GREEN T.I'S MAY BE ALSO DROPPED IN
THE EARLY PART OF THE ATTACK.

(C) A ~~MAZXXXX~~ MASTER BOMBER WILL GIVE AIMING INSTRUCTIONS TO THE
MAIN FORCE ~~WHOS XXXX~~ WHO SHOULD LISTEN OUT FROM H MINUS
15

CALL SIGN = MASTER BOMBER = SNODGRASS.
DEPUTY BOMBER = SNODGRASS 2.
MAIN FORCE = BOMBLOAD.
FREQUENCIES = 5145 KCS AND 5570 KCS.

(D) IN THE EVENT OF CLOUD OBSCURING THE GROUND MARKING SKYMARKING
FLARES RED/YELLOW STARS WILL BE DROPPED AT THE RELEASE POINT
THROUGHOUT THE ATTACK.

(E) IF THE MASTER BOMBER IS NOT HEARD. THE MAIN FORCE ARE TO AIM
THEIR BOMBS IN THE FOLLOWING ORDER OF PREFERENCE.

(1) AT THE CENTRE OF MIXED RED AND GREEN T.I'S.

(2) AT THE CENTRE OF THE RED T.I'S.

(3) AT THE CENTRE OF THE GREEN T.I'S.

(4) AT THE CENTRE OF THE SKYMARKING FLARES RED/YELLOW STARS
ON AN EXACT HEADING OF 068 DEGREES T. (073 DEGREES M)

N7. TACTICS.

(A) CLIMB ON TRACK TO RENDEZVOUS AT READING ABOVE LOW CLOUD
4/6000 FEET.

(B) CONTINUE CLIMBING TO BEACHY HEAD 6/8 000 FEET.

(C) REMAIN AT 6/8000 FT AS FAR AS 0430 E ON TRACK.

(D) FROM 0430E CLIMB TO BOMBING HEIGHT 19/22000 FT BY 5010N 0740E

(E) ~~KAIXXXXX~~ REMAIN AT THIS HEIGHT AS FAR AS 5045N 1145E

(F) FROM THIS POSITION LOSE HEIGHT AND GAIN SPEED TO BE AT
14/16000 FT BY 5020N 1000 E

(G) REMAIN AT THIS HEIGHT AS FAR AS 0400E ON RETURN

(H) FROM THIS POSITION LOSE HEIGHT TO 810000 FT BY THE
'CONTINENTAL COAST 'OUT''

(I) FROM CONTINENTAL COAST ''OUT'' REMAIN AT 8/10000 FT TO BASE
AREAS.

N8. WINDOW. TO FOLLOW WHEN AVAILABLE.

O ~~AXXXXXXX~~ ACKNOWLEDGE.

P 141305A

HDOD GPA 11/14

TOO 1422 BW

No. 170 Squadron, R.A.F. 14th January, 1945. BATTLE ORDER SERIAL NO. 47. O.C. FLYING: S/LDR. R. FRONDE, D.F.C.

A/C CR.	A/C NO.	PILOT	F/ENG.	A/B	NAV.	W.OP.	M.U.G.	R/G.
1.N.	PB 693	F/L BURTON D.F.M.	SGT GERNON	F/O ROWAN	F/O ROGERS	F/S STEWART	SGT SEARSON	SGT TOMLINSON
2.D.	ND 452	F/L HAYLEY	SGT GRANT	F/S CARTWRIGHT	F/O BRYER	F/S BYRNE	F/O TAYLOR	F/S MEASHAM
3.Q.	NN 739+	F/O WHYTE	SGT WALTERS	W/O PARKINSON	SGT PALMER	F/S HORNE	SGT GILMOUR	F/S KERNAHAN
4.S.	ME 306	F/L HUXLEY – PARLOUR	SGT EVANS	W/O SCHNEIDER	F/S SEITH	F/S LKER	F/S SLEIGHTHOLME	SGT FELLOWS
5.A.	NG 349+	F/O JARMAN	SGT HADCROFT	F/S STORRAR	F/O SLIPSON	F/S HULME	F/S CHALMERS	F/S CAMPBELL
6.P.	ND 658	F/O McAINSH	F/S LEWIS	F/S SUMMERS	F/S McCULLOUGH	SGT SYKES	F/S JONES (727)	SGT CROOT
7.W.	PB 728	F/O CLOSE	SGT DEWAR	F/S SWANSON	F/O ARCHIBALD	F/S HARRISON	F/S FREESTONE	F/S EDWARDS.
8.J.	PB 595	F/O CONSTABLE	SGT ASHTON	F/S PELLETZ	F/O SUMMERS	F/S HART	F/S LEFEIVER	F/S JOHNSTONE
9.E.	ND 863	F/O COURT	SGT GARRISON	F/S BURKE	F/S WRIGHT	F/S SMITH	F/S GILPIN	F/O PATRICK
10.U.	ME 302	F/O JEAVONS	SGT OLSON	W/O ANDERSON	F/S BAIRSTOW	F/S BAILEY	F/S THORBURN	SGT ROBINSON
11.R.	PB 704+	F/O DIXIE	SGT SCOTT	F/O WOODSIDE	F/O SQUIRES	W/O LONG	F/S CRABE	F/S FERNQUIST
12.L.	ME 320	F/O HAMPSON	SGT BOWERS	SGT REYNOLDS	SGT FRENCH	SGT HART (512)	SGT McWILLIAMS	F/S RIDDELL
13.T.	NG 202+	F/L ALEXANDRA	SGT MATTHEWS	F/O PEDERSEN	F/O O'REGAN	SGT MALKIN	SGT McSKIMMING	SGT NILES
14.F.	ND 385	F/L CODERRE	SGT MORRISON	F/O FLANIGAN	F/O COOPER	SGT LEWIS (204)	F/S PATERSON	F/S MacINNIS
15.G.	PB 480	F/O SULPHER	SGT MILLS	F/O JELLEY	F/S NORMAN	SGT SWANWICK	SGT LAMPEN	SGT ALLEN
16.V.	NN 744+	F/O QUINE	SGT WELLS	F/O GREENE	F/O SEATON	SGT BRASSINGTON	SGT HOWELL	SGT THOMPSON
17.M.	PB 752+	F/O JACKSON	SGT GORMAN	F/S ARMSTRONG	F/O MAXWELL	SGT UNDERHILL	F/S FREEBORN	F/S HEWGILL

+ = Mark 1.

DUTY CREWS								
		F/O McINTYRE		F/S CRAIGEN	F/S SYLATT	SGT JOHNSON	F/S McMILLAN	F/S RUTZOU
				F/O MOORE	SGT HART (267)		SGT DIXON	SGT KANE

RATIONS 119 @ 1/- To be distributed by F/S PERROTT at Locker Room 30 minutes after Main Briefing Time.

DESPATCHING F/O McINTYRE and F/O MOORE.

OPERATIONAL MEALS ordinary lunch.

NAVIGATION BRIEFING 1345 hours. MAIN BRIEFING 1430 hours.

(signature)

for Wing Commander, Commanding,
No. 170 Squadron, R.A.F.

The Battle Order for 170 Squadron, 14 January 1945, target Leuna.

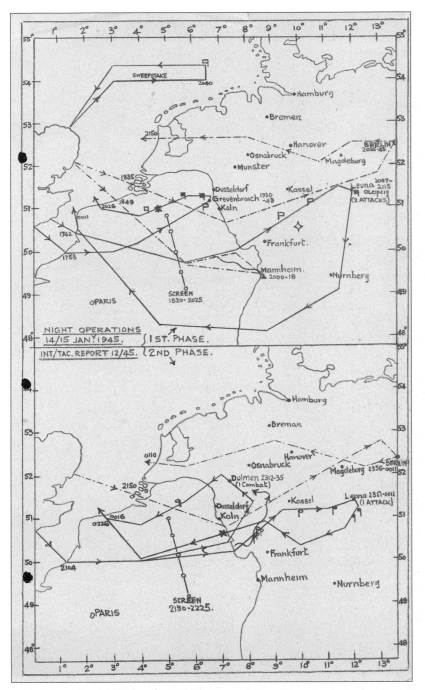

A plan of night operations for 14/15 January 1945 in two phases. Diversionary operation (Sweepstake) over the North Sea by 126 training aircraft; two attacks on Leuna three hours apart by 573 Lancasters and 14 Mosquitoes of 1, 5, 6 and 8 Groups; secondary raids on Grevenbroich by 151 Halifaxes, Mosquitoes and Lancasters of 6 and 8 Groups; and on Dulmen by 115 Halifaxes, Mosquitoes and Lancasters of 4 and 8 Groups; two attacks on Berlin three hours apart by 83 Mosquitoes, and one by 9 Mosquitoes on Mannheim; 58 RCM sorties flying Mandrel screens two hours apart.

Armourers collect American-made ANM65 1,000lb GP bombs from the bomb dump at Linton-on-Ouse, Yorkshire, for loading into the Lancasters of the base's resident Canadian bomber squadron, 408 (Goose) Squadron. (DND/UK 11739)

Groundcrew refuel Lancaster II LL725 'Z-Zombie' of 408 Squadron on 21 April 1944 for a night raid on Cologne, to be flown by Flg Off E.M.C. Franklin and crew. On 28/29 July 'Zombie' was one of four Lancasters lost by the squadron on operations to Hamburg, skippered on this occasion by Plt Off J.H.A. McCaffrey DFC, RCAF. (DND/PL 29074)

Armourers feed 2,000 rounds of belted .303in ammunition into the storage boxes inside the FN5 front gun turret of a 617 Squadron Lancaster at Woodhall Spa. (IWM CH18175)

An 8,000lb 'Blockbuster' is pushed into position beneath a Lancaster, ready to be lifted into the bomb-bay. (IWM CH12593)

and searchlight positions are also marked on this map by red and green celluloid overlays respectively. First, the SIO explains details of the target and why it has been chosen, followed by the signals, bombing and navigation leaders who explain the various routines for the night. Next comes the FCO who outlines engine start-up and marshalling times, and the runway to be used. Then the met officer gives a full briefing on wind speeds, cloud and the weather likely to be encountered over the target. The squadron wing commanders follow by speaking to the crews in detail about the operation before handing over to the station commander who then wishes everyone good luck and a safe return.

With the briefing over, pilots obtain their maps for the night from the station map stores and mark onto them their proposed routes. The wireless operators draw their flimsies on which are printed radio frequencies and the colours of the day. Crews hurry to the parachute stores to collect chutes and Mae Wests, then make for the locker rooms where valuables are handed in and escape kits collected before changing into flying kit.

Amid the usual babble of conversation and the jumble of parachutes, helmets and flying boots, each man struggles into his unwieldy flying gear, the gunners usually taking the longest with their layers of electrically heated clothing and the bulky Taylorsuits. Sandwiches and flasks of coffee for the return journey together with slabs of chocolate and barley sugar sweets are handed out to each crew member from wrappings of newspaper.

Outside the locker room the buses arrive to take the crews on the short ride to their aircraft, dispersed around the perimeter of the airfield. A corporal stands at the open door shouting out the letters by which each

Crews of 431 (Iroquois) and 434 (Bluenose) Squadrons are briefed for a raid on Essen. (DND/UK 16239)

Canadian aircrew don flying clothing in the locker room prior to boarding the crew bus to take them out to their aircraft, waiting on a distant dispersal pan.

aircraft is known. As space becomes available on a bus for that aircraft's crew, they climb on board and are taken out to their waiting aircraft.

Once on their respective dispersals, each pilot completes the formalities of signing the Form 700 for the groundcrew corporal after a careful check of the control surfaces, wheel tyres and undercarriage oleo-legs. Then after a last leak on the dewy grass beside the dispersal, he and the rest of his crew board the aircraft: flight engineer, pilot, navigator, bomb-aimer and the wireless operator make their way up the fuselage to the nose, the two gunners to their turrets. The pilot stows his 'chute and straps himself into his seat. Outside in the dark on the dispersal pan the groundcrew move the battery starter trolley into position under the port wing.

The crew of 9 Squadron's Lancaster ED831 'Y-Yoke' board their aircraft at Bardney, Lincolnshire, before taking off for the ten-hour round trip to Friedrichshafen on 20 June 1943, one of the longest they would be expected to make. Skippered by Sqn Ldr A.M. Hobbs DFC, RNZAF, they are Sgt F.W. Sanderson (N), Sgt K. Mott (BA), Sgt C.P. King (FE), Sgt E.C. Bishop (WOp), Sgt W.C. Rowlands (MU), and Flt Sgt F. Slater (RG). Six nights later Hobbs and his crew failed to return from an operation to Gelsenkirchen in 'Y-Yoke', shot down into the Ijsselmeer on the homeward trip by a nightfighter. All the crew perished.

The flight engineer checks to see that all the fuel cocks below his instrument panel are in their correct positions, then leans forward to the pilot and declares he is ready for engine start-up. The engineer looks out of the cockpit window and down to the ground beneath, calling back that the groundcrew are ready with their battery cart to start the port inner. When the pilot switches on the ignition, the fitter down beneath the wing shouts 'Contact!'. The engineer presses one of the four black starter buttons on his panel and the first of four engines coughs, splutters and finally roars into life. The same procedure is repeated until all four engines are running. The pilot checks the intercom to all crew positions, then opens up the engines and allows them to warm up to operating temperature.

Taxiing times for each individual aircraft were set at briefing and the time to taxi out for take-off has now arrived. The engineer stands behind the pilot, keeping watch on the array of dials on his engineer's panel and the bomb-aimer comes up from his station in the nose to assist the pilot at take-off. The rear hatch door is secured by the

Caught in the glare of the green Aldis light from the runway controller's van, the pilot releases the wheel brakes and opens the throttles of his Lancaster III to begin his take-off run. (Roy Conyers Nesbit collection)

groundcrew before the wheel chocks are pulled away and the pilot gently opens the throttles. On doughnut tyres the big bomber trundles and sways forward, following the aircraft in front around the perimeter track in slow procession towards the duty runway for the night, and joining the queue at the end. The pilot goes through his final cockpit check and the navigator outlines the flight plan and climb instructions. A green Aldis light flashes from the control van signalling to the pilot that it is his turn to line up for take-off.

The pilot runs up the engines against the brakes, which are then released and the aircraft begins to accelerate down the runway. Although the throttles are almost fully open, to build as much speed as possible he purposely holds the bomber's nose down as she strains to leave the ground, using the full length of the runway if necessary. The bomb-aimer eases the throttles through the gate for full take-off power and slams the clamp on to keep them from slipping back through vibration at the crucial moment. With both hands firmly grasping the control column, the pilot eases it back and the engine note changes as the

The pilot eases the heavily laden bomber off the end of the runway.

bomber claws its way into the sky at little more than 100mph, leaving the runway to slip away beneath. The wheel-brake lever is nipped to stop the wheels turning before the main gear retracts with a clunk. The red and green indicator lights go out on the pilot's instrument panel as each leg locks up and at last they are airborne.

The bomber continues in a shallow climb until the air speed has built sufficiently for the pilot to adjust the fuel mixture and engine revolutions to normal. The engineer eases the throttles back as the heavy bomber continues to climb. The flaps are now fully retracted and the power eased off again to suit the rate of climb selected. The navigator gives the pilot a course to steer for the group's assembly point

and with the reassuring red and green glow of navigation lights on the other aircraft in the sky all around them they fly in the climb towards the coast.

Once rendezvous has been made with the other aircraft of the group, navigation lights are turned out as the armada of bombers drones its way seawards at a speed of some 200mph – usually towards Cromer for bomber groups below the river Humber, Flamborough Head or Spurn Point for those to the north of this line – where they leave the shores of England behind.

The gunners now request permission to test-fire their guns over the sea as the bomber continues to climb towards the briefed height for crossing the enemy coast, now some ten

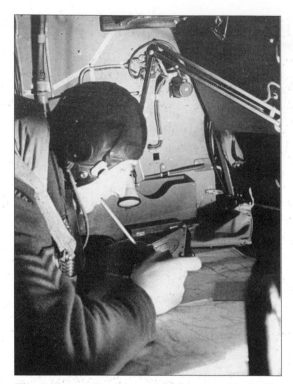

The navigator, hard at work in his curtained-off compartment behind the pilot.

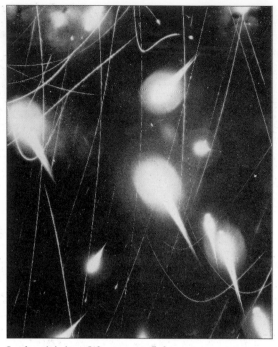

In the vicinity of the target, flak comes up to greet them. It was said that if you could see the red hot core of a flak shell on its way up, it was close; if you could smell the cordite when it exploded, it was too close for comfort. (Roy Conyers Nesbit collection)

minutes' flying time away. Continually scanning the sky for the first signs of enemy fighters, they swing their turrets from side to side. Behind the pilot, the flight engineer continues to monitor his instrument panel, checking fuel states, oil temperatures and pressures, and cross-feeding petrol when necessary. Meanwhile, the wireless operator tunes his set to listen in to the broadcast winds which come through at regular intervals. These are an average taken at group headquarters from meteorological data received from selected aircraft on the raid, and then rebroadcast to all aircraft to enable them to navigate using the same wind speeds and directions. The navigator tunes the brilliance knob on his Gee set to get a comfortable picture, while down in the nose the bomb-aimer keeps a look-out for

the enemy coast ahead, and the first puffs of flak coming up to greet them. Passing through the 5,000ft height band the order comes from the pilot to switch on oxygen.

After the enemy coast has been crossed, the navigator gives the pilot a new course to steer that will take them to the target, with an estimated time of arrival. It is about thirty to forty minutes' flying time from the Dutch coast to the Ruhr, but more than two hours to a more distant target like Berlin. The gently waving fingers of searchlights continue to probe the night sky as the bomber drones on its course to the target.

A strong Mandrel screen keeps the Germans guessing where the bombers will finally strike and a special Window force drops bundles of metal foil strips to swamp

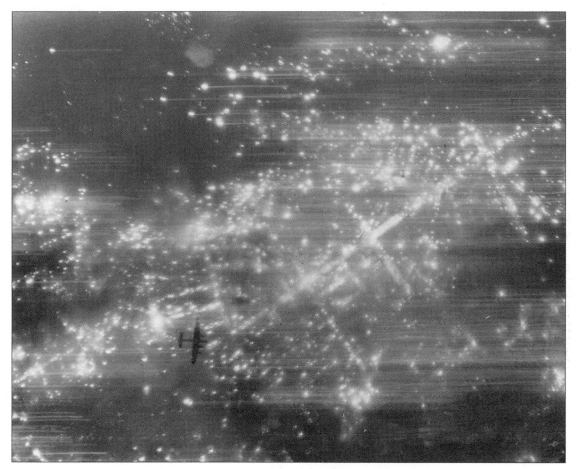

Hannover burns, the result of an attack by 504 RAF heavy bombers on the night of 8/9 October 1943. A Lancaster can be seen several thousand feet below, silhouetted against the mass of incendiary fires in the vicinity of the Sallestrasse. (Roy Conyers Nesbit collection)

the enemy radar screens with false returns. The aim is to put the enemy fighter and flak controllers off their stroke. Aircraft of the Pathfinder Force are timed to drop coloured route and target markers just before the arrival of the main force. On a typical raid against a target in the Ruhr in late 1944 involving a main force drawn from three heavy bomber groups, plus Pathfinders, the whole raid is timed to last just 14 minutes with 553 bombers being streamed over the target during this time.

Ahead, the heavy flak opens up with a vengeance as the Pathfinders begin to mark the target with the aid of H2S – route markers in green and target markers in red.

As the pilot turns onto the final leg to the target, the bomb-aimer goes down into the nose to check his bombsight and fusing panel; the engineer moves beyond the cockpit bulkhead to check the master fuel cocks; the wireless operator pushes bundles of Window down the flare chute at regular intervals to add to the confusion of enemy radar operators down below; the pilot calls up the gunners to keep their eyes peeled for enemy fighters; and the navigator's voice comes over the intercom to give the pilot the ETA on target. Each member of the crew is busy as the procession of aircraft begins its final run-in to the target.

With the bomb doors now open, the pilot holds the bomber on a straight and level course for its bombing run. Beneath, the target area is a sea of flame, punctuated by the red and green target markers dropped by the Pathfinders. Dozens of searchlight beams grope the sky, hoping to latch on to a bomber during its most vulnerable phase of the operation, so that the flak batteries below can get a bead on it and then attempt to blast it from the sky. The crew can hear the occasional dull thud of a shell bursting

close by, and perhaps the clattering on the fuselage as pieces of spent shrapnel hit it.

The bomb-aimer directs the pilot with calm instructions of 'Left, left, steady, right a bit. Hold it there, left a bit. Bombs gone!' The aircraft seems to rear up in the sky, relieved of her heavy cargo of bombs, but the pilot needs to fly straight and level for another 30 seconds to enable the aiming point photograph to be taken. Without it their operation will not count towards their tour of thirty operations. With the enemy defences now well awakened and throwing all they can at the slowly moving bomber stream overhead, most crews see this as the longest 30 seconds of their lives. Before they can leave the target area, the bomb-aimer

Coming home on a wing and a prayer. Damaged and with wounded crew on board, some bombers were lucky to make it home to a safe landing in England.

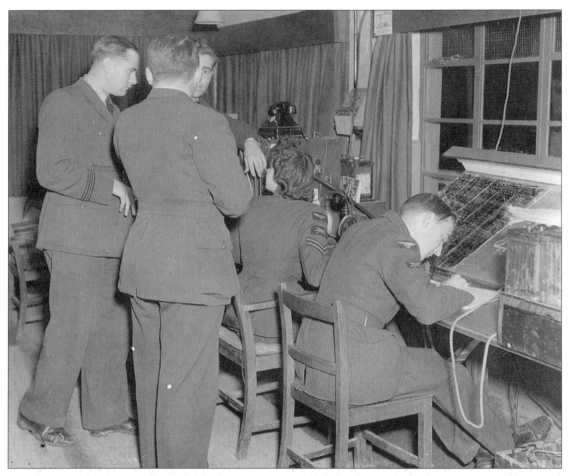

Tension lines the faces of flying control personnel at Fiskerton as they await the return of the first aircraft from Berlin in the early hours of 3 January 1944. Fiskerton's resident squadron, No. 49, lost two Lancasters that night. (IWM CH12207)

checks on his panel for signs of any bomb hang-ups which could mean another run over the target, but if all is well the bomb doors are closed and they turn for home.

Vigilance is still required on the long haul back across blacked-out Europe to the enemy coast. Flak and searchlights are still active and German nightfighters loiter for the unwary crew who have let down their guard now that the tension of the bomb run has passed, or the one that has lost its way from the relative safety of the bomber stream. Some, even,

have been shot down on the home straight by enemy intruders lurking in the circuit at their base as they prepare to land.

Once across the enemy coast and over the sea, the navigator picks up his Gee lattice line and they join the procession that will lead to home. In a short while, 50 miles from the English coast, the pilot calls up on VHF and identifies his aircraft. Once over England, the crew look out below for the Pundit beacon that flashes in Morse code the identification letters of their home airfield. A call is then

Lancaster JB362 'D-Dog' of 49 Squadron, skippered by Flt Sgt Clive Roantree, comes safely home from Berlin on 19 November 1943. The two outer engines have been shut down as Roantree taxies 'D-Dog' to her dispersal pan, guided by a groundcrewman with torches. (Roy Conyers Nesbit collection)

Cigarettes and mugs of tea help Sqn Ldr J. Martin DFC and his crew unwind while they are debriefed by the station intelligence officer, Flg Off G. Dunbar, following the Berlin raid of 22/23 November 1943. (Roy Conyers Nesbit collection)

Post-raid reconnaissance was undertaken by the RAF using five dedicated photo-reconnaissance squadrons, operating PR Spitfires and Mosquitoes from their base at Benson in Oxfordshire. This reconnaissance cover of Leuna was taken after the heavy RAF raid on the night of 14/15 January 1945 by 573 Lancasters and 14 Mosquitoes and reveals almost total devastation of the synthetic oil plant by fire and high explosive. (US National Archives)

made to the control tower asking for permission to join the circuit and land.

Once safely back on the ground the engines are throttled back for the first time in more than six hours, the white-hot exhausts making a reassuring crackle, and the bomber is marshalled to its dispersal. The engines are finally shut down and the exhausted crew climb out of their aircraft and are taken by crew bus to the briefing room where they are dropped off for interrogation by the station intelligence staff. They answer a lengthy questionnaire giving details of the operation they have just flown. A welcome mug of tea or coffee, laced with rum, and a much needed cigarette, helps the crew to unwind before interrogation is completed and they return their flying kit to the stores and lockers before retiring to their billets for a well-earned sleep.

The whole process starts all over again on the following evening.

CHAPTER 8

PERSONAL EQUIPMENT

UNIFORMS AND INSIGNIA

Both officers' and airmen's blue-grey tunics were worn on operations by bomber crews from the beginning of the war, either on their own or beneath a flying suit, until largely superseded by the battledress in 1941. The same tunics and battledresses were also worn by ground staff, although a number of unofficial variations crept into use by groundcrews who spent most of their working life outdoors on cold windswept dispersals.

An off-the-peg garment made from coarse and itchy unlined serge, the airman's uniform was much less comfortable to wear than the tailored and lined officer's barathea version. Different uniforms were worn by personnel of the dominions and air forces in exile, serving alongside their RAF comrades in Bomber Command. They retained the uniforms and insignia of their own national air forces, for example: Australia (dark blue), South Africa (brown) and Free French (black). However, the uniforms of the RCAF and Polish Air Force, for example, were identical to the RAF pattern except for buttons and insignia. Regrettably, it is beyond the scope of this book to consider these variations in any further detail.

OFFICERS' No. 1 DRESS

The RAF No. 1 dress tunic, as worn by commissioned officers and warrant officers

(WO) during the Second World War, dates from 1919 and was based on the Army cavalry officer's tunic, with rank displayed on the cuffs according to Royal Navy tradition. Uniforms were individually tailored by local gents' outfitters, or by national tailoring firms like Gieves or Alkit who specialised in service outfitting and who had branches in most of the major cities in England and Scotland. One newly commissioned RAF bomber pilot recalled the experience of buying his new uniform in 1943: 'Spent £25 on coat, trousers, 2 hats, 2 shirts, shoes, tie, etc. It all seems wonderfully light and so much softer than the uniform I have been accustomed to for so long . . . [it is] so well tailored it fits me like a glove.'

Made from fine blue-grey barathea woollen cloth, the No. 1 dress uniform was worn with blue-grey shirt and black tie and comprised a tunic and trousers, the quality and cut of which depended very much on what you were able to pay. The tunic was fastened at the front with four brass buttons and a waist belt with brass buckle. It featured lapels, pleated button-down patch breast pockets, and two side pockets each fastened by a single brass button. Officers' rank insignia was displayed on each cuff in the form of rings of black lace with a pale blue central stripe. Trade badges were not worns by officers and WOs with the exception of those designating

Officers' No. 1 dress tunic tailor-made in barathea cloth with service dress peaked cap, worn with observer's half-wing 'O' above the left breast pocket and cloth national identity flash 'CANADA' in blue-grey on the shoulders. The wearer is Flg Off George Pelter RCAF, who completed a tour of operations as a navigator with 425 and 408 Squadrons in 1944.

Officers' uniforms were individually tailored by local outfitters or national concerns such as Burberrys or Gieves.

branches, for example chaplain. The trousers had a button fly, slash pockets and were worn with service issue black lace-up shoes.

Headgear was either the service dress peaked cap or field service side cap, both in blue-grey. The former featured a black mohair band and fabric peak, gold bullion embroidered crown surmounting a gilt eagle and bullion laurel leaves badge on the front for all officer ranks up to group captain. For air ranks the badge had a gold embroidered wreath surrounding a gilt eagle, surmounted by a crown and lion. The peak was in black leather with gold oakleaf embroidery, one row for group captains, two for air ranks.

This unidentified sergeant wireless operator/air gunner wears an airmen's tunic in blue-grey serge with field service side cap, air gunner's half wing 'AG', RAF eagle arm badge, wireless operator's 'sparks' trade badge, and sergeant's stripes.

The field service side cap was made from lined barathea, with brass crown and eagle badge, and twin brass-buttoned front. A special version for air ranks featured pale blue piped edges and a miniature version of the air officers' cap badge.

AIRMEN'S TUNIC

The blue-grey serge unlined open-neck tailored four-pocket tunic (jacket, simplified, airmen) and trousers (trousers, blue-grey, other airmen) was issued from 1936 to all airmen up to and including the rank of flight sergeant (including air and groundcrews during the Second World War). It was worn with a blue-grey shirt and black tie, and like the officers' version it was fastened at the front with four brass buttons, a waist belt with brass buckle, and featured two pleated button-down patch breast pockets. However, the side pockets had simple unbuttoned flaps. The trousers were similar in cut and detailing to the officers' barathea version, but made from the coarser serge material.

A field service side cap in blue-grey serge was worn with this uniform for everyday use (a blue-grey cap with a shiny black plastic peak had been withdrawn from general use in December 1939) with the RAF airmen's cap badge in brass, featuring the letters 'RAF' surrounded by a laurel wreath and surmounted by a crown.

BATTLEDRESS

The 'suit, blue-grey, aircrews' – otherwise known as battledress – was introduced in 1941 for the sole use of RAF flying personnel when flying, but later became available for wear by all RAF personnel. Modelled on the British Army battledress, it was made from blue-grey serge and comprised a blouse and trousers. The blouse was fastened at the front with concealed buttons and a side-fastening buckle at the waist. It also featured button-down epaulettes, two large pleated patch pockets and was worn unbuttoned at the neck to reveal collar and tie. The aircrew whistle (for use in the event of ditching or being shot down, to attract the attention of fellow crew members) was

The same battledress pattern was issued to both officers and other ranks. Flt Lt Ken Letford wears a service dress peaked cap with battledress, bearing officer's rank braid on the epaulettes, pilot's wings and medal strip above the left breast pocket, and aircrew whistle attached to the left collar fastener. (IWM CH11694)

This unidentified bare-headed airman wears battledress with air gunner's half-wing 'AG' above the left breast pocket and sergeant's stripes on the right sleeve only.

worn only with the battledress and was attached to the collar fastener. The trousers had a concealed button fly and featured a flap pocket on the front left (later replaced by a simple button-up dressing pocket). They also had buttons at the ankles to enable them to be fastened more tightly to fit into flying boots. The same battledress pattern was issued to both officers and other ranks. Headgear was as for officers' or airmen's dress noted above.

GREATCOATS

When required, greatcoats could be worn by all ranks over their tunics or battledresses. They were long and double-breasted, the officers' version in fleece or melton cloth had five rows of buttons with fabric belt and gilt buckle; the airmen's in serge, without belt, had only four rows of buttons. The officers' coat had shoulder boards bearing rank insignia; the airmen's rank and arm badges were worn on their greatcoats, but not their trade badges.

145

Officers' greatcoat in Melton cloth, with shoulder boards bearing the rank insignia of a wing commander, worn with service dress cap over No. 1 dress tunic and trousers with regulation black lace-up shoes.

BADGES AND INSIGNIA

Both commissioned and non-commissioned ranks wore their flying brevets and medal ribbons above the left breast pocket, and 8 (PFF) Group crews wore the gilt Pathfinder badge on the left breast pocket flap below the medal ribbons, but not on operations for obvious reasons. Where applicable, brass 'VR' collar studs were worn by officers on each lapel and on the shoulder boards of great coats; VR badges were discontinued in mid-1943.

Cloth national identity flashes – for example 'CANADA' – were applied to each shoulder, embroidered in pale blue thread on a cloth ground, usually rectangular black for NCOs and airmen, and curved blue-grey for officers. There were forty-two such empire titles authorised for use.

NCO and airmen's rank distinctions were worn on each arm, embroidered warrant officers' crowns on the sleeve of each forearm. Airmen's trade badges were worn on the right sleeve only. The RAF eagle arm badge worn by all non-commissioned airmen below warrant officer rank and

The coveted pilot's wings of the Royal Air Force.

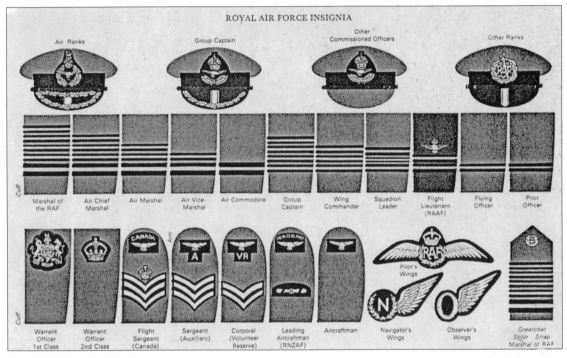

Royal Air Force insignia.

embroidered in light blue cotton thread on a blue-black fabric back-ground, was applied to each shoulder, together with cloth national identity flashes and cloth VR badges on a blue-black background, where applicable.

On battledress, officers' rank insignia was worn on each shoulder strap, airmen's and warrant officers' rank badges on the right arm only. Flying brevets, medal ribbons and the Pathfinder badge were worn as for the No. 1 dress and airmen's tunic.

The gilt Pathfinder eagle was worn on the left breast pocket flap.

FLYING CLOTHING AND EQUIPMENT

Apart from the ever-vigilant German defences and the unpredictability of the weather, the bomber crew's other enemy was the cold. Flying high to avoid enemy defences meant that aircrews needed additional protection against freezing temperatures, particularly in aircraft that had no effective cabin heating systems, and at heights above 10,000ft they also needed to breathe more oxygen. With increasing altitude there is a corresponding drop in air pressure, air temperature (1.98°C for every 1,000ft up to 36,000ft, after which it is assumed to remain constant at −56°C) and oxygen content of the atmosphere. Unassisted breathing above this height becomes progressively laboured unless wearing an oxygen mask, without which unconsciousness and death follow swiftly. In the first year of the war most RAF bomber operations were flown below 10,000ft and therefore below oxygen height, and at this altitude extreme cold was seldom encountered. But as the German defences became more of a threat and heavier more powerful bombers came into service with Bomber Command, the operating heights increased and with them the need for heated flying clothing and special breathing apparatus.

Protection from the cold for RAF aircrews – of which Bomber Command crews were the main beneficiaries – was solved by the backroom boffins at RAE Farnborough and in private industry. Their solutions included a range of thermally insulated and electrically heated flying clothing, including specially designed gloves and socks which gave protection to the bodily extremities most prone to frostbite.

To facilitate breathing at altitude a simple oxygen delivery system was devised in 1935 to pipe oxygen from a pressurised bottle and into a face mask worn by the airman. Although an improvement on what had gone before – that is to say, nothing – this constant-flow method of delivery was quickly found to be wasteful and led to the invention of the economiser flow system which eventually became a standard fit in the RAF's heavy bombers with oxygen released from the supply only when the wearer of the oxygen mask actually inhaled. Improved flying clothing and oxygen delivery systems continued to be developed through the war years.

The early months of the Second World War saw a variety of different flying clothing

A variety of early wartime flying clothing can be seen in this photograph of a Whitley crew taken in 1940. All except the airman in the middle (who wears an Irvin thermally insulated flying suit) wear 1930-pattern Sidcot suits. All carry parachute packs and wear observer-type parachute harnesses with quick-attach points, except for the airman second from the right who wears an Irvin 'Harnessuit' and carries a Type B helmet with Type D oxygen mask. The first, third and fifth airmen (from the left) each wear 1936-pattern boots; the second wears fleece-lined chestnut-brown 1930-pattern boots; the fourth, regulation black leather lace-up shoes.

styles being worn by RAF bomber crews and included much that had been standard issue to aircrew in the pre-war RAF: the one-piece 1930-pattern khaki 'Sidcot' suit (which could trace its origins to the First World War), or the white unlined cotton flying suits, Irvin 'Harnessuit' or heavy sheepskin flying jacket, the 1932-pattern Mae West life jacket, the Type B zip-eared flying helmet with Type D melton wool/chamois oxygen mask (the only type in use by the RAF at the

outbreak of war), and Mk III flying goggles, and 1930- or 1936-pattern all-leather flying boots, or service issue black lace-up shoes.

The coldest crew position in wartime heavy bomber aircraft was usually that of the gunners, particularly in the rear turret. Although the internal heating systems of bomber aircraft like the Halifax and Lancaster worked fairly effectively in the forward ends of the fuselage, they were none the less rudimentary affairs and not to be wholly relied upon. In the Lancaster, for example, the heating duct outlet was adjacent to the wireless operator's position, so he and the navigator were invariably hot. But while he and the navigator might be working in shirtsleeves or battledress, on the other side of the blackout curtain which shut off the navigator's compartment from the cockpit area, the pilot, flight engineer and bomb-aimer froze. It was a similar story aft of the main spar where the mid-upper and rear gunners could be shivering in their turrets in temperatures of −40°C, despite being wrapped up against the cold in five layers of thermally insulated and electrically heated flying clothing, boots and gloves. At the war's end about half the Lancaster force had been equipped with ducted heating to the rear turret, but Halifax aircraft rear turrets remained unheated.

The canary-yellow Taylor buoyant suit introduced in 1942 went some way towards improving the lot of the air gunner, but worn with electrically heated linings the circuitry in this kind of flying clothing was inclined to play up on a fairly regular basis, as recalled here by Ken Kemp, a Halifax rear gunner with 578 Squadron in 1944–5: 'The Taylorsuits we wore quite often short-circuited themselves. The first sign of trouble was a smell of burning, but it didn't usually get through very far because of the other layers of clothing beneath. Another problem with the electrics was caused by the normal movement of one's arms which caused the suit to become accidentally unplugged from the current.'

On the medium bomber squadrons of 2 Group which operated during daylight and invariably at low level, the aircrew need for protective flying clothing was limited, particularly during the warm summer months. (A similar situation would have applied to the heavy bomber crews who by 1944–5 were flying an increasing number of daylight sorties, although their flying clothing requirements would have depended upon the individual crew position, the time of year and operating height.) In any case American-built twin-engined medium bombers like the Boston and Mitchell had the Stewart Warner system of hot air ducts to all crew positions, which was particularly effective for the pilots and navigators in the sealed front compartments, but not so for their gunners to the rear who were exposed to the cold air of the slipstream thanks to their open gun hatches. They shared the discomfort of extreme cold with their comrades on 'heavies', and to protect themselves from sub-zero temperatures they needed to wrap up in heated flying suits or fur-lined Irvin jackets, worn over their battledress uniforms, with heated inner gloves underneath gauntlets. The Mosquito crews of 2, 5, 8 and 100 Groups were also blessed with very effective cabin heating in their aircraft, so much so that even in winter on high-level sorties they only needed to wear Sidcot suits over battledress to keep warm. In the summer, however, the cockpit could become too warm due to the greenhouse effect of the Perspex cockpit canopy.

In addition to battledress most medium bomber crews wore parachute harnesses, flying helmets with goggles and oxygen masks (although at low level, i.e. below 10,000ft, from mid-1944 the withdrawn Type E* oxygen mask was reissued with the breathing tubes removed for use solely as a microphone carrier), flying boots or service-issue shoes, and occasionally leather gauntlets or flying gloves. Some gunners and occasionally pilots were inclined to forgo their Sidcot suits or Irvin jackets, instead wearing a pair of flannelette pyjamas for extra warmth beneath their battledresses.

To protect their heads against shell splinters entering the aircraft from above on low-level operations, many Boston and Mitchell crews wore steel helmets over their leather flying helmets. Many also claimed to have sat on the steel helmets to protect their lower regions from possible injury caused by shell splinters entering the aircraft from beneath!

FLYING SUITS

A development of the First World War Sidcot suit, the **1930-pattern flying suit** was made from lightweight waterproofed green cotton and lined with linen. It was a one-piece overall-type suit with a large flap collar, full-length diagonal zip front and three-button fastening, zip sleeves and legs. Additional zip fastenings were at the crutch and at either side of the waist for access to the pockets. Sewn to the left breast was a large map pocket and two large fleece-lined patch pockets were sewn to the front of each thigh. The Sidcot could be worn over service dress uniform or battledress, or with one of a range of special button-in linings, and continued in use throughout the Second World War.

Made to the same pattern as the 1930-pattern suit, but from a heavy olive-coloured waterproof gabardine, the **1940-pattern flying suit** was light and roomy, but without any internal wiring. Electrically heated gloves and footwear could be worn provided the electrically heated linings were worn beneath the suit.

Similar to the 1940-pattern flying suit, the **1941 pattern** was the final development of the Sidcot suit. It was electrically wired and adaptable for use under extreme conditions by using a variety of Type D electrically heated linings, gloves and boot liners.

Made of reversed lambskin, the bulky dark brown **Irvin thermally insulated flying suit** actually comprised of jacket and trousers as separate items, but with a good

Wg Cdr H.R. Graham was the CO of 7 Squadron in 1941–2. He is pictured here wearing the 1930-pattern Sidcot flying suit, with Type B flying helmet and Type E oxygen mask, 1933-pattern flying gauntlets and regulation black lace-up shoes. He carries a pilot's seat-type parachute harness. (IWM CH4471)

overlap to ensure draught exclusion. The jacket, which soon became the hallmark of RAF aircrew, had a full-length zip down the front and at the wrists and had an adjustable belt at the waist. The heavy trousers, their weight supported by braces, wrapped around the legs from behind instead of being pulled on and were secured by zips running from ankle to waist, one on the inside of each leg. The electrically heated Type D lining could be worn underneath.

The Taylor buoyant suit – or 'Taylorsuit' – was designed to aid survival in the event of landing in water.

Used fairly widely in the first years of the war, by mid-1943 the Irvin suit had ceased to be standard issue flying clothing but continued to be available only to bomber crews.

Introduced from May 1940, the **Irvin Harnessuit** was created primarily with Bomber and Coastal Command crews in mind. Its novel design incorporated a life jacket bladder and a webbing parachute harness in a short-legged jerkin. The Harnessuit could be used with either seat or chest-type parachute packs.

Issued in small numbers to air gunners from 1942, the **Taylor buoyant suit (Taylorsuit)** was designed to aid survival in the unwelcome event of landing in water. It was made from heavy duty canary yellow fabric with a diagonal neck to waist zip fastener and two full-length leg zip fasteners to help in the putting on and removal of this cumbersome garment. Because of its weight the suit was fitted with integral braces. Fully lined in a heavy brown cotton and generously padded throughout with kapok, the Taylorsuit featured five pouches on the chest, legs and behind the neck for the insertion of additional kapok flotation pads. It could be worn with electrically heated RAE or Type D linings and also came with snap connectors at the cuffs and ankles for electrically heated gloves and bootees.

Operationally tested by Bomber Command's heavy and light bomber crews in 1943/4, the **Anti-flak suit** full body armour was intended for use by aircrews flying mainly the lightly armoured American-built bombers like the Boston and Mitchell. Made from steel plates wrapped in strong khaki canvas, the suits were heavy and bulky and as such were not popular with RAF bomber crews who rarely used them.

Identical to the unwired Irvinsuit, the RAE-pattern electrically wired version had a wiring loom sewn into leather channels that ran across the back and down each sleeve of the jacket, carrying current to heated gloves which connected to a two-prong plastic connector (visible on the forearm of the airman on the left) and, via matching trousers, to electrically heated footwear. Hanging below the same airman's right thigh is the standard aircraft metal plug connector for electrically heated clothing and the two-prong plastic connector for the trousers. (Roy Conyers Nesbit collection)

ELECTRICALLY HEATED LININGS

TYPE D SERIES
The **Type D heated waistcoat** could be worn as an alternative to the longer Type E lining.

Made of soft brown leather lined with woollen cloth, the **Type D flying gauntlets** were originally issued for use with the electrically heated **Type D lining** which was a fleece-lined black silk inner glove.

Type D socks were in fact ankle-length, felt-lined bootees fitted with an electrical heating cable. They were intended to be worn over thick socks and under the flying boots.

TYPE E SERIES
Heated by means of electrical elements sewn into the fabric, the **Type E full-length electrically heated lining** was specially designed for use by air gunners in Boulton

Paul power-operated turrets and offered specific protection to the knees.

TYPE F SERIES
Identical to the Type D, the **Type F waistcoat** integrated with the Type G high wattage electrically heated clothing system.

TYPE G SERIES
Identical to the Type D, but modified to take a higher wattage and included **Type G glove liners**, **Type G full-length suit liner**, **Type G socks** and **bootees**.

TYPE H SERIES
Standard issue from 1944, the Type H series of heated clothing featured a new style of heating element, namely gauze wire strips in place of the wire-type elements used in previous series. The **Type H full-length suit liner** was made of either brown cotton or rayon and lined with cotton twill, with a knitted shawl collar.

Externally similar to the 1941-pattern gauntlet, the **Type H gloves** featured a blanket-lined rayon lining carrying the gauze wire heating elements and a snap closure at the wrist instead of a zip. **Type H bootees** were almost identical to the Type D, but used gauze wire heating elements.

KAPOK QUILTED LININGS
A lining for the 1930-pattern suit was a one-piece kapok-lined quilted garment which buttoned into the flying suit and was introduced in 1940. Both 1940- and 1941-pattern linings were intended for use with the 1940- or 1941-pattern Sidcot flying suits and could be used over the electrically heated Type D lining to provide thermal insulation. However, the 1930-pattern suit could only be worn with the 1941-pattern lining if suitably modified.

FLYING BOOTS

Although officially obsolete in 1939, the knee-length **1930-pattern boot** was made from fleece-lined chestnut-brown suede, with zip-up front, and was still in use by bomber crews well into the first two years of war. The **1936-pattern** black all-leather fleece-lined **boot** was secured at the top by a buckled leather strap across a small V-shaped aperture and continued in use throughout the war by many bomber crews. Made to the same pattern as the all-leather 1936 pattern, the **1939-pattern boot** featured vulcanised green canvas uppers.

A fleece-lined brown sheepskin flying boot, very similar to the 1930 pattern, the **1940-pattern boot** had a zip-up front and wrap-around composite leather/ rubber sole, purposely loose-fitting around the ankle to accommodate electrically heated moccasins and allow the flying suit leg to be tucked inside. Both the 1940 and the 1943 pattern boots had calves interlined with thirty layers of parachute silk to help protect the wearer against injury from metal shrapnel splinters. For aircrew who had cause to bale out, the 1940-pattern boot was not popular because the boots often slipped off during their descent. The later **1941-pattern boot** was identical to the 1940 pattern, but with the addition of leather ankle straps to help prevent boot loss during parachute descents.

The so-called 'escape boot', developed by Major Clayton Hutton of MI9, the **1943-pattern boot** featured a lace-up black leather walking shoe with detachable zip-up black suede and sheepskin-lined upper section. In the event of the wearer finding himself down in enemy territory after crashing or baling out, the boot was also supplied with a concealed saw or knife

This photograph of a 75 (NZ) Squadron Stirling crew at Mepal, taken in early 1944, reveals a representative selection of flying kit as worn by a heavy bomber crew in the late war period. Left to right: Type C flying helmet with Type G oxygen mask, 1936-pattern boots; off-white knitted woollen pullover (Frock, White, Aircrew) over battledress, with sea-boot socks worn inside 1940-pattern brown suede zip-up boots; RAE-pattern electrically heated Irvinsuit and 1940-pattern boots; thermally insulated Irvin jacket with 1943-pattern escape boots; battledress and 1943-pattern boots; RAE-pattern electrically heated Irvin jacket over battledress with 1940-pattern boots. All wear Mae Wests and observer-type parachute harnesses.

blade inside the lining of the upper section. This enabled him to cut off the boot uppers, leaving the walking shoes which would not be as obvious to enemy observers as a pair of RAF flying boots. Aircrew who had cause to use these shoes when on the run in enemy territory reported them as most uncomfortable.

LIFE JACKETS

Popularly referred to as 'Mae Wests' because of their similarity to the ample bosoms of the American film star of the same name, the yellow RAF aircrew life jackets were a distinctive feature of bomber crew flying kit as revealed in photographs of this period. They came in two

Over their battledress tunics these two officers each wear a Life Jacket Mk I, more commonly known as the 'Mae West'. The flight lieutenant on the right also wears a pair of 1940-pattern boots and 1941-pattern flying gauntlets.

PARACHUTES

For operational flying there were two main types of parachute, **chest-type (observer)** and **seat-type (pilot)**. Most bomber crews wore the chest-type chute, but most pilots wore the seat-type, although this was not a hard and fast rule. The canopy itself was made from white silk but after 1943 it was gradually replaced by nylon; the shroud lines were also made from silk or nylon cord.

The parachute harness for both types of chute was made from a double-thickness white cotton and linen mixture webbing which was sewn together. Four straps passing over the shoulders and around the legs secured the harness to the airman's body. All four strap ends connected into a metal quick-release box situated over the belly area. Seat-type chutes were permanently fixed to the harness, while chest-type packs were clipped onto two metal snap hooks attached to the shoulder straps just above the quick-release box. Both types were provided with back pads attached to the harness by tabs and snap fasteners.

patterns, the first being the relatively old-fashioned **1932-pattern life jacket**. This was a thick khaki cotton twill waistcoat containing an orally inflated bladder, fastened at the front with three buttons and two buckled straps. The front panels were often painted yellow to make the wearer more visible in the water.

In mid-1941 the 1932 pattern was superseded by the newly introduced **Life Jacket Mk I** which remained in service for the duration of the war, with modifications. Dull yellow in colour and similar in cut to the 1932 pattern, the air bladder was inflated by a break-neck CO_2 cylinder situated on the lower right-hand side. The oral inflation tube was retained in order to top-up the air bladder if required.

HELMETS

Standard issue to all RAF aircrew between 1936 and 1941, the **Type B helmet** was designed to be worn with the Type D oxygen mask. It was made from dark brown chrome leather lined with chamois and fitted with brass-zipped leather-covered 'donut' ear pieces, a leather chinstrap and a buckle-fastened split at the back to facilitate a secure fit. Electrical wiring was external. The Type B was superseded by the Type C helmet in 1941, although some continued in use for much longer with minor modifications to accept the Type D oxygen mask.

Made of dark brown chrome leather with

The zip-eared Type B helmet with Type D oxygen mask worn here by a Stirling pilot in 1941. The helmet is fitted with brass guide plates for use with the Mk IV series goggles. (Roy Conyers Nesbit collection)

a chamois lining, the **Type C helmet** was issued from October 1941 for use in north-west Europe and utilised the external wiring harness from the Type B helmet, but was intended to take the Type E and F oxygen masks. The 'donut' ear pieces were replaced by smaller black moulded rubber cups to contain the radio receivers. The early Type C had a leather chinstrap with press-stud fastener, while the later version had an integral wiring loom and elasticated chinstrap. This pattern became the most widely used RAF flying helmet of the war and was also issued to the USAAF.

OXYGEN MASKS

A green cloth and chamois-lined mask, the **Type D mask** was fastened to the Type B helmet by four press studs. At the outbreak of war it was the only oxygen mask in use by the RAF, but gave a poor seal around the face. Used with the constant flow oxygen system it proved very wasteful. The mask could be fitted with one of three different types of microphone, the Type E carbon (1935), Type 10 magnetic (1939) or the Type 21 magnetic (1940).

Smaller in size than the Type D to

improve forward vision, and with modifications to eradicate freezing up of the oxygen inlet valve, the **Type E mask** was the first RAF oxygen mask to use the economiser flow system. Made from uncured rubber the Type D caused severe skin irritation to many wearers.

A black rubber mask designed to be worn with the Type C helmet, the **Type E* mask** was issued in February 1942 as an interim to the suivant Type G and incorporated the major improvements of the Type F mask which was never issued. The Type E* eradicated leaks around the face and used the newly designed oxygen economiser system with vastly improved results. Both Type E masks were withdrawn in July 1943 but were later reissued in August 1944 as microphone carriers only, with the breathing tubes removed.

Although production of this green rubber mask did not actually begin until 1942 and supplies were limited until mid-1943, the **Type G mask** was well liked by the aircrews. It featured a much improved oxygen system and so the problems caused by internal condensation were to a great extent alleviated, while the use of a finer quality cured rubber led to fewer skin problems. The Type G remained in use up until the last year of the war when it was largely superseded by the **Type H mask**. Virtually identical to the Type G mask, the Type H had a smaller and lighter microphone unit.

Type E, E* and G oxygen masks could be fitted with a range of different microphone assemblies, according to the type of helmet being worn and the radio equipment in the aircraft. These included: Type 26 magnetic, Type 28 carbon, Type 35 magnetic (virtually identical to Type 26), and Type 48 magnetic.

A **mask microphone heater and draught excluder hood** was first issued in 1943 and designed especially for air gunners in turrets. It incorporated a small electrical heating element which clipped onto the microphone inside the Type G oxygen mask which helped to prevent moisture from exhaled breath from freezing and blocking the microphone. The element was issued with a shoulder-length green cotton hood to protect the heating element and prevent draughts, a very welcome accessory in an exposed turret and particularly when the clear vision panel had been removed.

GOGGLES

In use from 1935 to 1942, the **Mk IIIa (1934-pattern) goggles** featured two single-piece curved celluloid lenses in a metal and leather frame. The celluloid lenses were prone to visual distortion and scratched easily, discouraging many airmen from wearing them. These goggles did not fit well with the Type B flying helmet then in use and once tested in action and found wanting they were soon replaced by the **Mk IV goggles**.

Offering improved vision and better protection to the eyes against injury in combat, the Mk IV goggles were introduced in June 1940 and featured an angular black-painted brass metal frame and two-piece right-angled lenses. It was also equipped with elasticated side cords for fitting over earphone covers and featured a side-fastening plate on each side. The Mk IV was the first goggle to feature the upward-hinging tinted visor. A lighter weight version of the Mk IV was the **Mk IVa goggles**, made from rigid black plastic instead of the heavy brass. Very few of this variation were produced.

First issued in August 1940 to Fighter Command pilots, the **Mk IVb goggles** were distributed to Bomber Command air gunners from 1941 and were issued in greater numbers than the previous two versions. They were equipped with elasticated side cords for fitting over earphone covers and featured a side-fastening plate on each side. Some were also fitted with an upward-hinging tinted visor. They were replaced by the **Mk VII goggles** in July 1942 which continued to use the two-piece lenses but integrated them into a better-contoured brass frame to fit the face more comfortably and complement more closely the new rubber oxygen masks then coming into use.

Introduced in October 1943, the **Mk VIII goggles** were the last to be issued before the RAF introduced 'bone domes' and wrap-around visors in the late 1950s. They still featured the two-piece lenses but in a more streamlined grey metal frame backed with leather cushioning.

CREW INTER-COMMUNICATIONS

A vital piece of equipment in any multi-crew aircraft was the intercom system, to which all crew members were connected for the purpose of speaking to one another. The oxygen masks they wore fulfilled a dual role, not only in helping the wearer to breathe at altitude, but also enabling him to speak to his fellow crewmembers with the aid of a built-in microphone connected by an electrical lead to the aircraft's internal communication (intercom) system.

In 1937 the Air Ministry had rejected the use of throat-type microphones as being dangerous and unreliable, instead opting for mask-type microphones. The RAF was thereby placed at odds with both the USAAF and the *Luftwaffe*, whose aircrews all used throat-type microphones during the Second World War. To enable RAF crews to listen in to both external radio transmissions and inter-crew conversations, a small earphone was wired into each earpiece of the flying helmet.

Type C helmet worn with Mk VIII flying goggles and Type G oxygen mask by Sgt W. Brown, a Stirling mid-upper gunner with 199 Squadron in mid-1944. (W. Brown/Stirling Aircraft Association)

The personal communications equipment (microphone and earphones) issued to each RAF bomber crew member was designed to work with the British TR9 intercom system, the standard equipment for RAF bomber aircraft. Personal comms equipment and the TR9 generally worked well together in the British-built aircraft for which they had been designed, but in the American-built Boston, Mitchell, Fortress and Liberator aircraft, where the Bendix intercom system had been designed for use with throat-type microphones, RAF crews experienced incompatibility problems with their personal comms equipment which at times made it very difficult for them to hear clearly what was being said.

If the intercom system failed completely owing to damage from enemy action, or occasionally because of equipment malfunction, it was not difficult for the crews in a Lancaster, Halifax or Mosquito to exchange handwritten notes to maintain contact. But it was a different story, for example, for crews in Bostons where each man was in a sealed crew compartment and therefore unable to see or physically reach his fellow crewmembers. This was mitigated in a rather curious way by a wire-and-pulley system that allowed the pilot to communicate with the rear gunner by clipping a handwritten message on to the pulley wire, but this facility was not available to the navigator. Mitchell crews fared slightly better, with interconnecting tunnels between crew positions through which they could wriggle if the situation required it.

Happily, both British and American bomber aircraft were equipped with call lights, also known as the Bendix signalling system, where each crew position was provided with a small unit fitted with three coloured light bulbs and three buttons. In the event of an intercom failure a signalling procedure worked out in advance enabled crewmembers to communicate with one another, although the captain always had priority. It was a vital back-up system, particularly for the tail gunner in heavy bombers, if the pilot ordered his crew to abandon aircraft. For example, in the Lancaster the call lights were installed in nine separate locations within the aircraft: the front turret, on the port side of the bomb-aimer's compart- ment, on the port side of the pilot's instrument panel, on the navigator's instrument panel, adjacent to the window in the wireless operator's station, at the

rest station aft of the main spar, at the flare station forward of the mid-upper turret, in the mid-upper turret, between formers 25 and 26, and in the rear turret. All lights at all crew positions were interconnected so that when any button was depressed all lights illuminated.

ESCAPE AND EVASION

Nearly 10,000 Bomber Command aircrew who were forced down over enemy occupied territory became prisoners of war, incarcerated in more than twenty camps scattered across Germany and Poland. They were the lucky ones. For every man who had survived to become a POW, five more had been killed in action, but a tiny number, probably no more than 1,000, evaded capture and escaped to freedom. These men owed their lives to the intervention of a number of factors, not the least of which were luck and circumstance, and the emphasis placed on escape and evasion techniques by their station intelligence staff during lectures on the subject.

Some evaders made their way unaided, while the great majority were assisted by men and women of the various escape lines established in occupied Europe under the guidance of MI9. But many who helped Allied airmen escape were ordinary citizens who risked their lives in so doing, and often paid with them if caught by the Gestapo.

Every bomber station intelligence library had a corner devoted to the important matters of escape and evasion, well stocked with relevant display material such as escape gadgets, maps, foreign currency and informative posters. Lectures were also given on a regular basis to all crews and to every new crew joining a squadron, occasionally by men who had been shot down themselves, evaded and returned to England.

Before take-off on a raid, every crew member was issued with an escape and survival pack to help them evade capture if forced down over enemy territory. However, few of those who were shot down, and survived, had much chance of using the small escape pack they all carried because they were quickly apprehended by German forces.

Escape packs were issued sealed and collected from crews on their return. They came in several different forms, fitting easily into a battledress pocket, and each contained a variety of useful items and ingenious gadgets to help its owner with his escape and survival. They included packets of real foreign currency and detailed waterproof maps of Europe printed on silk, some of which showed the best escape routes and frontiers. These were sometimes issued separately, occasionally sewn into battledress lining, and at other times as part of a complete escape pack.

The **Type 2 ration and escape pack**, made from clear acetate plastic in two closely fitting and waterproof sections, was known as an 'escape box'. It contained rations for 48 hours and a variety of aids for survival when living off the land, including high-energy foodstuffs such as Horlicks tablets, chewing gum, chocolate, barley sugar sweets, and a tube of condensed milk. The survival aids included matches, magnetised razor blades (to serve as a compass pointer), a small compass, a heliograph (to signal with), Benzedrine tablets (known to aircrew as 'wakey-wakey pills') to combat tiredness, water-purifying tablets, a rubber water bottle, needle and thread and fishing twine, a razor and soap. The contents varied from kit to kit and on what condensed rations were available at any given time.

Escape packs contained a variety of useful items, including real currency, to help an airman to survive and escape if shot down over enemy territory. This pack contains French and Belgian francs and Dutch guilders. (Courtesy of Mrs Anne Beard)

The **Mk IV escape box** was cleverly designed as a hollow circular container that could also double as a water bottle. Its contents included a silk escape map, Horlicks tablets, chocolate, water-purifying tablets, matches, needle and thread. To empty the contents, the side of the box had first to be removed and then replaced to form a bottle. The stopper unscrewed to reveal a tiny watch and compass.

In addition to the escape packs there were additional pieces of escape equipment and gadgets issued as personal items, or as articles of clothing and flying kit. These included the 1943 pattern flying boots that could be cut down to make a pair of walking shoes (*see page 154*), the standard issue British forces Bakelite razor that often contained a compass in the base, a magnetised fly-button compass, tunic and cap buttons that unscrewed to reveal a tiny compass, a tobacco pouch containing a map concealed inside the lining, and a pencil that if broken at a certain letter embossed on the pencil would reveal a tiny compass inside.

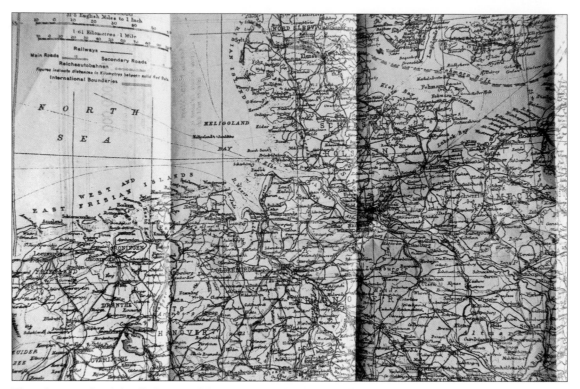

They also contained detailed maps of Europe, printed either on silk or rice paper, to assist an evader in finding his way home. This is a detail from a rice paper map contained in an escape pack that belonged to WO Doug Clarke DFC, a Lancaster air gunner with 218 Squadron in 1944. The opacity of the paper can be appreciated from the printing on the reverse of the map showing through. (Courtesy of Mrs Anne Beard)

'Pimpernel' pictures – sequences of passport-sized head and shoulders photographs – were sewn into battledress tunics and carried on all operations. The subject was photographed from different angles and with varying lighting effects to simulate his state of health as a civilian in the different countries of Europe. For example, he would be gaunt and under-nourished in Holland, but rosy-faced and well fed in France. The photographs were for use in the production of forged identity papers in the event of the airman making contact with the Resistance.

Only a few airmen took escape and evasion seriously enough to actually plan for

'Pimpernel' pictures were sewn into battledress tunics and carried on all operations. These passport-sized head and shoulders photographs were for use in the production of forged identity papers should the airman be shot down and make contact with the resistance. This 'Pimpernel' photograph is of Sgt Graham Evans, a Halifax rear gunner with 425 (Alouette) Squadron in early 1944. Evans had flown just three operations of his first tour before he was killed when his Halifax crashed and burned at Bradford-on-Avon, Wiltshire, during a night cross-country training flight on 26 March 1944.

the eventuality should it happen to them. One such man was Group Captain John Whitley, station commander of RAF Linton-on-Ouse in 1943, and later to become AOC 4 Group (*see page 197*). He concluded that the best way to escape was to avoid prompt capture and to fly equipped to travel through enemy territory. To this end he made his own simple escape kit which was carried in a small haversack that could easily be attached to his parachute harness should he need to bale out. It contained a civilian tie, the jacket of a lounge suit and a peaked cap. Whenever he flew on operations he wore the trousers of the lounge suit under his uniform trousers, and under his uniform shirt wore a blue check shirt with collar attached. In the pockets of his battledress he carried a number of personal items including a Rolls razor, tube of brushless shaving cream, toothbrush and tube of toothpaste, a nail file and tiny compass. Although his home-made escape kit caused much amusement among his aircrews, it certainly saved him from falling into the hands of the Germans when his Halifax was shot down over France on 10 April 1943 and enabled him to evade successfully.

CHAPTER 9

AWARDS AND MEDALS

In common with the other commands of the RAF during the Second World War, and indeed the other armed forces of the Crown, the air and groundcrews of Bomber Command were eligible for a variety of decorations for gallantry and meritorious service, campaign stars and medals.

DECORATIONS FOR GALLANTRY AND MERITORIOUS SERVICE

VICTORIA CROSS (VC)

The pre-eminent and most highly prized British and Commonwealth gallantry decoration, the VC is awarded to soldier, sailor or airman, regardless of rank, for 'some signal act of valour or devotion to their country in the presence of the enemy'. It is the rarest of all British decorations and takes precedence over all other Orders and medals. The award is open to civilians and also to women, but no such award has ever been made. Instituted by Queen Victoria in 1856, the VC is accompanied by an annual

Obverse of the Victoria Cross.

pension. In the 142 years of its existence, only three recipients have been awarded the VC with bar.

The decoration is simple in its execution and consists of a bronze cross pattée, 1½in across with raised edges. On the obverse, in the centre, is a lion passant guardant standing upon the royal crown, and below are the words 'For Valour' in capital letters on a semicircular scroll. Like the obverse, the reverse has raised edges, but with the date of the act for which the decoration has been awarded engraved in a circle in the centre. The cross is suspended by a plain link from a 'V', the latter integral with the clasp, ornamented with laurel leaves, through which the ribbon passes, and on the back of the clasp is engraved the name, rank and ship, regiment or squadron of the recipient. The ribbon is crimson and measures 1½in wide.

During the Second World War, 32 VCs were awarded to RAF and Commonwealth air forces personnel, of which 25 went to officers and 7 to NCOs; 27 of these recipients were pilots, 4 were wireless operators or air gunners, and 1 a flight engineer. Of the 32, 19 were awarded to men of Bomber Command (of which 7 were to Commonwealth airmen), 13 to officers and 6 to NCOs.

(Ribbon: crimson)

DISTINGUISHED SERVICE ORDER (DSO)

Established in 1886 for rewarding individual instances of 'meritorious or distinguished service in the field or before the enemy', the DSO can only be awarded to a person holding a commission in the British armed forces and who has been mentioned in dispatches for this bravery. The DSO is second only to the Victoria Cross and in common with many other service awards is not available to civilians. The maximum number of bars to one DSO is three, thus representing four DSOs.

The award consists of a gold cross, enamelled white and edged with gold, which hangs from its riband by a gold clasp ornamented with laurel, while another similar clasp is worn at the top of the ribbon. In the centre of the obverse is the imperial crown in gold within a wreath of laurel, enamelled green. On the reverse is the royal cypher surrounded by a similar wreath of laurel.

Obverse of the Distinguished Service Order.

During the Second World War 870 DSOs were awarded to RAF and Commonwealth air forces personnel, with 62 first bars (including Wing Commander Guy Gibson, first commanding officer of 617 Squadron, and Wing Commander Charles Pickard who died leading the Amiens prison raid); 8 second bars (including Group Captain Leonard Cheshire and Air Commodore Johnny Fauquier RCAF, both of whom were one-time wartime commanders of 617 Squadron); and 2 third bars (Air Vice-Marshal Sir Basil Embry, one-time commander of 107 Squadron and AOC 2 Group/2nd TAF, and Wing Commander J.B.'Willie' Tait another former commander of 617 Squadron).

(Ribbon: red with narrow blue borders)

DISTINGUISHED FLYING CROSS (DFC)

The DFC was instituted in 1918 following the formation of the RAF and was granted only to officers and warrant officers to recognise acts of 'valour, courage or devotion to duty performed whilst flying in active operations against the enemy'. From February 1942 onwards it could be given to personnel of dominion countries.

The DFC is in silver and consists of a cross flory terminated in the horizontal and base bars with bombs, the upper bar

Obverse of the Distinguished Flying Cross.

Bar for DFC, AFC, DFM and AFM.

terminating with a rose, surmounted by another cross composed of aeroplane propellers charged in the centre with a roundel within a wreath of laurels, a rose winged ensigned by an imperial crown thereon the letters RAF. On the reverse the royal cypher above the date. The whole attached to the clasp and ribbon by two sprigs of laurel.

During the Second World War over 20,000 DFCs were awarded, with 1,550 first bars and 42 second bars (the latter including Air Marshal Sir Ivor Broom, one-time 105 Squadron Blenheim pilot). Some were 'immediate' awards for specific acts of gallantry, while most were awarded at the end of a successful tour of operations.

(Ribbon: violet and white alternate diagonal stripes, running at an angle of 45 degrees from left to right)

AIR FORCE CROSS (AFC)

Instituted in 1918 at the same time as the DFC, DFM and AFM, its purpose was to reward those who distinguished themselves in 'acts of valour, courage or devotion to duty whilst flying, though not in active operations against the enemy'.

The cross is in silver and consists of a thunderbolt in the form of a cross, the arms conjoined by wings, the base bar terminating with a bomb surmounted by another cross composed of aeroplane propellers, the four ends inscribed with the letters G.R.VI.I. In the centre on a roundel is a representation of Hermes mounted on a hawk in flight bestowing a wreath. On the reverse is the royal cypher above the date 1918, and the whole cross is ensigned by an Imperial crown and attached to the clasp and ribbon by two sprigs of laurel.

From 1940 to 1945 a little more than 2,000 AFCs were awarded and in common with the DFC they were issued unnamed.

(Ribbon: red and white in alternate diagonal stripes running at an angle of 45 degrees from left to right)

CONSPICUOUS GALLANTRY MEDAL (CGM)

Instituted in 1855 as an award for NCOs of the Royal Navy and Royal Marines who had shown 'exceptional gallantry in the face of the enemy', the CGM was second only in status to the Victoria Cross and was the NCO's equivalent of the DSO.

The medal is of silver and has on the obverse the effigy of the reigning sovereign with the usual legend; on the reverse, in raised letters, are the words 'For Conspicuous Gallantry', with a crown above, and the whole design encircled by laurel branches.

Extended to Army and RAF personnel during the Second World War, by 1945 only 110 awards to RAF and Commonwealth NCO aircrew had been made, of which 89 were to members of Bomber Command, compared with a total of 870 DSOs to officer recipients (not including bars). 101 Squadron was exceptional in that eight CGMs were awarded to its NCO aircrew.

(Ribbon: light blue with narrow dark blue borders)

DISTINGUISHED FLYING MEDAL (DFM)

The DFM was instituted at the same time as the DFC to recognise acts of valour, courage and devotion to duty shown by aircrew NCOs while flying in active operations against the enemy.

The silver medal is oval in shape, bearing the effigy of the reigning sovereign on the

Reverse of the Distinguished Flying Medal.

obverse with the usual legend; on the reverse is a representation of the goddess Athena Nike seated on an aeroplane, a hawk rising from her right hand above the words 'For Courage'. The medal is ensigned by a bomb attached to the clasp and ribbon by two wings.

During the Second World War 6,638 DFMs were awarded with 58 first bars and just one second bar (to a Spitfire pilot). It is somewhat incomprehensible that with more than 70 per cent of Bomber Command aircrew being NCOs, the DFM should account for less than a quarter of the combined total of almost 27,000 DFCs and DFMs awarded during the Second World War.

(Ribbon: identical to DFC, but the diagonal stripes are narrower)

AIR FORCE MEDAL (AFM)

The junior of the four RAF awards, the AFM was issued to NCOs and men in the same way and for the same reasons as the AFC.

The AFM is in silver and oval-shaped, bearing the effigy of the reigning monarch on the obverse and on the reverse, within a wreath of laurel, a representation of Hermes mounted on a hawk in flight bestowing a wreath. The whole is ensigned by a bomb attached to the clasp and ribbon by two wings.

Like the DFM, but unlike the DFC and AFC, the AFM is issued with the service number, rank, surname and initials of the recipient engraved around the edge. Because even fewer NCOs and men were in a position to earn the AFM, this has been awarded on fewer occasions than the DFM; between 1939 and 1974 only 630.

(Ribbon: identical to the AFC, but the diagonal stripes are narrower)

SECOND WORLD WAR CAMPAIGN STARS AND MEDALS

THE CAMPAIGN STARS

A total of eight of these identically designed six-pointed campaign stars were first ready for issue in 1947, for services during the Second World War. However, the central royal cypher, surmounted by a crown, was partly surrounded by the name of the appropriate campaign, for example 'The Air Crew Europe Star'. It was decreed that a maximum of five stars could be earned by one man (or woman). Those who qualified for more received a clasp to the ribbon, although only one clasp to a ribbon was permitted. The stars for which personnel serving under the operational control of Bomber Command were eligible are listed below and could carry the following clasps:

1939–45 Star (Clasp: Battle of Britain)

Awarded for service between 3 September 1939 and 2 September 1945. Qualification for RAF personnel was for carrying out operations against the enemy but with the qualification that two months' service had been completed in an operational unit. Non-aircrew personnel had to complete six months' service in an area of an operational command. The exceptions to these rules were if operational service had been cut short by death, disability or wounds, or if the recipient had received an honour, decoration, mention in dispatches or King's Commendation. If any of these cases applied, then a recipient qualified for the award irrespective of their length of service.

(Ribbon: equal vertical bands of dark blue, red and light blue)

Atlantic Star (Clasps: Air Crew Europe or France and Germany)

Awarded to commemorate the battle of the Atlantic between 3 September 1939 and 8 May 1945. Qualification for RAF personnel was restricted to aircrew who had taken part in active operations within the specified area, so long as they had completed two months' service in an operational unit and qualified for the 1939–45 Star.

(Ribbon: equal watered vertical bands of dark blue, white and sea green)

Air Crew Europe Star (Clasps: Atlantic or France and Germany)

Awarded for operational flying from bases in the UK over Europe between 3 September 1939 and 5 June 1944. To qualify, recipients needed to have completed two months as aircrew and qualified for the 1939–45 Star.

(Ribbon: vertical bands comprising black edges bordered by two narrow yellow stripes enclosing a broad light blue centre stripe)

France and Germany Star (Clasps: Atlantic or Air Crew Europe)

This star was awarded for service in either France, Belgium, Holland or Germany, or for any operations flown over Europe between 6 June 1944 and 8 May 1945.

(Ribbon: equal vertical stripes of blue, white, red, white and blue)

The Defence Medal, 3 September 1939– 2 September 1945

Issued in cupro-nickel, the Defence Medal was awarded to members of the armed forces and civilians for three years' service at home, or for six months' service overseas in a non-operational area which was subjected to, or closely threatened by, air attack. It is the most common of the Second World War campaign stars and medals and was issued unnamed.

The obverse contains the uncrowned head of King George VI with the usual legend, while the reverse bears the royal crown resting on the stump of an oak tree flanked by two lions, with '1939–1945' at the top and 'The Defence Medal' in capital letters in the exergue.

(Ribbon: Thick equal vertical bands of green, orange, green, with two thin vertical black stripes)

The War Medal, 3 September 1939– 2 September 1945

Also issued in cupro-nickel, the War Medal was awarded to all full-time service personnel wherever they were serving, so long as the duration was for at least twenty-eight days irrespective of whether they were operational or non-operational.

The obverse contains the crowned head of King George VI with the usual legend, while the reverse contains a lion standing on a slain dragon.

(Ribbon: equal vertical stripes of red, blue, white, blue, red, with a thin vertical red centre stripe)

THE BOMBER COMMAND VCS

Flight Lieutenant R.A.B. Learoyd VC, 49 Squadron

Leading a formation of nine Hampdens in a low-level attack on the Dortmund–Ems canal on 12 August 1940, Learoyd's aircraft took the full force of the light flak defences. 'Babe' Learoyd brought his badly damaged Hampden safely back to Scampton after blowing up the aqueduct.

Sergeant John Hannah VC, 83 Squadron

As an eighteen-year-old wireless operator of a Hampden, on 15 September 1940 Hannah's aircraft was set on fire by flak while bombing invasion barges in Antwerp harbour. He had the opportunity to bale out but chose to stay with the aircraft and fought the flames, thus saving the life of his Canadian pilot who successfully flew the crippled Hampden back to Scampton. Hannah became the youngest member of the RAF to receive the VC, but was invalided out of the service in 1942 and died of TB in 1947.

Wing Commander Hughie Edwards VC, DFC, 105 Squadron

Although twice involved in earlier crashes and refusing ground appointments, this Australian followed his DFC by leading a formation of Blenheims at low level to bomb a vital target at Bremen on 4 July 1941. He later commanded the first Mosquito bomber squadron, No. 139, and was awarded the DSO and OBE before the war ended. He retired as an air commodore and later became governor of South Australia.

Sergeant James Ward VC, RNZAF, 75 (NZ) Squadron

As second pilot of a Wellington attacked and set on fire by a nightfighter during a raid on Munster on 7/8 July 1941, Ward climbed out onto the wing and smothered the flames with a tarpaulin engine cover, thereby preventing the flames from reaching the petrol tanks. Two months later, on 15/16 September 1941, as captain of his own Wellington, he was shot down and killed over Hamburg.

Squadron Leader J.D. Nettleton VC, 44 (Rhodesia) Squadron

Leading one section of twelve Lancasters in daylight over a distance of 500 miles at under 50ft to bomb the MAN diesel engine factory at Augsburg, Nettleton successfully bombed the target on 17 April 1942. During the arduous return flight he shepherded the remaining five aircraft safely home. As a wing commander, he was killed on 13 July 1943 returning from a raid on Turin.

Flying Officer L.T. Manser VC, 50 Squadron

On the first 1,000-bomber raid to Cologne on 30/31 May 1942, Manser was captain of a Manchester bomber that was hit by flak but he succeeded in bombing the target from 7,000ft. With his aircraft badly damaged and on fire, Manser ordered his crew to bale out, knowing he had little chance himself. Out of control, the bomber plunged to destruction soon afterwards, taking the selfless pilot to his death.

Flight Sergeant R.H. Middleton VC, RAAF, 149 Squadron

The first member of the Royal Australian Air Force to win the VC in the Second World War, Middleton was the captain of a Stirling detailed to bomb the Fiat works at Turin on 28/29 November 1942. Hit by flak over the target that severely wounded both pilots, in very difficult conditions Middleton succeeded in piloting the damaged bomber as far as the Kent coast where he ordered the crew to bale out. Only five were able to jump before the Stirling crashed into the sea, killing Middleton.

Squadron Leader L.H. Trent VC, DFC, RNZAF, 487 (NZ) Squadron

It was not until March 1946 that the details of Trent's last operation were revealed in his VC citation for the raid on 3 May 1943 when he led eleven Venturas against Amsterdam's power station. All were shot down by the overwhelming defences but

Trent and his navigator survived to become POWs. Trent broke out of Stalag Luft III in the Great Escape in March 1944 and escaped execution at the hands of the Gestapo.

Wing Commander Guy Gibson VC, DSO (2 Bars), DFC (2 Bars), 617 Squadron

Guy Gibson was awarded the VC for his epic leadership of the attack on the Ruhr dams on 16/17 May 1943 by Lancasters of 617 Squadron. Having dropped his bouncing bomb on the Möhne dam, Gibson continued to circle the target, drawing enemy fire away from the other aircraft until they had all completed their bomb runs. He was killed on 19/20 September 1944, returning from a raid on Rheydt where he had been acting as master bomber.

Flight Sergeant L.A. Aaron VC, DFM, 218 Squadron

On 12/13 August 1943, en route to bomb Turin, Arthur Aaron's Stirling aircraft was badly shot up over the Alps by another Stirling bomber, killing the navigator and mortally wounding Aaron. Despite his dreadful injuries Aaron directed his bomb-aimer to fly the Stirling to North Africa, where on the point of unconsciousness he helped to crash-land the aircraft, thereby saving the lives of his crew. Aaron died from his injuries a few hours later.

Flight Lieutenant W. Reid VC, 61 Squadron

Bill Reid was captain of a Lancaster bombing Düsseldorf on 3 November 1943, which was badly damaged in a head-on attack from a nightfighter, followed by a second attack which killed two of his crew. Badly wounded, Reid continued to fly a further 200 miles to bomb the target and eventually landed his crippled aircraft safely back in England.

Pilot Officer C.J. Barton VC, 578 Squadron

En route to bomb Nuremberg on the infamous raid of 30/31 March 1944, Cyril Barton's Halifax was attacked and heavily damaged by two nightfighters, causing half his crew to bale out. Without navigator, bomb-aimer or wireless operator he pressed on to drop his load and when almost home he ordered the remaining crew to prepare for a crash-landing as he struggled to avoid houses. The three crew survived but Barton was killed in the crash-landing.

Sergeant N.C. Jackson VC, 106 Squadron

As a flight engineer on his sixtieth operation, Norman Jackson's Lancaster was set on fire in a nightfighter attack after bombing Schweinfurt on 26 April 1944. Although wounded in the attack, he climbed out of the aircraft in a gallant attempt to extinguish the flames but was caught in the fire and badly burned. Swept over the trailing edge of the wing by the slipstream with his parachute already open, he fell thousands of feet to the ground where miraculously he survived. The aircraft crashed but four of the remaining crew members parachuted to safety.

Wing Commander G.L. Cheshire VC, DSO (2 Bars), DFC, 617 Squadron

On his fourth tour of operations in 1944 Leonard Cheshire was awarded the VC for four years of fighting against the bitterest opposition in the forefront of the battle. He requested demotion from group captain to wing commander in September 1943 to command 617 Squadron, piloting Lancasters and Mosquitoes as master bomber on many raids, pioneering dangerous low-level target marking techniques. His citation recorded that he had a reputation second to none in Bomber Command.

Pilot Officer A.C. Mynarski VC, RCAF, 419 (RCAF) Squadron

A Polish-Canadian from Manitoba, Mynarski was mid-upper gunner in a Lancaster detailed to attack Cambrai on the night of 12 June 1944. Set on fire in a nightfighter attack, both port engines failed and the aircraft became a flying inferno. Ordered to abandon the aircraft, Mynarski attempted in vain to save the trapped rear gunner before jumping himself. His clothing and parachute were well ablaze as he jumped from the aircraft and he fell, a human torch, to die later of terrible burns.

Squadron I.W. Bazalgette VC, DFC, 635 Squadron

Ian Bazalgette was the master bomber marking the V-1 flying bomb site at Trossy St Maxim on 4 August 1944 when his Lancaster was hit. Despite his blazing aircraft he pressed on to mark and bomb the target accurately before struggling bravely to bring his aircraft and crew to safety. With only one engine remaining he ordered his crew to bale out, but two who were wounded could not. Bazalgette attempted to crash-land after avoiding a French village but the Lancaster exploded on touching the ground.

Flight Sergeant G. Thompson VC, 9 Squadron

This airman was the wireless operator of a Lancaster which attacked the Dortmund–Ems canal in daylight on 1 January 1945. Hit by a heavy flak shell just after bombing, Thompson entered the blazing mid-upper and rear turrets to rescue the wounded gunners and suffered terrible burns in the process. After a crash-landing in Holland, Thompson was flown home for treatment but died three weeks later from his injuries.

Squadron Leader R.A.M. Palmer, VC, DFC & Bar, 109 Squadron

A veteran bomber pilot with 110 operations to his credit, Palmer was marker for a daylight raid on Cologne on 23 December 1944. Fighter attacks and flak set on fire the two engines of his Mosquito but he continued to bomb the marshalling yards accurately before his aircraft dived into the ground in flames.

Captain E. Swales VC, DFC, SAAF, 582 Squadron

Transferring from the 8th Army to the SAAF in 1943, Edwin Swales became a Pathfinder in 1944. On 23 February 1945 he was master bomber in a raid on Pforzheim when his Lancaster was crippled by an enemy fighter. Unperturbed, he continued to issue instructions to the main force and remained over the target until satisfied that the attack had been a success. He nursed his Lancaster to friendly territory on two engines where he ordered his crew to bale out before the aircraft crashed, carrying him to his death.

CHAPTER 10

THE COMMANDERS

To most people the name Bomber Harris is synonymous with the RAF's wartime bomber offensive and it is often the only name ever mentioned in this context. Yet there were four other wartime commanders who preceded Harris as commander-in-chief, but whose names have been largely overlooked by the random searchlight of history.

Each man followed a predictably similar path to high command, but there were some unexpected twists along the way. Ludlow-Hewitt, Portal, Peirse and Baldwin were all products of the English public school system; the latter two attended university, Ludlow and Baldwin entered Sandhurst. Harris was educated privately but ran away to Rhodesia when his parents insisted that he join the Army. Both Ludlow and Baldwin were commissioned into the Army, while Peirse was commissioned into the RNAS. Portal and Harris enlisted as private soldiers in the Army before taking a commission and transferring to the RFC. All fought with distinction during the First World War.

Ludlow-Hewitt was commander-in-chief of Bomber Command on the outbreak of war and had already steered it through the difficult years of expansion before the war, but realised in 1939 how woefully inadequate and under-prepared his squadrons were. In 1940 his insistence on the formation of more operational training

units may have cost him his job at Bomber Command headquarters, but his foresight proved vital to the survival of the Command when the big losses began to bite in 1942–3.

His successor was Sir Charles Portal who sensibly restricted the Command's vulnerable Hampdens, Wellingtons and Whitleys to night bombing in the wake of the disastrous losses in the first daylight raids. Portal did not stay long at Bomber Command: singled out for higher office, he was appointed Chief of the Air Staff in October 1940.

Sir Richard Peirse took over from Portal in October 1940 and presided over the first stages of Bomber Command's transition into a larger and better equipped force. Unfortunately his performance as a commander was under intense scrutiny from Portal who had become increasingly dissatisfied with the growing losses under Peirse's command. In January 1942 Peirse was posted away to the Far East.

Air Vice-Marshal 'Jack' Baldwin, AOC 3 Group, stepped in briefly as caretaker at Bomber Command headquarters in January 1942 until Peirse's successor could take over. Little more than a month later Sir Arthur Harris was appointed commander-in-chief and from there on he pursued with single-minded determination the systematic destruction of Germany through strategic bombing. A powerful personality with a clear sense of purpose, inflexible and impatient, Harris resisted most attempts by the Air Staff to switch his Command to precision bombing. But in the closing months of the war it became clear that Portal should have kept Harris on a tighter reign than he actually did.

THE HIGH COMMANDERS

Air Chief Marshal Sir Edgar LUDLOW-HEWITT GCB, GBE, CMG, DSO, MC, C-in-C 1937–40

Although not a very approachable man, Ludlow, as he was known, was widely respected for his immense knowledge of the RAF and lauded by Bomber Harris as the only officer in any of the services 'who so completely commanded and earned the faith and respect of his subordinates'. Ludlow-Hewitt was one of the few RAF commanders who kept abreast of new techniques and who actually bothered to maintain his skills as a pilot.

The son of a clergyman, Edgar Rainey Ludlow-Hewitt was born in Co. Cork on 9 June 1886 and educated at Radley and Sandhurst. Commissioned into the Royal Irish Rifles in 1905 he later learnt to fly at Upavon and was appointed to the RFC in August 1914. The following year he joined 1 Squadron in France where he saw action over the Western Front during the battle of Neuve Chapelle and in the fighting at Hill 60. Later he commanded 3 Squadron and was promoted wing commander and temporary lieutenant-colonel to command the 3rd Corps Wing at Bertangles. He was awarded the MC in 1916, the *Croix de Chevalier*, Legion of Honour in 1917, the DSO in 1918, and was mentioned in dispatches six times during the war, and in 1918 he was Chief Staff Officer at the RAF headquarters in France. Between the wars his career developed quickly with

As C-in-C from 1937 to 1940, Sir Edgar Ludlow-Hewitt steered Bomber Command through the difficult pre-war expansion period. He was widely respected for his knowledge of the RAF and lauded by Bomber Harris – rare indeed from such a tough commander.

appointments as Commandant of the RAF Staff College (1926–30), Director of Operations and Intelligence at the Air Ministry, and Deputy Chief of Staff (1933–5), AOC India (1935–7), followed in 1937 by appointment as C-in-C Bomber Command.

Ludlow-Hewitt steered Bomber Command through the difficult pre-war expansion period, but still remained realistic enough to recognise the deficiencies of the Command and its unreadiness for combat as war approached in September 1939. He could see that the problems it faced stemmed largely from the rapid expansion which had failed to address the crucial issues of night flying training, navigational aids, and the vulnerability of bombers to enemy fighter attack during daylight raids. By early in 1940 he acknowledged that the pre-war theory of the bomber always getting through had finally been dashed, and he was openly pessimistic about the capabilities of the RAF's bomber force.

In early 1940 Ludlow-Hewitt was posted away from Bomber Command in what some observers believe was a fit of pique by certain personalities within the Air Ministry, scornful of Ludlow's insistence on the formation of more OTUs at the expense of some front-line aircraft and crews to fuel the training programme. However, his appreciation of the value of operational training was to be the salvation of Bomber Command in the years that followed. Bomber Harris later commented that 'without this policy of Ludlow's, the dog would have eaten its own tail to hurting point within a few weeks, and would have been a dead dog beyond all hope of recovery, within a few months. Ludlow-Hewitt saved the situation – and the war – at his own expense.'

From 1940 to 1945 Ludlow-Hewitt became Inspector-General of the RAF and retired from the service in the year the war ended as an air chief marshal. In the same year he was appointed Chairman of the Board of Governors of the College of Aeronautics where he remained until 1953, whereupon he was made Deputy Lieutenant for Wiltshire. Ludlow-Hewitt died on 15 August 1973, aged eighty-seven.

Air Marshal Sir Charles PORTAL KG, GCB, OM, DSO, MC, C-in-C 1940

A quiet but likeable man, at forty-six years of age 'Peter' Portal was still relatively young when he succeeded Sir Edgar Ludlow-Hewitt on 4 April 1940 as C-in-C Bomber Command, but his prodigious intelligence and determination as a commander singled

Just six months into the job as Ludlow-Hewitt's successor at Bomber Command in 1940, 'Peter' Portal was singled out for higher office and appointed Chief of the Air Staff.

him out for higher office. Just six months into his command at High Wycombe he was appointed Chief of the Air Staff in October 1940, in which role he was later to become strongly committed to using Bomber Command in the fullest way possible to destroy Nazi Germany.

Born Charles Frederick Algernon Portal on 21 May 1893 at Hungerford, he was educated at Winchester and Christ Church, Oxford, before joining the Motor Cyclist Section of the Royal Engineers on the outbreak of war in 1914. As a corporal he was mentioned in dispatches the following month and was commissioned in September the same year. Transferring to the RFC as an observer in 1915, Portal was regarded as a pilot by 1916. He became a squadron commander in 1917 and a lieutenant-colonel, RAF, in June 1918, at the age of twenty-five, and with the MC and a DSO and bar.

Between the wars his RAF career progressed quickly, being promoted to wing commander in 1925 followed by the command of 7 (B) Squadron in 1927. In 1934, as a group captain, he was appointed commander of British forces in Aden, followed in 1937 by promotion to air vice-marshal and appointment as Director of Organisation at the Air Ministry where he served until appointed to the Air Council in 1939 as Air Member for Personnel. On the outbreak of war he was granted the rank of acting air marshal and remained on the Air Council until chosen to succeed Sir Edgar Ludlow-Hewitt as C-in-C Bomber Command in April 1940.

During his short time in command at High Wycombe, Portal steered Bomber Command through the dangerous summer of 1940. As a result of the disastrous daylight operation against the German fleet at Kristiansand in April, he sensibly restricted the Command's Hampdens and Wellingtons to night operations only, like the Whitleys.

He took office as Chief of the Air Staff in October 1940, where he remained for the duration of the war, and in April 1942 received substantive promotion to air chief marshal with seniority of May 1940. In January 1944 he was advanced to the highest rank of Marshal of the RAF.

Portal was a member of the Chiefs of Staff Committee in which capacity he played a full part in presenting to the Prime Minister and the War Cabinet the advice of the Chiefs of Staff on Allied strategy and other important matters of military policy. He was also present at all the wartime conferences of the Allied leaders, culminating in the meetings of 'the big three' at Teheran, Yalta and Potsdam.

The Portal–Harris axis in the Second World War proved very important for Bomber Command and had its genesis before the war when both men had commanded bomber squadrons at Worthy Down. The effective teamwork and close relationship that had grown up between them in the 1920s developed further during the war years, shaping the growth of Bomber Command in a significant way. Portal was acutely aware of the influence that Harris could exert on Churchill and he actively encouraged this liaison, even going so far as to help Harris plan his approaches to the Prime Minister, but then leaving him to proceed alone. Portal and Harris did have their differences, and at times these were forcibly expressed, but never did they allow such sentiments to affect their personal friendship or professional relationship.

Portal was created a baron in the honours announced on the resignation of the Churchill government in August 1945, and in the New Year honours of 1946 was raised to the dignity of a viscount. He was also one of the seven war leaders who were appointed Knights of the Garter in December 1946. From 1946 to 1951 Portal was Controller of Atomic Energy at the Ministry of Supply and in 1960 he was elected Chairman of the British Aircraft Corporation. As well as being an authority on falconry and a keen fisherman, he was also president of the MCC in 1958–9. He died on 22 April 1971, aged seventy-seven.

Air Marshal Sir Richard E.C. PEIRSE KCB, DSO, AFC, C-in-C 1940-42

Appointed by the Air Council in October 1940 to succeed Portal, Peirse had previously been Vice-Chief of the Air Staff where he had been closely involved in British bombing policy. During his fourteen-month tenure at High Wycombe he presided over the expansion of the bomber force and the introduction of the Stirling, Manchester and Halifax bombers which

Towards the end of 1941, Portal became increasingly dissatisfied with the performance of Ludlow's successor, Sir Richard Peirse, as C-in-C (1940–2), eventually posting him away to command the Allied Air Forces in SE Asia.

submarine bases and winning the DSO in 1915. In 1919 he was awarded the AFC and a permanent commission as squadron leader in the RAF, eventually rising to become commander of British forces in Palestine and Transjordan from 1933 to 1936. Returning to England, he was made an air vice-marshal in 1936 and in the following year became Director of Operations and Intelligence at the Air Ministry, and then Deputy Chief of the Air Staff (from April 1940 this post was redesignated Vice-Chief of the Air Staff). In 1939, Peirse was made an additional member of the Air Council and promoted acting air marshal.

Appointed C-in-C Bomber Command on 5 October 1940, Peirse was in command during a very difficult period that witnessed the painful transition from an inadequately equipped bomber force into the heavy force that his successor Sir Arthur Harris would take forward to victory. Towards the end of 1941 Portal became increasingly dissatisfied with Peirse's performance as commander-in-chief and alarmed at the growing losses being suffered by the Command. In January 1942 Peirse posted away to command the Allied air forces in South East Asia and retired as an air marshal in 1945. Sir Richard Peirse died on 6 August 1970, aged seventy-seven.

Air Vice-Marshal J.E.A. BALDWIN KBE, CB, DSO, DL, Acting C-in-C 1942

AVM 'Jack' Baldwin, AOC of 3 Group, acted as caretaker at Bomber Command headquarters until Peirse's successor could take over. It was during his brief tenure that the Channel Dash occurred, when the *Scharnhorst* and *Gneisenau* escaped from the French port of Brest and fled up the English Channel to the sanctuary of Kiel harbour in northern Germany, despite the attentions of 242 bomber aircraft of Bomber Command. (*See entry on page 181 for a full biography.*)

promised much, but which in reality failed to live up to expectations.

Born on 30 September 1892, Richard Peirse was an only child and came from a naval background. His father, an admiral, later became C-in-C East Indies, during the First World War. Richard was educated at Monkton Combe School near Bath, HMS *Conway*, and at King's College, London, before being commissioned into the Royal Naval Reserve for service in the RFC Naval Wing. He served with distinction as a pilot during the First World War, seeing much action along the Belgian coast, attacking

Air Chief Marshal Sir Arthur HARRIS GCB, OBE, AFC, C-in-C 1942–5

Known universally by his nickname 'Bomber', Sir Arthur Harris was the architect of Britain's strategic air offensive in the Second World War and for three years pursued the systematic destruction of Germany with a single-minded determination. Of all the Allied wartime commanders, Harris is arguably the most controversial and to this day his name is closely linked with the questionable policy of area bombing. Although he did not invent area bombing, he applied himself rigorously to its execution and demonstrated to the world the importance of strategic air power and the key role played by the RAF in the Allied war effort.

Harris was a man who could express himself clearly and who exuded a clear sense of purpose, although he was seen by some as unrefined and rude, lacking in sensitivity, impatient and totally inflexible. Yet generally he was regarded with affection by his bomber crews, and with awe by his many minions at Bomber Command headquarters.

When he was appointed commander-in-chief of Bomber Command in 1942, the bomber war had scarcely begun. In the thirty months that preceded his arrival at High Wycombe, Bomber Command had dropped about 90,000 tons of bombs and lost some 7,000 aircrew killed on operations; during the period of his command from 1942 to 1945, over 850,000 tons of bombs were dropped but aircrew casualties climbed to more than 40,000.

Although promoted Marshal of the RAF in 1945, unlike the other main leaders of the war years Harris did not receive a peerage in the 1946 New Year honours. Politicians, including Churchill himself, were quick to distance themselves from the bomber offensive now that the war had

'Cometh the hour, cometh the man.' Tough and uncompromising, 'Bomber' Harris was the C-in-C that Bomber Command desperately needed, a man who could express himself clearly and who exuded a strong sense of purpose.

been won, and Sir Arthur Harris and Bomber Command became victims of postwar political expediency.

Arthur Travers Harris was born at Cheltenham on 13 April 1892, the son of an official in the Indian Civil Service. He was educated privately but later fell out with his parents when they insisted on him joining the Army. Instead, the young Harris travelled across the world to Rhodesia where, at the age of sixteen, he tried his luck at gold mining, driving horses, and tobacco planting. When war broke out in 1914 he joined the Rhodesia Regiment as a bugler and fought in the campaign in German South West Africa. When the regiment disbanded on completion of the campaign he returned to England where he learned to fly at Brooklands and was commissioned into the RFC in November 1915. Harris was posted to France where he served on the Western Front until returning to England late in 1917. Promoted to major in 1918 he was given command of a home defence squadron (No. 44) and acquired something of a reputation as a pioneer in night flying and night fighting with 191 Squadron. He was awarded the AFC in November 1918 and granted a permanent commission in the RAF the following year.

During the interwar years Harris commanded several bomber squadrons in India and Iraq, demonstrating to those in authority his belief in the efficacy of large bomber aircraft and their direct employment against the enemy, and not as adjuncts to the other services. From 1925 to 1927 he commanded 58 (Bomber) Squadron at Worthy Down, during which time he effected great improvements in the squadron's navigational methods and in bombing by night. Between 1930 and 1933 he was employed on staff duties in the Middle East before returning home once more, this time as a group captain to command 210 Squadron, a flying boat unit based at Pembroke Dock, and where one of his flight commanders was a young and talented Australian named Don Bennett who would later become his AOC of the Pathfinder Force. Harris spent the next four years at the Air Ministry as Deputy Director, Operations and Intelligence, and later Director of Plans in which role he played a major part in inter-service planning. Promoted air commodore, he became the first AOC of the newly formed 4 Group in June 1937 where he remained until July the following year when he was posted overseas again, this time as AOC in Palestine and Transjordan with the unenviable task of

helping the Army keep civil order between Arab and Jew. He was invalided home to England in July 1939 suffering from a duodenal ulcer, but was soon given command of 5 Group in September where he remained until his appointment as Deputy Chief of the Air Staff in November 1940. Six months later he was chosen to head the RAF delegation in Washington and it was from this post that he was appointed in February 1942 to succeed Air Marshal Sir Richard Peirse as commander-in-chief Bomber Command.

As commander-in-chief, Harris presided over the rapid expansion of Bomber Command with the introduction of better aircraft in greater numbers, improved bombs and bombing tactics, and the effective use of radar technology. He succeeded in turning what had been a poorly equipped force with mediocre results into an efficient and deadly weapon of war, a situation brought about largely by dint of his personal commitment and strength of character. With the first 1,000-bomber raid in May 1942 Harris sent out a strong signal to Bomber Command's detractors, particularly in the Royal Navy, that he meant business, and that his command was not going to be dismembered and its resources shared out between the other two services.

Not surprisingly, Harris had very firm views about how his force should be employed: he resisted the formation of the Pathfinder Force in 1942 and fought every attempt to transfer Bomber Command's efforts from area to precision bombing. But after the heavy mauling of his bomber squadrons over the winter of 1943/4 in the battle of Berlin, the Air Staff became sceptical of his assertion that Bomber Command alone could bring Germany to its knees and insisted instead on selective attacks against industry. Despite the misgivings of Harris, Bomber Command was notably successful in the bombing of selective targets and in later precision attacks. In the closing months of the war, Bomber Command's aircraft could range far and wide over Germany with virtual impunity and strike at will in a manner that would have seemed inconceivable in 1941.

Promoted Marshal of the RAF in 1945, Harris retired from the RAF in the following year and with his wife and daughter left for South Africa where he ran a shipping line until 1953. He then returned to England where he lived in active retirement until his death on 5 April 1984, aged ninety-one.

THE GROUP COMMANDERS

Almost without exception, the men appointed to command Bomber Command's front-line groups during the Second World War were an able and determined elite, their skills in command being a major factor in the successful prosecution of the bomber offensive. Apart from a small handful of these men, most had been raised and educated in the closing years of Queen Victoria's long reign, a time when Britain's standing as a world power was truly great and unassailable. The globe was stained pink from pole to pole, denoting the disproportionate influence of one tiny island on the affairs of the world as a whole.

Many came from families whose menfolk had contributed to this global empire – conquering Africa, governing India and ministering to the great and good in the name of the 'Great White Queen'. They had enjoyed privileged upbringings and lifestyles which ranged from the aristocratic like the Hon. Sir Ralph Cochrane – a future commander of 5 Group – to the Indian Army like John Slessor, who would one day become a professional head of the RAF. For the majority, a public school education followed as a matter of course and then officer training for the British Army at Sandhurst.

War broke out in August 1914 and many of the future bomber group commanders saw active service as young subalterns on the Western Front in the four years of bitter conflict that ensued. However, by mid-war most had transferred from the Army to the Royal Flying Corps and a few from the Royal Navy to the Royal Naval Air Service. The formation of the RAF in 1918 marked the beginning for many of their climb to air rank and their eventual appointment to high command in a war yet to come.

Of those appointed to command Bomber Command's front-line and training groups during the Second World War, several stand out from the crowd for a number of very different reasons. At the age of thirty-three, Don Bennett was commander of the Pathfinders and the youngest air vice-marshal in the RAF – he was also 'colonial', the son of an Australian sheep farmer, and without a public school education. Together with Edward Addison, commander of the specialist bomber support and countermeasures 100 (BS) Group, he was one of only two wartime bomber group commanders whose specialist skills in navigation and electronics, respectively, were brought to bear on their jobs as group commanders.

With an exciting interwar career as an explorer and pioneer aviator behind him, 4 Group's Roddy Carr had the distinction of becoming the longest serving bomber group commander of the war, from 1941 to 1945. The only other group commander to come close to this was Edward Rice who commanded 1 Group from 1942 to 1945.

John Whitley was one of several younger and less experienced officers to whom Harris wanted to give group command experience before the war ended. As a station commander in 1943 he had flown on a raid 'unofficially' as a second pilot, only to be shot down over France. He evaded capture and made his way home to England via Spain with the help of the Resistance in a 'textbook' escape. In February 1945 Harris appointed him to command 4 Group, succeeding Roddy Carr.

Alec Coryton was a group commander who fell foul of Harris. Despite being respected as a first-rate commander of 5 Group who inspired his crews, Coryton has the distinction of being the only group commander to be sacked from his job by the commander-in-chief.

The thwarted career of Owen Boyd is perhaps the saddest tale of all. Apart from John Breen who commanded 1 Group from June to November 1940, Boyd's period of tenure as a bomber group commander was the shortest of the war. With his meteoric rise from squadron commander during the First World War to air marshal in 1940, his career looked set to take him all the way to the top. But on his way out to Egypt to take up a new appointment as AOC-in-C Middle East, Boyd's aircraft was forced down over Sicily and he was captured by the Italians, spending the next three years as a prisoner of war. Returning to England after the Italian capitulation, in February 1944 he was appointed to command 93 (OTU) Group. In July his wife divorced him and a week later he was dead from a heart attack. In the case of Owen Boyd, the fortunes of war proved not to be in his favour.

Air Vice-Marshal Edward B. ADDISON CB, CBE, OBE, MA, CENG, FIEE

AOC 100 (Bomber Support) Group, 1943–5
As a specialist in electrical engineering, Addison was the ideal candidate to head Bomber Command's newly formed 100 (BS) Group in November 1943 tasked primarily with the airborne jamming of enemy radar and communications systems.

Edward Addison held a master's degree from Cambridge and was the only wartime commander of 100 (Bomber Support) Group during its brief two-year existence. (IWM CH10907)

Edward Baker Addison was born on 4 October 1898 and served with the RFC and the RAF during the First World War after which he went up to Sidney Sussex College, Cambridge (1918–21), and then re-commissioned into the RAF in 1921. His studies continued, gaining his Master's degree from Cambridge in 1926 and the *Ingénieur Diplôme de l'École Supérieure d'Électricité* from Paris in 1927. Appointed AOC 100 (BS) Group in November 1943, he remained the group's only commander during its short (two-year) wartime existence. Addison retired from the RAF in 1955 but maintained a close involvement with the electronics field and on his retirement in 1975 was Director of Intercontinental Technical Services. He died at Weybridge, Surrey, on 4 July 1987, aged eighty-eight.

Air Marshal Sir John BALDWIN KBE, CB, DSO, DL

AOC 3 Group, 1939–42

A cavalry officer in the First World War, for a little over three years in the Second, John Baldwin presided over 3 Group, witnessing the heavy casualties of the early daylight raids, the transition to the night offensive and his group's re-equipment with the RAF's first four-engined monoplane heavy bomber, the Short Stirling. A popular officer, he occasionally flew on operations with his crews, a practice frowned upon and actively discouraged by Command headquarters.

Born on 13 April 1892, John Baldwin was educated at Rugby and Sandhurst before being commissioned into the 8th KRI Hussars in 1911. He transferred to the RAF in 1918 and was appointed ADC to King George V (1931–3). A succession of high-level appointments followed culminating with AOC 3 Group from 28 August 1939 to 14 September 1942. Baldwin's final RAF

For a little over three years, John Baldwin commanded 3 Group. At the beginning of 1942 he acted as caretaker at Bomber Command HQ until Peirse's successor, Harris, took over in February. Baldwin (extreme left) is pictured here at Waterbeach on 12 June 1942 in the company of King George VI, who is inspecting the staff and training crews of 1651 HCU. The king is shaking hands with Flt Lt Peter Boggis DFC.

appointment was as AOC 3rd Tactical Air Force in 1943–4 and he retired from the RAF at the end of the war. Thereafter he re-established links with his old regiment, the 8th KRI Hussars, and became their colonel from 1948 to 1958. Baldwin died at Stamford, Lincolnshire, on 28 July 1975, aged eighty-three.

Air Vice-Marshal Donald BENNETT CB, CBE, DSO

AOC 8 (PFF) Group, 1943–5

'His technical knowledge and his personal operational ability was altogether exceptional. His courage, both moral and physical [was] outstanding and as a technician he [was] unrivalled. He could not suffer fools gladly, and by his own high standards there were many fools.' Renowned for his bluntness and not disposed towards unnecessary flattery, this was praise indeed for Bennett from his high commander Bomber Harris. In 1944, at the age of thirty-three, Don Bennett became the youngest air vice-marshal in the history of the RAF.

Born in Toowoomba, Queensland, on 14 September 1910, the youngest son of an Australian sheep farmer, Donald Clifford Tyndall Bennett joined the Royal Australian Air Force in 1930 and travelled to England in the following year on attachment to the RAF. Initially posted to 29 (F) Squadron he later became an instructor on flying boats at RAF Calshot and when he left the RAF in 1935, transferring to the Reserve, he was a highly qualified pilot and air navigator. Joining Imperial Airways, Bennett flew the world's air routes in flying boats and landplanes, achieving several much publicised flying exploits including the *Mercury-Maia* composite flying boat flight across the North Atlantic in July 1938, and various in-flight refuelling experiments in 1939.

One of the outstanding bomber group commanders of the war was Don Bennett, appointed AOC of the newly formed Pathfinder Force in July 1942. When the war ended, Bennett remained the only bomber group commander not to receive a knighthood – a perceived snub that still rankles with former Pathfinder crews to this day. (Roy Conyers Nesbit collection)

In 1940 Bennett was selected to help set up the Atlantic Ferry organisation for the collection of American- and Canadian-built aircraft for delivery to England, and led the first formation flight of Hudsons across the Atlantic.

Recommissioned into the RAFVR in 1941, Bennett was promoted to wing commander in December and appointed to command 77 Squadron at Leeming. He later moved on to command 10 Squadron in April 1942 and was shot down on a raid to sink the

Tirpitz. He evaded and made his way home to England via Sweden.

The high point of Bennett's RAF career came in July 1942 when Harris asked him to form the Pathfinder Force, and which officially came into being the following month. Bennett was promoted air commodore in January 1943 and later air vice-marshal. That same year he was awarded the DSO.

The success of the Pathfinder Force was due in large measure to Bennett's relentless drive and vision: night after night for the remaining three years of the war, almost every main force raid was spearheaded by the Pathfinders who contributed in a major way to the successful prosecution of the RAF's strategic air offensive.

When the war ended, Bennett remained the only bomber group commander not to receive a knighthood. Nevertheless, his postwar achievements and activities were varied: he was one-time Liberal MP for Middlesbrough West, Director of British South American Airways, and a designer and builder of light aircraft and cars. He died on 15 September 1986, aged seventy-six.

Air Vice-Marshal 'Bobby' BLUCKE CB, CBE, DSO, AFC

AOC 1 Group, 1945

As a pilot with the RAE's Experimental Section at Farnborough in the mid-1930s, 'Bobby' Blucke flew many sorties to conduct experiments in the new science of electronics. On 26 February 1935, as a squadron leader, Bobby Blucke flew a Handley Page Heyford bomber through the beam of the BBC Daventry transmitter to demonstrate that radio waves bounced off his aircraft in flight. This demonstration had important repercussions and led successively to the development of Radio Direction Finding and, ultimately, radar.

Born on 22 June 1897, Robert Stewart Blucke was commissioned into the RAF in April 1918 and his first operational posting was as a flying officer pilot with 29 (F) Squadron, seven years later in 1925. He later spent time with the RAF in India between 1929 and 1932, at Karachi, before returning to England in 1933 to join the AA Cooperation Flight at Horsley. The following year he was posted to the RAE Farnborough where he became involved in the experiments with electronics. On the outbreak of war in 1939 Blucke was in charge of Blind Approach Training and later helped in the Allied scientific counter-offensive against the German *Knickebein* transmitters.

On 12 February 1945 Bobby Blucke was one of several less experienced officers to be given operational group command experience by Harris before the war ended. Appointed AOC of 1 Group, he remained there until January 1947 and on his retirement in 1952 he was C-in-C Transport Command. Bobby Blucke died on 2 October 1988, aged ninety-one.

Air Chief Marshal Sir Norman BOTTOMLEY KCB, CB, CIE, DSO, AFC

AOC 5 Group, 1940–1

From Senior Air Staff Officer at Bomber Command headquarters between 1938 and 1940, Norman Bottomley was appointed AOC 5 Group in November 1940 and was later promoted to Deputy Chief of the Air Staff in 1943. At the war's end he succeeded Bomber Harris as C-in-C Bomber Command.

Born in Yorkshire on 18 September 1891, Norman Bottomley was educated at Halifax School and the University of Rennes in Brittany before being commissioned into the Yorkshire Regiment with which he served until transferring to the RFC in 1915. Between the wars his appointments included service in the Middle East and the command

Norman Bottomley (second from right), AOC 5 Group from 1940 to 1941, poses for the camera on 1 February 1943 with Mosquito crews from 105 and 139 Squadrons. The day before they had taken part in a daring daylight attack on Berlin. At this time, Bottomley was Deputy Chief of the Air Staff. (IWM CH8527)

of 4 (AC) Squadron and 1 (Indian) Group. Bottomley's appointment as SASO at Bomber Command in 1938 marked the beginning of a rapid rise towards C-in-C by 1945. He became Inspector-General of the RAF in 1947 and retired the following year. Sir Norman Bottomley died on 13 August 1970, aged seventy-eight.

Air Vice-Marshal Owen BOYD CB, OBE, MC, AFC

AOC 93 (OTU) Group, 1944

Of all Bomber Command's wartime group commanders, Owen Boyd spent the shortest time in command of his appointed group. His life was cut tragically short at the age of fifty-four in August 1944, six months into his appointment as AOC of 93 (OTU) Group.

Owen Tudor Boyd was born on 30 August 1889 and educated at RMA Sandhurst before entering the Indian Army in 1909. He saw service in the First World War with the RFC and RAF, and commanded 66 Squadron. In 1938 he became C-in-C Balloon Command and two years later in 1940 was promoted air marshal and appointed Deputy to the AOC-in-C Middle East. On his way out to Egypt the aircraft in which he was a passenger was forced down over Sicily by enemy fighters and he became a POW in Italy. When Italy capitulated in September 1943, Boyd and two British Army generals (Neame and O'Connor, who had been captured in North Africa in 1941) made a bid for freedom and finally reached Allied lines. Life was not easy for Boyd on his return to England. In July 1944 his wife divorced him and little more than a week later on 5 August he was dead from a heart attack.

Air Marshal John BREEN CB, OBE

AOC 1 Group, 1940

Born John Joseph Breen on 8 March 1896, forty-four years later as an air commodore he was appointed AOC 1 Group in June 1940. His period of tenure was short, being succeeded five months later by Air Vice-Marshal R.D. Oxland.

Transferring to the RAF in 1918 as a staff captain, Breen was later on the staff at the Air Ministry's Directorate of Organisation and Staff Duties (1923) before promotion to squadron leader in 1925. There followed training as a pilot with 24 Squadron at Northolt in 1927, and an overseas posting to Iraq in April the next year saw Breen in command of an Armoured Car Wing. His newly acquired flying skills were put to better use six months later when he was moved on to command 84 Squadron, flying Wapitis from Shaibah.

Breen returned home in October 1929 to assume command of 33 Squadron at Eastchurch. A period of study followed at the Imperial Defence College in 1931, after successful completion of which he was promoted acting wing commander to join the Air Staff of the Western Area/Wessex Bombing Area, ADGB, at Andover in 1932. Another overseas posting followed in 1935 with an attachment to the HQ Staff of the Sudan Defence Force in Khartoum.

Breen was promoted group captain in July 1937 and returned home to become SASO at 4 Group under Air Commodore A.T. Harris in November the same year. There he remained until his appointment as AOC 1 Group on 27 June 1940. Six months later, as an air commodore, he was moved to the Air Ministry where he spent the next four years as Director General of Personnel (1940–4) and then as Head of the Postwar Planning Executive (1944–5). He retired from the RAF as an air marshal on 2 May 1946 and died on 9 May 1964 at a nursing home in Dublin, aged sixty-eight.

Air Vice-Marshal George BROOKES CB, OBE

AOC 6 (RCAF) Group, 1942–4

George Brookes had the formidable task of forming from scratch a complete bomber group on foreign soil and then organising it into a force ready for action. That he did so in such a short time and so effectively, is a testament to his professionalism. For organising and commanding 6 (RCAF) Group the British government recognised his services with the Order of the Bath. But 'Bomber' Harris had been 'alarmed' at the prospect of the new Canadian bomber group under his command. Brookes was looked upon in the RCAF more as a fatherly than a dynamic figure, and so the demanding Harris may not have considered his strength of personality exacting enough for the job.

Born in Yorkshire on 22 October 1894, George Eric Brookes emigrated to Canada with his parents in 1910 at the age of sixteen and settled in Owen Sound, Ontario. He enlisted in the Canadian Army Medical Corps in 1914 and served in France before accepting a commission in the RFC in 1916. Brookes was posted to 13 Squadron, flying the BE2, but he was wounded in combat the following year and as a result was taken off

A Yorkshireman by birth, George Brookes emigrated to Canada when in his teens and eventually joined the CAF. He later returned to England to become the first AOC of 6 (RCAF) Group from January 1943 to February 1944. (DND/PL142657)

William Callaway was the first AOC of 5 Group in August 1937, which was later to become Bomber Command's premier main force bomber group during the Second World War. (IWM CH10261)

front-line duties. He joined the RAF in 1918 as an instructor and transferred to the Canadian Air Force in 1921.

In 1939 he was a group captain at HQ Eastern Air Command in Halifax, Nova Scotia, planning Canada's coastal defence and convoy patrols. In May 1940, as an air commodore, he became AOC 1 Training Command in Toronto before being posted overseas to England and appointed AOC 6 (RCAF) Group on 24 October 1942 as an air vice-marshal. He was succeeded in February 1944 by 'Black Mike' McEwen and retired from the RCAF in November the same year.

After the war he was very active in the Royal Canadian Air Cadets and was the National President of the RCAF Association. He died in Toronto on 8 September 1982, aged eighty-seven.

Air Vice-Marshal William CALLAWAY CBE, AFC, DL

AOC 5 Group, 1937–9

As an air commodore, Callaway became the first AOC of the newly created 5 Group on 17 August 1937 and relinquished the appointment two years later to AVM Arthur Harris, who was later to become AOC-in-C Bomber Command.

The son of Royal Navy engineer captain, William Bertram Callaway was born on 15 October 1889 and educated privately before following his father into the Royal Navy in 1907. He spent nine years in the RN before transferring to the RNAS in 1916, when he won the AFC, and was commissioned into the RAF in 1918. As an air commodore, Callaway became the first AOC of the newly created 5 (Bomber) Group on 17 August 1937 and relinquished the appointment two years later to AVM Arthur Harris, who was later to become AOC-in-C Bomber Command. Promoted AVM in 1942, Callaway retired from the RAF in 1947 to become Divisional Controller, SW Division, Ministry of Civil Aviation, where he remained until his retirement in 1953. He lived at Lingfield in Surrey until his death on 28 August 1974, aged eighty-four.

Air Marshal Sir Roddy CARR CB, DFC, AFC

AOC 4 Group, 1941–5

'An officer much respected . . . he was the archetype English gentleman though born in New Zealand, with an easy manner and the gift of putting one completely at ease. His straightforwardness and lack of pomposity was reflected in his subordinates . . .', was how one Bomber Command staff officer, John Searby, recalled him. At nearly four years in post, Roddy Carr was unique among Harris's wartime group commanders in claiming the longest continuous period in command of the same group.

Born at Feilding, New Zealand, on 31 August 1891, Roderick Carr was educated at Wellington College, New Zealand, before travelling to Europe to fight in the First World War with the New Zealand Army. Later in the war he served with the RNAS and was transferred to the RAF in 1918 before journeying to north Russia in 1919 with the RAF contingent of the British Relief Force to help anti-Bolshevik forces in their (eventually) futile attempts to crush Lenin's forces. A distinguished interwar career saw him take part in Shackleton's Antarctic Expedition in 1921–2 and in 1927 he flew on the RAF's first long-distance flight from England to the Persian Gulf in a modified Hawker Horsley. Service in Egypt (1929–33) and on secondment to the Royal Navy (HMS *Eagle*, 1936–9) followed, and at the outbreak of war Carr was with the RAF's AASF in France. He became AOC RAF Northern Ireland in 1940 before his appointment as AOC 4 (Bomber) Group on 26 July 1941, where he remained until replaced by AVM J.R. Whitley in 1945. On retirement in 1947 Carr was AOC-in-C India. He died at Bampton, Oxfordshire, on 15 December 1971, aged eighty-one.

Air Chief Marshal the Hon. Sir Ralph A. COCHRANE GBE, KCB, AFC, FRAES

AOC 3 and 5 Groups, 1942–5

In the opinion of AVM Donald Bennett, Cochrane was a disaster: 'He would have been the best Group Commander in Bomber Command had he done ten trips – or if he had done any trips. But his knowledge of flying and of operations was nil.' But Bomber Harris, who had known Cochrane before the war, regarded him as 'a most brilliant, enthusiastic and hard working leader of men'. Objective truth or simply the clash of two powerful personalities?

Born on 24 February 1895, Cochrane was educated at the Royal Naval Colleges at Osborne and Dartmouth before entering the Royal Navy in 1912, but he transferred to the RAF in 1918. A number of overseas postings culminated in 1936 with his appointment as the first Chief of the Air Staff to the Royal New Zealand Air Force. In 1942 Cochrane became AOC 3 Group and with the sacking by Harris of AVM Coryton in February 1943 he assumed the command of 5 Group. Cochrane had been a flight commander of a squadron commanded by Bomber Harris in Mesopotamia during the 1920s and as such remained a strong supporter of the C-in-C, a loyalty that evidently was reciprocated. Nevertheless, Cochrane was a difficult man to get along with and was viewed by many as austere and humourless. After the war Cochrane became AOC Transport and Flying Training Commands, followed in 1950 by appointments as ADC to the King and Queen and then Vice-Chief of the Air Staff before retirement in 1952. He died on 17 December 1977, aged eighty-two.

Air Marshal Sir Arthur CONINGHAM KCB, KBE, CB, DSO, MC, DFC, AFC

AOC 4 Group, 1939–41
Arthur 'Mary' Coningham gained his nickname (a corruption of the word Maori) in recognition of his New Zealand upbringing. On 3 July 1939 he became the third AOC of 4 Group and presided over changes in November 1940 that saw one of its squadrons, No. 35, become the second ever front-line RAF unit to operate monoplane four-engined heavy bombers.

Born in Brisbane, Australia, in 1895, and educated in New Zealand, Coningham saw service early in the First World War with the New Zealand forces in the Pacific and Middle East before transferring to the RFC in 1916 and winning a string of gallantry decorations in rapid succession (MC, DSO, DFC). In 1926 he led a record-breaking 5,268-mile flight from Helwan in Egypt to Kaduna in Nigeria for which he was rewarded with the AFC. In July 1939 Coningham became AOC 4 Group and was succeeded two years later by Roddy Carr, but the pinnacle of his RAF career came with his appointment as AOC 2nd Tactical

Air Force in 1944, followed with the command of Flying Training Command in 1945. He retired from the RAF in 1947 and died on 30 January 1948, aged fifty-two.

Air Chief Marshal Sir H.A. CONSTANTINE KBE, CB, DSO

AOC 5 Group, 1945
As a group captain station commander of RAF Elsham Wolds, 'Connie' Constantine insisted on joining the first 1,000-bomber raid over Cologne in May 1942 – an unusual occurrence for an officer of his rank. He was awarded the DSO the same year while commanding Elsham Wolds, and was mentioned in dispatches four times.

Born on 23 May 1908, Hugh (Alex) Constantine was educated at Christ's Hospital and the RAF College Cranwell where he excelled at boxing and rugby. He began his RAF career as a fighter pilot but soon moved to Bomber Command where he became a protégé of Bomber Harris. As SASO with 1 Group between 1943 and 1944, Constantine was handpicked by Harris to become Deputy SASO at Bomber Command headquarters, before being appointed to succeed Sir Ralph Cochrane as AOC 5 Group in January 1945. During his time with 5 Group, Constantine worked closely with the scientist Barnes Wallis of bouncing bomb fame, also winning praise from General Montgomery for the accurate bombing carried out by his squadrons in support of the Allied crossing of the Rhine in March 1945. After the war he became Deputy Chief of Staff at SHAPE in Paris and later C-in-C Flying Training Command before retirement in 1964. For the next thirteen years, he continued to work part-time at the Ministry of Defence as coordinator of Anglo-American community relations. He died on 16 April 1992, aged eighty-three.

Despite being a first-rate group commander, Alec Coryton was sacked by Harris.

Air Chief Marshal Sir Alec CORYTON KCB, KBE, MVO, DFC

AOC 5 Group, 1942–3

According to John Searby's posthumous memoirs, 'Alec Coryton was a first-rate group commander, knowledgeable, thrusting and capable of inspiring his crews.' Yet, in February 1943, he was sacked by Harris for refusing to send a small force of Lancasters from his group on a sneak raid to Berlin in bad weather.

(William) Alec Coryton was born at Pentillie Castle, Cornwall, on 16 February 1895. He was commissioned into the Rifle Brigade in the First World War and transferred to the RAF in 1918. Coryton served in India in 1920 and rose to become Director of Operations (Overseas) at the Air Ministry (1938–41). Appointed to command 5 Group on 25 April 1942, he presided over the introduction of the first Avro Lancasters into Bomber Command service and bitterly resented the release of his best squadron, No. 83, to the newly formed Pathfinder Force in August. After he was

sacked by Harris in February 1943 he moved to the Air Ministry where he became Assistant Chief of Air Staff (Operations) before appointment one year later as Air Commander, 3rd Tactical Air Force with SEAC (1944–5).

He retired from the RAF in 1951 and died at Langton Matravers, Dorset, on 20 October 1981, aged eighty-six.

Air Marshal Sir John D'ALBIAC KCVO, KBE, CB, DSO

AOC 2 Group, 1942–3

Born on 28 January 1894, John Henry D'Albiac was educated at Seabrook Lodge School, Kent, Framlingham College and the RMC Sandhurst where he was commissioned into the Army in 1914. Seconded to the RNAS in 1915 he served in France and was awarded the DSO in 1917. Transferring to the RAF in the following year he went on to fill a number of overseas staff appointments during the interwar years. At the outbreak of the Second World War he was AOC RAF Palestine but was later appointed to command 2 Group on 29 December 1942, a position he held until June 1943 when he became AOC 2nd Tactical Air Force. On retirement from the RAF in 1946, D'Albiac was Director-General Personnel at the Air Ministry. Postwar, he became commandant of the newly opened London Heathrow Airport in 1947 where he remained for ten years before his appointment as Deputy Chairman of the Air Transport Advisory Council (1957–61). He died at Beaconsfield, Buckinghamshire, on 20 August 1963, aged sixty-nine.

Air Vice-Marshal W.F.MacN. FOSTER CB, CBE, DSO, DFC, MA Oxon (Hon.)

AOC 6 (Training) Group, 1939–42

Born William Foster MacNeece in Co. Donegal on 21 August 1889, the son of an Army officer, he assumed the surname of Foster by royal licence in 1927. Educated at Cheltenham

College and RMC Sandhurst, he was commissioned into the RFC on the outbreak of the First World War and was awarded the DSO in 1917 and the DFC in 1918. During the interwar years his appointments included British Air Representative to the Council of the League of Nations (1926–9) and command of 1 Air Defence Group HQ (1929–34). He retired from the RAF in 1937 but was recalled to command 6 Group at the outbreak of war where he remained until April 1942. A number of important committee appointments followed at home, in the USA and in China, which included membership of the Combined Chiefs of Staff Committee (1942–3). Foster reverted to the retired list in 1946 and became actively involved in the local politics of Oxford, culminating in his election to the office of Lord Mayor in 1966. He enjoyed writing and submitted occasional verses to *The Times* and *Spectator*. His 'An Airman's Te Deum' was printed in 1936 to music by Sir Walford Davies and in 1937 to music by Dr Martin Shaw. Foster died in Aldeburgh, Suffolk, on 28 March 1978, aged eighty-eight.

Air Vice-Marshal J.A. GRAY CB, CBE, DFC, GM

AOC 91 (OTU) Group, 1944–5

During the inter-war years, John Gray spent much of his time on the developmental side of military aviation, with three years each at AAE Martlesham Heath (1922–5) and RAE Farnborough in the Experimental Section (1925–9), followed by two years at Felixstowe with the Marine Aircraft Experimental Establishment (1930–2). His spell at the MAEE coincided with the RAF's third and final attempt on the Schneider Trophy in 1931 where Gray found himself serving alongside Flight Lieutenant John Boothman (who won the trophy outright for Britain on 13 September 1931) and an (as yet) unknown young flying officer named Frank Whittle.

John Astley Gray was born on 23 July 1899 and saw service as an officer with the Royal Engineers in the closing years of the First World War before transferring to the RAF in April 1918. His career at the RAF's main experimental establishments was interspersed with an eighteen-month posting to 55 (B) Squadron at Hinaidi in 1929, followed after 1931 by a series of home-based staff appointments at HQ ADGB, RAF College Cranwell, and 23 (Training) Group, by which point the Second World War had broken out. Gray was promoted group captain in 1940, air commodore in 1943 and acting air vice-marshal in February 1944 when he was appointed AOC of 91 (OTU) Group, and there he remained for the duration of the war.

John Gray became SASO Transport Command in 1949, followed in 1951 by an overseas posting to Egypt on his appointment as AOC Administrative Staff, MEAF HQ, at Ismailia. He retired from the RAF in May 1954.

Air Commodore Harold HAINES CBE, DFC, MA

AOC 92 (OTU) Group, 1942–3

Born on 22 November 1899 at Salcombe Regis in Devon, Harold Haines was educated at Peterhouse College, Cambridge before joining the RNAS in 1917. Transferring to the RAF in 1918, he was later appointed to command 92 (OTU) Group at its head-quarters in Winslow, Buckinghamshire, on 14 May 1942. His final appointment before retirement in 1948 was as Commandant of the RAF Regiment Depot. Haines died on 26 June 1955, aged fifty-five.

Air Vice-Marshal Richard HARRISON, CB, CBE, DFC, AFC

AOC 3 Group, 1943–6

Born at Pocklington, Yorkshire, on 29 June 1893, Richard Harrison was educated at Highgate School, Scarborough College and Sheffield University before seeing service in the First World War. During the interwar years he served with the RAF in Palestine, Iraq (where he was twice mentioned in dispatches), and Egypt. During the Second World War he was three times mentioned in dispatches and was appointed AOC of 3 Group on 27 February 1943. Harrison retired from the RAF in 1946 and died on 18 May 1974, aged eighty.

Air Vice-Marshal George HODSON CB, CBE, AFC

AOC 93 (OTU) Group, 1944–5
George Stacey Hodson was born in London on 2 May 1899 and was educated at Dulwich School. He succeeded AVM Owen Boyd as AOC 93 (OTU) Group on 9 August 1944, and later became Air Officer Training at Bomber Command headquarters in 1945. Subsequent postwar appointments included AOA Coastal Command (1946), AOC 205 Group RAF Mediterranean and Middle East (1947), and was SASO Home Command on his retirement in 1951. Hodson died at Bognor Regis on 1 October 1976, aged seventy-seven.

Air Chief Marshal Sir Alan LEES KCB, CBE, DSO, AFC

AOC 2 Group, 1941–2
Born on 23 May 1895 at Ashton-under-Lyne, Alan Lees was educated at Wellington College, Berkshire and the RMC Sandhurst before joining the RFC, in which he served throughout the First World War. Lees spent several periods overseas during the interwar years: in Iraq (1923–6), and on the north-west Frontier of India (1933–7). With the outbreak of the Second World War he succeeded AVM Stevenson as AOC 2 Group on 17 December 1941, where he remained until replaced by AVM J. D'Albiac on 29 December 1942. At the end of the war Lees became AOC-in-C Reserve Command (1946–9) whereupon he retired from the

RAF. He died on 14 August 1973, aged seventy-eight.

Air Vice-Marshal Percy MAITLAND CB, CBE, MVO, AFC

AOC 93 (OTU) Group, 1942–3
The son of a naval surgeon-captain, Percy Eric Maitland was born on 26 October 1895. His career in the British forces, ultimately to span nearly fifty years, began in 1908 at the tender age of thirteen when he attended the Royal Naval Colleges at Osborne and Dartmouth. Maitland's naval service continued though the First World War with secondment in 1915 to the newly formed RNAS airship branch. In April 1918 he transferred to the RAF as a captain specialising in navigation. His career during the interwar years was interesting and varied with service in Egypt and Iraq, followed by a record-breaking long-distance flight to Australia in which he was the navigator. Maitland was Staff Officer for the Royal Review in 1935 and served in the Far East up until the outbreak of war in 1939, by which time he was a group captain. He spent 1939–40 with Flying Training Command before joining Bomber Command, which led to his appointment as AOC 93 (OTU) Group on 15 June 1942. In February 1943 he moved to a staff job at the Air Ministry where he became Director of Operational Training. A succession of commands followed at the end of the war and he finally retired from the RAF in 1950. Percy Maitland died at Wallingford on 22 August 1985, aged eighty-nine.

Air Vice-Marshal Cuthbert MACLEAN CB, DSO, MC

AOC 2 Group, 1938–40
Born in Wanganui, New Zealand on 18 October 1886, the son of a clergyman, Cuthbert Trelawder MacLean was educated

at Wanganui Collegiate School and at Auckland University, New Zealand. He came to England before the First World War whereupon he was seconded to the RFC in 1915, transferring to the RAF in 1918. MacLean was promoted air vice-marshal in 1935 and his postings included AOC-in-C Middle East (1934–8) and concluded with his appointment as AOC 2 Group on 16 May 1938. He retired from the RAF in April 1940 and died at Cirencester, Gloucestershire, on 25 February 1969, aged eighty-two.

Air Vice-Marshal Clifford ('Black Mike') McEWEN CB, MC, DFC & Bar

AOC 6 (RCAF) Group, 1944–5

The forceful, dynamic leadership of 'Black Mike' McEwen as AOC of 6 (RCAF) Group earned him high praise from 'Bomber' Harris. He assumed command at a critical point in the strategic air offensive when the tide of war was finally turning in the Allies' favour, but also when the *Luftwaffe* fighter force was once more in the ascendancy. One of McEwen's first initiatives on taking command in February 1944 was to institute a full-scale programme of flying training for all aircrew, regardless of whether they were freshmen or on second tours. While crews grumbled about the training programme, it later paid dividends in a low casualty rate.

Born at Griswold, Manitoba, on 2 July 1896, Clifford Mackay McEwen was educated at the University of Saskatchewan before enlisting in the 196th Battalion, Canadian Expeditionary Force, in 1916. He was commissioned in England the following year and was seconded to the RFC with whom he learned to fly. McEwen served as a pilot with 28 Squadron RFC in Italy, shooting down twenty-two enemy aircraft and winning the MC, DFC & Bar, and the Italian Bronze Medal for Valour. He was promoted captain before the First World

A Canadian fighter pilot hero from the First World War, during which he was credited with shooting down twenty-two enemy aircraft, 'Black Mike' McEwen succeeded George Brookes as AOC of 6 (RCAF) Group in February 1944. (DND/PL24444)

War ended and joined the fledgling Canadian Air Force.

During the interwar years 'Black Mike' (as he became known – a nickname acquired while training at Camp Borden thanks to his tendency to sun-tan quickly) was a flying instructor and attended the RAF Staff College in 1930. On the outbreak of war in 1939 he was a group captain at the big training base at Trenton, Ontario, but in 1941 was promoted air commodore and given command of the RCAF's 1 Group in Coastal Command at St John's, Newfoundland, waging a vital war against German U-boats in the North Atlantic.

McEwen had been overseas in England for more than a year as a station commander before he was promoted air vice-marshal and appointed to command 6 (RCAF) Group on 28 February 1944. A stickler for discipline and a leader by example, he flew on operations over Germany on a number of occasions. When the war ended, he was designated commander of the bomber group planned to be sent to the Pacific theatre to fight the Japanese, but with the collapse of Japan in August the plan was scrapped. McEwen retired from the RCAF in 1946 and became a private consultant to aircraft manufacturers. For two years he was a director of Trans-Canada Air Lines. He died on 6 August 1967, aged seventy-one.

Air Vice-Marshal Robert OXLAND CB, CBE, OBE

AOC 1 Group 1940–3

Born on 4 April 1889 and educated at Bedford Modern School, Robert Dickinson Oxland joined the RFC in 1915 and transferred to the RAF in 1918. As a qualified meteorological observer his first postings were in Iraq as a specialist staff officer. Returning home in 1925 as a squadron leader he joined 502 Squadron at Aldergrove, then moved on to 2 FTS at Digby in 1927.

Oxland was promoted wing commander in 1930 and from then until 1938 he took a series of staff appointments at home and overseas before promotion to air commodore and the post of Director of Personal Services at the Air Ministry in 1938. In November 1940 he was promoted to command 1 Group where he remained until succeeded by Air Vice-Marshal Edward Rice in February 1943. Oxland retired from the RAF in 1946 and died on 27 October 1959, aged sixty.

Robert Oxland, who had trained as a meteorological observer in the RFC in 1915, was appointed to command 1 Group in November 1940. He is pictured here in the company of Polish Air Force officers shortly before the war. (IWM C750)

Air Vice-Marshal Sir Edward RICE KBE, CB, CBE, MC

AOC 1 Group 1942–5

A chance meeting between Edward Rice and the head of the engineering firm Rose Brothers led to the design of the successful Rose-Rice twin 0.50in Browning tail turret for Lancasters of 1 Group. Despite a lack of any official interest, Rice went ahead and helped Alfred Rose with the winning design and the Air Ministry placed an initial production order for the turret in June 1943.

Despite the lack of official interest, Edward Rice collaborated with armament engineer Alfred Rose to produce the winning design of the Rose Rice twin 0.50in Browning tail turret for Lancasters in Rice's 1 Group. (IWM CH15534)

The son of a Berkshire doctor, Edward Rice was born on 19 December 1893 and educated privately before transferring to the RFC from the Army in 1915. After a succession of overseas postings during the 1920s and '30s, he was promoted air commodore in 1940 and appointed AOC RAF West Africa from 1941 to 1942. Returning to England in 1942, Rice was promoted air vice-marshal to command 1 Group until February 1945 when he was appointed AOC 7 (Training) Group, where he remained until his retirement from the service in 1946. He died soon afterwards on 14 April 1948, aged fifty-four.

Air Vice-Marshal Alan RITCHIE CBE, AFC

AOC 93 (OTU) Group 1943–4

Born on 7 April 1899, Alan Ritchie saw service during the First World War and transferred to the RAF in 1918, training as a pilot at CFS Upavon in 1921. His first posting was to 100 Squadron at Spittlegate in 1922, equipped with the DH9a, followed by a period at Staff College (1924–5), then a three-year spell as CO of the RAF's Home Communication Flight at Northolt (1925–9). Ritchie spent the next three years from early in 1929 on Air Staff Intelligence Duties at Khartoum in the Sudan and on his return home went to the Air Ministry Directorate of Operations and Intelligence (1932–5). It was here that he served under and alongside many of the future high and group commanders of Bomber Command, including Ludlow-Hewitt, Peirse, Portal, Cochrane and Coryton.

He was posted out to the Middle East once again in 1935 where he spent the next two years as CO of 47 (B) Squadron in Khartoum, flying the Fairey Gordon and Vickers Vincent. A return to staff duties followed in June 1937 when Ritchie joined the Combined General Headquarters, Palestine and Transjordan, as a wing commander. He remained in the Middle East until after the outbreak of war and returned home to England in 1940 as a group captain.

As an acting air vice-marshal, Ritchie was appointed AOC 93 (OTU) Group on 25 February 1943 and was succeeded one year later by AVM Owen Boyd. He retired from the RAF in December 1945 and became Deputy Lieutenant of Suffolk in 1950. Alan Ritchie died on 17 August 1961, aged sixty-two.

Air Chief Marshal Sir James ROBB GCB, KBE, DSO, DFC, AFC

AOC 2 Group 1940–1

One of the most valuable gifts James Robb gave to the RAF in the Second World War came about through his involvement in establishing the Commonwealth Air Training Plan in Canada during the late thirties, which later provided Bomber Command with a steady stream of trained aircrew when it needed them most. Later appointed AOC 2 Group on 17 April 1940, he soon witnessed the severe mauling his squadrons received in the desperate battle of France.

Born on 26 January 1895 at Hexham,

The establishment of the Commonwealth Air Training Plan in Canada before the war owes much to the foresight of James Robb, AOC 2 Group from 1940 to 1941.

Northumberland, the son of a JP, James Robb was educated at George Watson's School and Durham University. During the First World War he served with the Northumberland Fusiliers and the RFC and was twice wounded. He soon acquired a reputation as an ace pilot, shooting down seven enemy aircraft, and was awarded the DFC. After the war he was given an RAF permanent commission and in 1936 became Commandant of the CFS at Upavon. During 1938–9 Robb was closely involved in setting up the Commonwealth Air Training Scheme in Canada which soon began to pay dividends for the RAF once the casualties of war began to mount. Robb's RAF career developed rapidly thereafter with a series of key appointments, starting in 1944 as the Chief of Staff (Air) to Eisenhower, followed in 1945 by AOC-in-C RAF Fighter Command, Vice-Chief of the Air Staff in 1948 and finally as Inspector General of the RAF on his retirement in 1951. Robb died at Bognor Regis on 18 December 1968, aged seventy-three.

Marshal of the RAF Sir John SLESSOR GCB, DSO, MC, DL

AOC 5 Group 1941–2

John Slessor was the only one of the RAF's wartime bomber group commanders ultimately to become the professional head of the RAF, as Marshal of the RAF.

Born on 3 June 1897 at Rhanikhet, India, the son of a British Army officer, John Cotesworth Slessor served with the RFC in the First World War in the London Air Defence, and in France, Egypt and the Sudan. The interwar years saw him appointed to several staff positions and the commands of 4 Squadron (1925–8) and 3 (Indian) Wing (1935). This was followed in 1937–41 by Director of Plans at the Air

As AOC of 5 Group from 1941 to 1942, John Slessor was the only RAF wartime bomber group commander to become the professional head of the Service.

Ministry during which time he was also appointed ADC to the King. On 12 May 1941 he became AOC 5 Group but was succeeded less than a year later on 25 April 1941 by AVM Alec Coryton. Promotion followed swiftly to Assistant Chief of the Air Staff (Policy) (1942–3), AOC-in-C Coastal Command (1943), C-in-C RAF Mediterranean and Middle East (1944–5), Air Member for Personnel (1945–7), Marshal of the RAF (1950), and Chief of the Air Staff (1950–2). Following his retirement from the RAF he maintained a busy personal schedule as a JP, county councillor and High Sheriff for Somerset. He also found time to write several books on strategy which

included *The Central Blue* (1956) and *The Great Deterrent* (1959). He died on 12 July 1979, aged eighty-two.

Air Vice-Marshal Donald STEVENSON CB, CBE, OBE, DSO, MC & Bar

AOC 2 Group 1941–2

In 1941, the light bombers of 2 Group were ordered to attack and sink all enemy coastal shipping that put to sea between the Brittany peninsula and Germany. As the group commander, Donald Stevenson followed his orders to the letter but the resulting cost in aircraft and crews was painfully high and earned for him the nickname 'Red Steve'.

The son of an Army officer, Donald Stevenson was born on 7 April 1895 and served with the British forces in the First World War before transferring to the RFC in 1916, winning the MC and bar, and a DSO. He became Air ADC to King George VI in 1939–40 before taking up an Air Ministry appointment which preceded his move to command 2 Group in February 1941. Here he stayed for little more than ten months before accepting a command posting to the Far East. His final RAF command was as AOC 9 (Fighter) Group in 1943. Stevenson was High Commissioner to Romania from 1944 to 1947 after which he retired from the RAF. He died on 10 July 1964, aged sixty-nine.

Air Vice-Marshal Henry THOROLD CB, CBE, DSC, DFC, AFC

AOC 92 (OTU) Group 1943–5

Born on 11 May 1896 and educated at Marlborough College, Henry Thorold served throughout the First World War with the RNAS. Transferring to the RAF in 1918, his career between the wars took him to Iraq twice and later saw him command

10 (Bomber) and 70 (BT) Squadrons between 1933 and 1936. Promoted group captain in 1937, he commanded RAF station Mildenhall. From 1938, a number of staff appointments at home and overseas preceded his command of 92 (OTU) Group in March 1943, where he remained until succeeded by AVM Hodson in February 1945. Later that same year he became head of the Air Section to the British Military Mission in Moscow, followed in 1946 as SASO Flying Training Command. Thorold retired in the following year and died on 10 April 1966, one month short of his seventieth birthday.

Air Marshal Sir Hugh WALMSLEY

AOC 91 (OTU) Group 1942–4, AOC 4 Group 1945

Awarded the MC in 1918, the DFC in 1922, and mentioned in dispatches five times during the Second World War, Hugh Walmsley was born in 1898 and educated at Dover College. During the First World War he saw service with the Royal North Lancashire Regiment before secondment to the Royal Flying Corps in 1916. Walmsley received a permanent commission in the RAF in 1922 and as a group captain became AOC 91 (OTU) Group in 1942. He took over as AOC 4 Group from AVM John Whitley on 7 May 1945 before moving on to become Air Officer, Transport Command, SE Asia (1945–6) and then AOC Air HQ, India (1946–7). A succession of senior command appointments followed with Deputy Chief of the Air Staff in 1948, and then in 1950 AOC Flying Training Command. Walmsley retired from the RAF in 1952 and became managing director of Air Service Training Ltd and later principal of the College of Air Training until he retired again in 1960. He died at Lymington in August 1985, aged eighty-seven.

Air Marshal Sir John WHITLEY KBE, CB, DSO, AFC & Bar

AOC 4 Group 1945

As part of Harris's plan to give group command experience to less experienced officers before the war ended, AVM John Whitley assumed command of 4 Group in February 1945 from the long-serving and much respected AVM Roddy Carr. He was also an airman who took escape and evasion seriously. Thanks to his preparedness for such an eventuality Whitley made good his escape from France to England via Spain after he was shot down in 1943.

John Rene Whitley was born on 7 September 1905, the son of a civil engineer, and spent his early childhood in Chile where his father was in charge of building what was then the highest railway in the world. After his mother's death he was brought up in France by his grandparents. Educated at Haileybury, Whitley joined the RAF on a short service commission in 1926 and a year later his first posting was to 7 Squadron at Worthy Down. In 1931 he moved to 101 Squadron before being offered a permanent commission and a posting to India where he was given command of the Bomber Transport Flight at Lahore. In India he piloted the Viceroy and made many long-range flights into South East Asia, but his involvement in humanitarian relief operations following the Quetta earthquake in 1935 saw him awarded the AFC.

Returning home to England in 1937 he was promoted to squadron leader and posted in August to 38 (B) Squadron at Marham as a flight commander. In the following August he was posted to 24 Squadron at Hendon, a communications squadron, where he commanded the VIP flight and his log book recorded flying such men as Churchill, Chamberlain, Bomber Harris, Noel Coward and David Niven to a host of destinations. In May 1940 Whitley was promoted wing commander and given command of 149 Squadron at Mildenhall flying Wellingtons, but in November he was posted to Bomber Command head-quarters as an operations officer.

Whitley served with distinction in 4 Group from 1941 and as a group captain he was appointed to command RAF station Linton-on-Ouse on 23 May 1941. Almost two years later on 10 April 1943, Whitley was flying as second pilot to Flight Lieutenant Hull of 76 Squadron on a raid to Frankfurt when their Halifax was intercepted over Belgium by a German nightfighter and shot down. Whitley and three others survived the crash, but he soon made contact with the French Resistance and eventually made good his escape to England via Spain in an attempt widely regarded as a classic of its kind.

After a period of rest following his escape, Whitley was appointed to command RAF station Lissett in September 1943, but promotion to air commodore followed swiftly and with it command of Driffield Base in April 1944. In February 1945, Whitley recalled 'being rung up by the AOC's PA and told that the AOC wanted to see me, but the PA didn't know why. So I drove into 4 Group HQ at Heslington Hall wondering what I'd done wrong. I was shown into the AOC's office and there was the great man. He greeted me and told me to sit in his chair. Having done so I felt somewhat foolish but not for long as he said "Well John, it's all yours", meaning of course that I was being promoted to air vice-marshal and AOC 4 Group.'

Whitley was duly appointed as AOC 4 Group on 12 February 1945, where he remained for just three months before he turned down a posting to the Far East as Deputy AOC to Hugh Pugh Lloyd, and instead became AOC of 8 (PFF) Group until November when he joined HQ Air Command South East Asia as Air Commodore Air Staff.

Returning home in 1948 he was promoted successively and his appointments included AOC 1 Group, 1953–6, Air Member for Personnel, 1957–9 (promoted air marshal), and Inspector-General of the RAF, 1959–62, whereupon he retired from the service. Whitley became Controller of the RAF Benevolent Fund between 1962 and 1968 and at the time of his death on Boxing Day 1997, aged ninety-two, he was the last surviving wartime RAF bomber group commander.

Air Vice-Marshal Arthur WRIGHT AFC

AOC 1 Group 1939–40

During his short tenure as AOC 1 Group, Arthur Wright witnessed the virtual annihilation of his aircrew and aircraft as the AASF in France during the desperate spring of 1940. On returning home to England in June, he relinquished command in favour of Air Commodore John Breen.

Born on 19 September 1888, Arthur Claude Wright transferred to the RAF in 1918 as a major in the Aeroplane and Seaplane Branch. His first appointment was on the staff at RAF HQ Middle East in Cairo in 1921, returning home in 1924 to a two-year posting at the Supermarine Southampton flying boat base at Calshot, Hampshire. He was promoted wing commander in 1925 and the following year took over as CO of 502 Squadron at Aldergrove, equipped with the Vickers Vimy and later the Handley Page Hyderabad, where he remained for the next three years. Two years' further training at staff college saw Wright posted overseas in January 1931 to command 205 Squadron at Seletar in Singapore, flying Southamptons. Returning home in 1933, he took the first of four staff posts that led to his promotion to air commodore and his eventual appointment as SASO 1 Group in March 1938. On the outbreak of war Wright succeeded AVM P. Playfair as group AOC and remained in command until 27 June 1940. He retired from the RAF in March 1942 and died on 23 April 1977, aged eighty-eight.

CHAPTER 11

THE MEN WHO WERE BOMBER COMMAND

In much the same way as Bomber Command was an international force of men from the far-flung corners of the empire, so too was it a remarkable confluence of great personalities and individual achievement. For some men the war was an opportunity for great adventure; for others it was a job of work that had to be done – a regrettable but unavoidable interruption to their peacetime careers. But however it was perceived, its demands and its effects left indelible and far-reaching impressions upon the lives of the thousands who spent their war with Bomber Command, be they air or groundcrew, bomber station or command headquarters staff, or Air Ministry policy-makers.

The war careers of some like Wing Commander Guy Gibson or Group Captain Charles Pickard were as shooting stars, their exploits burning bright for a brief moment before being snuffed out. Others like Michael Beetham, Ivor Broom and John Curtiss survived into the uneasy peace that followed VE-Day in 1945, rising to air rank and carving for themselves successful careers in the postwar air force.

The one-time air gunner Denholm Elliott left blue serge behind and instead channelled his efforts into bright lights and greasepaint in a wholly new and fulfilling life on stage and screen.

For 'Skeets' Kelly, who flew operationally as a cameraman with the RAF Film Unit, the love of flying stayed with him long after the war ended. He became a much sought-after aerial cameraman in the film business but died tragically in a helicopter accident during filming in Ireland.

Whatever paths these men chose to follow in the years after the war, they all share a fund of common experience – of camaraderie, danger, of survival against the odds, and of having played a part in the great events of the Second World War that have shaped our postwar world.

Ekanayake Edward AMERESEKERE (1917–74)

A native of Ceylon, Ameresekere volunteered for the RAF in September 1941 and trained as a navigator, serving with 35, 158 and 640 Squadrons. He flew in Halifaxes on fifty-two bomber operations and was demobbed in November 1946. Returning to Ceylon he spent some time as an air traffic controller at Colombo before joining the Royal Ceylon Air Force on its formation in 1951. Rising to the rank of air vice-marshal he became the first Ceylonese to command the RCeyAF from 1962 to 1971. He died in March 1974, aged fifty-seven.

Michael BEETHAM GCB, CBE, DFC, AFC, ADC (b. 1923)

In common with John Slessor, another aspiring star of wartime Bomber Command, Michael Beetham later achieved the rare distinction of becoming the professional head of the RAF.

Beetham joined the RAF in 1941 and after flying training was posted to 50 Squadron at Skellingthorpe where as a pilot he completed a tour of operations on Lancasters, and during which time he won the DFC. After a spell instructing at 5 LFS, he joined 57 Squadron at East Kirkby for a second tour a few months before the end of the war.

His postwar career included command in 1958–60 of the RAF's first air-to-air refuelling squadron, No. 214. It was during this tour flying Valiants that Beetham established the London–Capetown/ Capetown–London non-stop records which still stand. A number of senior staff appointments followed including Commandant of the RAF Staff College, Deputy C-in-C Strike Command and C-in-C RAF Germany, before he was appointed Chief of the Air Staff in 1977. By now Sir Michael Beetham GCB, CBE, DFC, AFC, ADC, he became Marshal of the RAF before eventually retiring from the service in 1982. Since then he has been Chairman of the Trustees of the RAF Museum, Hendon.

Gerry BLACKLOCK OBE, DFC, DFM (b. 1914)

On 4 August 1940 Flying Officer Gerry Blacklock DFM made RAF history in being nominated as captain of a Short Stirling I, the first monoplane four-engined heavy bomber in Bomber Command. Blacklock had already completed a first tour of operations

Gerry Blacklock DFC, DFM, Bomber Command's first captain of a four-engine monoplane heavy bomber. (Gerry Blacklock)

with 99 Squadron on Wellingtons between September 1939 and July 1940, for which he was awarded the DFM. A second tour with 7 Squadron on Stirlings – the first RAF squadron to equip with the new generation of four-engined heavy bombers – saw the award of an immediate DFC for his part in a raid against Bremen on 28 June 1941. Born near Skipton, Yorkshire, of Scottish parents, Gerry Blacklock began his RAF career as a Halton apprentice and reached the rank of group captain before his retirement from the RAF in 1961.

Ivor BROOM KCB, CBE, DSO, DFC & two Bars, AFC (b. 1920)

To rise through the ranks from sergeant pilot to air marshal is impressive, but Ivor

Broom is also among the very few (forty-two, in fact) wartime aircrew to achieve a triple DFC.

When Broom joined the RAF his first posting was to 114 Squadron as a sergeant pilot flying Blenheims in 1941. Commissioned later that year he moved to 107 Squadron before completing his tour of ops and taking up an instructor's post at 1655 Mosquito Training Unit. From 1943 to 1945 he flew Mosquitoes with 571 and 128 Squadrons of the PFF's Light Night Striking Force, and later commanded 163 Squadron, also a PFF unit. His distinguished wartime career as bomber pilot and squadron commander was marked by the award of the DFC in 1942, followed by a first bar to the decoration in 1944, then a second in 1945, and a DSO.

The peak of his postwar RAF career came in 1970 with his appointment as AOC 11 (Fighter) Group, Strike Command. Sir Ivor retired from the RAF in 1972 to pursue a second career with the Civil Aviation Authority.

Leonard CHESHIRE VC, OM, DSO, DFC (1917–92)

Born in Chester on 7 September 1917, Leonard Cheshire was one of those rare individuals who went on to achieve so much in both war and peace and upon whom was bestowed the two highest awards for valour and merit that are in the gift of a British sovereign: the Victoria Cross and the Order of Merit. His outstanding career as a bomber pilot between 1940 and 1944 was rewarded with the VC, DSO and two bars, and the DFC. Unusually, his VC was awarded not for a single act but for four years of valour, his citation underlining 'a record second to none in Bomber Command'.

His first posting was to 102 Squadron in June 1940 and promotion followed swiftly to squadron commander of 76 Squadron in

Unusually, Leonard Cheshire's award of the VC was not for a single act but for four years of valour, his citation underlining 'a record second to none in Bomber Command'.

August 1942. In March 1943 at the age of twenty-five, he became the youngest group captain in the RAF, commanding the bomber station at Marston Moor in Yorkshire. So that he could return to an operational flying command, he later reverted to the rank of wing commander and the command of 617 Squadron in November 1943. He personally developed the squadron's low-level marking techniques and as a result 617 Squadron achieved a bombing accuracy that was the envy of the Pathfinders. Cheshire was taken off operations in July 1944 and on 15 August 1945 was official British observer of the second A-bomb to be dropped on Japan. This cataclysmic event became a defining moment in his life and eventually led to his single-minded devotion in peacetime to the care of the physically handicapped and incurably ill. With his second wife Sue Ryder, he founded the Cheshire Homes for the disabled which today number more than 270 in Britain and in fifty countries abroad. Leonard Cheshire died on 31 July 1992, aged seventy-four.

Peter CLAPHAM DFC & Bar
A fighter controller declared medically unfit for operational flying duties, by the war's end Peter Clapham had flown nearly seventy operations and had been awarded the DFC and bar, although without aircrew status or pay.

Clapham had been personally selected in 1941 by Wing Commander Basil Embry (later AVM and AOC 2 Group) to be his regular AI operator/navigator. Despite his official status as an administrative branch officer, this unique aircrew partnership continued until the end of the war, but it was not until 1945 that Clapham received official recognition as a navigator from the Air Ministry.

Syd CLAYTON DSO, DFC, DFM (1916–76)
As a 24-year-old sergeant navigator, Syd Clayton joined 107 Squadron in 1940 and went on to achieve seventy-two ops in Blenheims at a time of the war when this was virtually unheard of, winning the DFM. He was commissioned in 1941 and instructed for a short while before joining 105 Squadron in June 1942, the first RAF squadron to equip with the de Havilland Mosquito. With his pilot from the Blenheim days, Roy Ralston, Clayton flew a further twenty-eight bomber ops on Mosquitoes before completing his 100th on 1 April 1943. By now a veteran with the DSO, DFC and DFM to his name, he left 105 Squadron to undergo pilot training. In August 1944 Clayton was posted to 464 (RAAF) Squadron

in 2nd Tactical Air Force and flew in Mosquitoes once more, this time in the pilot's seat, completing a further forty-six ops which brought his total by the war's end to 146.

After the war, Clayton left the RAF and ran a hotel in Morecambe for some years before acquiring a chain of newsagents. These he sold in 1971 and joined the civil service, but died five years later in tragic circumstances.

Iliffe COZENS CB, AFC (1904–95)
When Air Commodore Iliffe Cozens was station commander at RAF Hemswell in the winter of 1943/4 at the height of the battle of Berlin, he made a 16mm colour film which he called *Night Bombers*, shot on a clockwork camera and which followed a real bombing raid on Berlin, from take-off to landing. It was intended to help new crews gain some idea of what bombing operations were actually like. The film remained unknown to the public at large until in 1978, after release from the restrictions of the thirty-year rule, and with a soundtrack and commentary added by a BBC producer, it was shown on BBC television. The film is unique in being shot, directed and edited by Cozens, and on colour film stock which was virtually unavailable in Britain during the war.

Alec CRANSWICK DSO, DFC (1919–44)
Killed in action, aged twenty-four
After the war, Air Vice-Marshal Donald Bennett, commander of the Pathfinder Force, described Alec Cranswick as 'not a flamboyant roistering character but simply a quiet honest Englishman . . . so simply courageous and so selfless in his sacrifice'. This modest Englishman flew four operational bomber tours – two as a Pathfinder – but was killed on his 107th sortie.

Alec Cranswick defied the odds by flying four tours of operations as a bomber pilot, two of them as a Pathfinder. He was killed on his 107th sortie.

Volunteering for the RAF in 1939, Alec Cranswick joined his first operational unit in June 1940 and completed twenty-nine operations with 214 Squadron flying Wellingtons. He later volunteered for duties in the Middle East where he was posted to 148 Squadron and also spent a short spell ferrying aircraft in West Africa. He returned to England in April 1942, as a flight lieutenant DFC, and was posted to 419 (Moose) Squadron, but flew only five sorties before volunteering for the Pathfinders. Joining 35 (PFF) Squadron at Graveley, he flew thirty sorties (his ninety-sixth overall) before being rested for six months at PFF headquarters, but returned to 35 (PFF) Squadron in April 1944 for a fourth tour. On the night of 4/5 July, Squadron Leader Cranswick's crew was acting as deputy master bomber when their Lancaster was hit by flak after bombing the rail marshalling yards at Villeneuve St Georges. Severely damaged, it was not long before the main spar snapped and the aircraft disintegrated in flames before crashing to earth. Only the wireless operator survived.

John CURTISS (b. 1922)
Educated at Radley and Worcester College Oxford, John Curtiss joined the RAF in 1942 and served as a sergeant navigator flying in Halifaxes with 578 and 158 Squadrons in 1944–5. After the war he took a permanent commission in the RAF and saw service with Transport, Training and Fighter Commands between 1946 and 1964, followed by a number of staff appointments. He eventually rose to the rank of air marshal before his retirement from the service in 1983.

As AOC 18 Group from 1980 to 1983, Sir John Curtiss, as he had now become, was in overall command of all RAF air operations in the South Atlantic during the Falklands conflict in 1982.

Roberts DUNSTAN DSO (1923–89)
Roberts Dunstan was the only Australian air gunner to receive the DSO during the Second World War, and probably the only Commonwealth air gunner to be so honoured. He was also an amputee.

Having lost his right leg in the first siege of Tobruk in 1941 while serving as a sapper with the Australian Imperial Force in North Africa, Roberts Dunstan was invalided home to his native Australia where he was medically discharged from the Army. However, he soon found civilian life dull and persuaded the RAAF to accept him for aircrew training in 1942. Dunstan joined 460 (RAAF) Squadron as a tail gunner flying Lancasters from Binbrook, with which he completed a full tour of thirty ops commencing in June 1943. In

Roberts Dunstan was the only Australian air gunner to receive the DSO during the Second World War. He was also an amputee. (Victor Doree via Don Darbyshire)

Denholm ELLIOTT (1922–92)

Better known for his postwar role as a star of stage and screen, Denholm Elliott enjoyed a brief wartime career as a sergeant wireless operator/air gunner with 76 Squadron, under the command of Wing Commander Leonard Cheshire.

It was on 23/24 September 1942 that Elliott's crew was one of several from 76 Squadron that took part in a raid on the German U-boat pens at Flensburg. Descending through low cloud to bomb the target, Elliott's Halifax II was hit by flak on its bomb run which later caused it to ditch in the North Sea near Sylt. Elliott survived the ordeal with two other crew members to spend the rest of the war as a POW at Stalag VIIIB, Lamsdorff, in Upper Silesia.

Born on 31 May 1922, Denholm Mitchell Elliott was educated at Malvern and as a POW in Germany during the Second World War he became involved in amateur dramatics. Repatriated at the war's end, his acting career began to flourish and his first stage appearance came in *The Guinea Pig* at The Criterion in 1946; three years later he landed his first film role in *Sound Barrier*. At the time of his death aged seventy from an AIDS-related illness at his home on Ibiza on 6 October 1992, Elliott had risen to become a highly acclaimed international actor of stage and screen, with almost forty feature films to his credit (including *Alfie, A Room with a View* and *Raiders of the Lost Ark*), not to mention dozens of stage appearances. He was also the winner of many richly deserved BAFTA awards for best film actor.

Basil EMBRY KBE, DSO & two Bars, DFC, AFC (1902–77)

As an energetic, untiring squadron and group commander with little time for bureaucracy and Air Ministry red tape, or for those who did everything 'by the book', Basil Embry was looked up to by those

October that year he was commissioned and awarded the DSO two months later. Dunstan was fêted by the British and Australian wartime press and returned home to a hero's welcome.

He pursued a very full postwar career and served as a Liberal Party Member in the State of Victoria from 1956 to 1982, and as a Minister from 1970 to 1978. Dunstan was also something of a newspaper film critic, reviewing some 2,500 movies over a period of nineteen years. He died in Melbourne in 1989, aged sixty-six.

under his command as an inspiring leader of men.

Flying one final sortie on 26 May 1940 before he was due to be grounded, Wing Commander Basil Embry led his squadron of Blenheims to bomb German troops advancing on the beleaguered British forces holed up in Dunkirk. On the bomb run, Embry's Blenheim was hit by light flak which killed his gunner and forced Embry and his observer to bale out. Embry was captured by the Germans but succeeded in escaping and was then on the run for two months in occupied Europe, eventually making good his escape to England via Spain and Gibraltar. His adventures are related in *Wingless Victory* by Anthony Richardson (Odhams, 1950) who was adjutant of 107 Squadron at the time.

Embry moved to Fighter Command as Sector Commander at Wittering before secondment to the Desert Air Force from October 1941 to March 1942, and on return resumed his command at Wittering before appointment as SASO at 10 Group Fighter Command. On 27 May 1943 he was given command of 2 Group Bomber Command shortly before it was transferred to 2nd Tactical Air Force. As an air vice-marshal he still led from the front, flying on numerous operations as 'Wing Commander Smith', and being closely involved with the planning and execution of many low-level precision attacks on key targets. After the war he became C-in-C Fighter Command from 1949 to 1953 and retired from the RAF in 1956.

Richard ENGLAND DSO, DFC (1916–43)
Killed in action aged twenty-seven
Wing Commander R.G. 'Dickie' England DFC assumed command of 107 Squadron on 10 April 1943 which at the time was flying Bostons from Great Massingham with 2 Group. Born in the same year as the infamous battle of the Somme, England's family roots were, paradoxically, in the Welsh valleys at Lisvane, Glamorgan. He became a highly regarded bomber squadron commander who led by example and met his death on the afternoon of 22 October 1943, leading his squadron in a low-level attack on an aero-engine repair works at Courcelles in Belgium. Flying in his personal Boston bearing the inscription 'ENGLAND EXPECTS' below the cockpit window, his aircraft took a direct hit from flak and flew into the ground shortly after crossing the Dutch coast. Ironically, the next day his award of the DSO was gazetted, the citation paying tribute to his 'inspiring leadership, great courage and exceptional skill'. Sir Basil Embry later wrote of England: 'His loss is a severe blow to the whole Group. He was a great leader who commanded universal respect and admiration.'

Howard FARMILOE DSO (b. 1922)
As a 22-year-old pilot officer with 61 Squadron, Howard Farmiloe was one of the most junior commissioned officer in the RAF to be awarded the DSO during the Second World War, for a feat of bravery and determination that could easily have ended in disaster for him and his crew.

On the last raid of the battle of Berlin on 24/25 March 1944, Farmiloe was captain of Lancaster 'H-Hellzapoppin' that suffered an engine failure outward bound over the North Sea. On his bomb run the second engine on the same wing failed, but he managed to bomb on target from 18,500ft before setting a course for home. With one of the two damaged engines on fire, 'Hellzapoppin' became difficult to hold straight and level and height was lost. Ken Vowe, the bomb-aimer, spent three hours with his arm locked around the starboard rudder pedal to help Farmiloe control the

Dickie England (third from right), the inspirational leader of 107 Squadron, was killed leading his squadron of Bostons on a daylight sortie on 22 October 1943. (via Martin W. Bowman)

badly damaged Lancaster which was side-slipping and continuing to lose height. Against the odds they made it home to a successful emergency landing at Little Snoring at 2.15 a.m. For his fortitude Farmiloe was awarded an immediate DSO, his bomb-aimer Ken Vowe and wireless operator Eddie Davidson each received a well-deserved DFM, and the navigator a bar to his DFC. After the war was over, Howard Farmiloe left the RAF to become a chartered surveyor and auctioneer.

Johnny FAUQUIER DSO & two Bars, DFC (d. 1981)

Probably the most celebrated Canadian bomber pilot of the war, from April 1943

Fauquier commanded 405 (Vancouver) Squadron – the Canadian PFF squadron – and as a group captain was given command of 617 Squadron in December 1944. A tough CO and a former Canadian bush pilot, Fauquier was remembered by Hamish Mahaddie as 'giving me the most trouble by returning more potential Pathfinders than any other CO . . . Johnny was surely the Billy Bishop of World War 2. Only the war ending when it did denied him the highest award.'

James Fraser BARRON DSO & Bar, DFC, DFM (1921–44)
Killed in action aged twenty-three

Flying his 79th sortie on 19/20 May 1944 as master bomber against the rail marshalling

One of the most junior commissioned officers in the RAF to be awarded the DSO during the Second World War, Howard Farmiloe nursed his seriously damaged Lancaster home from Berlin on 25 March 1944, to make a successful emergency landing in England. (Howard Farmiloe)

March 1942 after completing his first tour and spent a time instructing before joining 7 Squadron as a Pathfinder in September of the same year. Barron completed a second tour on Stirlings with the squadron in February 1943, followed by nine months of instructional duties before he returned to 7 Squadron as a flight commander with the rank of squadron leader. Promoted to wing commander in February 1944, when the CO Wing Commander W.G. Lockhart was killed in action on 27/28 April, Barron was appointed to take his place. When he too was killed less than a month later, the squadron had lost three COs in as many months.

Guy GIBSON VC, DSO & Bar, DFC & Bar (1918–44)
Killed in action aged twenty-six

Alongside Leonard Cheshire, Guy Gibson is probably the most famous RAF bomber pilot of all time. Precocious, arrogant, and with an unrelenting enthusiasm for operations, he went on to win undying fame for his role leading the attack on the Ruhr dams in May 1943 for which he was awarded the VC. Gibson flew operationally from the day war was declared completing 177 operational sorties, with few breaks, up until his final fateful flight in September 1944.

Born on 12 August 1918, he was commissioned into the RAF in 1937 and his first posting was to 83 Squadron as a bomber pilot. His early career in the service was undistinguished but the war was to change all of that. Completing his first tour in August 1940, Gibson was posted to instruct at an OTU before transferring to Fighter Command and a posting to 29 Squadron flying Beaufighter nightfighters. In ninety-nine operational sorties he claimed three enemy aircraft destroyed and was promoted to squadron leader with a bar to his DFC on completion of his tour in December 1941. A short spell instructing was followed by a

yards at Le Mans, Wing Commander James Fraser Barron DSO, DFC, DFM, met his death, possibly as the result of a mid-air collision. Group Captain Hamish Mahaddie, group training inspector for the Pathfinders, was later to comment that he would question if anyone in the Command had amassed the operational experience of James Fraser Barron in such a relatively short time.

Born at Dunedin in New Zealand on 9 January 1921, Barron enlisted in the RNZAF in 1940 and trained as a pilot. He travelled to England where he completed his training and joined 15 Squadron at Wyton in June 1941, flying Stirlings. He was commissioned in

Pictured here when commander of 106 Squadron, Guy Gibson won fame and the VC for leading 617 Squadron on the epic dams raid of 16/17 May 1943. (US National Archives)

posting back to Bomber Command and the command of 106 Squadron. He completed his second bomber tour in March 1943 as a wing commander, DSO and Bar, DFC and Bar, before he was told to form 617 Squadron on 21 March. He led nineteen Lancasters on the famous dams raid on 16/17 May, in which the Möhne and Eder dams were successfully breached, but eight Lancasters failed to return. Gibson was awarded the VC and remained with the squadron until August when he was officially taken off operations.

Between then and D-Day he became a celebrity figure at home and in the USA, a protégé of Winston Churchill, a prospective Conservative Party candidate for Macclesfield, and the author of what later became a best-selling account of the bomber air war, *Enemy Coast Ahead*. However, he was desperate to get back to operational flying and in September 1944 Harris finally relented and granted him one final sortie. Gibson piloted a 627 Squadron Mosquito as master bomber in a raid on Rheydt and Mönchengladbach on 19 September, but on the return journey his aircraft inexplicably flew into the ground and exploded, killing Gibson and his navigator Squadron Leader James Warwick.

Ronald IVELAW-CHAPMAN GCB, KBE, DFC, AFC (1899–1978)

In May 1944 Air Commodore Ronald Ivelaw-Chapman became the most senior RAF officer to be taken prisoner while serving in Bomber Command. Because of his knowledge of the D-Day plans, gained during a spell as a staff officer in 1943, Churchill ordered the French Resistance to do all they could to help him return to England – but to kill him if he was in danger of capture by the Germans, fearing he might give the game away if interrogated by the Gestapo.

'Chaps' joined the RFC in 1917 and trained as a pilot, seeing service over the Western Front in the closing eleven months of war with 10 Squadron, flying Bristol Fighters. Twenty-two years later at the outbreak of the Second World War, now a wing commander, he found himself on the operations staff at Bomber Command headquarters, but in June 1940 was promoted to group captain and given command of the 4 Group bomber airfield at Linton-on-Ouse. In 1941 Chaps returned to the Air Ministry as a staff officer where he became involved in planning for D-Day. There he remained until posted to Lincolnshire late in 1943 to become Base Commander at Elsham Wolds, in 1 Group.

On 6/7 May 1944, Chaps flew as second pilot with a 576 Squadron Lancaster crew against the ammunition dump at Aubigne, 25 miles north of Le Mans, but his aircraft was shot down by a nightfighter. He was on the run for a month, watched over by the Resistance, but was captured by the Gestapo on 8 June. Luckily, Churchill's worries were unfounded because the Germans never realised his importance and treated him as an ordinary POW.

After the war, Chaps rose to the rank of air chief marshal and was appointed Vice-Chief of the Air Staff in 1952, finally retiring from the service in 1957.

'Skeets' KELLY DFC (1914–70)

As a flying officer film cameraman with the RAF Film Unit, Skeets Kelly's dramatic footage of 2 Group's daring low-level daylight attack on the Philips factory at Eindhoven on 6 December 1942, shot from an 88 Squadron Boston, made newsreel history when it was screened in cinemas across the land.

Kelly began his film career with British & Dominion Studios at Elstree as a junior camera assistant before the war. By 1940 he was camera operator to the famous Director of Photography Freddie Young and worked with him on the movie *The 49th Parallel*. Joining the RAF Film Unit after war broke out, Kelly flew on twenty-three bomber operations with a number of different squadrons in 2 Group before he was shot down on 27 August 1943, his twenty-fourth op. Flying as a cameraman in a 107 Squadron Boston skippered by Flying Officer Jim Allison, their target was the electrical power station at Gosnay in northern France. From the moment they crossed the enemy coast, they were involved in a running fight with German Focke Wulf Fw 190 fighters that trailed them all the way to Gosnay. Allison managed to bomb the target from very low level before turning for home, but the enemy fighters finally succeeded in bringing the badly damaged bomber down in a grain field. Miraculously none of the crew was hurt and all evaded successfully, except for Kelly who was later captured by the Germans and spent the rest of the war as a POW. When he was repatriated at the war's end and returned home, he discovered that he had been awarded the DFC.

Kelly's postwar career in the film industry with MGM saw him become a most experienced, skilful and sought-after airborne cinematographer. Moving on to Second Unit work, he was camera operator

As a film cameraman with the RAF Film Unit, 'Skeets' Kelly flew on twenty-three daylight bomber operations with 2 Group before he was shot down and made a POW. After the war he returned to the film business and became a much sought-after airborne cinematographer. He is pictured here (extreme left) during the making of *The Battle of Britain* (1969).

to Freddie Young on *Lawrence of Arabia* (1962) and one of two cameramen who shot the dramatic flying sequences for *The Battle of Britain* (1969). Skeets Kelly died tragically on 18 August 1970 while filming for *Zeppelin* off the Irish coast. A replica SE5A biplane crashed into the camera helicopter in which he was flying, killing him and three others.

J. Gilles LAMONTAGNE

A sergeant pilot with the French-Canadian manned 425 (Alouette) Squadron in Bomber Command's 6 (RCAF) Group, Lamontagne was captain of a Wellington bomber that was shot down by a nightfighter while returning from a raid on Essen on 12/13 March 1943. The aircraft crashed in Holland and all survived to become POWs, but Lamontagne managed to evade capture for several days before he too was apprehended by the Germans, spending the rest of the war in a POW camp. When after the war details were learned of his actions to save his crew by bringing the blazing bomber down to a crash-landing, he was mentioned in dispatches. After the war Lamontagne entered politics and thirty-five years later, following the 1980 general election in Canada, he was appointed Canadian Minister of National Defence.

Jimmy MARKS DSO, DFC (1922–42)
Killed in action aged twenty

'A brilliant pilot, a wonderful leader and a man that this country could not afford to lose' was how Jimmy Marks's flight engineer remembered him. Wing Commander J.H. Marks DSO, DFC was a pre-war regular and a veteran of the early years of the bomber offensive. He became the first CO of one of the four founder squadrons of the Pathfinder Force to be lost on operations. Marks was commanding 35 (PFF) Squadron when his Halifax was shot down over the Marne on 19/20 September 1942 by a nightfighter, killing him and two other crew members. He was succeeded in command by Wing Commander Basil Robinson.

Hamish MAHADDIE DSO, DFC, AFC, CZMC (1911–97)

In February 1943, Wing Commander Hamish Mahaddie received the DSO, DFC, AFC and Czech Military Cross in the same ceremony at Buckingham Palace – surely an RAF record. A short, stocky Scot from Edinburgh, Mahaddie joined the RAF as part of the 17th Entry at Halton in 1928. He trained as a pilot in the Middle East and gained his wings in 1935. During the Second World War he completed two tours of operations as a bomber pilot, the first with 77 Squadron flying Whitleys, and the second with 7 Squadron on Stirlings, before joining the headquarters staff of the Pathfinder Force. His job as Don Bennett's 'horse thief' was to find, select and train future Pathfinder crews from the main force squadrons. It was his skill in selecting crews that helped make the Pathfinder Force the elite band that it had become by the war's end.

After the war Hamish helped introduce the Canberra bomber into RAF service and upon his retirement in 1958, as a group captain, he acted as a technical adviser to the British film industry. His terrific sense of

It was the skill of Hamish Mahaddie, Don Bennett's 'horse thief', in finding, selecting and training future Pathfinder crews that helped make the Pathfinder Force so successful.

humour and legendary storytelling skills concealed a deep-rooted commitment to the RAF and a lifelong loyalty to his Pathfinder 'boss' Don Bennett. He died on 16 January 1997, aged eighty-five.

Mick MARTIN KCB, DSO, DFC & two Bars, AFC (1918–88)

As an operational bomber pilot, Mick Martin was regarded by none other than Leonard Cheshire as 'the greatest that the Air Force ever produced'. Born in New South Wales on 27 February 1918, Martin joined the RAF in England in 1940 and trained as a pilot. His first operational posting was to 455 Squadron RAAF in October 1941, although he completed his first tour with 50 Squadron. Personally selected by Wing Commander Guy Gibson to join his newly formed 617 Squadron for his low-flying skills, Martin flew on the Ruhr dams raid in May and survived to be given temporary command of the squadron on Gibson's departure. When Wing Commander Leonard Cheshire was appointed CO in the summer of 1943, Martin continued to build an enviable reputation as a low-level bombing specialist flying Lancasters, but was eventually taken off operations after a 'dicey do' on a sortie to the Antheor viaduct on 12/13 February 1944. Flying a desk at group headquarters was not for him, however, and he soon talked his way back into operations, flying Mosquito intruder sorties with 515 Squadron from Little Snoring. He was taken off operations for the last time in late 1944, having flown a total of eighty-three sorties, and was awarded a second bar to his DFC. He remained in the RAF after the war and retired in 1974 as Air Marshal Sir Harold Martin.

Andrew McPHERSON DFC (1918–40)
Killed in action aged twenty-two

A Scot from the city of Glasgow, Flying Officer Andrew McPherson DFC was the pilot of the first British aircraft of the Second World War to cross the German coast. On 4 September 1939, flying Blenheim N6125 of 139 Squadron, he was tasked with photographing the German fleet north of the port of Wilhelmshaven. His crew on this occasion included observer Commander Thompson RN and gunner Corporal Vincent Arrowsmith; the latter was dead before the month was out, killed on a reconnaissance flight.

McPherson was to lose his own life on 12 May 1940 bombing German armoured columns near Lanaken in Belgium, flying the very aircraft in which he had made

Andrew McPherson was the pilot of the first British aircraft to cross the German coast in the Second World War, flying a Blenheim IV of 139 Squadron. He is pictured here before the war in RAF full dress uniform. (Scottish Media Newspapers Ltd)

history eight months before. He was shot down on the way to the target area soon after first light by a swarm of Me 109s which were waiting for his squadron. By the day's end 139 Squadron had suffered grievous losses of seven aircraft and fifteen men.

Derrick NABARRO DCM

As a young sergeant pilot, Derrick Nabarro became a POW after his 10 Squadron Whitley was shot down by flak over Kiel Bay in the early hours of 28 June 1941. After six hours adrift in a dinghy he and the three other surviving crew members were rescued from the sea by the Germans and taken prisoner. Nabarro refused to remain captive

In recognition of his successful escape from a German POW camp in 1941, Sgt Plt Derrick Nabarro of 10 Squadron became the first RAF recipient of the Distinguished Conduct Medal (DCM).

As a warrant officer navigator with 15 Squadron in 1941, Richard Pape was shot down over Holland and spent the next three years evading and escaping from German POW camps. He was tortured and eventually repatriated to England on health grounds. In 1965 he returned his Military Medal (MM) to the Queen as a protest against the award of the MBE to the Beatles.

and escaped, making his way across occupied Europe to Gibraltar, and ultimately to England and freedom. He wrote a gripping account of his escape which was published in 1952 under the title *Wait for the Dawn*. Nabarro became the first RAF recipient of the DCM in recognition of his successful escape.

Richard PAPE, MM (1916–95)

A tough, red-headed Yorkshireman, Richard Pape began his career on the *Yorkshire Post* but joined the RAF on the outbreak of war. He trained as a navigator and joined 15 Squadron at Wyton but his Stirling was shot down by flak returning from Berlin on 7/8 September 1941 and crashed on the Dutch–German border. He evaded with the

help of the Dutch Resistance but was later captured and became a prisoner-of-war. He escaped twice and was recaptured twice, but after the second attempt he was subjected to severe torture by his captors. Eventually he was repatriated on health grounds, almost three years to the day after he had been shot down.

After the war, he turned his exploits as an escaped prisoner into a best-selling book, *Boldness be my Friend*, which was published in 1952. Pape was something of an eccentric and an adventurer, driving from the northern tip of Norway to Cape Town in 1955 in an Austin. He described his experiences along the way in *Cape Cold to Cape Hot*. In 1965 he returned his Military Medal to the Queen as a protest against the award of the MBE to the Beatles. He died in Australia on 19 June 1995, aged seventy-nine.

Peter PAYNTER CB (1898–1998)

As chief intelligence officer at Bomber Command headquarters between 1942 and 1945, Air Commodore Peter Paynter was a key member of Bomber Harris's staff and

Peter Paynter was a key member of Bomber Harris's staff and his reports lay behind many of the RAF's raids on German cities in this period. At the end of the war he became Director of Intelligence at the Air Ministry. (IWM CH20032)

his reports lay behind many of the RAF's raids on German cities in this period. He insisted to the end that intelligence sources had led him to believe that the Germans were stockpiling munitions in historic towns like Dresden in the belief that the Allies would never bomb them. Paynter established a close working relationship with Harris and at the end of the war he became Director of Intelligence at the Air Ministry. His loyalty to his old boss was such that, when the Attlee government refused to give Harris a place at the victory celebrations, he resigned his commission in protest. However, he was soon found another job, as a director of MI5, where he remained as a senior officer until his retirement in 1962. Peter Paynter died on 16 March 1998, aged ninety-nine.

'Percy' PICKARD DSO & two Bars, DFC (1915–44)
Killed in action aged twenty-eight

'Percy' Pickard is remembered primarily for his leadership on the Amiens prison raid on 18 February 1944, when he met his death, but he is also associated with the wartime film *Target for Tonight* (1941, Dir. Harry Watt) as the skipper of Wellington 'F for Freddie'. He was a pre-war regular pilot, joining 214 Squadron in September 1937 and serving on a succession of bomber squadrons (Nos 7, 99, 311, 9) until his appointment as CO of 51 Squadron in November 1941, with almost seventy ops to his credit. Under his expert direction, the squadron played an important part in the daring Combined Operations plan to capture key parts of a German *Würzburg* radar apparatus from Bruneval in northern France on 27/28 February 1942, when Whitleys of his squadron dropped 119 paratroops onto the radar site. The operation was a success and Pickard was awarded a well-deserved bar to his DSO,

Charles 'Percy' Pickard had a very full war before he met his death on the famous Amiens prison raid in February 1944. He had flown almost seventy bomber operations by late 1941, starred in the docu-drama *Target for Tonight* that same year and played a key part in the daring Bruneval raid in 1942. Pickard flew dozens of special duties sorties from Tempsford before moving on to command in turn several bomber squadrons, a bomber station and a wing in 2nd Tactical Air Force. He is pictured here in 1943 when commanding RAF Sculthorpe, accompanied by his dog Ming. (IWM CH10251)

originally awarded for his work with 311 Squadron.

After a short spell with 61 Squadron, Pickard was posted to 161 Squadron at Tempsford in October 1942, the secret 'cloak-and-dagger' airfield in Bedfordshire ferrying Allied agents to and from occupied Europe. He flew dozens of special duties sorties from Tempsford before receiving promotion to group captain in July 1943 and a posting to command the light bomber station at RAF Sculthorpe in Norfolk. In October he was appointed commander of

140 Wing in the newly formed 2nd Tactical Air Force, comprising three Mosquito squadrons and tasked with low-level precision bombing in daylight.

It was leading a special operation early the following year that had been requested by senior members of the French Resistance, that Pickard was killed in action. Operation 'Jericho' was the code name given to the daring plan to breach the walls of Amiens jail in northern France by low-level precision bombing, thereby releasing dozens of imprisoned Resistance fighters facing certain execution by the Gestapo. The operation by three squadrons of Mosquitos of 140 Wing was a success and 400 prisoners poured through the breached walls, 258 making good their escape. Leaving the target, Pickard's Mosquito was attacked from behind by a Focke-Wulf Fw190 fighter and shot down, killing him and his navigator Bill Broadley.

Basil ROBINSON DSO, DFC & Bar (1912–43)
Killed in action aged thirty-one

When fire broke out in the bomb bay of his 35 (PFF) Squadron Halifax II over the Alps on 18 November 1942, Wing Commander Basil Robinson DSO, DFC, ordered his crew to bale out. Just as he prepared to make his exit he noticed the flames had died away. Returning to the cockpit, 'Robbie', as he was known on the squadron, flew the Halifax home single-handedly to make a successful landing in England during the early hours of the 19th, for which he received a bar to his DFC.

Born in Gateshead in 1913, Basil Vernon Robinson was commissioned into the RAF in 1933, quickly establishing for himself a reputation as a fine rugby player. His oppo John Searby recalled him as 'not one for talking much – unless the subject was rugby football . . . he was a convinced Pathfinder and believed it was the only solution to the problem of getting bombs on the target'. Robinson was promoted to group captain and appointed station commander at Graveley. He lost his life on the first night of the battle of Berlin, 23/24 August 1943, when he flew to the 'Big City' as second pilot to a 35 (PFF) Squadron crew and was shot down by a nightfighter.

Vivian ROSEWARNE (1916–40)
Killed in action aged twenty-four

The anonymous author of 'An Airman's Letter to his Mother' published in *The Times* in June 1940, Vivian Rosewarne was one of the small band of RAF aircrew with a regular commission on the outbreak of war in 1939. Born in London in 1916, he joined the RAF in 1937 and was posted to 38 Squadron at Marham in March the following year. He flew fifteen bombing sorties in Wellingtons as a flying officer pilot before being shot down and killed over Belgium on 30 May 1940.

His posthumously published letter, intended to be given to his mother in the event of him failing to return from operations, was intercepted by his station commander at Marham, Group Captain Hilton Keith, and with the permission of Rosewarne's mother it was published in *The Times* on 18 June 1940. The letter captured the patriotic fervour of those desperate times and achieved massive acclaim both in Britain and overseas. By the year's end more than 500,000 copies of the letter had been reprinted, reproduced as a four-page leaflet. But not until long after the war had ended was Rosewarne finally identified as the author of this celebrated letter.

However, doubt has since been expressed in some quarters that he was actually the true author of the letter; and it has also been alleged that he was an active member of Oswald Mosley's Blackshirts during the mid-1930s.

Sir Robert SAUNDBY KCB, MC, DFC (1896–1971)

Appointed Senior Air Staff Officer at Bomber Command in 1940, Bob Saundby later became the right-hand man to Bomber Harris following the latter's appointment as commander-in-chief in 1942. Saundby had been a pilot with the RFC in the First World War and had been awarded the MC for shooting down an enemy airship. As a squadron leader he was awarded the DFC for gallantry during the troubles in Aden in 1925. By 1939 he was Director of Operational Requirements at the Air

An eccentric English gentleman, Sir Robert Saundby became Harris's right-hand man following the latter's appointment as C-in-C Bomber Command in 1942.

John STRACHEY PC, MP (1901–63)

The Labour politician and political writer John Strachey, educated at Eton and Magdalen College, is perhaps better remembered as the man who introduced postwar bread rationing and for his close links with the ill-fated ground nuts scheme in East Africa, than for his wartime confrontation with Bomber Harris. As a squadron leader on a temporary commission during the Second World War, he held an important appointment in the Air Ministry's Directorate of Bombing Operations.

Before the war Strachey had been Labour MP for Aston, but in 1931 followed Sir Oswald Mosley when he left the Labour Party to form his New Party. Concluding that the new body was too Fascist in its leanings and that he was on the wrong side of the political divide, Strachey became a Marxist. On the advice of the leader of the British Communist Party, Palme Dutt, he became a clandestine communist and maintained contact with communist leaders including those in the Russian Embassy in London.

Strachey joined the RAF in 1940 and was posted to the Air Ministry as a public relations officer in the Directorate of Bombing Operations. In this role he made a series of official radio broadcasts explaining the life and background of the men who flew on operations with Bomber Command. At this time Bomber Harris was becoming concerned about the possible internal security risks posed to his command. Following a tip-off from a member of his staff who identified Strachey as a person with an unstable political background, Harris demanded that the Air Ministry remove him at once, but thanks presumably to friends in high places, Strachey remained where he was and this fact aggravated Harris for the rest of the war.

Ministry and became Deputy AOC-in-C Bomber Command in 1943. He retired in 1946 as an air marshal.

Born on 26 April 1896, the son of a physician, Bob Saundby was an eccentric English gentleman, placid and mild-mannered with an eye for detail and a tremendous support for his chief. However, he was totally in awe of Harris and never made a decision without first consulting him. Saundby was an accomplished fly fisherman and it was this interest that led him to code-name every German city with the name of a fish – Berlin, for example was Whitebait, Nuremburg was Grayling. He died on 25 September 1971, aged seventy-five.

When the new Labour government under Clement Attlee came to power at the end of the war, Lord Stansgate (formerly William Wedgwood Benn, the wartime Director of Public Relations at the Air Ministry) became Secretary of State for Air and John Strachey was appointed his Under-Secretary. It is alleged that Strachey then set about destroying the reputation of Bomber Command and its wartime leader in revenge for Harris's treatment of him during the war.

In a letter to Brendan Bracken in April 1952, Harris wrote: 'It has always infuriated me, but never surprised me, that in pursuit of his personal spites and vengeance on my person that turncoat Strachey would willingly smear those fine [bomber] boys as a whole – after all they suffered, and all they achieved for England.'

Sir Gus WALKER GCB, CBE, DSO, DFC, AFC, MA (1912–86)

'He [Gus Walker] possessed first-hand knowledge of the fears, frustrations and fatigue which were the almost daily portion of the bomber crews. He spoke our language and dealt with our problems accordingly.' This was how one of his pilots, John Searby, recalled him. In 1943, at the age of thirty, he became the youngest air commodore in the RAF. (The only other youngster promoted to air rank at this time was the AOC 8 (PFF) Group, Don Bennett, who was two years Walker's senior.)

As a group captain commanding RAF station Syerston, Walker lost his right arm when a blazing Lancaster exploded next to the perimeter track on 8 December 1942. On seeing the fire from his vantage point in the control tower, he climbed aboard a fire tender and drove to the burning Lancaster. Walker began to rake away the burning incendiaries from beneath the aircraft's bomb bay in a courageous – but futile – attempt to try and prevent the 4,000lb 'cookie' from detonating. Without warning it exploded, seriously injuring Walker and killing one of the fire crew. Yet, within two months Walker was back on duty again as Syerston's station commander.

He later became air commodore commanding 42 Base at Pocklington and finally retired from the RAF as an air chief marshal.

Sir Arnold WILSON KCIIE, CSI, CMG, DSO (1884–1940)
Killed in action aged fifty-six

Late in the evening of 31 May 1940, air gunner Pilot Officer Sir Arnold Wilson was killed when his 37 Squadron Wellington crashed near Eringhem, south of Dunkirk, probably the victim of flak. In so doing, at the age of fifty-six he became probably the oldest and most highly decorated RAF airman to die on operations during the whole of the Second World War.

The son of a clergyman, Wilson's military career had begun when he graduated from the Royal Military College, Sandhurst in 1903 where he was awarded the King's Medal and Sword of Honour. Commissioned into the 32nd Sikh Pioneers of the Indian Army, he eventually rose to the rank of lieutenant-colonel. Before volunteering for aircrew duties in the RAF in October 1939 Wilson had enjoyed a distinguished career in the Indian Political Department and was appointed Deputy Civil Commissioner of India in 1916, followed in 1920 by a knighthood in recognition of his political services to the British Empire. Further diplomatic service postings took him to Persia and he later became something of an expert

At fifty-six, Sir Arnold Wilson (extreme right) became probably the oldest and most highly decorated RAF airman to die on operations during the whole of the Second World War. He is seen here before the war in his capacity as Conservative MP for Hitchin at a presentation to the Labour politician Herbert Morrison (second from left). (Hitchin Museum)

on Middle Eastern affairs, publishing several books on the subject. Returning home he sat on a number of government committees and in 1933 was elected National Conservative Member of Parliament for Hitchin, Hertfordshire, a seat he held until 1940.

John WOOLDRIDGE DSO, DFC, DFM (1919–58)

Born in Yokohama, Japan and educated at St Paul's School, London, John Wooldridge

joined the RAF in 1938 as a sergeant pilot. By 1943 he had risen to become a wing commander, DSO, DFC, DFM, with a total of ninety-seven operational sorties over Germany to his credit. After service with 44, 76, 61 and 207 Squadrons, in 1942 he became a flight commander with 106 Squadron under Guy Gibson's command before being appointed CO of 105 Squadron in 1943. With this squadron Wooldridge became an expert in low-level precision daylight bombing

John 'Dim' Wooldridge rose from sergeant pilot
in 1938 to wing commander DSO, DFC, DFM,
by 1943, with ninety-seven operational bombing
sorties to his credit. As commander of 105
Squadron in 1943 he became an expert in low-level
precision daylight bombing, flying the Mosquito.

flying the Mosquito. At this point he
found time to write a book, *Low Attack*
(Sampson Low, 1944), which is an
authentic account of the operational
activities of 105 and 139 Squadrons
between 1940 and 1943.

After the war he left the RAF and
devoted himself chiefly to the
composition of music for the big screen.
He also wrote the screenplay and score for
Appointment in London (1953) starring Dirk
Bogarde, a film portraying life on an RAF
heavy bomber squadron during 1943.
John Wooldridge's potentially high-flying
career as a screenplay writer and
composer was cut tragically short when he
was killed in a car accident in 1958, aged
thirty-nine.

REMEMBERING BOMBER COMMAND

BOMBER COMMAND TODAY IN MUSEUMS NATIONWIDE

Bomber Command ceased to exist in name in 1968 when it merged with its equally illustrious counterpart, Fighter Command, to form Strike Command. The pivotal role it played in the Allied war effort during the Second World War has not been forgotten and is recognised today in some two dozen museums and exhibitions scattered across eastern England, from Yorkshire down to London. They range from the impressive Bomber Command Museum at Hendon in north London, to the many smaller museums located in humble village halls or on deserted windswept airfields that once played host to the men and machines of the wartime Command. The strength of these museums lies in the variety of their exhibits, complemented in many cases by the uniqueness of their locations.

The list that follows is intended as a guide for visitors to the various Bomber Command-related museums and exhibitions in England (to the best of the author's knowledge there are none in Wales or Scotland). Some concentrate exclusively on the Command and its achievements, while others include just a few artefacts or

As controversial in death as he ever was in life, the commemoration of 'Bomber' Harris with this statue in the precinct of St Clement Danes Church in central London aroused strong feelings when it was unveiled in May 1992. The statue, and in particular the role played by the Queen Mother who unveiled it, prompted demonstrations and a bitter debate in Britain and dismay in Germany, where it was thought insensitive.

Many towns and villages along the length of eastern England have their own memorials to the men of Bomber Command who flew from neighbouring airfields during the Second World War. On the village green at Tholthorpe in North Yorkshire is a memorial to the four wartime RCAF squadrons that flew from the nearby airfield with 6 (RCAF) Group, and the airfield staff who supported them.

Bomber Command Museum
Royal Air Force Museum
Aerodrome Road, Hendon, London NW9 5LL
Telephone: 0181 205 2266

Hours of opening:
All year, every day 1000–1800
Closed Christmas and New Year
Admission charge, on-site parking, refreshments, shop

Located adjacent to the main RAF Museum building, the Bomber Command collection is exhibited in a building specially designed to house the large aircraft displayed within. The museum consists of three interconnecting walkways and exhibition pavilions, the latter filled with exhibits ranging from small-scale models and display cases to a full-size reconstruction of Dr Barnes Wallis's office at Weybridge. Most aspects of the bomber story are highlighted by essay and photographic panels which are arranged to complement the exhibits. Pride of place goes to the aircraft exhibits which include a Wellington X, MF628, used in the making of *The Dam Busters*; Halifax II Series I, W1048 (in its unrestored condition); Avro Lancaster I, R5868, veteran of 137 operational sorties; Mosquito T3, TW117, star of the film *633 Squadron*; and a B-25J Mitchell.

specific items that relate to the Command as part of a wider or more general collection.

To the best of the author's knowledge the information that follows is accurate, but to avoid disappointment it is always advisable to double-check all details with individual museums prior to making any visit.

How to get there:
Situated 8 miles north-west of central London. By road, signposted from the end of the M1 and on the North Circular Road.

By London Underground, take the Northern Line northbound from central London to Colindale. The museum is signposted and a 15-minute walk away.

The Yorkshire Air Museum at former RAF Elvington in North Yorkshire is a living memorial to the aircrews of 4 and 6 (RCAF) Groups, whose squadrons were stationed at many airfields across the county during the war. Centrepiece of the museum is this superbly restored Halifax III, painted to represent LV907 'Friday the 13th' of 158 Squadron.

Yorkshire Air Museum and Allied Air Forces Memorial
Halifax Way, Elvington, York YO4 5AU
Telephone: 01904 608595

Hours of opening:
Monday–Friday 1030–1600
Weekends and bank holidays 1030–1700
Admission charge, on-site parking, refreshments, shop

The sympathetic restoration of the wartime control tower and adjacent buildings has brought back to life this former 4 Group airfield at Elvington. These buildings now contain a number of Bomber Command-related exhibitions. A newly erected T2 hangar is used to house several static aircraft exhibits (from a total of more than twenty), including the impressively restored/reconstructed Handley Page Halifax III, LV907 'Friday the 13th', the only surviving example of a Mk III in the world.

How to get there:
Situated 5 miles east-south-east of York. By road, from the A64 York bypass take the Hull exit and on the large roundabout with traffic lights take the Hull exit (A1079), and then immediately filter right, signposted

Elvington and Howden (B1228). After about 2 miles you will see the end of the airfield on the right followed shortly afterwards by a signpost to the museum, also to the right.

Battle of Britain Memorial Flight Visitor Centre

Memorial Flight Visitor Centre, RAF Coningsby, Lincs
Telephone: 01526 344041

Hours of opening:
Weekdays 1000–1700 (last tour 1530)
Closed weekends, bank holidays and two weeks over Christmas
Admission charge, on-site parking, refreshments

The Battle of Britain Memorial Flight is a living tribute to all RAF air and groundcrews who gave their lives in the Second World War and comprises airworthy examples of the Lancaster, Hurricane, Spitfire and Dakota. Lancaster PA474 is arguably the star attraction and with the Flight's other aircraft can be seen at airshows across the UK during the display season. The guided ground tours of these famous aircraft last about one hour.

How to get there:
On the A153, 9 miles south of Horncastle.

50 and 61 Squadrons Museum
The Lawn, Union Road, Lincoln
Telephone: 01522 560306

Hours of opening:
Daily
Admission free, adjacent pay-and-display car parking

A small museum dedicated to 50 and 61 Squadrons which operated from RAF Skellingthorpe. The collection includes a model of the airfield, archive photographs and records, aircraft equipment and memorabilia, as well as the squadrons' books of remembrance.

How to get there:
Located on Union Road just off Lincoln city centre, close to The Lawn Hospital and castle walls.

Lincoln Cathedral
Minster Yard, Lincoln
Telephone: 01522 544544

Hours of opening:
All year. Late May–August 0715–2000, Sunday 0715–1800
September–May 0715–1800,
Sunday 0715–1700
Voluntary admission charge

The Airmen's Chapel of St Michael houses the Memorial Books to 1, 5 and 6 (Bomber) Groups, 7 (HCU) Group, and 91, 92 and 93 (OTU) Groups, RAF Bomber Command, containing the names of 25,611 personnel who were killed flying from the airfields in or near Lincolnshire. The four stained-glass windows in the chapel include one dedicated to Bomber Command.

Metheringham Airfield Visitor Centre
Westmoor Farm, Martin Moor, Metheringham, Lincs LN4 3BQ
Telephone: 01526 378270

Hours of opening:
Easter to October, Wednesdays 1200–1600
Weekends, bank holidays 1200–1700
Admission free, on-site parking, souvenir shop

Home to 106 Squadron from 1943 to 1945, the airfield's former ration store now

REMEMBERING BOMBER COMMAND

houses an exhibition of photographs and memorabilia recalling life on an operational wartime bomber airfield. Close by are the remains of the concrete runways and perimeter track, and the memorial to 106 Squadron.

How to get there:
The Visitor Centre is situated at Westmoor Farm approximately 2½ miles from Metheringham village on the B1189, directly opposite the B1191 turning to Martin and Woodhall Spa.

Newark Air Museum

The Airfield, Winthorpe, Newark, Notts NG24 2NY
Telephone: 01636 707170

Hours of opening:
April–September daily, 1000–1700
Weekends and bank holidays 1000–1800
October–March daily, 1000–1700
November–February daily 1000–1600
Admission charge, on-site parking, refreshments, shop

Wartime home to 1661 HCU, the former RAF Winthorpe airfield now houses the Newark Air Museum, one of the largest privately managed aviation museums in the UK. The centrepieces of this impressive collection are forty-five aircraft supported by extensive artefact displays including the 'Lancaster Corner', which incorporates Dambuster memorabilia, a fuselage and a wingtip section, and several Rose Brothers rear turrets.

How to get there:
On the north-east outskirts of Newark with easy access from the A1, A46, A1133 and the Newark bypass. By public transport the museum is a short taxi ride from Newark's two railway stations and bus station.

Norfolk & Suffolk Aviation Museum

Flixton, Bungay, Suffolk
Telephone: 01502 574119

Hours of opening:
April–October, Sundays and bank holidays, 1000–1700
School summer holiday, Sundays, Tuesdays–Thursdays 1000–1700

In addition to an outdoor static display of more than fifteen aircraft, the indoor display includes the front fuselage section of a Lancaster containing the wireless operator's and navigator's stations; the fuselage centre section of a Halifax with Boulton Paul mid-upper turret; wreckage of Wellington I L4288 of 9 Squadron; and smaller displays of personal items from Bomber Command crews who flew from East Anglia, including memorabilia belonging to Bill Reid VC.

How to get there:
At Flixton on the B1062, 6 miles west-south-west of Beccles.

North Kesteven Airfield Trail

North Kesteven District Council, Sleaford Tourist Information Centre, The Mill, Money's Yard, Sleaford, Lincs NG34 7TW
Telephone: 01529 414294
Contact Sleaford TIC for full details

Created by North Kesteven District Council's tourism department, the airfield trail is located in south Lincolnshire between Lincoln and Sleaford where visitors can discover twelve active and former RAF airfields, including the one-time Second World War bomber stations at Waddington, Metheringham, Swinderby and Skellingthorpe. The trail can be followed comfortably in a day's drive. Regular airfield tours, special events and lectures are organised by the District Council's tourism department.

How to get there:
North Kesteven is easily accessible by road from the north via the A1 and A57 to Lincoln, from the south via the A1 and A15, and from East Anglia via the A17 and A15.

By rail to Lincoln and Sleaford; by coach from London and other major cities to Lincoln.

Petwood House and the Dambusters' Memorial
Stixwould Road, Woodhall Spa, Lincs LN10 6QF
Telephone: 01526 352411

Petwood House was taken over during the war years by several bomber squadrons, including No. 617, as their officers' mess. Now a hotel, the Squadron Bar houses much memorabilia. There is a large memorial to 617 Squadron in the centre of Woodhall Spa built in the shape of a breached dam.

How to get there:
Situated 4 miles north-north-west of Coningsby off the B1191.

RAF Skellingthorpe Heritage Room
Community Centre, Lincoln Road, Skellingthorpe, Lincs

Hours of opening:
April–October daily, 1000–1700
November–March daily, 1000–1600

An exhibition of photographs which tells the story of this 5 Group wartime bomber airfield, satellite to RAF Swinderby, and its association with 50 and 61 Squadrons.

How to get there:
Situated 4 miles west of Lincoln in the village of Skellingthorpe, west of the A46.

RAF Swinderby Exhibition
Methodist Hall, Swinderby, Lincs

Hours of opening:
April–October daily, 1000–1700
November–March daily, 1000–1600

The history of RAF Swinderby from 1940 to 1993, wartime home to four bomber squadrons and two HCUs, is recorded in photographs.

How to get there:
Situated in Swinderby village, 9 miles south-west of Lincoln, off the A46.

Thorpe Camp Visitor Centre
Ex-RAF Woodhall Spa, Tattershall Thorpe, near Coningsby, Lincs
Telephone: 01526 342249

Hours of opening:
May–October, Sundays and bank holidays, 1400–1730
School and group visits by arrangement

Housed on the former No. 1 Communal Site of RAF Woodhall Spa airfield, one-time satellite to RAF Coningsby and the wartime home of 617 Squadron, the Visitor Centre charts the history of the airfield and wartime life in Lincolnshire.

How to get there:
Signposted on the B1192 south-east of Woodhall Spa.

Bomber County Aviation Museum
Hemswell airfield, near Gainsborough, Lincs

Hours of opening:
Sundays and bank holidays, 1100–1800

The museum is situated within the headquarters and admin sites of the former 1 Group airfield, wartime home at various times to eight bomber squadrons, and combines a static park of aircraft and a small indoor display including flying clothing, equipment and aircraft engines.

How to get there:
Signposted off the A631 east of Gainsborough, on the former Hemswell airfield.

Dambusters Heritage Centre
23 The High Street, Scampton, Lincs LN1 2SD
Telephone: 01522 731333 and 730200

Hours of opening:
Telephone for details
Admission free, on-street parking

A small private museum dedicated to 617 Squadron's famous raid on the Ruhr dams in May 1943. The display which is steadily growing in size includes a skin section from Lancaster ED910 lost on the outbound leg of the raid, a Lancaster radio set, and one of the makeshift hand-held 'coat-hanger' triangular bombsights. There is a small memorial plaque outside the centre.

How to get there:
Situated in Scampton village beside the local post office stores.

Lincolnshire Aviation Heritage Centre
East Kirkby, Spilsby, Lincs PE23 4DE
Telephone: 01790 763207

Hours of opening:
Easter Monday to October, Monday–Saturday 1000–1700
November to Easter Monday, Monday–Saturday 1000–1600
Closed Sunday
Admission charge, on-site parking, refreshments

Situated on the former East Kirkby airfield, the wartime home of 57 and 630 Squadrons, the centrepieces of this museum are Avro Lancaster VII, NX611, which has been fully restored to taxiing condition, and the well-renovated control tower. The museum, run by the Panton brothers who farm the land on which the former airfield was built, is dedicated to the memory of their brother Christopher who was killed flying with Bomber Command on the fateful Nuremberg raid in March 1944. There are a number of other airframes on show and several small exhibitions.

How to get there:
Situated 15 miles north of Boston. By road, 4 miles south-west of Spilsby on the A155.

Brooklands Museum
The Clubhouse, Brooklands Road, Weybridge, Surrey KT13 0QN
Telephone: 01932 859000

Hours of opening:
Tuesday–Sunday 1000–1700 summer, 1000–1600 winter
Closed Monday
Admission charge, on-site parking

Centred on the famous old Brooklands Circuit, the museum combines automotive and aeronautical exhibits. The centrepiece of the aviation exhibits is the fully restored Vickers Wellington Ia, N2980, veteran of the battle of Heligoland in December 1939, which was salvaged from the depths of Loch Ness in 1985.

How to get there:
Situated 1 mile south of Weybridge station. By road, on the B374 Weybridge to Byfleet road, Brooklands is on the right. Access also from M25 Junctions 10 or 11. The nearest rail stations are Weybridge and West Byfleet.

Imperial War Museum
Lambeth Road, London SE1 6HZ
Telephone: 0171 416 5000

Hours of opening:
All year, every day, 1000–1800
Closed Christmas and New Year's Days
Admission free, no on-site parking (meter parking on the main road outside the museum), refreshments, shop

The museum exists to collect, preserve and display material and information relating to the two world wars and other military operations since August 1914, in which Great Britain and other members of the Commonwealth have been involved. In addition to a variety of small exhibits that relate to Bomber Command displayed in different galleries around the museum, the newly refurbished aviation gallery displays the nose sections of Lancaster I, DV372, and Halifax AVIII, PN323.

How to get there:
By road, the museum is well signposted south of the River Thames in the vicinity of Waterloo, Lambeth and Kennington. By rail, the museum is a 10-minute walk from Waterloo station, or 5 minutes from the nearest London Underground station, Elephant and Castle (Northern Line).

Imperial War Museum
Duxford Aerodrome, Duxford, Cambs CB2 4QR
Telephone: 01223 835000

Hours of opening:
Mid-March to end October 1000–1800
Remainder of year 1000–1600
Closed December 24–26, New Year's Day
Admission charge, on-site parking, refreshments, shop

Most exhibits are of general interest to anyone concerned with the history of military aviation, although in particular the beautifully restored airworthy Blenheim IV, Z5722, can be seen here.

How to get there:
By road, 7 miles south of Cambridge on the A505, just off M11 Junction 10.

Mosquito Aircraft Museum
Salisbury Hall, London Colney, St Albans, Herts AL2 1BU
Telephone: 01727 822051

Hours of opening:
March to end of October
Tuesdays, Thursdays, Saturdays 1400–1730
Bank holidays and Sundays 1030–1730
Admission charge, on-site parking, refreshments, shop
Facilities for disabled

Set in the grounds of Salisbury Hall the museum has on display twenty types of de Havilland aircraft ranging from DH Moths to modern military and civil jets. It was here that the prototype Mosquito was designed and built in 1940, and today this very aircraft, W4050, forms the centrepiece of the museum. Also on display are Mosquito B35, TA643, the fuselage of FBVI, TA122, and the nose section of TJ118, as well as a variety of Mosquito-related exhibits.

How to get there:
By road, off the B556 1 mile south-east of London Colney, with access off M25 Junction 22. The nearest rail station is Radlett (3 miles).

Wellesbourne Wartime Museum
Wellesbourne Mountford Aerodrome, Stratford-upon-Avon, Warks

Hours of opening:
All year round
Sundays and bank holidays 1000–1600
Admission charge, on-site parking

One-time home to the Wellingtons of 22 OTU, the wartime story of the airfield is told in great detail inside the airfield's restored battle headquarters.

How to get there:
Situated on the western side of Wellesbourne Mountford aerodrome, south of Wellesbourne Mountford and off the A429, 4 miles east of Stratford-upon-Avon.

Wellington Aviation Museum
Moreton-in-Marsh, Glos GL56 0BG
Telephone: 01608 650323

Hours of opening:
Tuesday–Sunday 1000–1200, 1400–1730
Closed Mondays
Admission charge, limited on-site parking, shop

A small but comprehensive one-room museum with a range of photographs, artefacts, aircraft parts and other ephemera relating to former RAF Moreton-in-Marsh, wartime home to the Wellingtons of 21 OTU.

How to get there:
Situated just off the A429, 17 miles south of Stratford-upon-Avon. At the roundabout in the centre of Moreton-in-Marsh turn onto the A44 towards Evesham. The museum is little more than ½ mile along on the left.

Former RAF Witchford
Grovemere Holdings, Lancaster Business Park, Witchford, Cambs
Telephone: 01353 664934

Hours of opening:
Monday–Friday 0900–1630
Other times by appointment

A small collection of memorabilia from former RAF Witchford and RAF Mepal covering the years 1943–6 is on public display in the foyer of Grovemere Holdings' premises, including a roll of honour for all those who died flying from Witchford.

How to get there:
By road, off the A142 between Ely and Witchford.

Once the tide of war had receded and the Canadians had returned home, the airfield at Tholthorpe was closed in September 1945 and its watch tower quickly became a derelict shell. During the late 1980s, however, it was restored and converted into a family home.

THE BOMBER COMMAND WAR DIARY 1939–45

1939

September

3 War is declared on Germany by Britain and France. Blenheim of 139 Squadron becomes first aircraft to cross the German coast on a reconnaissance flight

3/4 10 Whitleys of 7 and 51 Squadrons fly first night of leaflet dropping over Germany

4 Blenheims and Wellingtons make first attack on the German fleet at Wilhelmshaven and Brunsbüttel. First casualties of the war with 17 bomber aircrew dead

October

1/2 Whitley of 10 Squadron becomes first British aircraft of the war to fly over Berlin

December

3 24 Wellingtons attack German warships at Heligoland; beginning of anti-mining patrols over German seaplane bases

17 EATS agreement signed

14 Enemy convoy in Schillig Roads attacked by 12 Wellingtons. 5 aircraft shot down

18 Attack on warships at Wilhelmshaven by 22 Wellingtons. 12 Wellingtons shot down by German fighters. Bomber Command realises that daylight operations by unescorted bombers are not viable

21 Spitfires mistakenly shoot down 2 Hampdens returning from N Sea shipping search

1940

January

11/13 First night sorties of the war for Wellingtons and Hampdens mark a move towards night operations

12/13 Whitleys flying from forward airfields in France bomb Prague and Vienna, without loss

March

11 U-boat sunk off Borkum by Blenheim of 82 Squadron Bomber Command

19/20 50 Whitleys and Hampdens attack the seaplane base at Hörnum in the biggest bomber operation of the war so far

28 Air Marshal Sir Charles Portal becomes C-in-C Bomber Command

April

9 German forces invade Denmark and Norway

11 Attack on Stavanger airfield by 6 Wellingtons is the first of the war on a mainland European target

13/14 First minelaying operation of the war by 14 Hampdens of Bomber Command, in sea lanes off Denmark

May

10 German forces invade the Low Countries

11/12 First Bomber Command raid of the war on mainland Germany, target Mönchengladbach

12–14 German forces cross the River Meuse, heavy losses suffered by AASF

15 Bombing operations east of the River Rhine authorised by the War Cabinet

15/16 Attack by 99 bombers on 16 oil and railway targets in the Ruhr, marking the first strategic bombing raid of the war

17 12 Blenheims of 82 Squadron attack German troop concentrations at Gemblaux, 11 bombers shot down

17/18 53 bombers operate against Meuse crossings, 78 attack oil and rail targets in Hamburg, Bremen and Cologne

27/28 First German nightfighter of the war falls to the guns of a 10 Squadron Whitley bomber

26 May–4 June Evacuation of 336,000 Allied troops from Dunkirk

June

10 Italy declares war on France and Great Britain

11/12 Whitleys raid Turin in the first attack on Italy

15/17 Remnants of the AASF rejoin Bomber Command

17 France sues for peace

20 Air Ministry Directive to Bomber Command to take steps to reduce the scale of German air attack on Britain

July

1/2 First 2,000lb bomb dropped by a Hampden of 83 Squadron Bomber Command, flown by Flg Off Guy Gibson, target *Scharnhorst* at Kiel

10 Beginning of the Battle of Britain

August

12 Beginning of intensive air attacks on Britain

13 *Luftwaffe 'Adler Tag'* attacks attempt to break Fighter Command

12/13 Dortmund–Ems aqueduct badly damaged by Hampdens of 49 and 83 Squadrons. Flt Lt R.A.B. Learoyd awarded first Bomber Command VC of the war

24/25 First German bombs land on central London

25/26 War Cabinet sanctions first Bomber Command raid on Berlin

September

2/3 First Bomber Command raid of the war on German U-boat bases. 32 Hampdens attack Lorient

7/8 Beginning of German heavy air attacks on London

8 Bomber Command attacks enemy airfields and ports

10/11 First attacks on German invasion barges in Channel ports

15/16 Antwerp docks bombed

23/24 Berlin attacked by 119 bombers

October

5 Air Marshal Sir Richard Peirse becomes C-in-C Bomber Command

25 Air Chief Marshal Sir Charles Portal becomes Chief of the Air Staff

30 First Air Ministry Directive sanctioning area bombing

31 Battle of Britain ends

November

14/15 Devastating German attack on Coventry by 457 bombers, 568 people killed

16/17 130 bombers attack Hamburg

December

16/17 First major area attack by Bomber Command. 134 bombers raid Mannheim in retaliation for recent German attacks on Coventry and Southampton

1941

January

1–4 Bremen bombed on three consecutive nights

15 New Air Ministry Directive makes bombing of enemy oil targets a priority

February

10/11 First operation by the Short Stirling when 3 Stirlings of 7 Squadron bomb oil tanks at Rotterdam

11/12 Dense fog over airfields in England causes 22 out of 79 bombers to crash returning from a raid on Bremen

24/25 First operation by the Avro Manchester when 6 Manchesters of 207 Squadron bomb German warships at Brest

March

9 Air Ministry's Battle of the Atlantic Directive gives priority to bombing attacks on U-boat and long-range aircraft threats

10/11 First operation by the Handley Page Halifax, when 6 Halifaxes of 35 Squadron bomb Le Havre

12/13 First occasion on which Halifaxes and Manchesters attack Germany, target Hamburg

13/14 First Manchester aircraft lost on raid to Hamburg

30/31 109 aircraft bomb the *Scharnhorst* and *Gneisenau* at Brest in the first of a series of attacks

30/1 April The first two 4,000lb bombs are dropped by Wellingtons on Emden, one aircraft each from 9 and 149 Squadrons

April

7/8 The largest raid of the war so far to a single target when 229 aircraft bomb Kiel

17/18 11 aircraft lost on this night: the largest total lost in night operations so far in the war

May

8/9 A record number of sorties despatched on this night when 359 aircraft attack Hamburg and Bremen

8–12 3 raids in 4 nights on Hamburg, killing 227 and making nearly 3,000 homeless

27 64 Wellingtons and Stirlings search the sea for the cruiser *Prinz Eugen*, but without success

June

7/8 33 Wellingtons and Stirlings bomb the *Prinz Eugen* at Brest, but score no hits

12/13 First operational flight by a Canadian bomber squadron when 4 Wellingtons of 405 Squadron bomb Schwerte

22 Operation 'Barbarossa' – Germany invades the Soviet Union

23 The first chain of three Gee stations is completed

July

8 First raid of the war by Bomber Command Fortress aircraft of 90 Squadron, in daylight, target Wilhelmshaven docks

24 100 aircraft bomb the *Gneisenau* at Brest and meet with stiff fighter opposition. 12 bombers shot down. 15 Halifaxes bomb the *Scharnhorst* at La Pallice

August

11/12 First trial of Gee by 2 Wellingtons of 115 Squadron, target Mönchengladbach

12 Daylight attack on Knapsack and Quadrath power stations near Cologne by 53 Blenheims

18 Butt Report is published and reveals that only one in four crews who claim to have bombed a target in Germany are found to have been within 5 miles of the target

29/30 First sortie by an Australian bomber squadron is flown by a Hampden of 455 Squadron to Frankfurt

September

2/3 The station commander of North Luffenham and the CO of resident 61 Squadron, both of whom are flying in the same aircraft, are shot down and killed over Berlin

25 Last daylight raid by a Bomber Command Fortress aircraft, target Emden

November

7/8 Berlin is raided by 169 aircraft, but 21 are lost. In the light of this, the Air Ministry orders only limited operations to be carried out for the coming months. The future of Bomber Command hangs in the balance

December

7 Japanese bombers launch an unprovoked attack on Pearl Harbor

7/8 First operational trials of Oboe by Stirlings of 7 and 15 Squadrons, target Brest

8–9 Great Britain, the Commonwealth countries, the USA and China unite to declare war on Japan

18 47 aircraft bomb the *Scharnhorst* and *Gneisenau* in Brest harbour during daylight

27 First Combined Operations raid of the war to the island of Vaagsö off Norwegian coast is supported by 29 bomber aircraft

1942

January

5–10 3 night attacks in 5 days to bomb the *Scharnhorst* and *Gneisenau* at Brest

29/30 *Tirpitz* is bombed by 16 aircraft at Trondheim

31/1 February *Scharnhorst* and *Gneisenau* bombed by 72 aircraft at Brest

February

12 Channel Dash – the *Scharnhorst*, *Gneisenau* and *Prinz Eugen* sail from Brest to Germany through the Dover Straits. 242 bomber aircraft attempt to attack the ships in the biggest daylight operation of the war so far. All three ships reach the safety of German ports

22 Air Marshal Sir Arthur Harris is appointed C-in-C of Bomber Command

26/27 49 aircraft bomb Keil where the *Gneisenau* is badly damaged

March

3/4 Night attack on Renault lorry factory at Billancourt, W of Paris, by 235 aircraft. The greatest number to a single target so far in the war, but 367 French civilians accidentally killed

First operational use of Lancaster – sea mining off NW coast of Germany by 4 aircraft of 44 Squadron

8/9 First operational use of Gee – 211 aircraft bomb Essen

10/11 First use of Lancaster on a bombing raid – 2 aircraft of 44 Squadron are part of a force of 126 bombers attacking Essen

13/14 First effective Gee-led raid, target Cologne

27/28 62 bombers used to support Combined Operations raid to destroy dock gates at St Nazaire

April

10/11 Bomber Command's first 8,000lb bomb dropped by 76 Squadron Halifax, target Essen

17 Daylight attack on MAN diesel engine factory at Augsburg by 12 Lancasters of 44 and 97 Squadrons. 7 Lancasters shot down

23–27 Rostock raided in 4 consecutive nights of area attacks

27/28 German battleship *Tirpitz* attacked in Trondheim fjord by 43 Lancasters and Halifaxes

Last front-line operation by Whitley (except OTU) when 2 aircraft of 58 Squadron bomb Dunkirk

May

30/31 First 1,000-bomber raid, target Cologne. Actual figure 1,047 aircraft, including 365 OTU aircraft used for the first time on a bombing raid

31 First Mosquito operation. 5 aircraft of 105 Squadron dispatched to photograph Cologne and drop bombs. 1 Mosquito lost

June

1/2 Second 1,000-bomber raid, target Essen. Actual figure 956 aircraft

25/26 Raid by 960 aircraft, target Bremen

July

11/12 Daylight low-level attack on Danzig U-boat yards by 44 Lancasters

August

15 Pathfinder Force (PFF) formed in 3 Group

17 US 8th AF VIII Bomber Command flies its first operation when 12 B-17s bomb Rouen rail yards

17/18 Last operation by Blenheim. Single aircraft of 18 Squadron attacks Leeuwarden, Holland

18/19 First PFF attack. 118 aircraft, including 31 PFF, attack Flensburg

19 Bombers used again in support of Combined Operations at Dieppe. 62 Bostons of 2 Group lay smoke and drop bombs

27/28 9 Lancasters of 106 Squadron fly 950 miles to bomb German aircraft carrier *Graf Zeppelin* at Gdynia. Haze prevents bombing

September

4/5 PFF introduce illuminator, visual marker and back-up marking techniques, target Bremen

10/11 First 4,000lb incendiary target marker dropped by PFF, target Düsseldorf

14/15 4 aircraft of 408 Squadron fly last front-line Hampden sorties

October

1/2 12 out of 27 Halifaxes of 4 Group lost on raid to Flensburg

17 Daylight attack on Schneider armaments factory at Le Creusot by 94 Lancasters of 5 Group

22/23 First raid of over 100 aircraft on Italy, target Genoa

24 Daylight attack on Milan by 88 Lancasters of 5 and 8 Groups to coincide with opening of 8th Army campaign at El Alamein

November

7 6 Mosquitoes of 105 Squadron in successful low-level daylight attack on German ship *Essberger* in Gironde estuary

28/29 First 8,000lb bomb dropped on Italy, target Turin

December

6 All operational aircraft of 2 Group in low-level daylight attack on Philips radio and valve factory at Eindhoven. 14 aircraft lost

20/21 Oboe first used operationally by small force of 109 Squadron Mosquitoes, target Lutterade power station, Holland

1943

January

14/15 6 Group's first operation. 15 aircraft sent to Lorient

16/17 Target indicator bombs used for the first time, target Berlin. First raid by an all four-engine bomber force

25 8 Group reformed to take over PFF

27 9 Mosquitoes make successful low-level attack on a Copenhagen diesel engine factory

27/28 Oboe Mosquitoes carry out ground marking for first time, target Düsseldorf

30 First daylight raid on Berlin, by 6 Mosquitoes of 105 and 139 Squadrons

30/31 H2S first used operationally by PFF Halifaxes and Stirlings, target Hamburg

February

2/3 Germans obtain H2S set from crashed Stirling on only the second occasion that the new device had been used operationally

13/14 Ordinary Main Force squadrons of Bomber Command drop 1,000 tons of bombs for first time, target Lorient

March

3 Molybdenum mines at Knaben, Norway, attacked by 10 Mosquitoes of 139 Squadron

5/6 Battle of the Ruhr begins with first attack on Essen by 442 aircraft

15/16 Railway workshops at Paderborn, 200 miles inland from coast, attacked by 16 Mosquitoes

April

2 First sortie of newly formed 1409 Met Flt, to Brittany

4/5 Largest non-1,000 raid of war so far: 577 aircraft to Kiel

28/29 Heaviest loss of war for RAF aircraft on minelaying sorties: 22 aircraft lost off Heligoland and Denmark

May

3 Power station attacked near Amsterdam by 11 Venturas of 487 Squadron. 10 shot down

16/17 Ruhr dams attacked by 19 Lancasters of 617 Squadron
23/24 Largest non-1,000 raid of war so far: 826 aircraft to Dortmund
27 Jena Zeiss optical factories attacked by 14 Mosquitoes of 105 and 139 Squadrons. 5 aircraft lost
31 2 Group's final operation in Bomber Command

June
20/21 Zeppelin works at Friedrichshafen attacked by 60 Lancasters which fly on to land in N Africa in first shuttle-bombing raid of war
23/24 Shuttle bombing Lancasters return to UK, bombing La Spezia in Italy on the way home

July
3/4 First use by Germans of *Wilde Sau* fighters over a target city, Cologne
12/13 Wg Cdr J.D. Nettleton VC killed returning from raid on Turin
24/25 Window first used operationally, target Hamburg
24–3 August Hamburg attacked on 4 nights, huge civilian casualties caused by resulting firestorm

August
16/17 Last attack on Italian targets which had begun in June 1940, target Turin
17/18 Peenemünde rocket research establishment attacked by 596 aircraft. First use of Master Bomber technique
23/24 Battle of Berlin begins with first attack by 727 aircraft. The loss of 56 aircraft was Bomber Command's biggest single loss on one night in the war so far
31/1 September First reported use of fighter flares by enemy fighters, target Berlin. Stirling casualties 16 per cent. Goebbels orders evacuation from Berlin of all children and adults not engaged on war work

September
8/9 5 US 8th AF B-17s join Bomber Command on their first night bombing sortie of war, target Boulogne

15/16 12,000lb HC bombs dropped for first time by 8 Lancasters of 617 Squadron, target Dortmund–Ems canal
22/23 First feint attack, target Oldenburg, by 29 aircraft of 8 Group. Main target Hanover. 711 aircraft attacked in the first of four heavy raids between 22 September and 19 October

October
7/8 First aircraft equipped with ABC from 101 Squadron operated this night, target Stuttgart
8/9 Last operational use of Wellington with Bomber Command by 300 and 432 Squadrons

November
3/4 First use of G-H on a bombing raid, target Dusseldorf, by Lancasters of 3 and 6 Groups
19/20 First operational use of FIDO at Graveley
22/23 Stirlings withdrawn from Main Force operations following this attack on Berlin

December
16/17 Mosquitoes and Beaufighters of 141 Squadron operated for first time as Intruders in Bomber Command, using 'Serrate' device, in patrols along routes of Berlin raid

1944

January
21/22 Bomber Command's heaviest loss of the war so far on night operations: 62 aircraft missing from attack on Magdeburg, 1 from diversionary attack on Berlin

February
8/9 Gnome-Rhone aero-engine factory at Limoges attacked by 12 Lancasters of 617 Squadron. Wg Cdr Leonard Cheshire uses low-level marking technique for first time with heavy bomber
15/16 Heaviest attack of war on Berlin (2,643 tons) and largest non-1,000 force sent to any target so far
23/24 17 Mosquitoes raid Düsseldorf. 1

Mosquito of 692 Squadron is first Mosquito to drop 4,000lb HE bomb

March

6/7 First raid of Transportation Plan in preparation for invasion of Europe, target Trappes marshalling yard, France

24/25 Final attack of Battle of Berlin and the last major raid of the war on the German capital, by 811 aircraft

30/31 Bomber Command's biggest single loss of the war, target Nuremberg. 795 aircraft despatched, 95 lost

April

5/6 Aircraft factory at Toulouse successfully attacked by 144 Lancasters and 1 Mosquito of 5 Group. Target marking carried out by 617 Squadron, not PFF. 5 Group now operates as independent bombing force using its own target marking techniques

May

3/4 Bomber Command suffers heavy losses in attack on German military base at Mailly-le-Camp, France. 342 aircraft despatched, 42 Lancasters lost

12/13 Mosquitoes used for first time to lay sea mines, Kiel Canal

22/23 Last attack on a German industrial cities, Dortmund and Brunswick, until 24/25 July

June

5/6 D-Day. 1,211 sorties flown during night. 5,000 tons of bombs dropped, biggest tonnage of war so far

6/7 Communications targets in France bombed by 1,065 aircraft

8/9 First 12,000lb Tallboy bombs dropped on Saumur railway tunnel by Lancasters of 617 Squadron

12/13 Nordstern synthetic oil plant at Gelsenkirchen attacked by 303 aircraft in first raid of new oil campaign

14 The beginning of a series of heavy bomber raids in daylight, the first since 2 Group left Bomber Command in May 1943, target Le Havre

16/17 First raids of the new campaign against V1 flying bomb sites in the Pas-de-Calais area

July

7 Heavy bombing in the vicinity of Caen by 467 aircraft in support of Allied troops

18 Further heavy bombing in vicinity of Caen by 942 aircraft in support of Operation 'Goodwood'

24/25 Offensive against German industrial cities resumed with an attack on Stuttgart by 461 aircraft

August

7/8 Massive bombing attack south of Caen by 1,019 aircraft in support of Allied troops

14 German troop positions bombed by 805 aircraft in support of Canadian advance on Falaise

15 Luftwaffe fighter airfields in Holland and Belgium attacked by 1,004 aircraft

27 First major daylight bombing raid on Germany since August 1941, target Rheinpreussen synthetic oil refinery at Meerbeck (Homberg)

September

8 Last bombing raid by Stirlings when 4 aircraft of 149 Squadron are part of a force that attacked Le Havre

10/11 Heavy bombing of Le Havre in support of attacking Allied troops

11/12 Darmstadt attacked in controversial fire raid by 243 aircraft

16/17 Operations in support of the airborne landings at Arnhem and Nijmegen by British and American forces

19/20 Wg Cdr Guy Gibson VC killed returning from raid on Rheydt

23/24 Dortmund–Ems canal breached by 2 direct hits from Tallboy-equipped Lancasters of 617 Squadron

25 Directive issued to RAF and USAAF giving priority to attacks on oil targets

October

3 Sea wall at Westkapelle on Walcheren island breached in attack by 259 aircraft

6/7 Opening of 'Second Battle of the Ruhr' with attack by 523 aircraft on Dortmund

Last of 32 major raids of the war on Bremen

7 Kembs dam on River Rhine, north of Basel, breached by Tallboy bombs dropped from Lancasters of 617 Squadron

14/15 Duisberg attacked by day and night in two consecutive raids by 1,013 and 1,005 aircraft respectively, Bomber Command's biggest night operation of the war

23/24 Heaviest raid of the war on Essen by 1,055 aircraft

25 Essen hit again by 771 aircraft. Krupps suffer serious damage and is finished as a major steel and armaments producer

28 Cologne badly damaged in attack by 733 aircraft

29 *Tirpitz* attacked in Tromsö by 37 Tallboy-equipped Lancasters of 9 and 617 Squadrons, but no hits scored

30–1 November Cologne hit and badly damaged in two consecutive attacks by 905 and 493 aircraft respectively

November

2/3 992 aircraft bomb Düsseldorf

4/5 749 aircraft bomb Bochum. Dortmund–Ems canal breached once again, in attack by 176 aircraft

6 Nordstern synthetic oil refinery at Gelsenkirchen attacked by 738 aircraft

12 *Tirpitz* capsizes at Tromsö after attack by 30 Tallboy-equipped Lancasters of 9 and 617 Squadrons

16 Close air support given to US 1st and 9th Armies for the first time by Bomber Command with daylight attacks on Jülich, Düren and Heinsberg by 1,188 aircraft

21/22 Mittelland canal near Gravenhorst breached in attack by 144 aircraft

December

6/7 First major attack on an oil target in Eastern Germany, at Leuna near Merseburg, by 487 aircraft

12/13 540 aircraft attack Essen in last heavy night raid

16 von Rundstedt's offensive opens in the Ardennes

19/26 Attacks on communication and airfield targets in attempt to thwart the German offensive in the Ardennes

26 294 aircraft bomb German troop positions near St Vith

31 12 Mosquitoes of 627 Squadron attack Gestapo HQ in Oslo

1945

January

1 104 aircraft attack the Dortmund–Ems canal causing breaches along the Ladbergen section

1/2 157 aircraft attack the Mittelland canal again, causing further breaches along the Gravenhorst section

4/5 354 aircraft attack Royan in SW France to soften up German garrison, but faulty intelligence reports mean that RAF bombs kill 800 French civilians

5/6 664 aircraft bomb Hannover; 140 aircraft mount successful attack on German communications links at Houffalize in the Ardennes

7/8 654 aircraft bomb Munich in the last major attack on the city

14/15 587 aircraft bomb synthetic oil refinery at Leuna-Merseburg

28/29 Last large RAF raid of the war on Stuttgart, by 602 aircraft

February

2/3 Last major raid of the war on Karlsruhe by 261 aircraft

7/8 Goch and Kleve attacked in support of British advance across the German frontier near the Reichswald

13/14 Dresden bombed by 803 aircraft in what was to become the most controversial raid of the war. More than 50,000 people perished in the

firestorm that followed; 368 aircraft bomb the Braunkole-Benzin synthetic oil refinery at Böhlen
20/21 The first of 36 consecutive night raids on Berlin by Mosquitoes
21/22 Dortmund, Düsseldorf, Monheim and the Mittelland canal bombed in the first of a series of attacks against communications targets to isolate the Ruhr
23/24 Bomber Command's last VC of the war is won posthumously by Capt E. Swales SAAF of 582 Squadron this night during a raid on Pforzheim

March
2 858 aircraft take part in the final RAF raid of the war on Cologne
3/4 Luftwaffe mounts Operation *Gisela*, sending 200 fighters to follow RAF bombers home to England. 20 bombers shot down
5/6 760 aircraft bomb Chemnitz
7/8 531 aircraft bomb Dessau, another new target in Eastern Germany
11 1,079 aircraft bomb Essen in the largest raid of the war so far
12 1,108 aircraft bomb Dortmund in the largest raid of the whole war
14 The first 22,000lb Grand Slam bomb is dropped on Bielefeld viaduct by Lancasters of 617 Squadron, causing it to collapse
23/24 218 aircraft bomb Wesel in preparation for the British Army's amphibious crossing of the Rhine
27 U-boat pens at Farge, north of Bremen, are destroyed by 2 Grand Slam bombs dropped by Lancasters of 617 Squadron

April
6 Official end of area bombing

8/9 440 aircraft bomb Hamburg in the last major Bomber Command raid of the war
9/10 599 aircraft bomb Kiel harbour, sinking the *Admiral Scheer* and badly damaging the *Admiral Hipper* and the *Emden*
14/15 512 aircraft bomb Potsdam
16 18 Lancasters of 617 Squadron attack and sink the *Lützow* at Swinemunde with Tallboy bombs
18 969 aircraft attack the German naval base at Heligoland
20/21 The final RAF raid of the war on Berlin
22 767 aircraft bomb Bremen in preparation for a ground attack by British troops
25 482 aircraft bomb coastal batteries on the island of Wangerooge; 375 aircraft bomb Hitler's 'Eagle's Nest' retreat at Berchtesgaden
25/26 Final heavy bomber raid of the war, target Tonsberg oil refinery in southern Norway
26 April–7 May Operation 'Exodus', Bomber Command assists in the repatriation of British POWs. 469 flights bring home 75,000 men to England
29 April–7 May Operation 'Manna', food supplies are dropped by Bomber Command to the starving people of Holland

May
2/3 The final Bomber Command losses of the war. During an attack on Kiel, 2 Halifaxes of 199 Squadron collide on their bomb run; 1 Mosquito of 109 Squadron crashes on a low-level attack against Jagel airfield near Kiel. All crews are killed
7 Unconditional surrender of Germany at midnight
8 The war is over

THE SQUADRONS

The information that follows is a record of every front-line squadron that operated with RAF Bomber Command between September 1939 and May 1945. The data is arranged as follows: number (and name) of squadron, the date from which it became operational/ceased operations with Bomber Command in the Second World War (if operational on the outbreak of war and served throughout the war without a break, no date is given), the bomber group(s) in which it served in chronological order, squadron code letter(s), the RAF station(s) at which it was based in chronological order, aircraft types operated and when, total sorties flown, aircraft losses and a comprehensive listing of commanding officers.

7 SQUADRON (from 10/40) (3, 8) (MG)
Based: Oakington; *aircraft*: Stirling (08/40–08/43), Lancaster (05/43–08/45); *total sorties*: 5,060; *aircraft losses*: 165

Wg Cdr P. Harris 08/40
Wg Cdr H.R. Graham 04/41
Wg Cdr B.D. Sellick 04/42
Wg Cdr O.R. Donaldson 10/42
Wg Cdr H.H. Burnell 05/43
Grp Capt K.R. Rampling 09/43
Wg Cdr W.G. Lockhart 03/44
Wg Cdr J.F. Barron 04/44
Wg Cdr R.W. Cox 05/44

9 SQUADRON (3, 5) (WS)
Based: Honington, Waddington, Bardney; *aircraft*:

Wellington (01/39–08/42), Lancaster (09/43–07/46); *total sorties*: 5,828; *aircraft losses*: 177

Wg Cdr H.P. Lloyd 01/39
Wg Cdr R.A.A. Cole 09/39
Wg Cdr A. McKee 01/40
Wg Cdr A.E. Healy 07/40
Wg Cdr R.G.C. Arnold 01/41
Wg Cdr K.M.M. Wasse 06/41
Wg Cdr W.I.C. Inness 01/42
Wg Cdr L.V. James 05/42
Wg Cdr J.M. Southwell 06/42
Wg Cdr K.B.F. Smith 03/43
Wg Cdr P. Burnett 04/43
Wg Cdr E.L. Porter 11/43
Wg Cdr J.M. Bazin 06/44

10 SQUADRON (4) (ZA)
Based: Dishforth, Leeming, Melbourne; *aircraft*: Whitley (03/37–12/41), Halifax (12/41–05/45); *total sorties*: 6,233; *aircraft losses*: 156

Wg Cdr W. Staton 06/38
Wg Cdr N.C. Singer 04/40
Wg Cdr S.O. Bufton 07/40
Wg Cdr V.B. Bennett 04/41
Wg Cdr J. Tuck 09/41
Wg Cdr J.B. Tait 05/42
Wg Cdr D.C.T. Bennett 06/42
Wg Cdr R.K. Wildey 07/42
Wg Cdr W. Carter 10/42
Wg Cdr D.W. Edmonds 02/43
Wg Cdr J.F. Sutton 10/43

Wg Cdr D.S. Radford 04/44
Wg Cdr U.Y. Shannon 10/44
Wg Cdr A.C. Dowden 01/45

12 SQUADRON (from 06/40) (1) (PH)
Based: Binbrook, Thorney Island, Eastchurch, Wickenby; *aircraft*: Battle (02/38–11/40), Wellington (11/40–11/42), Lancaster (11/42–07/46); *total sorties*: 5,160; *aircraft losses*: 171

Wg Cdr R.W.G. Lywood 05/38
Wg Cdr A.G. Thackray 09/39
Wg Cdr V.Q. Blackden 06/40
Wg Cdr R.H. Maw 04/41
Wg Cdr B.J.R. Roberts 10/41
Wg Cdr A Golding 01/42
Wg Cdr R.C. Collard 04/42
Wg Cdr H.I. Dabinett 07/42
Wg Cdr R.S.C. Wood 02/43
Wg Cdr J.G. Towle 08/43
Wg Cdr D.M.H. Craven 09/43
Wg Cdr J.D. Nelson 03/44
Wg Cdr M. Stockdale 08/44

15 SQUADRON (from 12/39) (3) (MG)
Based: Wyton, Alconbury, Bourn, Mildenhall; *aircraft*: Battle (06/38–12/39), Blenheim (12/39–10/40), Wellington (11/40–05/41), Stirling (04/41–12/43), Lancaster (12/43–03/47); *total sorties*: 5,787; *aircraft losses*: 166

Wg Cdr J.L. Wingate 03/39
Wg Cdr R.G.L. Lywood 12/39
Wg Cdr J.Cox 06/40
Wg Cdr H.R. Dale 12/40
Wg Cdr P.B.B. Ogilvie 05/41
Wg Cdr J. MacDonald 01/42
Wg Cdr D.J.H. Lay 06/42
Wg Cdr S.W.B. Menaul 12/42
Wg Cdr J.D. Stephens 05/43
Wg Cdr A.J. Elliott 09/43
Wg Cdr N.D.G. Watkins 04/44
Wg Cdr N.G. MacFarlane 11/44

18 (Burma) SQUADRON (from 05/40 to 11/42) (2) (WV)
Based: Gatwick, West Raynham, Great Massingham, Oulton, Horsham St Faith, Manston, Wattisham; *aircraft*: Blenheim (05/39); *total sorties*: 1,242; *aircraft losses*: 40

Wg Cdr W.A. Opie 05/39
Wg Cdr G. Bartholomew 05/40
Wg Cdr A.C.H. Sharp 10/40
Wg Cdr C.A. Hill 03/41
Wg Cdr G.C.O. Key 04/41
Wg Cdr T.N. Partridge 06/41
Wg Cdr D.C. Smythe 07/41
Wg Cdr J.R. Cree 03/42
Wg Cdr J.H. Newberry 04/42
Wg Cdr H.G. Malcolm 07/42

21 SQUADRON (from 09/39 to 12/41; 03/42 to 05/43) (2) (UP, YH)
Based: Watton, Bodney, Methwold, Oulton; *aircraft*: Blenheim (08/38–07/42), Ventura (05/42–09/43); *total sorties*: 1,419; *aircraft losses*: 39

Sqn Ldr L.T. Keens 07/38
Wg Cdr L.C. Bennett 04/40
Wg Cdr M.V. Delap 07/40
Wg Cdr G.A. Bartlett 03/41
Wg Cdr P.F. Webster 05/41
Wg Cdr J.O.C. Kercher 07/41
Wg Cdr W.K. Selkirk 09/41
Wg Cdr P.F. Webster 04/42
Wg Cdr R.J. Pritchard 08/42
Wg Cdr R.H.S. King 02/43

23 SQUADRON (from 06/44) (100) (YP)
Based: Little Snoring; *aircraft*: Mosquito (06/42–06/52); *total sorties*: 1,067; *aircraft losses*: 8

Wg Cdr A.M. Murphy 12/43
Wg Cdr S.P. Russell 12/44

35 (Madras Presidency) SQUADRON (from 11/40) (4, 8) (TL)
Based: Leeming, Linton-on-Ouse, Graveley; *aircraft*: Halifax (11/40–03/44), Lancaster

(03/44–09/49); *total sorties*: 4,709; *aircraft losses*: 127

Wg Cdr R.W.P. Collings 11/40
Wg Cdr B.V. Robinson 08/41
Wg Cdr J.H. Marks 03/42
Wg Cdr D.F.E.C. Dean 05/43
Wg Cdr S.P. Daniels 11/43
Gp Capt D.F.E.C. Dean 07/44
Wg Cdr H.J. Legood 02/45

37 SQUADRON (FJ) (until 11/40) (3) (FJ)
Based: Feltwell; *aircraft*: Wellington (05/39); *total sorties*: 688; *aircraft losses*: 15

Wg Cdr F.J. Fogarty 09/38
Wg Cdr W.H. Merton 06/40

38 SQUADRON (until 11/40) (3) (HD)
Based: Marham; *aircraft*: Wellington (11/38); *total sorties*: 659; *aircraft losses*: 7

Wg Cdr C.D. Adams 02/39
Wg Cdr J.E.W. Bowles 12/39
Wg Cdr W.P.J. Thompson 08/40

40 SQUADRON (from 03/40, re-numbered 156 Squadron 02/42) (2, 3) (BL)
Based: Wyton, Alconbury; *aircraft*: Blenheim (11/39–11/40), Wellington (11/40–02/42); *total sorties*: 1,256; *aircraft losses*: 53

Sqn Ldr H.C. Parker 02/38
Wg Cdr D.H.F. Barnett 06/40
Wg Cdr E.J.P. Davey 12/40
Wg Cdr L.G. Stickley 08/41
Wg Cdr P.G.Heath 11/41
Wg Cdr R.E. Ridgeway 05/42

44 (Rhodesia) SQUADRON (5) (KM)
Based: Waddington, Dunholme Lodge, Spilsby; *aircraft*: Hampden (02/39–12/41), Lancaster (12/41–09/47); *total sorties*: 6,405; *aircraft losses*: 192

Wg Cdr J.N. Boothman 09/39
Wg Cdr W.J.M. Ackerman 12/39
Wg Cdr D.W. Reid 03/40
Wg Cdr S.T. Misselbrook 03/41
Wg Cdr R.A.B. Learoyd 12/41
Wg Cdr P.W. Lynch-Blosse 05/42
Wg Cdr K.P. Smales 05/42
Wg Cdr J.D. Nettleton 02/43
Wg Cdr E.A. Williams 07/43
Wg Cdr R.L. Bowes 08/43
Wg Cdr F.W. Thompson 02/44
Wg Cdr R.A. Newmarch 11/44
Wg Cdr S.E. Flett 04/45

49 SQUADRON (5) (XU, EA)
Based: Scampton, Fiskerton, Fulbeck; *aircraft*: Hampden (09/38–04/42), Manchester (04–06/42), Lancaster (06/42–03/50); *total sorties*: 6,501; *aircraft losses*: 163

Wg Cdr J.S. Chick 02/39
Wg Cdr W.C. Sheen 12/39
Wg Cdr J.W.Gillan 04/40
Wg Cdr J.N.Jefferson 12/40
Wg Cdr R.D. Stubbs 07/41
Wg Cdr L.C. Slee 05/42
Wg Cdr P.W. Johnson 04/43
Wg Cdr A.A. Adams 10/43
Wg Cdr M. Crocker 05/44
Wg Cdr L.E. Botting 06/44

50 SQUADRON (5) (VN)
Based: Waddington, Lindholme, Swinderby, Skellingthorpe; *aircraft*: Hampden (12/38–04/42), Manchester (04–06/42), Lancaster (05/42–10/46); *total sorties*: 7,135; *aircraft losses*: 176

Wg Cdr L.Young 07/38
Wg Cdr R.T. Taafe 04/40
Wg Cdr N.D. Crockart 06/40
Wg Cdr G.W. Golledge 06/40
Wg Cdr G. Walker 12/40
Wg Cdr R.J. Oxley 10/41
Wg Cdr W.M. Russell 10/42

Wg Cdr R. McFarlane 08/43
Wg Cdr F. Pullen 12/43
Wg Cdr A.W. Heward 01/44
Wg Cdr R.T. Frogley 06/44
Wg Cdr J. Flint 03/45

51 SQUADRON (4) (MH)
Based: Linton-on-Ouse, Dishforth, Snaith, Leconfield; *aircraft*: Whitley (02/38–10/42), Halifax (11/42–05/45); *total sorties*: 5,959; *aircraft losses*: 158

Wg Cdr J. Silvester 04/38
Wg Cdr A.H. Owen 03/40
Wg Cdr N.F. Brescon 10/40
Wg Cdr J.B. Tait 12/40
Wg Cdr R.C. Wilson 01/41
Wg Cdr R.K. Burnett 05/41
Wg Cdr P.C. Pickard 11/41
Wg Cdr J.A.H. Tuck 05/42
Wg Cdr A.V. Sawyer 10/42
Wg Cdr A.D. Franks 04/43
Wg Cdr D.S.S. Wilkerson 11/43
Wg Cdr R.C. Ayling 02/44
Wg Cdr C.W.M. Ling 04/44
Wg Cdr H.A.R. Holford 11/44
Wg Cdr E.F.E. Barnard 04/45

57 SQUADRON (from 05/40) (2, 3, 5) (DX,DJ)
Based: Scampton, East Kirkby; *aircraft*: Blenheim (03/38–11/40), Wellington (11/40–09/42), Lancaster (09/42–11/45); *total sorties*: 5,151; *aircraft losses*: 172

Wg Cdr H.M.A. Day 08/39
Wg Cdr A.H. Garland 10/39
Wg Cdr R.H. Haworth-Booth 12/39
Wg Cdr A.H. Garland 02/40
Wg Cdr S.S. Bertram 02/41
Wg Cdr J.M. Southwell 05/41
Wg Cdr M.V. Petters-Smith 03/42
Wg Cdr E.J. Laine 07/42
Wg Cdr F.C. Hopcroft 09/42
Wg Cdr W.R. Haskell 07/43
Wg Cdr H.W.H. Fisher 08/43

Wg Cdr H.Y. Humphreys 04/44
Wg Cdr J.N. Tomes 01/45

58 SQUADRON (until 04/42) (4) (BW)
Based: Linton-on-Ouse; *aircraft*: Whitley (10/37–12/42); *total sorties*: 1,757; *aircraft losses*: 49

Wg Cdr J. Potter 04/37
Wg Cdr J.J.A. Sutton 02/40
Wg Cdr K.B.F. Smith 11/40
Wg Cdr R.W.M. Clark 06/41

61 SQUADRON (5) (QR)
Based: Hemswell, North Luffenham, Woolfox Lodge, Syerston, Skellingthorpe, Coningsby; *aircraft*: Hampden (02/39–10/41), Manchester (06/41–06/42), Lancaster (04/42–06/46); *total sorties*: 6,082; *aircraft losses*: 156

Sqn Ldr C.H. Brill 03/37
Wg Cdr C.M. De Crespigny 09/39
Wg Cdr F.M. Denny 02/40
Wg Cdr G.H. Sheen 05/40
Wg Cdr G.E. Valentine 11/40
Wg Cdr C.T. Weir 09/41
Wg Cdr C.M. Coad 06/42
Wg Cdr W.M. Penman 02/43
Wg Cdr R.N. Stidolph 10/43
Wg Cdr A.W. Doubleday 04/44
Wg Cdr W.D. Paxton 09/44
Wg Cdr C.W. Scott 02/45

75 Squadron (from 04/40) (3) (AA)
Based: Feltwell, Mildenhall, Newmarket, Mepal; *aircraft*: Wellington (07/39–11/42), Stirling (11/42–04/44), Lancaster (03/44–10/45); *total sorties*: 8,017; *aircraft losses*: 193

Wg Cdr M.W. Buckley 04/40
Wg Cdr C.E. Kay 11/40
Wg Cdr R. Sawrey-Cookson 09/41
Wg Cdr E.G. Olson 04/42
Wg Cdr V. Mitchell 07/42
Sqn Ldr G.T. Fowler 12/42

Wg Cdr G.A. Lane 01/43
Wg Cdr M. Wyatt 05/43
Wg Cdr R.D. Max 08/43
Wg Cdr R.J.A. Leslie 05/44
Wg Cdr R.J. Newton 12/44
Wg Cdr C.H. Baigent 01/45

76 SQUADRON (from 05/41) (4) (MP)
Based: Linton-on-Ouse, Holme-on-Spalding
Moor; *aircraft*: Halifax (05/41–05/45); *total
sorties*: 5,123; *aircraft losses*: 139

Wg Cdr D.S. Allan 09/39
Wg Cdr S.O. Bufton 04/40
Wg Cdr G.T. Jarman 05/41
Wg Cdr J.J.A. Sutton 09/41
Sqn Ldr J.T. Bouwens 11/41
Wg Cdr D.O. Young 12/41
Wg Cdr C.C. Calder 07/42
Wg Cdr G.L. Cheshire 08/42
Wg Cdr D.C. Smith 04/43
Wg Cdr D. Iveson 12/43
Wg Cdr R.K. Cassels 08/44
Wg Cdr L.G.A. Whyte 01/45

77 SQUADRON (4) (KN)
Based: Driffield, Linton-on-Ouse, Topcliffe,
Leeming, Elvington, Full Sutton; *aircraft*: Whitley
(11/38–10/42), Halifax (10/42–08/45); *total
sorties*: 5,379; *aircraft losses*: 131

Wg Cdr J. Bradbury 02/39
Wg Cdr C.H. Appleton 11/39
Wg Cdr J. MacDonald 06/40
Wg Cdr G.T. Jarman 08/40
Wg Cdr D.P. Hanafin 05/41
Wg Cdr D.O. Young 09/41
Wg Cdr D.C.T. Bennett 12/41
Wg Cdr J.R.A. Embling 04/42
Wg Cdr A.E. Lowe 12/42
Wg Cdr J.A. Roncoroni 10/43
Wg Cdr D.S. Clark 09/44
Wg Cdr J.D.R. Forbes 12/44

78 SQUADRON (from 07/40) (4) (EY)
Based: Dishforth, Middleton St George, Croft,
Linton-on-Ouse, Breighton; *aircraft*: Whitley
(07/37–03/42), Halifax (03/42–07/45); *total
sorties*: 6,237; *aircraft losses*: 192

Wg Cdr R.Harrison 03/37
Wg Cdr M. Wiblin 01/40
Wg Cdr G.T. Toland 02/41
Wg Cdr B.V. Robinson 03/41
Wg Cdr T. Sawyer 07/41
Wg Cdr E.J. Corbally 01/42
Wg Cdr A.S. Lucas 05/42
Wg Cdr J.B. Tait 07/42
Wg Cdr G.B. Warner 11/42
Wg Cdr G.K. Lawrence 08/43
Wg Cdr A. Markland 04/44
Sqn Ldr F.A. Hurley 09/44
Wg Cdr J.L. Young 11/44

82 (United Provinces) SQUADRON (until
03/42) (2) (OZ)
Based: Watton; *aircraft*: Blenheim (03/38–03/42);
total sorties: 1,436; *aircraft losses*: 62

Wg Cdr S.H. Ware 07/39
Wg Cdr The Earl of Bandon 12/39
Wg Cdr E.C. de Virac Lart 07/40
Wg Cdr J.C. MacDonald 08/40
Wg Cdr S.C. Elworthy 12/40
Wg Cdr L.V.E. Atkinson 05/41

83 SQUADRON (5, 8, 5) (OL)
Based: Scampton, Wyton, Coningsby; *aircraft*:
Hampden (11/38–01/42), Manchester
(12/41–06/42), Lancaster (05/42–07/46); *total
sorties*: 5,521; *aircraft losses*: 143

Wg Cdr R.B. Jordan 08/39
Wg Cdr L.S. Snaith 10/39
Wg Cdr J.C. Sisson
Wg Cdr D.A. Boyle 12/40
Wg Cdr W.W. Stainthorpe 02/41
Wg Cdr R.A.B. Learoyd 02/41
Wg Cdr H.V. Satterly 06/41

Wg Cdr S.O. Tudor 09/41
Wg Cdr M.D. Crichton-Biggie 04/42
Wg Cdr J.R. Gillman 02/43
Gp Capt J.H. Searby 05/43
Wg Cdr R. Hilton 11/43
Wg Cdr W. Abercromby 12/43
Grp Capt L.C. Deane 01/44
Grp Capt J.A. Ingham 08/44

85 SQUADRON (from 05/44) (100) (VY)
Based: Swannington; *aircraft*: Mosquito
(02/42–10/51); *total sorties*: 1,190; *aircraft losses*: 7

Wg Cdr C.M. Miller 03/44
Wg Cdr F.S. Gonsalves 10/44
Wg Cdr W.K. Davison 01/45

88 (Hong Kong) SQUADRON (from 07/41 to 05/43) (2) (RH)
Based: Swanton Morley, Attlebridge, Oulton; *aircraft*: Blenheim (02/41–02/42), Boston (02/41–06/43); *total sorties*: 655; *aircraft losses*: 11

Wg Cdr K.H. Riversdale-Elliott 03/39
Wg Cdr G.S. Ellison 02/40
Wg Cdr C.E. Harris 11/41
Wg Cdr J.E. Pelly-Fry 06/42

90 SQUADRON (from 05/41) (2, 3) (WP, JN)
Based: Watton, West Raynham, Polebrook, Ridgewell, West Wickham, Tuddenham; *aircraft*: Fortress (05/41–02/42), Stirling (11/42–06/44), Lancaster (05/44–09/47); *total sorties*: 4,613; *aircraft losses*: 86

Wg Cdr J. MacDougall 05/41
Wg Cdr P.F. Webster 07/41
Wg Cdr J.C. Clayton 11/42
Wg Cdr J.H. Giles 06/43
Wg Cdr G.T. Wynne-Powell 12/43
Wg Cdr F.M. Milligan 01/44
Wg Cdr A.J. Ogilvie 06/44
Wg Cdr P.F. Dunham 12/44
Wg Cdr Scott 02/45

97 (Straits Settlement) SQUADRON (from 05/40) (4, 5, 8, 5) (OF)
Based: Waddington, Coningsby, Woodhall Spa, Bourn; *aircraft*: Manchester (02/41–02/42), Lancaster (01/42–07/46); *total sorties*: 3,934; *aircraft losses*: 109

Wg Cdr D.F. Balsdon 02/41
Wg Cdr J.H. Kynoch 12/41
Wg Cdr J.D.D. Collier 03/42
Wg Cdr G.D. Jones 10/42
Gp Capt N.H. Fresson 07/43
Wg Cdr E.J. Carter 01/44
Wg Cdr A.W. Heward 06/44
Gp Capt P.W. Johnson 10/44

98 SQUADRON (VO) (from 09/42 to 05/43) (2) (VO)
Based: West Raynham, Foulsham; *aircraft*: Mitchell (02/42–09/45); *total sorties*: 70; *aircraft losses*: 2

Wg Cdr L.A. Lewer 09/42

99 (Madras Presidency) SQUADRON (until 12/42) (3) (LN)
Based: Newmarket, Waterbeach; *aircraft*: Wellington (10/38–08/44); *total sorties*: 1,786; *aircraft losses*: 43

Wg Cdr H.E. Walker 06/37
Wg Cdr J. Griffith 09/39
Wg Cdr R.J.A. Ford 06/40
Wg Cdr F.W. Dixon-Wright 01/41
Wg Cdr P. Heath 12/41
Sqn Ldr J.B. Black 06/42

100 SQUADRON (from 12/42) (1) (HW)
Based: Grimsby, Elsham Wolds; *aircraft*: Lancaster (12/42–05/46); *total sorties*: 3,984; *aircraft losses*: 92

Wg Cdr J.G.W. Swain 12/42
Wg Cdr R.V. McIntyre 04/43
Wg Cdr D.W. Holford 11/43

Wg Cdr J.F. Dilworth 12/43
Wg Cdr R.V.L. Pattison 03/44
Wg Cdr A.F. Hamilton 09/44
Wg Cdr T.B. Morton 03/45

101 SQUADRON (2, 3, 1) (LU, SR)
Based: West Raynham, Oakington, Bourn
Stradishall, Holme-on-Spalding Moor, Ludford
Magna; *aircraft*: Blenheim (04/39–07/41),
Wellington (04/41–10/42), Lancaster
(10/42–08/46); *total sorties*: 6,766; *aircraft losses*:
171

Wg Cdr J.H. Hargroves 04/39
Wg Cdr N.C. Singer 07/40
Wg Cdr D. Addenbrooke 04/41
Wg Cdr J. McDougall 04/41
Wg Cdr D.R. Briggs 05/41
Wg Cdr T.H.L. Nicholls 01/42
Wg Cdr E.C. Eaton 06/42
Wg Cdr D.A. Reddick 04/42
Wg Cdr G.A. Carey-Foster 07/43
Wg Cdr R.I. Alexander 01/44
Wg Cdr M.H. de L. Everest 07/44
Wg Cdr I.M. Gundrey-White 01/45

102 (Ceylon) SQUADRON (4) (DY)
Based: Driffield, Leeming, Linton-on-Ouse,
Dalton, Pocklington; *aircraft*: Whitley
(10/38–02/42), Halifax (12/41–09/45); *total
sorties*: 6,106; *aircraft losses*: 192

Wg Cdr C.F. Toogood 10/38
Wg Cdr S.R. Groom 05/40
Wg Cdr F. Cole 01/41
Wg Cdr C.V. Howes 04/41
Wg Cdr L. Howard 10/41
Wg Cdr S.B. Bintley 01/42
Wg Cdr G.W. Holden 10/42
Wg Cdr H.R. Coventry 04/43
Wg Cdr F.R.C. Fowle 07/43
Wg Cdr S.J. Marchbank 09/43
Wg Cdr L.D. Wilson 07/44
Wg Cdr E.F.E. Barnard 01/45
Wg Cdr D.F. Hyland-Smith 03/45

103 SQUADRON (from 07/40) (1) (GV, PM)
Based: Newton, Elsham Wolds; *aircraft*: Battle
(07/38–10/40), Wellington (10/40–07/42),
Halifax (07–10/42), Lancaster (10/42–11/45);
total sorties: 5,840; *aircraft losses*: 179

Wg Cdr H.J. Gemmell 01/39
Wg Cdr T.C. Dickens 03/40
Sqn Ldr C.E.R. Tait 11/40
Wg Cdr C.E. Littler 12/40
Wg Cdr B.E. Lowe 04/41
Wg Cdr R.S. Ryan 08/41
Wg Cdr J.F.H. Du Boulay 03/42
Wg Cdr R.A.C. Carter 09/42
Wg Cdr J.A. Slater 04/43
Wg Cdr E.D. McK. Nelson 10/43
Wg Cdr H.R. Goodman 05/44
Wg Cdr J.R. St John 05/44
Wg Cdr D.F. MacDonald 12/44

104 SQUADRON (from 04/41) (4) (PU, EP)
Based: Driffield (overseas 02/42); *aircraft*:
Wellington (04/41–11/43); *total sorties*: 373;
aircraft losses: 13

Sqn Ldr D.B.G. Tomlinson 04/41
Sqn Ldr P.R. Beare 04/41
Wg Cdr W.S.G. Simonds 05/41
Wg Cdr P.R. Beare 07/41
Sqn Ldr W.M. Protheroe 10/41

105 SQUADRON (from 06/40) (2, 8) (GB)
Based: Honington, Watton, Swanton Morley,
Horsham St Faith, Marham, Bourn; *aircraft*:
Blenheim (06/40–12/41), Mosquito
(12/41–02/46); *total sorties*: 6,187; *aircraft losses*:
58

Sqn Ldr G.C.O. Key 06/40
Wg Cdr J.G. Hawtrey 06/40
Wg Cdr C.K.J. Coggle 08/40
Wg Cdr A.L. Christian 12/40
Wg Cdr H.I. Edwards 05/41
Wg Cdr D.W. Scivier 09/41
Wg Cdr F.A. Harte SAAF 09/41

Wg Cdr P.H.A. Simmons 10/41
Wg Cdr H.I. Edwards 08/42
Wg Cdr G.P. Longfield 02/43
Wg Cdr J.W. Deacon 02/43
Wg Cdr J. de L. Wooldridge 03/43
Wg Cdr J.H. Cundall 07/43
Wg Cdr K.J. Somerville 09/44

106 SQUADRON (from 09/40) (5) (XS, ZN)
Based: Finningley, Coningsby, Syerston, Metheringham; *aircraft*: Hampden (05/39–03/42), Manchester (02–06/42), Lancaster (05/42–02/46); *total sorties*: 5,745; *aircraft losses*: 169

Wg Cdr P.J. Polglase (to 04/41)
Wg Cdr R.S. Allen 04/41
Wg Cdr G.P. Gibson 03/42
Wg Cdr J.H. Searby 03/43
Wg Cdr R.E. Baxter 05/43
Wg Cdr E.K. Piercy 03/44
Wg Cdr M.M.J. Stevens 08/44
Wg Cdr L. Levis 03/45

107 SQUADRON (until 05/43) (2) (OM, BZ)
Based: Wattisham, Great Massingham; *aircraft*: Blenheim (08/38–02/42), Boston (01/42–03/44); *total sorties*: 1,599; *aircraft losses*: 84

Wg Cdr Haylock 04/39
Wg Cdr B. Embry 09/39
Wg Cdr L.R. Stokes 05/40
Wg Cdr J.W. Duggan 09/40
Wg Cdr W.E. Cameron 01/41
Wg Cdr Birch 04/41
Wg Cdr L.V.E. Petley 05/41
Wg Cdr A.F.C. Booth 07/41
Wg Cdr F.A. Harte SAAF 07/41
Wg Cdr Dunlevie 12/41
Wg Cdr L.H. Lynn 01/42
Wg Cdr D.H. Dutton 09/42
Wg Cdr A.C.P. Carver 12/42
Sqn Ldr I.J. Spence 02/43
Wg Cdr G.R. England 04/43

109 SQUADRON (from 08/42) (8) (HS)
Based: Wyton, Marham, little Staughton; *aircraft*: Mosquito (12/42–07/52); *total sorties*: 5,421; *aircraft losses*: 18

Wg Cdr H.E. Bufton 07/42
Wg Cdr R.M. Cox 03/44
Wg Cdr G.F. Grant 05/44
Wg Cdr R.C.F. Law 12/44

110 (Hyderabad) SQUADRON (until 03/42) (2) (VE)
Based: Wattisham; *aircraft*: Blenheim (01/38–06/42); *total sorties*: 1,402; *aircraft losses*: 38

Sqn Ldr I. McL. Cameron 06/37
Sqn Ldr J.S. Sabine 10/39
Wg Cdr R.M. Foster 12/39
Wg Cdr L.F. Sinclair 05/40
Wg Cdr W.P. Sutcliffe 10/40
Wg Cdr T.M. Hunt 05/41
Wg Cdr J.R. Cree 07/41
Wg Cdr E.L. Walter 03/42

114 (Hong Kong) SQUADRON (until 11/42) (2) (FD)
Based: Wyton, Horsham St Faith, Oulton, West Raynham; *aircraft*: Blenheim (03/37–09/42); *total sorties*: 731; *aircraft losses*: 39

Wg Cdr G.R.C. Spencer 06/39
Wg Cdr C.M.H. Outram 11/39
Wg Cdr J.H. Powle 11/39
Wg Cdr P.W.M. Wright 05/40
Wg Cdr G.R.A. Elsmie 12/40
Wg Cdr G.L.B. Hull 04/41
Wg Cdr J.F.G. Jenkins 08/41
Wg Cdr G.L.B. Hull 04/42
Wg Cdr A.A.N. Malan 08/42

115 SQUADRON (3) (BK, IL)
Based: Marham, Mildenhall, East Wretham, Little Snoring, Witchford; *aircraft*: Wellington (03/39–03/43), Lancaster (03/43–09/49); *total sorties*: 7,753; *aircraft losses*: 208

Wg Cdr H.G. Rowe 03/39
Wg Cdr G.H. Mills 12/39
Wg Cdr H.I. Dabinett 06/40
Wg Cdr A.C. Evans-Evans 01/41
Wg Cdr T.O. Freeman 07/41
Wg Cdr F.W. Dixon-Wright 01/42
Wg Cdr A.G.S. Cousens 07/42
Wg Cdr A.F.M. Sisley 12/42
Wg Cdr J.B. Sims 03/43
Wg Cdr F.F. Rainsford 06/43
Wg Cdr R.H. Annan 12/43
Wg Cdr W.G. Devas 06/44
Wg Cdr R.H. Shaw 11/44
Wg Cdr H. Stanton 04/45

128 SQUADRON (from 09/44) (8) (M5)
Based: Wyton; *aircraft*: Mosquito (09/44–03/46);
total sorties: 1,531; *aircraft losses*: 2

Wg Cdr K.J. Burrough 09/44

138 SQUADRON (from 08/42) (3) (NF)
Based: Newmarket, Stradishall, Tempsford,
Tuddenham; *aircraft*: Halifax (08/41–08/44),
Stirling (06/44–03/45), Whitley (08/41–11/42),
Lysander (08/41–03/42), Lancaster
(03/45–09/47); *total sorties*: c. 2,578 (SD ops);
105 (bomber); *aircraft losses*: 70

Wg Cdr E.V. Knowles 08/41
Wg Cdr W.K. Farley 11/41
Wg Cdr R.C. Hockey 04/42
Wg Cdr R.D. Speare 06/43
Wg Cdr W.J. Burnett 05/44
Wg Cdr T.B.C. Murray 12/44

139 (Jamaica) SQUADRON (2, 8) (SY, XD)
Based: Wyton, Horsham St Faith, Oulton,
Marham, Upwood; *aircraft*: Blenheim
(07/37–11/42), Mosquito (06/42–01/53); *total
sorties*: 5,544; *aircraft losses*: 70

Wg Cdr L.W. Dickens 03/37
Wg Cdr D.F. Lascelles 07/40
Wg Cdr W.H. Kyle 12/40

Wg Cdr I.W. Braye 04/41
Wg Cdr N.E. Pepper 05/41
Wg Cdr E. Nelson 06/41
Wg Cdr D.R. Halliday 07/41
Wg Cdr A.R. Oakeshott
Wg Cdr W.P. Shand 07/42
Wg Cdr R.W. Reynolds 05/43
Wg Cdr L.C. Slee 08/43
Wg Cdr G.H. Womersley 02/44
Wg Cdr J.B. Voyce 10/44
Wg Cdr J.R.G. Ralston 03/45

141 SQUADRON (from 12/43) (100) (TW)
Based: West Raynham; *aircraft*: Beaufighter
(05/43–01/44), Mosquito (11/43–12/51); *total
sorties*: 1,214; *aircraft losses*: 11

Wg Cdr K.C. Roberts 10/43
Wg Cdr F.P. Davies 02/44
Wg Cdr C.V. Winn 06/44

142 SQUADRON (from 05/40) (1, 8) (QT, 4H)
Based: Waddington, Binbrook, Eastchurch,
Grimsby, Kirmington, Gransden Lodge (overseas
12/42–10/44); *aircraft*: Battle (03/38–11/40),
Wellington (11/40–10/44), Mosquito
(10/44–09/45); *total sorties*: 2,231; *aircraft losses*:
53

Wg Cdr C.L. Falconer 03/39
Wg Cdr W.R. Sadler 10/40
Wg Cdr R.L. Kippenberger 07/41
Wg Cdr S.S. Bertram 11/41
Wg Cdr D.G. Simmons 04/42
Wg Cdr T.W. Bamford 11/42
Wg Cdr B.G.D. Nathan 10/44

144 SQUADRON (until 04/42) (5) (NV)
Based: Hemswell, North Luffenham; *aircraft*:
Hampden (03/39–03/43); *total sorties*: 2,045;
aircraft losses: 62

Wg Cdr J.C. Cunningham 09/39
Wg Cdr R.B. Jordan 09/39
Wg Cdr A.N. Luxmoore 05/40

Wg Cdr J.J. Watts 05/40
Wg Cdr J. Gwyll-Murray 06/40
Wg Cdr W.S. Gardner 01/41
Wg Cdr D.D. Christie 11/41
Wg Cdr G.F. Simond 01/42

149 (East India) SQUADRON (3) (OJ)
Based: Mildenhall, Lakenheath, Methwold;
aircraft: Wellington (01/39–12/41), Stirling
(11/41–09/44), Lancaster (08/44–11/49); *total
sorties*: 5905; *aircraft losses*: 131

Wg Cdr E.H. Richardson 10/37
Wg Cdr P. Kellett 09/39
Wg Cdr J.R. Whitley 05/40
Wg Cdr J.A. Powell 11/40
Wg Cdr G.J. Spence 11/41
Wg Cdr C. Charlton-Jones 05/42
Wg Cdr K.M. Wasse 09/42
Wg Cdr G.E. Harrison 04/43
Wg Cdr C.R.B. Wigfall 09/43
Wg Cdr M.E. Pickford 05/44
Wg Cdr L.H. Kay 01/45
Wg Cdr P.L. Chilton 02/45

150 SQUADRON (from 06/40) (1) (DG, JN, IQ)
Based: Stradishall, Newton, Snaith,
Kirmington, Fiskerton, Hemswell (overseas
12/42–09/44); *aircraft*: Battle (08/38–09/40),
Wellington (10/40–10/44), Lancaster
(11/44–11/45); *total sorties*: 2,557; *aircraft
losses*: 56

Wg Cdr A. Hesketh 03/39
Wg Cdr G.J.C. Paul 12/40
Wg Cdr K.J. Mellor 12/41
Wg Cdr E.J. Carter 06/42
Wg Cdr R.A.C. Barclay 12/42
Wg Cdr G.G. Avis 11/44
Wg Cdr P.A. Rippon 04/45

153 SQUADRON (from 10/44) (1) (P4)
Based: Kirmington, Scampton; *aircraft*: Lancaster
(10/44–09/45); *total sorties*: 1,041; *aircraft losses*:
22

Wg Cdr F.S. Powley 10/44
Wg Cdr G.F. Rodney 04/45

156 SQUADRON (from 02/42) (3, 8) (GT)
Based: Alconbury, Warboys, Upwood; *aircraft*:
Wellington (02/42–01/43), Lancaster
(01/43–09/45); *total sorties*: 4,584; *aircraft losses*: 143

Wg Cdr P.G.R. Heath 02/42
Wg Cdr H.L. Price 05/42
Wg Cdr R.N. Cook 07/42
Wg Cdr T.S. Rivett-Carnac 10/42
Grp Capt R.W.P. Collings 06/43
Wg Cdr E.C. Eaton 01/44
Wg Cdr T.L. Bingham-Hall 04/44
Wg Cdr D.B. Falconer 11/44
Wg Cdr T.E. Ison 12/44
Wg Cdr A.J.L. Craig 04/45

157 SQUADRON (from 05/44) (100) (RS)
Based: Swannington, West Malling; *aircraft*:
Mosquito (01/42–08/45); *total sorties*: 1,510;
aircraft losses: 6

Wg Cdr H.D.U. Denison 03/44
Wg Cdr W.K. Davison 06/44
Wg Cdr K.H.P. Beauchamp 09/44

158 SQUADRON (from 02/42) (4) (NP)
Based: Driffield, East Moor, Rufforth, Lissett;
aircraft: Wellington, Halifax; *total sorties*: 5368;
aircraft losses: 159

Wg Cdr P. Stevens 02/42
Wg Cdr C.G. Robinson 10/42
Wg Cdr T.R. Hope 03/43
Wg Cdr C.C. Calder 08/43
Wg Cdr P. Dobson 06/44
Wg Cdr G.B. Read 03/45

161 SQUADRON (from 02/42) (3) (MA)
Based: Tempsford; *aircraft*: Halifax
(09/42–10/44), Stirling (09/44–06/45),
Lysander (02/42–06/45), Hudson
(02/42–08/44), Whitley (02–12/42), Albemarle

(10/42–04/43), Havoc (10/42–12/43); *total sorties*: 1,749; *aircraft losses*: 49

Wg Cdr E.H. Fielden 02/42
Wg Cdr P.C. Pickard 10/42
Wg Cdr L.M. Hodges 05/43
Wg Cdr G. Watson 01/45
Wg Cdr M.A. Brogan 02/45
Wg Cdr L.F. Ratcliff 03/45

162 SQUADRON (from 12/44) (8) (CR)
Based: Bourn; *aircraft*: Mosquito (12/44–07/46); *total sorties*: 913; *aircraft losses*: 1

Wg Cdr J.D. Bolton 12/44
Wg Cdr M.K. Sewell 04/45

163 SQUADRON (from 01/45) (8) (?)
Based: Wyton; *aircraft*: Mosquito (01–08/45); *total sorties*: 636; *aircraft losses*: 3

Wg Cdr I.G. Broom 01/45

166 SQUADRON (from 01/43) (1) (AS)
Based: Kirmington; *aircraft*: Wellington (01–09/43), Lancaster (09/43–11/45); *total sorties*: 5,068; *aircraft losses*: 153

Wg Cdr R.A.C. Barclay 01/43
Wg Cdr R.J. Twamley 07/43
Wg Cdr C. Scragg 12/43
Wg Cdr F.S. Powley 01/44
Wg Cdr D.A. Garner 04/44
Wg Cdr R.L. Vivian 12/44

169 SQUADRON (from 12/43) (100) (VI)
Based: Little Snoring, Great Massingham; *aircraft*: Mosquito (01/44–08/45); *total sorties*: 1,247; *aircraft losses*: 13

Wg Cdr E.J. Gracie 10/43
Wg Cdr R.G. Slade 02/44
Wg Cdr N.B.R. Bromley 04/44
Wg Cdr T.A. Heath 09/44
Wg Cdr N.E. Reeves 01/45

170 SQUADRON (from 10/44) (1) (TC)
Based: Kelstern, Dunholme Lodge, Hemswell; *aircraft*: Lancaster (10/44–11/45); *total sorties*: 980; *aircraft losses*: 13

Wg Cdr P.D. Hackforth 10/44
Wg Cdr Templeman-Rooke 02/45

171 SQUADRON (from 09/44) (100) (6Y)
Based: North Creake; *aircraft*: Stirling (09/44–01/45), Halifax (10/44–07/45); *total sorties*: 258; *aircraft losses*: 4

Wg Cdr M.W. Renaut 09/44

180 SQUADRON (from 09/42 to 05/43) (2) (EV)
Based: West Raynham, Foulsham; *aircraft*: Mitchell (02/42–09/45); *total sorties*: 151; *aircraft losses*: 4

Wg Cdr C.C. Hodder 09/42
Wg Cdr G.R. Magill 01/43

186 SQUADRON (from 10/44) (3) (AP)
Based: Tuddenham, Stradishall; *aircraft*: Lancaster (10/44–07/45); *total sorties*: 1,254; *aircraft losses*: 8

Wg Cdr J.H. Giles 10/44
Wg Cdr F.L. Hancock 03/45

189 SQUADRON (from 10/44) (5) (CA)
Based: Bardney, Fulbeck; *aircraft*: Lancaster (10/44–11/45); *total sorties*: 1,254; *aircraft losses*: 8

Wg Cdr J.S. Shorthouse 10/44

192 SQUADRON (from 01/43) (3, 100) (DT)
Based: Gransden Lodge, Feltwell, Foulsham; *aircraft*: Wellington (01/43–01/45), Halifax (03/43–08/45), Mosquito (01/43–08/45); *total sorties*: 2,565; *aircraft losses*: 19

Wg Cdr C.D.V. Willis 01/43
Wg Cdr E.P.M. Fernbank 03/44
Wg Cdr E.W. Donaldson 06/44

195 SQUADRON (from 10/44) (3) (A4)
Based: Witchford, Wratting Common; *aircraft*:
Lancaster (10/44–08/45); *total sorties*: 1,384;
aircraft losses: 14

Wg Cdr D.H. Burnside 10/44
Wg Cdr A.E. Cairnes 04/45

196 SQUADRON (from 11/42 to 11/43) (4, 3)
(7T)
Based: Leconfield, Witchford; *aircraft*: Wellington
(12/42–07/43), Stirling (07/43–03/46); *total
sorties*: 683; *aircraft losses*: 24

Wg Cdr R.H. Waterhouse 10/42
Wg Cdr A.G. Duguid 03/43
Wg Cdr N. Alexander 06/43

199 SQUADRON (from 11/42) (1, 3, 100) (EX)
Based: Blyton, Ingham, North Creake; *aircraft*:
Wellington (11/42–06/43), Stirling
(07/43–03/45), Halifax (02–07/45); *total sorties*:
2,863; *aircraft losses*: 32

Wg Cdr C.R. Hattersley 11/42
Wg Cdr A.S.B. Blomfield 12/42
Sqn Ldr G.T. Wynne-Powell 02/43
Wg Cdr L.W. Howard 03/43
Wg Cdr N.A.N. Bray 10/43
Sqn Ldr W.A. Betts 08/44
Wg Cdr Bennington 11/44

207 SQUADRON (from 11/40) (50 (EM)
Based: Waddington, Bottesford, Langar, Spilsby;
aircraft: Manchester (11/40–03/42), Lancaster
(03/42–08/49); *total sorties*: 4,563; *aircraft losses*:
148

Wg Cdr N.C. Hyde 11/40
Sqn Ldr C. Kydd 04/41
Wg Cdr K.P. Lewis 06/41
Wg Cdr C. Fothergill 10/41
Wg Cdr F.R. Jeffs 05/42
Wg Cdr T.A.B. Parselle 12/42
Wg Cdr P.N. Jennings 05/43

Wg Cdr V.J. Wheeler 02/44
Wg Cdr J. Grey 03/44
Wg Cdr Black 10/44

214 (Federated Malay States) SQUADRON (3,
100) (BU)
Based: Methwold, Stradishall, Honington,
Chedburgh, Downham Market, Sculthorpe,
Oulton; *aircraft*: Wellington (03/39–04/42),
Stirling (04/42–02/44), Fortress (01/44–07/45);
total sorties: 4,189; *aircraft losses*: 112

Wg Cdr W. Sanderson 11/38
Wg Cdr F.E. Nuttall 02/40
Wg Cdr G.H. Loughnan 10/40
Wg Cdr R.B. Jordan 03/41
Wg Cdr G.L. Cruickshanks 08/41
Wg Cdr R.D.B. MacFadden 09/41
Wg Cdr E.J.P. Davy 02/42
Wg Cdr K.D. Knocker 04/42
Wg Cdr A.H. Smythe 09/42
Wg Cdr M.V.M. Clube 03/43
Wg Cdr D.J. McGlinn 07/43
Wg Cdr D.D. Rogers 08/44
Wg Cdr R.L. Bowles 03/45

218 (Gold Coast) SQUADRON (2, 3) (HA)
Based: Mildenhall, Oakington, Marham,
Downham Market, Woolfox Lodge, Methwold,
Chedburgh; *aircraft*: Battle (01/38–05/40),
Blenheim (07–11/40), Wellington
(11/40–02/42), Stirling (01/42–08/44),
Lancaster (08/44–08/45); *total sorties*: 5,302;
aircraft losses: 130

Wg Cdr L.B. Duggan 12/37
Wg Cdr A.R. Combe 07/40
Wg Cdr G.N. Amison 02/41
Wg Cdr Kirkpatrick 05/41
Wg Cdr P. Holder 01/42
Wg Cdr O.A. Morris 08/42
Wg Cdr D. Saville 03/43
Wg Cdr W.G. Oldbury 08/43
Wg Cdr R.M. Fenwick-Wilson 03/44
Wg Cdr W.J. Smith 10/44

223 SQUADRON (from 08/44) (100) (6G)
Based: Oulton; *aircraft*: Liberator (08/44–06/45),
Fortress (04–07/45); *total sorties*: 625; *aircraft
losses*: 3

Wg Cdr D.J. McGlinn 08/44
Wg Cdr H.H. Burnell 09/44

226 SQUADRON (from 05/41 to 05/43) (2)
(MQ)
Based: Wattisham, Manston, Swanton Morley;
aircraft: Blenheim (05–12/41), Boston
(11/41–06/43); *total sorties*: 740; *aircraft losses*: 28

Wg Cdr R.G. Hurst 01/41
Wg Cdr V.S. Butler 07/41
Wg Cdr W.E. Surplice 03/42
Wg Cdr J.M. Warfield 12/42
Wg Cdr C.E.R. Tait 04/43

227 SQUADRON (from 10/44) (5) (9J)
Based: Bardney, Balderton, Strubby; *aircraft*:
Lancaster (10/44–09/45); *total sorties*: 815;
aircraft losses: 15

Wg Cdr E.R. Millington 10/44
Wg Cdr D.M. Balme 03/45

239 SQUADRON (from 12/43) (100) (HB)
Based: West Raynham; *aircraft*: Mosquito
(01/44–07/45); *total sorties*: 1,394; *aircraft losses*: 9

Wg Cdr P.M.J. Evans 09/43
Wg Cdr W.F. Gibb 09/44

300 (Masovian) SQUADRON (from 07/40) (1) (BH)
Based: Bramcote, Swinderby, Hemswell, Ingham,
Faldingworth; *aircraft*: Battle (07–11/40),
Wellington (12/40–03/44), Lancaster
(04/44–10/46); *total sorties*: 3,684; *aircraft losses*:
77

Lt-Col W. Makowski 07/40
Maj S. Cwynar 07/41
Maj R. Sulinski 01/42

Maj W. Dukszto 08/42
Maj A. Kropinski 11/42
Maj M. Kucharski 05/43
Maj K. Kuzian 11/43
Maj A. Kowalczyk 01/44
Maj T. Pozyczka 04/44
Maj B. Jarkowski 02/45

301 (Pomeranian) SQUADRON (from 07/40 to
04/43) (1) (GR)
Based: Swinderby, Hemswell; *aircraft*: Battle
(07–11/40), Wellington (10/40–04/43); *total
sorties*: 1,260; *aircraft losses*: 29

Lt-Col R. Rudkowski 07/40
Maj W. Piotrowski 07/41
Maj S. Krzystyniak 04/42
Maj M. Brzozowski 06/42
Maj H. Kolodziejek 07/42
Maj A. Dabrowa 09/42
Maj S. Krol 04/43

304 (Silesian) SQUADRON (from 08/40 to
05/42) (1) (QD)
Based: Bramcote, Syerston, Lindholme; *aircraft*:
Battle (08–11/40), Wellington (11/40–06/43);
total sorties: 464; *aircraft losses*: 18

Wg Cdr J. Bialy 08/40
Wg Cdr P. Dudzinski 12/40
Wg Cdr S. Poziomek 11/41

305 (Ziemia Wielkopolska) SQUADRON (from
08/40 to 08/43) (1) (SM)
Based: Bramcote, Syerston, Lindholme,
Hemswell, Ingham; *aircraft*: Battle (08–11/40),
Wellington (11/40–08/43); *total sorties*: 1,063;
aircraft losses: 30

Wg Cdr J. Jankowski 09/40
Wg Cdr B. Kleczynski 04/41
Wg Cdr R. Beill 08/41
Maj K. Sniegula 06/42
Maj T. Czolowski 01/43
Maj K. Konopasek 07/43

311 (Czechoslovak) SQUADRON (from 07/40 to 04/42) (3) (KX)
Based: Honington, East Wretham; *aircraft*: Wellington (08/40–06/43); *total sorties*: 1,029; *aircraft losses*: 19

Wg Cdr K.F.J. Toman 08/40
Wg Cdr J. Schrjbal 05/41
Wg Cdr J. Ocelka 07/41

320 (Dutch) SQUADRON (from 03/43 to 08/43) (2) (NO)
Based: Attlebridge; *aircraft*: Mitchell (03/43–08/45); *total sorties*: 0; *aircraft losses*: 0

Cdr Bakker

342 (Lorraine) SQUADRON (from 04/43 to 05/43) (2) (OA)
Based: West Raynham; *aircraft*: Boston (04/43–04/45); *total sorties*: 0; *aircraft losses*: 0

Wg Cdr A.C.P. Carver 04/43
Wg Cdr H. de Rancourt 04/43

346 (Guyenne) SQUADRON (from 05/44) (4) (H7)
Based: Elvington; *aircraft*: Halifax (05/44–11/45); *total sorties*: 1,371; *aircraft losses*: 15

Lt-Col G.E. Venot 05/44

347 (Tunisie) SQUADRON (from 06/44) (4) (L8)
Based: Elvington; *aircraft*: Halifax (06/44–11/45); *total sorties*: 1,355; *aircraft losses*: 15

(no data available)

405 (Vancouver) SQUADRON (from 04/41–10/42; and 03/43–09/45) (4, 6) (LQ)
Based: Driffield, Pocklington, Topcliffe, Leeming, Gransden Lodge; *aircraft*: Wellington (05/41–04/42), Halifax (04/42–09/43), Lancaster (08/43–09/45); *total sorties*: 3,852; *aircraft losses*: 112

Sqn Ldr D.G. Tomlinson 04/41
Wg Cdr P.A. Gilchrist 05/41
Wg Cdr R.M. Fenwick-Wilson 08/41
Wg Cdr G.D. MacAllister 02/42
Wg Cdr J.E. Fauquier 02/42
Wg Cdr R.J. Lane 01/44
Wg Cdr C.W. Palmer 08/44
Wg Cdr H.A. Morrison 09/44
Grp Capt W.F.M. Newson 11/44

408 (Goose) SQUADRON (from 06/41) (5, 4, 6) (EQ)
Based: Lindholme, Syerston, Balderton, Leeming, Linton-on-Ouse; *aircraft*: Hampden (06/41–09/42), Halifax (09/42–10/43; 09/44–05/45), Lancaster (10/43–09/44; 05–09/45); *total sorties*: 4,453; *aircraft losses*: 129

Wg Cdr N.W. Timmerman 06/41
Wg Cdr A.C.P. Clayton 03/42
Wg Cdr J.D. Twigg 05/42
Wg Cdr W.D.S. Ferris 09/42
Wg Cdr A.C. Mair 10/43
Wg Cdr D.S. Jacobs 11/43
Wg Cdr R.A. McLernon 05/44
Wg Cdr F.R. Sharp 11/44

415 (Swordfish) SQUADRON (from 07/44) (6) (6U)
Based: East Moor; *aircraft*: Halifax (07/44–05/45); *total sorties*: 1,526; *aircraft losses*: 13

Wg Cdr F. Ball 07/44
Wg Cdr J.G. McNeill 08/44
Wg Cdr F.W. Ball 10/44

419 (Moose) SQUADRON (from 12/41) (3, 4, 6) (VR)
Based: Mildenhall, Leeming, Topcliffe, Croft, Middleton St George; *aircraft*: Wellington (01–11/42), Halifax (11/42–04/44), Lancaster (03/44–09/45); *total sorties*: 4,293; *aircraft losses*: 129

Wg Cdr J. Fulton 12/41
Wg Cdr A.P. Walsh 08/42
Wg Cdr M.M. Fleming 09/42
Wg Cdr G.A. McMurdy 10/43
Wg Cdr W.P. Pleasance 10/43
Wg Cdr D.C. Hagerman 08/44
Wg Cdr C.M.E. Ferguson 01/45

420 (Snowy Owl) SQUADRON (from 12/41;
overseas 05-11/43) (5, 4, 6) (PT)
Based: Waddington, Skipton-on-Swale, Middleton
St George, Dalton, Tholthorpe; *aircraft*:
Hampden (01–08/42), Wellington
(08/42–10/43), Halifax (12/43–05/45); *total
sorties*: 3,479; *aircraft losses*: 60

Wg Cdr J.D.D. Collier 12/41
Wg Cdr D.A.R. Bradshaw 03/42
Wg Cdr D. McIntosh 04/43
Wg Cdr G.A. McKenna 04/44
Wg Cdr G.J. Edwards 10/44
Wg Cdr W.G. Phelan 11/44
Wg Cdr F.S. McCarthy 01/45
Wg Cdr R.J. Gray 04/45

424 (Tiger) SQUADRON (from 10/42; overseas
05-10/43) (4, 6) (QB)
Based: Topcliffe, Leeming, Dalton, Skipton-on-
Swale; *aircraft*: Wellington (10/42–10/43),
Halifax (12/43–01/45), Lancaster (01–10/45);
total sorties: 2,531; *aircraft losses*: 33

Wg Cdr H.M. Carscallen 10/42
Wg Cdr G.A. Roy 04/43
Wg Cdr A.N. Martin 12/43
Wg Cdr J.D. Blane 01/44
Wg Cdr G.A. Roy 08/44
Wg Cdr C.C.W. Marshall 10/44
Wg Cdr R.W. Norris 03/45

425 (Alouette) SQUADRON (from 06/42;
overseas 05–10/43) (4, 6) (KW)
Based: Dishforth, Tholthorpe; *aircraft*: Wellington
(08/42–10/43), Halifax (12/43–05/45); *total
sorties*: 2,927; *aircraft losses*: 39

Wg Cdr J.M.W. St Pierre 06/42
Wg Cdr B.D. Richer 09/43
Sqn Ldr R.A. McLernon 02/44 (Acting)
Wg Cdr J. Lecomte 05/44
Wg Cdr H.C. Ledoux 08/44

426 (Thunderbird) SQUADRON (from 10/42)
(4, 6) (OW)
Based: Dishforth, Linton-on-Ouse; *aircraft*:
Wellington (10/42–06/43), Lancaster
(07/43–05/44), Halifax (04/44–05/45); *total
sorties*: 3,207; *aircraft losses*: 68

Wg Cdr S.S. Blanchard 10/42
Wg Cdr L. Crooks 02/43
Wg Cdr W.H. Swetman 08/43
Wg Cdr E.C. Hamber 04/44
Wg Cdr C.W. Burgess 07/44
Wg Cdr F.C. Carling-Kelly 01/45
Wg Cdr C.M. Black 01/45

427 (Lion) SQUADRON (from 11/42) (4, 6)
(ZL)
Based: Croft, Leeming; *aircraft*: Wellington
(11/42–05/43), Halifax (05/43–03/45),
Lancaster (03/45–05/46); *total sorties*: 3,309;
aircraft losses: 69

Wg Cdr D.H. Burnside 11/42
Wg Cdr R.S. Turnbull 09/43
Wg Cdr G.J. Cribb 06/44
Wg Cdr E.M. Bryson 08/44
Wg Cdr V.F. Ganderton 09/44
Wg Cdr E.M. Bryson 04/45

428 (Ghost) SQUADRON (from 11/42) (4, 6)
(NA)
Based: Dalton, Middleton St George; *aircraft*:
Wellington (11/42–06/43), Halifax
(06/43–06/44), Lancaster (06/44–09/45); *total
sorties*: 3,433; *aircraft losses*: 67

Wg Cdr A. Earle 11/42
Wg Cdr D.W.M. Smith 02/43
Wg Cdr Suggitt 09/43

Wg Cdr D.T. French 10/43
Wg Cdr W.A.G. McLeish 05/44
Wg Cdr A.C. Hull 08/44
Wg Cdr M.W. Gall 12/44

429 (Bison) SQUADRON (from 11/42) (4, 6) (AL)
Based: East Moor, Leeming; *aircraft*: Wellington
(11/42–08/43), Halifax (08/43–03/45),
Lancaster (03/45–05/46); *total sorties*: 3,175;
aircraft losses: 78

Wg Cdr J.A.P. Owen 11/42
Wg Cdr J.L. Saward 06/43
Wg Cdr J.A. Piddington 06/43
Wg Cdr J.D. Pattison 07/43
Sqn Ldr Kenny 03/44
Wg Cdr A.F. Avant 05/44
Wg Cdr E.H. Evans 04/45

431 (Iroquois) SQUADRON (from 11/42) (4, 6) (SE)
Based: Burn, Tholthorpe, Croft; *aircraft*: Wellington
(12/42–07/43), Halifax (07/43–10/44), Lancaster
(10/44–09/45); *total sorties*: 2,578; *aircraft losses*: 75

Wg Cdr J. Coverdale 11/42
Wg Cdr W.F.M. Newson 06/43
Wg Cdr H.R. Dow 05/44
Wg Cdr E.M. Mitchell 07/44
Wg Cdr R.F. Davenport 01/45
Wg Cdr W.F. McKinnon 03/45

432 (Leaside) SQUADRON (from 05/43 (6)
(QO)
Based: Skipton-on-Swale, East Moor; *aircraft*:
Wellington (05–11/43), Lancaster
(10/43–02/44), Halifax (02/44–05/45); *total
sorties*: 3,100; *aircraft losses*: 65

Wg Cdr H.W. Kerby 05/43
Wg Cdr W.A. McKay 07/43
Wg Cdr J.F.K. MacDonald 05/44
Wg Cdr A.D.R. Lowe 07/44
Wg Cdr J.F. K. MacDonald 09/44
Wg Cdr S.H. Minhinnick 01/45
Wg Cdr K.A. France 02/45

433 (Porcupine) SQUADRON (from 09/43) (6) (BM)
Based: Skipton-on-Swale; *aircraft*: Halifax
(11/43–01/45), Lancaster (01–10/45); *total
sorties*: 2,316; *aircraft losses*: 31

Wg Cdr C.B. Sinton 09/43
Wg Cdr A.J. Lewington 06/44
Wg Cdr G.A. Tambling 11/44

434 (Bluenose) SQUADRON (from 06/43) (6) (WL)
Based: Tholthorpe, Croft; *aircraft*: Halifax
(06/43–12/44), Lancaster (12/44–09/45); *total
sorties*: 2,597; *aircraft losses*: 58

Wg Cdr C.E. Harris 06/43
Wg Cdr C.S. Bartlett 03/44
Wg Cdr F. Watkins 06/44
Wg Cdr A. P. Blackburn 07/44
Wg Cdr J.C. Mulvihill 04/45

455 (Australian) SQUADRON (from 08/41 to
04/42) (5) (UB)
Based: Swinderby, Wigsley; *aircraft*: Hampden
(07/41–12/43); *total sorties*: 424; *aircraft losses*: 14

Flt Lt J.H.W. Lawson 05/41
Wg Cdr J. Gyll-Murray 07/41
Wg Cdr G.M. Lindeman 12/41

458 (Australian) SQUADRON (from 10/41 to
02/42) (4) (MD)
Based: Holme-on-Spalding Moor; *aircraft*: Wellington
(08/41–09/43); *total sorties*: 65; *aircraft losses*: 3

Wg Cdr N.G. Mulholland 10/41

460 (Australian) SQUADRON (from 03/42) (1)
(AR, UV)
Based: Breighton, Binbrook; *aircraft*: Wellington
(11/41–09/42), Halifax (08–10/42), Lancaster
(10/42–10/45); *total sorties*: 6,238; *aircraft losses*: 169

Wg Cdr A.L.G. Hubbard 11/41
Wg Cdr K.W. Kaufmann 09/42
Wg Cdr J. Dilworth 12/42

Wg Cdr C.E. Martin 02/43
Wg Cdr R.A. Norman 09/43
Wg Cdr F.A. Arthur 10/43
Wg Cdr H.D. Marsh 01/44
Wg Cdr J.K. Douglas 05/44
Wg Cdr K.R.J. Parsons 10/44
Wg Cdr J. Clark 11/44
Wg Cdr J. Roberts 12/44
Wg Cdr M.G. Cowan 01/45

462 (Australian) SQUADRON (from 08/44) (4, 100) (Z5)
Based: Driffield, Foulsham; *aircraft*: Halifax (08/44–09/45); *total sorties*: 1,165; *aircraft losses*: 13

Wg Cdr D.E.S. Shannon 08/44
Wg Cdr P.M. Paull 12/44

463 (Australian) SQUADRON (from 11/43) (5) (JO)
Based: Waddington, Skellingthorpe; *aircraft*: Lancaster (11/43–09/45); *total sorties*: 2,525; *aircraft losses*: 69

Wg Cdr R. Kingsford Smith 11/43
Wg Cdr D.R. Donaldson 06/44
Wg Cdr W.A. Forbes 06/44
Wg Cdr K.M. Kemp 02/45

464 (Australian) SQUADRON (from 08/42 to 05/43) (2) (SB)
Based: Feltwell, Methwold; *aircraft*: Ventura (09/42–11/43); *total sorties*: 226; *aircraft losses*: 6

Wg Cdr R.H. Young 09/42
Wg Cdr H.J.W. Meaken 04/43

466 (Australian) SQUADRON (from 10/42) (4) (HD)
Based: Driffield, Leconfield; *aircraft*: Wellington (10/42–09/43), Halifax (09/43–08/45); *total sorties*: 3,328; *aircraft losses*: 65

Wg Cdr R.E. Bailey 10/42
Wg Cdr D.T. Forsyth 09/43
Wg Cdr H.W. Connolly 05/44
Wg Cdr A. Wharton 10/44
Wg Cdr A. Hollings 04/45

467 (Australian) SQUADRON (from 11/42) (5) (PO)
Based: Scampton, Bottesford, Waddington; *aircraft*: Lancaster (11/42–09/45); *total sorties*: 3,833; *aircraft losses*: 104

Wg Cdr C.L. Gomm 11/42
Sqn Ldr A.S. Raphael 08/43
Wg Cdr J.R. Balmer 08/43
Wg Cdr W.L. Brill 05/44
Wg Cdr J.K. Douglas 10/44
Wg Cdr E.le P. Langlois 02/45
Wg Cdr I.H. Hay 03/45

487 (New Zealand) SQUADRON (from 11/42 to 05/43) (2) (EG)
Based: Feltwell, Methwold; *aircraft*: Ventura (09/42–09/43); *total sorties*: 273; *aircraft losses*: 15

Wg Cdr F.C. Seavill 08/42
Wg Cdr G.J. Grindell 12/42
Wg Cdr A.G. Wilson 05/43

514 SQUADRON (from 09/43) (3) (A2, JI))
Based: Foulsham, Waterbeach; *aircraft*: Lancaster (09/43–08/45); *total sorties*: 3,675; *aircraft losses*: 66

Wg Cdr A.J. Samson 09/43
Wg Cdr M. Wyatt 05/44
Wg Cdr P.L.B. Morgan 02/45

515 SQUADRON (from 12/43) (100) (3P)
Based: Little Snoring; *aircraft*: Mosquito (02/44–06/45); *total sorties*: 1,366; *aircraft losses*: 21

Wg Cdr F.F. Lambert 01/44
Wg Cdr H.C. Kelsey 12/44

550 SQUADRON (from 11/43) (1) (BQ)
Based: Grimsby, North Killingholme; *aircraft*: Lancaster (11/43–10/45); *total sorties*: 3,582; *aircraft losses*: 59

Wg Cdr J.J. Bennett 11/43
Wg Cdr P.E.G.G. Connolly 05/44
Wg Cdr A.F.M. Sisley 07/44
Sqn Ldr B.J. Ramond 09/44

Wg Cdr B. Bell 09/44
Wg Cdr J.C. McWatters 02/45

571 SQUADRON (from 04/44) (8) (8K)
Based: Downham Market, Graveley, Oakington;
aircraft: Mosquito (04/44–09/45); *total sorties*:
2,681; *aircraft losses*: 8

Wg Cdr J.M. Birkin 04/44
Wg Cdr R.J. Gosnell 11/44
Wg Cdr R.W. Bray 04/45

576 SQUADRON (from 11/43) (1) (UL)
Based: Elsham Wolds, Fiskerton; *aircraft*: Lancaster
(11/43–09/45); *total sorties*: 2,788; *aircraft losses*: 66

Wg Cdr G.T.B. Clayton 11/43
Wg Cdr B.D. Sellick 06/44
Wg Cdr McAllister 02/45

578 SQUADRON (from 01/44) (4) (LK)
Based: Snaith, Burn; *aircraft*: Halifax
(01/44–03/45); *total sorties*: 2,721; *aircraft losses*: 40

Wg Cdr D.S.S. Wilkerson 01/44
Wg Cdr A.G.T. James 08/44
Wg Cdr E.L. Hancock 02/45

582 SQUADRON (from 04/44) (8) (6O)
Based: Little Staughton; *aircraft*: Lancaster
(04/44–09/45); *total sorties*: 2,157; *aircraft losses*: 28

Wg Cdr C.M. Dunnifliffe 04/44
Wg Cdr P.H. Cribb 07/44
Wg Cdr S.P. Coulson 11/44

608 (North Riding) SQUADRON (from 08/44) (8) (6T)
Based: Downham Market; *aircraft*: Mosquito
(08/44–08/45); *total sorties*: 1,726; *aircraft losses*: 9

Wg Cdr W.W.G. Scott 08/44
Wg Cdr R.C. Alabaster 11/44
Wg Cdr K. Gray 04/45

617 SQUADRON (from 03/43) (50 (AJ, KC, YZ)
Based: Scampton, Coningsby, Woodhall Spa;

aircraft: Lancaster (03/43–09/46), Mosquito
(04/44–03/45); *total sorties*: 1,599; *aircraft losses*: 32

Wg Cdr G.P. Gibson 03/43
Wg Cdr G.W. Holden 08/43
Sqn Ldr H.B. Martin 09/43
Wg Cdr G.L. Cheshire 11/43
Wg Cdr J.B. Tait 07/44
Wg Cdr J. Fauquier 12/44
Wg Cdr J.E. Grindon 04/45

619 SQUADRON (from 04/43) (5) (PG)
Based: Woodhall Spa, Coningsby, Dunholme
Lodge, Strubby; *aircraft*: Lancaster
(04/43–07/45); *total sorties*: 3,011; *aircraft losses*: 77

Wg Cdr I.J. McGhie 04/43
Wg Cdr W. Abercromby 08/43
Wg Cdr J.R. Jeudwine 12/43
Wg Cdr J.R. Maling
Wg Cdr R.A. Milward 07/44
Wg Cdr S.G. Birch 02/45

620 SQUADRON (from 06 to 11/43) (3) (QS)
Based: Chedburgh; *aircraft*: Stirling
(06/43–07/45); *total sorties*: 339; *aircraft losses*: 17

Wg Cdr D.H. Lee 06/43

622 SQUADRON (from 08/43) (3) (GI)
Based: Mildenhall; *aircraft*: Stirling
(08/43–01/44), Lancaster (12/43–08/45); *total
sorties*: 3,000; *aircraft losses*: 51

Sqn Ldr J. Martin 08/43 (Acting)
Wg Cdr G.H.N. Gibson 08/43
Wg Cdr I.C.K. Swales 02/44
Wg Cdr G.K. Buckingham 10/44

623 SQUADRON (from 08-12/43) (3) (IC)
Based: Downham Market; *aircraft*: Stirling
(08–12/43); *total sorties*: 150; *aircraft losses*: 10

Wg Cdr E.J. Little 08/43
Wg Cdr G.T. Wynne-Powell 09/43
Wg Cdr F.M. Milligan 11/43

625 SQUADRON (from 10/43) (1) (CF)
Based: Kelstern; *aircraft*: Lancaster
(10/43–10/45); *total sorties*: 3,385; *aircraft losses*:
66

Wg Cdr T. Preston 10/43
Wg Cdr D.D. Haig 03/44
Wg Cdr MacKay 09/44
Wg Cdr J.R. Barker 11/44

626 SQUADRON (from 11/43) (1) (UM)
Based: Wickenby; *aircraft*: Lancaster
(11/43–10/45); *total sorties*: 2,728; *aircraft losses*: 49

Wg Cdr P. Haynes 11/43
Wg Cdr Q.W.A. Ross 02/44
Wg Cdr G.F. Rodney 04/44
Wg Cdr J.H.N. Molesworth 09/44
Wg Cdr D.F. Dixon 04/45

627 SQUADRON (from 11/43) (8, 5) (AZ)
Based: Oakington, Woodhall Spa; *aircraft*:
Mosquito (11/43–09/45); *total sorties*: 1,535;
aircraft losses: 19

Wg Cdr R.P. Elliott 11/43
Wg Cdr G.W. Curry 06/44
Wg Cdr B.R.W. Hallows 01/45
Wg Cdr R. Kingsford-Smith 04/45

630 SQUADRON (from 11/43) (5) (LE)
Based: East Kirkby; *aircraft*: Lancaster
(11/43–07/45); *total sorties*: 2,453; *aircraft losses*: 59

Wg Cdr M. Crocker 11/43
Wg Cdr J.D. Rollinson 12/43
Wg Cdr W. Deas 02/44
Wg Cdr L.M. Blome-Jones 07/44
Wg Cdr J.E. Grindon 09/44
Wg Cdr F.W.L. Wild 04/45

635 SQUADRON (from 03/44) (8) (F2)
Based: Downham Market; *aircraft*: Lancaster

(03/44–08/45); *total sorties*: 2,225; *aircraft losses*:
34

Wg Cdr A.G.S. Cousens 03/44
Wg Cdr W.T. Brooks 04/44
Wg Cdr S. Baker 07/44
Wg Cdr J.W. Fordham 03/45

640 SQUADRON (from 01/44) (4) (C8)
Based: Leconfield; *aircraft*: Halifax
(01/44–05/45); *total sorties*: 2,423; *aircraft losses*:
40

Wg Cdr D.J.H. Eayrs 01/44
Wg Cdr W Carter 04/44
Wg Cdr M.T.Maw 06/44
Wg Cdr J.M. Viney 08/44
Wg Cdr E.D. Badcoe 01.45

692 (Fellowship of the Bellows) SQUADRON
(from 01/44) (8) (P3)
Based: Graveley; *aircraft*: Mosquito (01/44–09/45);
total sorties: 3,237; *aircraft losses*: 17

Wg Cdr W.G. Lockhart 01/44
Wg Cdr S.D. Watts 03/44

1409 (Met) FLIGHT (from 04/43) (no code)
Based: Oakington; *aircraft*: Mosquito
(04/43–5/45); *total sorties*: 1364; *aircraft losses*: 3

Sqn Ldr D.A. Braithwaite 04/43
Sqn Ldr The Hon P.I. Cunliffe-Lister 05/43
Flt Lt G.H. Hatton 07/43
Flt Lt V.S. Moore 11/43
Sqn Ldr J.M. Birkin 01/44
Sqn Ldr N. Bicknell 04/44
Sqn Ldr R.D. Mclaren 11/44
Sqn Ldr D.G. Johnson 03/45

(**Note:** data for sorties and aircraft losses has
been extracted from *The Bomber Command War
Diaries*, with acknowledgement.)

APPENDIX III

THE AIRFIELDS

ABINGDON, Berks
Opened: 09/32; currently in use by Army; *location*: NW Abingdon town
User sqns/units: 97 Sqn 09/39–04/40; 166 Sqn 09/39–04/40; 10 OTU 04/40–09/46

ALCONBURY, Cambs
Opened: 05/38; *closed*: 1997; *location*: 4 miles NW Huntingdon
User sqns/units: 15 Sqn 04–05/40; 40 Sqn 02/41–02/42; 156 Sqn 02–08/42
Transferred to USAAF 08/42

ATTLEBRIDGE, Norfolk
Opened: 06/41; *closed*: 03/59; *location*: 8 miles NW Norwich
User sqns/units: 88 Sqn 08/41–09/42; 320 Sqn 03/43–08/43
Transferred to USAAF 03/44

BALDERTON, Notts
Opened: 06/41; *closed*: 1954; *location*: 3 miles SSE Newark-on-Trent
User sqns/units: 25 OTU 06–11/41; 408 Sqn 12/41–09/42; 1668 HCU 08–11/43; 227 Sqn 10/44–04/45
Transferred to USAAF 01/44
Returned to RAF 10/44

BARDNEY, Lincs
Opened: 04/43; *closed*: 1963; *location*: 10 miles E Lincoln
User sqns/units: 9 Sqn 04/43–07/45; 227 Sqn 10/44; 189 Sqn 10–11/44, 04–10/45

BARFORD St JOHN, Oxon
Opened: 06/41; *closed*: 03/46; *location*: 4½ miles SSE Banbury
User sqns/units: 16 OTU 12/42–03/46

BASSINGBOURN, Cambs
Opened: 03/38; currently in use by Army; *location*: 3½ miles NW Royston
User sqns/units: 104 Sqn 05/38–09/39; 108 Sqn 05/38–09/39; 215 Sqn 09/39–04/40; 35 Sqn 12/39–02/40; 11 OTU 04/40–10/42
Transferred to USAAF 10/42

BENSON, Oxon
Opened: 04/39; currently in use by RAF; *location*: 2 miles NE Wallingford
User sqns/units: 103 Sqn 04–09/39; 150 Sqn 04–09/39; 52 Sqn 09/39–04/40; 63 Sqn 09/39–04/40; 207 Sqn 04/40; 12 OTU 04/40–09/41; 1 PRU 11/40–10/42
Transferred to Coastal Command 09/41

BICESTER, Oxon
Opened: 1917; currently in use by RAF; *location*: 1 mile NNE Bicester town
User sqns/units: 104 Sqn 09/39–04/40; 108 Sqn 09/39–04/40; 13 OTU 04/40–06/43; 1551 Flt 11/42–04/43; 307 FTU 12/42–03/43
Transferred to Fighter Command 06/43

BINBROOK, Lincs
Opened: 06/40; *closed*: 1988; *location*: 9 miles SW Grimsby
User sqns/units: 12 Sqn 07–08/40, 09/40–09/42; 142 Sqn 07–08/40, 09/40–11/41; 460 Sqn 05/43–07/45

BIRCOTES, Notts
Opened: 11/41; *closed*: 08/44; *location*: 1 mile W Bawtry
User sqns/units: 25 OTU 06/41–01/43; 18 OTU 10/43–08/44

BITTESWELL, Leics
Opened: 02/42; currently in use by British Aerospace; *location*: 6 miles N Rugby
User sqns/units: 18 OTU 02/42–06/43; 29 OTU 06/43–11/44
Transferred to Transport Command 11/44

BLYTON, Lincs
Opened: 11/42; *closed*; 1954; *location*: 16 miles NW Lincoln
User sqns/units: 199 Sqn 11/42–02/43; 1662 HCU 02/43–04/45

BODNEY, Norfolk
Opened: 03/40; *closed*: 11/45; *location*: 4 miles W Watton
User sqns/units: 82 Sqn 03/40–04/41; 105 Sqn 05–07/41; 21 Sqn 03–10/42
Transferred to USAAF 05/43

BOTTESFORD, Lincs
Opened: 09/41; *closed*: 1945; *location*: 7 miles NW Grantham
User sqns/units: 207 Sqn 11/41–09/42; 90 Sqn 11–12/42; 467 Sqn 11/42–11/43; 1668 HCU 07/44–03/46
Transferred to USAAF 11/43
Returned to RAF 07/44

BOURN, Cambs
Opened: 04/41; *closed*: 1948; *location*: 7 miles W Cambridge
User sqns/units: 101 Sqn 02–08/42; 15 Sqn 08/42–04/43; 97 Sqn 04/43–04/44; 105 Sqn 03/44–06/45; 162 Sqn 12/44–07/45

BRAMCOTE, Warks
Opened: 06/40; currently in use by Army; *location*: 4 miles SE Nuneaton

User sqns/units: 18 OTU 06/40–03/43; 300 Sqn 07–08/40; 301 Sqn 07–08/40; 304 Sqn 08–12/40; 305 Sqn 08–12/40
Transferred to Transport Command 04/43

BREIGHTON, Yorks
Opened: 01/42; *closed*: 1946; *location*: 13 miles SE York
User sqns/units: 460 Sqn 01/42–05/43; 1656 HCU 10/42; 78 Sqn 06/43–09/45

BRUNTINGTHORPE, Leics
Opened: 11/42; *closed*: 1962; *location*: 10 miles S Leicester
User sqns/units: 29 OTU 06/43–06/45

BURN, Yorks
Opened: 11/42; *closed*: 1946; *location*: 2 miles S Selby
User sqns/units: 1653 HCU 06–10/42; 431 Sqn 11/42–07/43; 578 Sqn 02/44–04/45

CARNABY, Yorks
Opened: 03/44; *closed*: 1963; *location*: 2 miles SW Bridlington
User sqns/units: none. FIDO-equipped Emergency Landing Ground under control of 4 Group

CASTLE DONINGTON, Leics
Opened: 01/43; currently in use as East Midlands Airport; *location*: 9 miles SE Derby
User sqns/units: 28 OTU 01/43–10/44
Transferred to Transport Command 10/44

CHEDBURGH, Suffolk
Opened: 09/42; *closed*: 10/52; *location*: 6 miles SW Bury St Edmunds
User sqns/units: 214 Sqn 10/42–12/43; 620 Sqn 06–11/43; 1653 HCU 11/43–12/44; 218 Sqn 12/44–08/45

CHEDDINGTON, Bucks
Opened: 03/42; currently in use by MOD; *location*: 6 miles ENE Aylesbury
User sqns/units: 26 OTU 03–09/42
Transferred to USAAF 10/42

CHIPPING WARDEN, Oxon
Opened: 08/41; *closed*: 12/46; *location*: 5 miles NNE Banbury
User sqns/units: 12 OTU 07/41–06/45

CHURCH BROUGHTON, Derby
Opened: 08/42; *closed*: 06/45; *location*: 8 miles W Derby
User sqns/units: 27 OTU 08/42–06/45; 1429 OTF 08/42–06/45; 93 Group Instructors' Pool 04/43–06/45

CONINGSBY, Lincs
Opened: 11/40; currently in use by RAF; *location*: 7 miles SSW Horncastle
User sqns/units: 106 Sqn 02/41–10/42; 97 Sqn 03/41–03/42, 04/44–11/46; 617 Sqn 08/43–01/44; 619 Sqn 01–04/44; 61 Sqn 01–04/44; 83 Sqn 04/44–11/46

COTTESMORE, Rutland
Opened: 03/38; currently in use by RAF; *location*: 5 miles NNE Oakham
User sqns/units: 185 Sqn 08/39–04/40, 04–05/40; 106 Sqn 09–10/39; 14 OTU 04/40–08/43
Transferred to USAAF 09/43

CRANFIELD, Beds
Opened: 07/37; currently in use as Institute of Technology; *location*: 7 miles SW Bedford
User sqns/units: 35 Sqn 08–12/39; 207 Sqn 08–12/39, 04/40
Transferred to Fighter Command 05/41

CROFT, Yorks
Opened: 10/41; *closed*: 1946; *location*: 4 miles S Darlington
User sqns/units: 419 Sqn 10–11/42; 427 Sqn 11/42–05/43; 1664 HCU 05–12/43; 431 Sqn 12/43–06/45; 434 Sqn 12/43–06/45

CROUGHTON, Northants
Opened: 07/41; *closed*: 05/46; *location*: 3 miles SSW Brackley
User sqns/units: 16 OTU 06/41–07/42
Transferred to Flying Training Command 07/42

DALTON, Yorks
Opened: 11/41; *closed*: 12/45; *location*: 4 miles S Thirsk
User sqns/units: 102 Sqn 11/41–06/42; 1652 HCU 07–08/42; 428 Sqn 11/42–06/43; 424 Sqn 05/43; 1666 HCU 05–10/43; 420 Sqn 11–12/43

DESBOROUGH, Northants
Opened: 09/43; *closed*: 1946; *location*: 6 miles NNW Kettering
User sqns/units: 84 OTU 09/43–06/45

DISHFORTH, Yorks
Opened: 09/36; currently in use by Army; *location*: 4 miles E Ripon
User sqns/units: 10 Sqn 01/37–07/40; 78 Sqn 02/37–12/39, 07/40–04/41; 51 Sqn 12/39–05/42; 425 Sqn 06/42–05/43, 11–12/43; 426 Sqn 10/42–06/43

DONCASTER, Yorks
Opened: 01/16; *closed*: 05/54; *location*: 1 mile SE Doncaster town
User sqns/units: 18 OTU 06/43–01/45

DOWNHAM MARKET, Norfolk
Opened: 07/42; *closed*: 10/46; *location*: 10 miles S Kings Lynn
User sqns/units: 218 Sqn 07/42–03/44; 623 Sqn 08–12/43; 214 Sqn 12/43–01/44; 635 Sqn 03/44–09/45; 571 Sqn 04/44; 608 Sqn 08/44–08/45

DRIFFIELD, Yorks
Opened: 07/36; currently in use by Army; *location*: 13 miles N Beverley
User sqns/units: 102 Sqn 07/38–08/40; 77 Sqn 07/38–08/40; 97 Sqn 04–05/40; 88 Sqn 06/40; 104 Sqn 04/41–02/42; 405 Sqn 04–06/41; 158 Sqn 02–06/42; 466 Sqn 10–12/42, 06/44–09/45; 196 Sqn 11–12/42; 462 Sqn 08–12/44

DUNHOLME LODGE, Lincs
Opened: 05/43; *closed*: 1964; *location*: 5 miles NE Lincoln

User sqns/units: 44 Sqn 05/43–09/44; 619 Sqn 04–09/44; 170 Sqn 10–11/44

EAST KIRKBY, Lincs
Opened: 08/43; *closed*: 04/70; *location*: 4 miles SW Spilsby
User sqns/units: 57 Sqn 08/43–11/45; 630 Sqn 11/43–07/45

EAST MOOR, Yorks
Opened: 06/42; *closed*: 06/46; *location*: 7 miles N York
User sqns/units: 158 Sqn 06–11/42; 429 Sqn 11/42–08/43; 432 Sqn 09/43–05/45; 1679 HCU 05–12/43; 415 Sqn 07/44–05/45

EAST WRETHAM, Norfolk
Opened: 03/40; *closed*: 07/46; *location*: 6 miles NE Thetford
User sqns/units: 311 Sqn 09/40–04/42; 1429 Flt 01–07/42; 115 Sqn 11/42–08/43; 1678 HCU 03–08/43
Transferred to USAAF 10/43

EDGEHILL, Warks
Opened: 10/41; *closed*: 06/45; *location*: 3 miles SE Kineton
User sqns/units: 21 OTU 10/41–04/43; 12 OTU 04/43–06/45

ELGIN, Moray
Opened: 06/40; *closed*: 1947; *location*: 1½ miles SW Elgin town
User sqns/units: 21 Sqn 06–10/40; 57 Sqn 06–08/40; 20 OTU 06/40–06/45

ELSHAM WOLDS, Lincs
Opened: 07/40; *closed*: 1947; *location*: 5 miles NNE Brigg
User sqns/units: 103 Sqn 07/42–11/45; 576 Sqn 11/43–10/44; 100 Sqn 04–12/45

ELVINGTON, Yorks
Opened: 10/42; *closed*: 03/92, now the Yorkshire Air Museum; *location*: 5 miles ESE York

User sqns/units: 77 Sqn 10/42–05/44; 346 Sqn 05/44–10/45; 347 Sqn 06/44–10/45

ENSTONE, Oxon
Opened: 09/42; *closed*: 1947; *location*: 5 miles E Chipping Norton
User sqns/units: 21 OTU 04/43–08/45

FALDINGWORTH, Lincs
Opened: 10/43; *closed*: 11/72; *location*: 5 miles SW Market Rasen
User sqns/units: 300 Sqn 03/44–10/46; 1667 HCU 10/43–02/44

FELTWELL, Norfolk
Opened: 04/37; *closed*: 05/58; *location*: 5 miles NW Brandon
User sqns/units: 37 Sqn 04/37–11/40; 75 Sqn 04/40–08/42; 57 Sqn 11/40–09/42; 464 Sqn 08/42–04/43; 487 Sqn 08/42–04/43; 192 Sqn 04–11/43; Bombing Development Unit (BDU) 04–11/43, 01–06/45; 320 Sqn 04–05/43; 1473 RCM Flt 09–11/43; 3 LFS 11/43–01/45

FINMERE, Bucks
Opened: 1941; *closed*: 07/45; *location*: 3½ miles W Buckingham
User sqns/units: 13 OTU 08/42–11/43; 307 FTU 03–05/43
Transferred to Flying Training Command 11/43

FINNINGLEY, Yorks
Opened: 09/36; *closed*: 09/95; *location*: 7 miles SE Doncaster
User sqns/units: 76 Sqn 04/37–09/39; 106 Sqn 10/39–02/41; 98 Sqn 03–04/40; 7 Sqn 04–05/40, 09/40; 12 Sqn 06–07/40; 25 OTU 03/41–01/43; 18 OTU 03/43–01/45; Bomber Command Instructors' School (BCIS) 12/44–01/47

FISKERTON, Lincs
Opened: 01/43; *closed*: 12/45; *location*: 4½ miles E Lincoln
User sqns/units: 49 Sqn 01/43–10/44; 576 Sqn 10/44–09/45; 150 Sqn 11/44

FORRES, Moray

Opened: 04/40; *closed*: 10/44; *location*: 13 miles WSW Elgin

User sqns/units: 19 OTU 04/40–10/44

FOULSHAM Norfolk

Opened: 05/42; *closed*: 1945; *location*: 8½ miles NNE Dereham

User sqns/units: 98 Sqn 10/42–08/43; 180 Sqn 10/42–08/43; 514 Sqn 09–11/43; 678 HCU 09–11/43; 192 Sqn 11/43–08/45; 462 Sqn 12/44–09/45

FULBECK, Lincs

Opened: 1940; *closed*: 1970; *location*: 6½ miles ESE Newark on Trent

User sqns/units: 49 Sqn 10/44–04/45; 189 Sqn 11/44–04/45

To USAAF control 10/43

Returned to RAF 10/44

FULL SUTTON, Yorks

Opened: 05/44; *closed*: 04/63; *location*: 8 miles E York

User sqns/units: 77 Sqn 05/44–08/45

GAMSTON, Notts

Opened: 12/42; *closed*: 1957; *location*: 3 miles S East Retford

User sqns/units: 82 OTU 06/43–06/44; 86 OTU 06–10/44; 30 OTU 02–06/45

Opened in Flying Training Command 12/42

To Bomber Command 05/43

GAYDON, Warks

Opened: 06/42; *closed*: 10/74; *location*: 7½ miles SSE Leamington Spa

User sqns/units: 12 OTU 06–09/42; 22 OTU 09/42–07/45

GRANSDEN LODGE, Beds

Opened: 04/42; *closed*: 1955; *location*: 10 miles W Cambridge

User sqns/units: 1418 Flt 04–07/42; 1474 Flt 07/42–01/43; 1 BDU 07/42–04/43

192 Sqn 01–04/43; PFF Navigation Training Unit 04–06/43; 405 Sqn 04/43–05/45; 97 Sqn 08–09/43; 142 Sqn (LNSF) 10/44–09/45

GRAVELEY, Hunts

Opened: 03/42; *closed*: 12/68; *location*: 5 miles S Huntingdon

User sqns/units: 161 Sqn 03–04/42; 35 Sqn 08/42–09/46; 692 Sqn (LNSF) 01/44–06/45; 571 Sqn (LNSF) 04/44

GREAT MASSINGHAM, Norfolk

Opened: 09/40; *closed*: 04/58; *location*: 7½ miles WSW Fakenham

User sqns/units: 18 Sqn 09/40–04/41; 107 Sqn 05/41–08/43; 90 Sqn 05–08/41

Fortress I; 98 Sqn 09–10/42; 342 Sqn 07–09/43; 1692 BSTU; 169 Sqn 06/44–08/45

GRIMSBY/WALTHAM, Lincs

Opened: 11/41; *closed*: 1946; *location*: 9 miles S Grimsby

User sqns/units: 142 Sqn 11/41–12/42; 100 Sqn 12/42–04/45; 550 Sqn 10/43–01/44

HAMPSTEAD NORRIS, Berks

Opened: 09/40; *closed*: 1945; *location*: 11 miles WNW Reading

User sqns/units: 15 OTU 09/40–03/44

To 38 Group control 03/44

HARRINGTON, Northants

Opened: 11/43; *closed*: 01/63; *location*: 5 miles W Kettering

User sqns/units: None

Declared surplus to RAF requirements and transferred to USAAF control 03/44

HARWELL, Oxon

Opened: 02/37; *closed*: 1945; currently Atomic Energy Research Establishment; *location*: 6 miles S Abingdon

User sqns/units: 75 Sqn 09/39–04/40; 148 Sqn 09/39–04/40; 15 OTU 04/40–03/44

To 38 Group control 04/44

HEMSWELL, Lincs

Opened: 01/37; *closed*: 1967; *location*: 7 miles E Gainsborough

User sqns/units: 61 Sqn 03/37–07/41; 44 Sqn 03/37–07/41; 300 Sqn 07/41–05/42, 01–06/43; 301 Sqn 07/41–04/43; 305 Sqn 07/42–06/43; 83 Sqn 04/44–01/56; 1 LFS 01–11/44; 150 Sqn 11/44–11/45; 170 Sqn 11/44–11/45

HINTON-IN-THE-HEDGES, Northants

Opened: 11/40; *closed*: 07/45; *location*: 6 miles ESE Banbury

User sqns/units: 13 OTU 11/40–07/42; 16 OTU 07/42–04/43; 1478 Flt 04/43–07/44; Signals Development Unit (SDU) 06/43–07/44

HIXON, Staffs

Opened: 05/42; *closed*: 11/57; *location*: 7 miles NE Stafford

User sqns/units: 30 OTU 06/42–02/45

HOLME-ON-SPALDING-MOOR, Yorks

Opened: 08/41; *closed*: 10/45; *location*: 5 miles SW Market Weighton

User sqns/units: 458 Sqn 08/41–03/42; 101 Sqn 09/42–06/43; 76 Sqn 06/43–08/45

Transferred to Transport Command 05/45

HONEYBOURNE, Worcs

Opened: 10/41; *closed*: 01/46; *location*: 4½ miles E Evesham

User sqns/units: 24 OTU 03/42–07/45

Opened in Ferry Command 10/41

Transferred to Bomber Command 03/42

HONILEY, Warks

Opened: 05/41; *closed*: 03/58; *location*: 7 miles SW Coventry

User sqns/units: Signals Flying Unit (26 Gp) 07/44–06/46

Opened under Fighter Command control 05/41

Transferred to Bomber Command 07/44

HONINGTON, Suffolk

Opened: 05/37; currently in use by RAF regiment; *location*: 7 miles NNE Bury St Edmunds

User sqns/units: 9 Sqn 07/39–08/42; 103 Sqn 06–07/40; 105 Sqn 06–07/40; 311 Sqn 07–09/40; 214 Sqn 01/42

Transferred to USAAF 09/42

HORSHAM St FAITH, Norfolk

Opened: 05/40; currently in use as Norwich Airport; *location*: 4 miles N Norwich

User sqns/units: 139 Sqn 06/40–07/41, 10–12/41; 114 Sqn 06–08/40; 18 Sqn 07–11/41, 12/41; 105 Sqn 12/41–09/42

Transferred to USAAF 09/42

HUSBANDS BOSWORTH, Leics

Opened: 1943; *closed*: 1956; *location*: 10 miles NE Rugby

User sqns/units: 14 OTU 08/43–06/44; 85 OTU 06/44–07/45

INGHAM, Lincs

Opened: 05/42; *closed*: 01/45; *location*: 8 miles NNW Lincoln

User sqns/units: 300 Sqn 05/42–01/43, 06/43–03/44; 199 Sqn 02–06/43; 305 Sqn 06–09/43

KELSTERN, Lincs

Opened: 09/43; *closed*: 05/45; *location*: 5 miles NW Louth

User sqns/units: 625 Sqn 10/43–04/45; 170 Sqn 10/44

KIMBOLTON, Cambs

Opened: 11/41; *closed*: 1946; *location*: 8 miles W Huntingdon

User sqns/units: 460 Sqn 11/41–01/42

Transferred to USAAF 07/42

KINLOSS, Moray

Opened: 1939; currently in use by RAF; *location*: 9 miles W Elgin

User sqns/units: 19 OTU 05/40-06/45

Opened in Flying Training Command 1939

Transferred to Bomber Command 04/40

KIRMINGTON, Lincs

Opened: 10/42; currently in use as Humberside Airport; *location*: 6 miles NE Brigg

User sqns/units: 150 Sqn 10–12/42; 142 Sqn 12/42–01/43; 166 Sqn 01/43–11/45; 153 Sqn 10/44

LAKENHEATH, Suffolk

Opened: 06/41; currently in use by USAF; *location*: 4½ miles SW Brandon

User sqns/units: 20 OTU 11/41–01/42; 149 Sqn 04/42–05/44; 199 Sqn 06/43–05/44; Closed for rebuilding to Very Heavy Bomber (VHB) station standard 05/44

LANGAR, Notts

Opened: 09/42; *closed*: 09/68; *location*: 9 miles SE Nottingham

User sqns/units: 207 Sqn 09/42–10/43; 1669 HCU 11/44–03/45.

To USAAF control 10/43

To RAF Bomber Command control 10/44

LECONFIELD, Yorks

Opened: 12/36; currently in use by Army; *location*: 2½ miles N Beverley

User sqns/units: 97 Sqn 01/37–09/39; 196 Sqn 12/42–07/43; 466 Sqn 12/42–06/44; 640 Sqn 01/44–05/45; 51 Sqn 04–08/45

To Fighter Command 10/39

Closed for runway building 12/41

To Bomber Command 12/42

LEEMING, Yorks

Opened: 06/40; currently in use by RAF; *location*: 7 miles SW Northallerton

User sqns/units: 7 Sqn 08–10/40; 10 Sqn 07/40–08/42; 102 Sqn 08–09/40; 35 Sqn 11–12/40; 77 Sqn 09/41–05/42; 419 Sqn 08/42; 408 Sqn 09/42–08/43; 1659 HCU 10/42–03/43; 405 Sqn 03–04/43; 424 Sqn 04–05/43; 427 Sqn 05/43–05/46; 429 Sqn 08/43–05/46

LICHFIELD, Staffs

Opened: 08/40; *closed*: 04/58; *location*: 3 miles NE Lichfield

User sqns/units: 27 OTU 04/41–07/45

LINDHOLME, Yorks

Opened: 06/40; currently in use as HM Prison; *location*: 7 miles ENE Doncaster

User sqns/units: 50 Sqn 07/40–07/41; 408 Sqn 06–07/41; 304 Sqn 07/41–05/42; 305 Sqn 07/41–07/42; 1656 HCU 10/42–11/45; 1667 HCU 06–10/43; 1 LFS 11/43–01/44

Opened as Hatfield Woodhouse 06/40

Name changed to Lindholme 08/40

LINTON-ON-OUSE, Yorks

Opened: 05/37; currently in use by RAF; *location*: 8½ miles NW York

User sqns/units: 51 Sqn 04/38–12/39; 58 Sqn 04/38–09/39, 02/40–04/42; 78 Sqn 12/39–07/40, 09/42–06/43; ?7 Sqn 08–10/40; 102 Sqn 10–11/40; 35 Sqn 12/40–08/42; 76 Sqn 05–06/41, 09/42–06/43; 426 Sqn 06/43–05/45; 408 Sqn 08/43–06/45; 405 Sqn 05–06/45

LISSETT, Yorks

Opened: 02/43; *closed*: 08/45; *location*: 6 miles SSW Bridlington

User sqns/units: 158 Sqn 04/43–08/45; 640 Sqn 01/44–05/45

LITTLE HORWOOD, Bucks

Opened: 09/42; *closed*: 01/46; *location*: 2½ miles NE Winslow

User sqns/units: 26 OTU 09/42–08/44, 10/44–03/46

LITTLE SNORING, Norfolk

Opened: 07/43; *closed*: 10/58; *location*: 3½ miles NE Fakenham

User sqns/units: 115 Sqn 08/43–11/43; 1678 HCU 08–09/43; 23 Sqn 06/44–09/45; 169 Sqn 12/43–06/44; 515 Sqn 12/43–06/45

LITTLE STAUGHTON, Hunts

Opened: 12/42; *closed*: 12/45; *location*: 8½ miles NNE Bedford

User sqns/units: 582 Sqn 04/44–09/45; 109 Sqn 04/44–09/45

Opened as USAAF bomber station 12/42

Transferred to RAF Bomber Command 03/44

LONG MARSTON, Gloucs
Opened: 11/41; *closed*: 1954; *location*: 3½ miles SSW Stratford-upon-Avon
User sqns/units: 24 OTU 03/42–07/45; 23 OTU 1943

LOSSIEMOUTH, Moray
Opened: 1939; currently in use by RAF; *location*: 4½ miles N Elgin
User sqns/units: 20 OTU 05/40–07/45; 21 Sqn 06–10/40; 57 Sqn 06–08/40

LUDFORD MAGNA, Lincs
Opened: 06/43; *closed*: 05/63; *location*: 6 miles E Market Rasen
User sqns/units: 101 Sqn 06/43–10/45

MARHAM, Norfolk
Opened: 04/37; currently in use by RAF; *location*: 10 miles SE King's Lynn
User sqns/units: 38 Sqn 05/37–11/40; 115 Sqn 06/37–09/42; 218 Sqn 11/40–07/42; 1418 Flt 01–03/42; 105 Sqn 09/42–03/44; 139 Sqn 09/42–07/43; 1655 Mosquito Training Unit (MTU) 1943; 109 Sqn 07/43–04/44
Closed for redevelopment to VHB station standard 03/44

MARKET HARBOROUGH, Leics
Opened: 05/43; *closed*: 05/47; *location*: 2 miles NW Market Harborough town
User sqns/units: 14 OTU 08/43–06/45

MARSTON MOOR, Yorks
Opened: 11/41; *closed*: 11/45; *location*: 8½ miles W York
User sqns/units: 1652 HCU 01–07/42, 08/42–06/45

MELBOURNE, Yorks
Opened: 1940; *closed*: 03/46; *location*: 12 miles SE York
User sqns/units: 10 Sqn 08/42–08/45

MEPAL, Cambs
Opened: 06/43; *closed*: 1963; *location*: 6 miles W Ely
User sqns/units: 75 Sqn 06/43–07/45

METHERINGHAM, Lincs
Opened: 10/43; *closed*: 02/46; *location*: 10 miles SE Lincoln
User sqns/units: 106 Sqn 11/43–02/46

METHWOLD, Suffolk
Opened: 09/39; *closed*: 06/58; *location*: 5 miles NW Brandon
User sqns/units: 214 Sqn 09/39–02/40; 21 Sqn 10/42–04/43; 57 Sqn 01–09/42; 320 Sqn 03/43; 464 Sqn 04–07/43; 487 Sqn 04–07/43; 149 Sqn 05/44–04/46; 218 Sqn 08–12/44

MIDDLETON St GEORGE, Co. Durham
Opened: 01/41; currently in use as Teesside Airport; *location*: 5 miles E Darlington
User sqns/units: 78 Sqn 04–10/41, 06–09/42; 76 Sqn 06/41–09/42; 420 Sqn 10/42–05/43; 419 Sqn 11/42–06/45; 428 Sqn 06/43–05/45

MILDENHALL, Suffolk
Opened: 10/34; currently in use by USAF; *location*: 12 miles NW Bury St Edmunds
User sqns/units: 149 Sqn 04/37–04/42; 419 Sqn 12/41–08/42; 115 Sqn 09–11/42; 15 Sqn 04/43–08/46; 622 Sqn 08/43–08/45

MOLESWORTH, Hunts
Opened: 05/41; currently in use by USAF; *location*: 10½ miles WNW Huntingdon
User sqns/units: 460 Sqn 11/41–01/42
Transferred to USAAF 06/42

MORETON-IN-MARSH, Gloucs
Opened: 01/41; currently in use as Fire Service Training College; *location*: 14 miles S Stratford-upon-Avon
User sqns/units: 21 OTU 03/41–11/46; 1446 Flt 05/42–05/43

MOUNT FARM, Oxon
Opened: 07/40; *closed*: 07/46; *location*: 8 miles SE Oxford
User sqns/units: 12 OTU 07/40–07/41; 140 Sqn 05/42–03/43

To Coastal Command control 01/42
To USAAF control 02/43

NEWMARKET, Suffolk

Opened: 1939; *closed*: 05/45; *location*: 1 mile W Newmarket town
User sqns/units: 99 Sqn 09/39–03/41; 7 Sqn 03–04/41; 138 Sqn 08–12/41; 215 Sqn 12/41–01/42; 161 Sqn 02–03/42; 75 Sqn 11/42–06/43; Bombing Development Unit 09/43–02/45;

NEWTON, Notts

Opened: 1937; *closed*: 04/95; *location*: 7 miles E Nottingham
User sqns/units: 103 Sqn 07/40–07/41; 150 Sqn 07/40–07/41
To Flying Training Command 07/41

NORTH CREAKE, Norfolk

Opened: 11/43; *closed*: 09/47; *location*: 2 miles NW Little Walsingham
User sqns/units: 199 Sqn 05/44–07/45; 171 Sqn 09/44–07/45

NORTH KILLINGHOLME, Lincs

Opened: 11/43; *closed*: 10/45; *location*: 10 miles NW Grimsby
User sqns/units: 550 Sqn ?1/44–10/45

NORTH LUFFENHAM, Rutland

Opened: 12/40; *closed*: 1998; *location*: 6 miles SW Oakham
User sqns/units: 61 Sqn 07–09/41; 144 Sqn 07/41–04/42; 29 OTU 04/42–07/43; 1653 HCU 11/44–10/45
To Flying Training Command 04/44
To Bomber Command 11/44

NUNEATON, Leics

Opened: 02/43; *closed*: 09/46; *location*: 4½ miles NNE Nuneaton town
User sqns/units: 18 OTU 02–03/43
To Transport Command 04/43

OAKINGTON, Cambs

Opened: 07/40; currently in use by Army Air Corps; *location*: 5 miles NW Cambridge
User sqns/units: 101 Sqn 07/41–02/42; 218 Sqn 07–11/40; 7 Sqn 10/40–07/45; 3 PRU 11/40–07/41; Navigation Training Unit (NTU) 03–06/43; 1409 Met Flt 04/43–01/44; 627 Sqn 11/43–04/44; 571 Sqn 04/44–07/45

OAKLEY, Bucks

Opened: 05/42; *closed*: 08/45; *location*: 11 miles WSW Aylesbury
User sqns/units: 11 OTU 08/42–08/45

OSSINGTON, Notts

Opened: 01/42; *closed*: 08/46; *location*: 8 miles NNW Newark-on-Trent
User sqns/units: 82 OTU 06/43–01/45
To Flying Training Command 01/42
To Bomber Command 05/43

OULTON, Norfolk

Opened: 07/40; *closed*: 11/47; *location*: 3 miles W Aylsham
User sqns/units: 114 Sqn 08/40–03/41; 18 Sqn 04–07/41, 11–12/41; 139 Sqn 07–10/41, 12/41–01/42; 88 Sqn 09/42–03/43; 21 Sqn 04–08/43; 214 Sqn 05/44–07/45; 1699 CU 05/44–07/45; 223 Sqn 08/44–07/45

PERSHORE, Worcs

Opened: 02/41; *closed*: 1978; *location*: 8 miles ESE Worcester
User sqns/units: 23 OTU, 04/41–03/44
Transferred to Ferry Command control 03/44

POCKLINGTON, Yorks

Opened: 06/41; *closed*: 09/46; *location*: 12 miles ESE York
User sqns/units: 405 Sqn, 06/41–08/42; 102 Sqn, 08/42–09/45

POLEBROOK, Northants

Opened: 06/41; *closed*: 01/67; *location*: 3½ miles ESE Oundle

User sqns/units: 17 OTU, 12/40–09/41; 90 Sqn, 08/41–02/42; 1653 HCU, 01–06/42

RICCALL, Yorks
Opened: 09/42; *closed*: 1946; *location*: 10 miles S York
User sqns/units: 1658 HCU, 10/42–04/45
Transferred to Transport Command control 04/45

RIDGEWELL, Essex
Opened: 12/42; *closed*: 03/57; *location*: 7½ miles NW Halstead
User sqns/units: 90 Sqn, 12/42–05/43
Transferred to USAAF control 05/43

RUFFORTH, Yorks
Opened: 11/42; *closed*: 1954; *location*: 3½ miles W York
User sqns/units: 158 Sqn, 11/42–02/43; 1663 HCU, 03/43–05/45

SALTBY, Leics
Opened: 08/41; *closed*: 09/55; *location*: 8 miles NE Melton Mowbray
User sqns/units: 14 OTU 08/41–08/43
Transferred to USAAF 02/44

SANDTOFT, Lincs
Opened: 02/44; *closed*: 11/45; *location*: 11½ miles NE Doncaster
User sqns/units: 1667 HCU 02/44–11/45

SCAMPTON, Lincs
Opened: 08/36; *closed*: 1996; *location*: 5 miles N Lincoln
User sqns/units: 49 Sqn 03/38–01/43; 83 Sqn 03/38–08/42; 98 Sqn 03/40; 57 Sqn 09/42–08/43; 1661 HCU 11–12/42; 467 Sqn 11/42; 617 Sqn 03–08/43; 153 Sqn 10/44–09/45; 625 Sqn 04–10/45

SCULTHORPE, Norfolk
Opened: 01/43; *closed*: 1994; *location*: 4 miles WNW Fakenham

User sqns/units: 342 Sqn 05–07/43; 464 Sqn 07–12/43; 487 Sqn 07–12/43; 21 Sqn 09–12/43; 214 Sqn 01–05/44
Closed for conversion to VHB station standard 05/44

SEIGHFORD, Staffs
Opened: 01/43; *closed*: 01/66; *location*: 2 miles NW Stafford
User sqns/units: 30 OTU 01/43–10/44

SILVERSTONE, Northants
Opened: 03/43; *closed*: 11/46; *location*: 4 miles S Towcester
User sqns/units: 17 OTU 04/43–11/46

SKELLINGTHORPE, Lincs
Opened: 10/41; *closed*: 1952; *location*: 3 miles W Lincoln
User sqns/units: 50 Sqn 11/41–06/42, 10/42–06/45; 61 Sqn 11/43–01/44, 04/44–06/45

SKIPTON-ON-SWALE, Yorks
Opened: 08/42; *closed*: 10/45; *location*: 4 miles W Thirsk
User sqns/units: 420 Sqn 08–10/42; 432 Sqn 05–09/43; 433 Sqn 09/43–10/45; 424 Sqn 11/43–10/45

SNAITH, Yorks
Opened: 07/41; *closed*: 04/46; *location*: 7 miles W Goole
User sqns/units: 150 Sqn 07/41–10/42; 51 Sqn 10/42–04/45; 578 Sqn 01–02/44

SPILSBY, Lincs
Opened: 09/43; *closed*: 03/58; *location*: 3 miles E Spilsby town
User sqns/units: 207 Sqn 10/43–07/45; 44 Sqn 09/44–07/45

STANTON HARCOURT, Oxon
Opened: 09/40; *closed*: 01/46; location: 5 miles W Oxford
User sqns/unit: 10 OTU 09/40–01/45

STEEPLE MORDEN, Cambs
Opened: 09/40; *closed*: 09/46; *location*: 3 miles W Royston
User sqns/units: 11 OTU 09/40–09/42; 17 OTU 01–05/43
Transferred to USAAF 07/43

STRADISHALL, Suffolk
Opened: 02/38; *closed*: 08/70; *location*: 5 miles NE Haverhill
User sqns/units: 75 Sqn 07–09/39; 148 Sqn 04–05/40; 150 Sqn 06–07/40; 214 Sqn 02/40–10/42; 138 Sqn 12/41–03/42; 215 Sqn 01–02/42; 109 Sqn 0–08/42; 101 Sqn 08–09/42; 1657 HCU 10/42–12/44; 186 Sqn 12/44–07/45

STRATFORD, Warks
Opened: 07/41; *closed*: 11/45; *location*: 2½ miles SSE Stratford-upon-Avon
User sqns/units: 22 OTU 09/41–11/42, 03–12/44; 23 OTU 11/42–03/44

STRUBBY, Lincs
Opened: 04/44; *closed*: 09/72; *location*: 3½ miles N Alford
User sqns/units: 619 Sqn 09/44–06/45; 227 Sqn 04–06/45

STURGATE, Lincs
Opened: 09/44; *closed*: 1964; *location*: 4 miles ESE Gainsborough
User sqns/unit: 1520 BAT Flt 09/44–05/45

SWANNINGTON, Norfolk
Opened: 04/44; *closed*: 11/47; *location*: 3 miles SE Reepham
User sqns/units: 85 Sqn 05–07/44, 08/44–06/45; 157 Sqn 05–07/44, 08/44–08/45

SWANTON MORLEY, Norfolk
Opened: 09/40; currently in use by Army; *location*: 3 miles N East Dereham
User sqns/units: 88 Sqn 07–08/41, 03–08/43; 105 Sqn 10/40–12/41; 226 Sqn 12/41–02/44; 98 Sqn 08/43–10/44; 305 Sqn 09–11/43; 2 GSU 04–12/44; BSDU 11/44–05/45

SWINDERBY, Lincs
Opened: 08/40; *closed*: 03/96; *location*: 9 miles SW Lincoln
User sqns/units: 300 Sqn 08/40–07/41; 301 Sqn 08/40–07/41; 455 Sqn 06/41–02/42; 50 Sqn 07–11/41, 6–10/42; 1660 HCU 10/42–11/43, 01/45–11/46; 1654 HCU 06/43

SYERSTON, Notts
Opened: 12/40; currently in use by RAF; *location*: 5 miles SW Newark-on-Trent
User sqns/units: 304 Sqn 12/40–07/41; 305 Sqn 12/40–07/41; 408 Sqn 07–12/41; 61 Sqn 05/42–11/43; 106 Sqn 10/42–11/43; 49 Sqn 04–09/45

TATENHILL, Staffs
Opened: 08/40; *closed*: 01/47; *location*: 5 miles W Burton upon Trent
User sqns/units: 27 OTU, 11/41–08/42
Transferred to Flying Training Command control 11/42

TEMPSFORD, Beds
Opened: 1941; *closed*: 02/63; *location*: 9 miles ENE Bedford
User sqns/units: 11 OTU, 12/41–04/42; 109 Sqn 01–04/42; 1418 Flt 03–04/42; 138 Sqn 03/42–03/45; 161 Sqn

THIRSK, Yorks
Location: ½ mile W Thirsk town
User sqns/units: 226 Sqn, 06/40
Racecourse used occasionally as emergency landing ground for Topcliffe and Skipton

THOLTHORPE, Yorks
Opened: 08/40; *closed*: 09/45; *location*: 12 miles NW York
User sqns/units: 77 Sqn 08–12/40; 434 Sqn 06–12/43; 431 Sqn 07–12/43; 420 Sqn 12/43–06/45; 425 Sqn 12/43–06/45

TILSTOCK, Salop
Opened: 08/42; *closed*: 03/46; *location*: 3 miles SSE Whitchurch
User sqns/units: 81 OTU 09/42–01/44
To 38 Group, 01/44

TOPCLIFFE, Yorks

Opened: 09/40; currently in use by Army Air Corps and RAF; *location*: 2½ miles SW Thirsk

User sqns/units: 77 Sqn 10/40–09/41; 102 Sqn 11/40–11/41; 405 Sqn 08–10/42, 03/43; 419 Sqn 08–10/42; 424 Sqn 10/42–04/43; 1659 HCU 03/43–09/45

TUDDENHAM, Suffolk

Opened: 10/43; *closed*: 07/63; *location*: 7 miles NW Bury St Edmunds

User sqns/units: 90 Sqn 10/43–11/46; 186 Sqn 10–12/44; 138 Sqn 03/45–11/46

TURWESTON, Bucks

Opened: 11/42; *closed*: 09/45; *location*: 9 miles E Aylesbury

User sqns/units: 12 OTU 11/42–04/43; 13 OTU 04–08/43; 17 OTU 08/43–07/45

UPPER HEYFORD, Oxon

Opened: 10/27; *closed*: 09/94; *location*: 5 miles NW Bicester

User sqns/units: 18 Sqn 10/31–09/39; 57 Sqn 09/32–09/39; 7 Sqn 09/39–04/40; 76 Sqn 09/39–04/40; 16 OTU 04/40–03/46; 1473 Flt 07/42–01/43

UPWOOD, Hunts

Opened: 01/37; *closed*: 09/95; *location*: 6 miles N Huntingdon

User sqns/units: 90 Sqn 09/39–04/40; 35 Sqn 02–04/40; 17 OTU 04/40–04/43; PFF Navigation Training Unit (NTU) 06/43–03/44; 139 Sqn 02/44–02/46; 156 Sqn 03/44–06/45

WADDINGTON, Lincs

Opened: 11/16; currently in use by RAF; *location*: 4 miles S Lincoln

User sqns/units: 44 Sqn 06/37–05/43; 50 Sqn 05/37–07/40; 142 Sqn 06–07/40; 207 Sqn 11/40–11/41; 97 Sqn 02–03/41; 420 Sqn 12/41–08/42; 9 Sqn 08/42–04/43; 467 Sqn 11/43–06/45; 463 Sqn 11/43–07/45

WARBOYS, Hunts

Opened: 09/41; *closed*: 1963; *location*: 5½ miles NE Huntingdon

User sqns/units: 156 Sqn 08/42–03/44; 1655 MCU 03–12/44; PFF NTU 03/44–06/45

WATERBEACH, Cambs

Opened: 01/41; currently in use by Army; *location*: 5 miles N Cambridge

User sqns/units: 99 Sqn 03/41–02/42; 1651 HCU 01/42–11/43; 514 Sqn 11/43–08/45; 1678 CF 11/43–06/44; Bomber Command Film Unit 09/44–06/45

WATTISHAM, Suffolk

Opened: 03/39; currently in use by Army Air Corps; *location*: 9 miles NW Ipswich

User sqns: 107 Sqn 05/39–05/41; 110 Sqn 05/39–03/42; 114 Sqn 05–06/40; 226 Sqn 05–12/41; 18 Sqn 12/41–08/42 Transferred to USAAF 09/42

WATTON, Suffolk

Opened: 01/39; currently in use as HM Prison; *location*: 11 miles NE Thetford

User sqns/units: 21 Sqn 03/39–06/40, 10/40–12/41; 82 Sqn 08/39–03/42; 18 Sqn 05/40; 105 Sqn 07–10/40; 90 Sqn 05/41 Transferred to USAAF 05/43

WELLESBOURNE MOUNTFORD, Warks

Opened: 04/41; *closed*: 1964; *location*: 5 miles E Stratford-upon-Avon

User sqns/units: 22 OTU 04/41–07/45

WESTCOTT, Bucks

Opened: 09/42; currently in use by MOD; *location*: 7 miles NW Aylesbury

User sqns/units: 11 OTU 09/42–08/45

WESTON-ON-THE-GREEN, Oxon

Opened: 07/18; currently in use by RAF; *location*: 3 miles SW Bicester

User sqns/units: 104 Sqn 09/39–04/40; 108 Sqn 09/39–04/40; 13 OTU 04–10/40 Transferred to Flying Training Command 11/40

WEST RAYNHAM, Norfolk

Opened: 05/39; currently in use by RAF; *location*: 5½ miles SW Fakenham

User sqns/units: 101 Sqn 05/39–07/41; 90 Sqn 09/39, 05–08/41; 76 Sqn 04–05/40; 139 Sqn 05–06/40; 18 Sqn 06–09/40, 08–11/42; 114 Sqn 07/41–11/42; 98 Sqn 09–10/42; 180 Sqn 09–10/42; 342 Sqn 04–05/43; 141 Sqn 12/43–07/45; 239 Sqn 12/43–07/45

WICKENBY, Lincs

Opened: 09/42; *closed*: 1956; *location*: 9 miles NE Lincoln

User sqns/units: 12 Sqn 09/42–09/45; 626 Sqn 11/43–10/45

WIGSLEY, Notts

Opened: 02/42; *closed*: 07/58; *location*: 7 miles W Lincoln

User sqns/units: 455 Sqn 02–04/42; 1654 HCU 06/42–08/45

WING, Bucks

Opened: 11/41; *closed*: 04/60; *location*: 4 miles W Leighton Buzzard

User sqns/units: 26 OTU 01/42–03/46

WINTHORPE, Notts

Opened: 09/40; *closed*: 07/59; *location*: 1 mile NE Newark-on-Trent

User sqns/units: 1661 HCU 01/43–08/45

WITCHFORD, Cambs

Opened: 06/43; *closed*: 03/46; *location*: 2 miles SW Ely

User sqns/units: 196 Sqn 07–11/43; 513 Sqn 09–11/43; 115 Sqn 11/43–09/45; 195 Sqn 10–11/44

WOMBLETON, Yorks

Opened: 10/43; *closed*: 1949; *location*: 3 miles E Helmsley

User sqns/units: 1666 HCU 10/43–08/45; 1679 HCU 12/43–01/44

WOODBRIDGE, Suffolk

Opened: 11/43; currently in use by Army; *location*: 11 miles ENE Ipswich

User sqns/units: none. FIDO-equipped Emergency diversion runway 3,000 yd × 250 yd with undershoots and overshoots of 500 yd each. Busiest of the three diversion airfields with 4,120 emergency landings made by end 06/45.

WOODHALL SPA, Lincs

Opened: 02/42; *closed*: 1964; *location*: 6 miles SW Horncastle

User sqns/units: 97 Sqn 03/42–04/43; 619 Sqn 04/43–01/44; 617 Sqn 01/44–06/45; 627 Sqn 04/44–09/45

WOOLFOX LODGE, Rutland

Opened: 12/40; *closed*: 01/66; *location*: 6 miles NW Stamford

User sqns/units: 14 OTU 12/40–08/41; 61 Sqn 09/41–05/42; 1429 (Czech) Operational Training Flight (OTF) 07–08/42; 1665 HCU 06/43–01/44; 218 Sqn 03–08/44; 1651 HCU 11/44–07/4

Transferred to USAAF 09/44

Reverted to RAF 10/44

WORKSOP, Notts

Opened: 11/43; *closed*: 12/60; *location*: 4 miles W East Retford

User sqns/units: 18 OTU 11/43–01/45

WRATTING COMMON, Cambs

Opened: 05/43; *closed*: 04/46; *location*: 3½ miles NNW Haverhill

User sqns/units: 90 Sqn 05–10/43; 1651 HCU 11/43–11/44; 195 Sqn 11/44–08/45

Opened as West Wickham 05/43

Renamed Wratting Common 08/43

WYMESWOLD, Leics

Opened: 05/42; *closed*: 1957; *location*: 3½ miles ENE Loughborough

User sqns/units: 28 OTU 05/42–10/44

Transferred to Transport Command 10/44

WYTON, Hunts

Opened: 07/36; currently in use by RAF; *location*: 3 miles NE Huntingdon

User sqns/units: 114 Sqn 12/36–12/39; 139 Sqn 09/36–12/39; 40 Sqn 12/39–02/41; 15 Sqn 12/39–04/40, 05/40–08/42; 57 Sqn 05, 06, 11/40; 109 Sqn 08/42–07/43; 83 Sqn 08/42–04/44; 1409 Met Rec Flt 01/44–05/45; 128 Sqn 09/44–05/45; 163 Sqn 01–08/45

ORDERS OF BATTLE:
1939, 1943 AND 1945

27 SEPTEMBER 1939

No. 1 GROUP, HQ: Forming at Benson, Oxon

No. 2 GROUP, HQ: Wyton, Cambs

21 Sqn 82 Sqn	} 79 Wing	Watton	Blenheim I, IV
114 Sqn 139 Sqn	} 82 Wing	Wyton	Blenheim I, IV
107 Sqn 110 Sqn	} 83 Wing	Wattisham	Blenheim I, IV
101 Sqn		West Raynham	Blenheim IV

No. 3 GROUP, HQ: Mildenhall, Suffolk

9 Sqn Honington Wellington I
37 Sqn Feltwell Wellington I
38 Sqn Marham Wellington I
99 Sqn Mildenhall Wellington I
115 Sqn Marham Wellington I
149 Sqn Mildenhall Wellington I
214 Sqn Feltwell Wellington I
215 Sqn Bassingbourn Wellington I, Harrow

No. 4 GROUP, HQ: Linton-on-Ouse, Yorks

10 Sqn Dishforth Whitley IV
51 Sqn Linton-on-Ouse Whitley II, III
58 Sqn Linton-on-Ouse Whitley III
77 Sqn Driffield Whitley III, V
78 Sqn Dishforth Whitley I, IVa, V
102 Sqn Driffield Whitley III

No. 5 GROUP, HQ: St Vincent's, Grantham, Lincs

44 Sqn Waddington Hampden
49 Sqn Scampton Hampden
50 Sqn Waddington Hampden
61 Sqn Hemswell Hampden
83 Sqn Scampton Hampden
106 Sqn Cottesmore Hampden
144 Sqn Hemswell Hampden
185 Sqn Cottesmore Hampden

FEBRUARY 1943

No. 1 GROUP, HQ: Bawtry Hall, Yorks

12 Sqn Wickenby Lancaster I, III
101 Sqn Holme Lancaster I, III
103 Sqn Elsham Wolds Lancaster I, III
166 Sqn Kirmington Wellington III, X
199 Sqn Ingham Wellington III
300 Sqn Hemswell Wellington III
301 Sqn Hemswell Wellington IV
305 Sqn Hemswell Wellington IV
460 Sqn Breighton Lancaster I, III

No. 2 GROUP, HQ: Castlewood House, Huntingdon

21 Sqn Methwold Ventura I, II
88 Sqn Oulton Boston III
98 Sqn Foulsham Mitchell II
105 Sqn Marham Mosquito IV
107 Sqn Great Massingham Boston III, IIIa

139 Sqn Marham Mosquito IV
180 Sqn Foulsham Mitchell II
226 Sqn Swanton Morley Boston III, IIIa
464 Sqn Feltwell Ventura I, II
487 Sqn Feltwell Ventura II

No. 3 GROUP, HQ: Exning, Suffolk

15 Sqn Bourn Stirling I, III
75 Sqn Newmarket Stirling I
90 Sqn Ridgewell Stirling I
115 Sqn East Wretham Wellington III
138 Sqn Tempsford Halifax II, V
149 Sqn Lakenheath Stirling I, III
161 Sqn Tempsford Lysander, Halifax, Hudson, Havoc, Albemarle
192 Sqn Gransden Lodge Wellington I, III, X, Mosquito IV
214 Sqn Chedburgh Stirling I, III
218 Sqn Downham Market Stirling I, III

No. 4 GROUP, HQ: Heslington Hall, Yorks

10 Sqn Melbourne Halifax II
51 Sqn Snaith Halifax II
76 Sqn Linton-on-Ouse Halifax II/V
77 Sqn Elvington Halifax II
78 Sqn Linton-on-Ouse Halifax II
102 Sqn Pocklington Halifax II
158 Sqn Rufforth Halifax II
196 Sqn Leconfield Wellington X
429 Sqn East Moor Wellington III, X
466 Sqn Leconfield Wellington X

No. 5 GROUP, HQ: St Vincent's, Grantham, Lincs

9 Sqn Waddington Lancaster I, III
44 Sqn Waddington Lancaster I, III
49 Sqn Fiskerton Lancaster I, III
50 Sqn Skellingthorpe Lancaster I, III
57 Sqn Scampton Lancaster I, III
61 Sqn Syerston Lancaster I, III
97 Sqn Woodhall Spa Lancaster I, III
106 Sqn Syerston Lancaster I, III
207 Sqn Langar Lancaster I, III
467 Sqn Bottesford Lancaster I, III

No. 6 (RCAF) GROUP, HQ: Allerton Park, Yorks

405 Sqn det Beaulieu, Hants Halifax II
408 Sqn Leeming Halifax II
419 Sqn Middleton St George Halifax II
420 Sqn Middleton St George Wellington III, X
424 Sqn Topcliffe Wellington III, X
425 Sqn Dishforth Wellington III
426 Sqn Dishforth Wellington III
427 Sqn Croft Wellington III, X
428 Sqn Dalton Wellington III

No. 8 (PFF) GROUP, HQ: Wyton, Hunts

7 Sqn Oakington Stirling I, III
35 Sqn Graveley Halifax II
83 Sqn Wyton Lancaster I,III
109 Sqn Wyton Mosquito IV
156 Sqn Warboys Wellington III, Lancaster I, III

22 MARCH 1945

No. 1 GROUP, HQ: Bawtry Hall, Yorks

12 Sqn Wickenby Lancaster I, III
100 Sqn Grimsby Lancaster I, III
101 Sqn Ludford Magna Lancaster I, III
103 Sqn Elsham Wolds Lancaster I, III
150 Sqn Hemswell Lancaster I, III
153 Sqn Scampton Lancaster I, III
166 Sqn Kirmington Lancaster I, III
170 Sqn Hemswell Lancaster I, III
300 Sqn Faldingworth Lancaster I, III
460 Sqn Binbrook Lancaster I, III
550 Sqn North Killingholme Lancaster I, III
576 Sqn Fiskerton Lancaster I, III
625 Sqn Kelstern Lancaster I, III
626 Sqn Wickenby Lancaster I, III

No. 3 GROUP, HQ: Exning, Suffolk

15 Sqn Mildenhall Lancaster I, III
75 Sqn Mepal Lancaster I, III
90 Sqn Tuddenham Lancaster I, III
115 Sqn Witchford Lancaster I, III
149 Sqn Methwold Lancaster I, III
186 Sqn Stradishall Lancaster I, III
195 Sqn Wratting Common Lancaster I, III

218 Sqn Chedburgh Lancaster I, III
514 Sqn Waterbeach Lancaster I, III
622 Sqn Mildenhall

No. 4 GROUP, HQ: Heslington Hall, Yorks

10 Sqn Melbourne Halifax III
51 Sqn Snaith Halifax III
76 Sqn Holme Halifax III, VI
77 Sqn Full Sutton Halifax III, VI
78 Sqn Breighton Halifax III
102 Sqn Pocklington Halifax III, VI
158 Sqn Lissett Halifax III
346 Sqn Elvington Halifax III, VI
347 Sqn Elvington Halifax III, VI
466 Sqn Driffield Halifax III
640 Sqn Leconfield Halifax III, VI

No. 5 GROUP, HQ: Moreton Hall, Swinderby, Lincs

9 Sqn Bardney Lancaster I, III
44 Sqn Spilsby Lancaster I, III
49 Sqn Fulbeck Lancaster I, III
50 Sqn Skellingthorpe Lancaster I, III
57 Sqn East Kirkby Lancaster I, III
61 Sqn Skellingthorpe Lancaster I, III
106 Sqn Metheringham Lancaster I, III
189 Sqn Fulbeck Lancaster I, III
207 Sqn Spilsby Lancaster I, III
227 Sqn Balderton Lancaster I, III
463 Sqn Waddington Lancaster I, III
467 Sqn Waddington Lancaster I, III
617 Sqn Woodhall Spa Lancaster I, III, Mosquito VI
619 Sqn Strubby Lancaster I, III
630 Sqn East Kirkby Lancaster I, III

On loan fron No. 8 (PFF) GROUP

83 Sqn (PFF) Coningsby Lancaster I,III
97 Sqn (PFF) Coningsby Lancaster I, III
627 Sqn (PFF) Woodhall Spa Mosquito IV, IX, XVI, XX, XXV

No. 6 (RCAF) GROUP, HQ: Allerton Park, Yorks

408 Sqn Linton-on-Ouse Halifax VII
415 Sqn East Moor Halifax III, VII
419 Sqn Middleton St George Lancaster X
420 Sqn Tholthorpe Halifax III

424 Sqn Skipton-on-Swale Lancaster I, III
425 Sqn Tholthorpe Halifax III
426 Sqn Linton-on-Ouse Halifax VII
427 Sqn Leeming Lancaster I, III, Halifax III
428 Sqn Middleton St George Lancaster X
429 Sqn Leeming Lancaster X, Halifax III
431 Sqn Croft Lancaster X
432 Sqn East Moor Halifax VII
433 Sqn Skipton-on-Swale Lancaster I, III, Halifax III
434 Sqn Croft Lancaster I, III, X

No. 8 (PFF) GROUP, HQ: Castle Hill House, Hunts

7 Sqn Oakington Lancaster I, III
35 Sqn Graveley Lancaster I, III
105 Sqn Bourn Mosquito IX, XVI
109 Sqn Little Staughton Mosquito IX, XVI
128 Sqn Wyton Mosquito XVI
139 Sqn Upwood Mosquito IX, XVI, XX, XXV
142 Sqn Gransden Lodge Mosquito XXV
156 Sqn Upwood Lancaster I, III
162 Sqn Bourn Mosquito XX, XXV
163 Sqn Wyton Mosquito XXV
405 Sqn Gransden Lodge Lancaster I, III
571 Sqn Oakington Mosquito XVI
582 Sqn Little Staughton Lancaster I, III
608 Sqn Downham Market Mosquito XX, XXV
635 Sqn Downham Market Lancaster I, III
692 Sqn Graveley Mosquito XVI

No. 100 (SD) GROUP, HQ: Bylaugh Hall, East Dereham, Norfolk

23 Sqn Little Snoring Mosquito VI
85 Sqn Swannington Mosquito XXX
141 Sqn West Raynham Mosquito VI, XXX
157 Sqn Swannington Mosquito XIX, XXX
169 Sqn Great Massingham Mosquito VI, XIX
171 Sqn North Creake Halifax III
192 Sqn Foulsham Halifax III, Mosquito IV, XVI
199 Sqn North Creake Halifax III, Stirling III
214 Sqn Oulton Fortress III
223 Sqn Oulton Liberator IV
239 Sqn West Raynham Mosquito XXX
462 Sqn Foulsham Halifax III
515 Sqn Little Snoring Mosquito VI

BIBLIOGRAPHY

PRIMARY SOURCES

MOD AIR HISTORICAL BRANCH, LONDON

RAF squadron histories

PUBLIC RECORD OFFICE, KEW

AIR 27 Class – RAF Squadron Operations Record Books – various piece numbers

LETTERS, DIARIES AND INTERVIEWS

Howard Farmiloe, pilot, 61 Squadron 1943–4, letter to the author, 10 October 1997
Leslie Fry, flight engineer, 429 Squadron RCAF, unpublished diary, 92 pp, March–October 1944
Ken Kemp, air gunner, 578 Squadron 1944–5, interview with the author, 7 September 1988
Air Marshal Sir John Whitley, AOC 4 Group 1945, unpublished memoirs (not dated)

OTHER SOURCES

Air Diagrams 3952, Aircrew Clothing:
    Sheet 1, *Well-dressed Aircrews*
    Sheet 2, *Flying Suits* (Air Ministry, April 1943)
The Air Force List (various)

SECONDARY SOURCES

BOOKS

Ashworth, C., *RAF Bomber Command 1936–1968* (Sparkford, PSL, 1995)

Bennett, D.C.T., *Pathfinder* (London, Frederick Muller, 1958)
Blanchett, C., *From Hull, Hell and Halifax: An Illustrated History of 4 Group 1937–1948* (Leicester, Midland Counties Publications, 1992)
Bowyer, C., *Bomber Barons* (London, William Kimber, 1983)
Bowyer, M.J.F., *2 Group RAF: A Complete History 1936–1945* (London, Faber & Faber, 1974)
Bowyer, M.J.F. and Rawlings, J.D.R., *Squadron Codes 1937–56* (Cambridge, PSL, 1979)
Bramson, A., *Master Airman: A Biography of Air Vice-Marshal Donald Bennett* (Shrewsbury, Airlife Publishing, 1985)
Brickhill, P., *Escape or Die* (London, Pan, 1952)
Brookes, A., *Bomber Squadron at War* (Shepperton, Ian Allan, 1983)
Chorley, W.R., *To See the Dawn Breaking: 76 Squadron Operations* (privately published, W.R. Chorley, 1981)
Chorley, W.R., *Bomber Command Losses* (Leicester, Midland Publishing, various volumes)
Cormack, A. and Volstad, R., *Men at Arms 225: The Royal Air Force 1939–45* (London, Osprey, 1996)
Cosgrove, E., *Canada's Fighting Pilots* (Toronto, Clark, Irwin & Co., 1965)
Delve, K., *The Source Book of the RAF* (Shrewsbury, Airlife Publishing, 1994)
Elliott, S. and Turner, B., *Denholm Elliott: Quest for Love* (London, Headline, 1994)
Everitt, C. and Middlebrook, M., *The Bomber Command War Diaries* (London, Viking, 1985)
Eyton-Jones, A.P., *Day Bomber* (Stroud, Sutton Publishing, 1998)
Falconer, J., *RAF Bomber Airfields of World War 2* (Shepperton, Ian Allan, 1992)

Green, W. and Swanborough, G., *RAF Bombers Parts 1 & 2* (London, Macdonald and Jane's, 1979, 1981)

Greenhous, B. *et al.*, *The Official History of the RCAF, vol. III: The Crucible of War 1939–1945* (University of Toronto Press, 1994)

Greer, L. and Harold, A., *Flying Clothing: The Story of its Development* (Shrewsbury, Airlife Publishing, 1979)

Harris, Sir A., *Bomber Offensive* (London, Collins, 1947)

Harris, Sir A., *Despatch on War Operations, 23 February 1942 to 8 May 1945* (London, Frank Cass, 1995)

Hastings, M., *Bomber Command* (London, Michael Joseph, 1979)

Ivelaw-Chapman, J., *High Endeavour: The Life of Air Chief Marshal Sir Ronald Ivelaw-Chapman* (Barnsley, Leo Cooper, 1993)

James, J., *The Paladins: The Story of the RAF up to the Outbreak of World War II* (London, Macdonald, 1990)

Jefford, Wing Commander C.G., *RAF Squadrons* (Shrewsbury, Airlife Publishing, 1988)

Joslin, E.C., *The Observer's Book of British Awards & Medals* (London, Frederick Warne, 1974)

Marriot-Smith, A.J., *Aeronautica: Collectables relating to Military and Naval Airforces of the World 1914–1984* (London, Arms & Armour Press, 1989)

Mason, F.K., *The British Bomber since 1914* (London, Putnam, 1994)

Merrick, K.A., *Halifax: An Illustrated History of a Classic World War II Bomber* (Shepperton, Ian Allan, 1980)

Middlebrook, M. (ed.), *The Everlasting Arms: The War Memoirs of Air Commodore John Searby* (London, William Kimber, 1988)

Munson, K., *Aircraft of World War II* (Shepperton, Ian Allan, 1972)

Musgrove, G., *Operation Gomorrah: The Hamburg Firestorm Raids* (London, Jane's, 1981)

Price, A., *Bomber Aircraft* (London, Arms & Armour Press, 1989)

Prodger, M.J., *Luftwaffe vs. RAF: Flying Clothing of the Air War 1939–45* (Atglen, PA, USA, Schiffer Publishing, 1997)

Richards, D., *The Hardest Victory: RAF Bomber Command in the Second World War* (London, Hodder & Stoughton, 1994)

Saward, D., *'Bomber' Harris* (London, Cassell, 1984)

Streetly, M., *Confound & Destroy: 100 Group and the Bomber Support Campaign* (London, Jane's, 1978)

Tapprell Dorling, Captain H., *Ribbons and Medals* (London, George Philip, 1940)

Townsend Bickers, R., *Home Run* (London, Leo Cooper, 1992)

Wallace-Clarke, R., *British Aircraft Armament vol. 1: RAF Gun Turrets from 1914 to the Present Day* (Sparkford, PSL, 1993)

Wallace-Clarke, R., *British Aircraft Armament vol. 2: RAF Guns and Gunsights from 1914 to the Present Day* (Sparkford, PSL, 1994)

Webster, C. and Frankland, N., *The Strategic Air Offensive Against Germany 1939–1945*, 4 volumes (London, HMSO, 1961)

Wells, M.K., *Courage and Air Warfare: The Allied Aircrew Experience in the Second World War* (London, Frank Cass, 1995)

Who Was Who, vol. IV 1941–50 (London, A & C Black, 1952)

Who Was Who, vol. V 1951–60 (London, A & C Black, 1961)

Who Was Who, vol. VI 1961–70 (London, A & C Black, 1972)

Who Was Who, vol. VII 1971–80 (London, A & C Black, 1981)

Who Was Who, vol. VIII 1981–90 (London, A & C Black, 1991)

Who's Who, 1995 (London, A & C Black, 1995)

JOURNALS, MAGAZINES, NEWSPAPERS

Ellis, K., 'British Aviation Museums' (Stamford, Key Publishing, 1994)

FlyPast Magazine (various issues)

The Times and the Daily Telegraph (various editions)

INDEX

This is a selective index covering the prologue, epilogue and chapters 1 to 11 inclusive. It does not include the appendices. All the squadrons listed in this index are bomber squadrons unless designated otherwise, e.g. (F), (AC), etc.